Alexander the Great and the Hellenistic Age
Part I

Professor Jeremy McInerney

THE TEACHING COMPANY ®

PUBLISHED BY:

THE TEACHING COMPANY
4840 Westfields Boulevard, Suite 500
Chantilly, Virginia 20151-2299
1-800-TEACH-12
Fax—703-378-3819
www.teach12.com

ISBN 1-56585-856-5

Jeremy McInerney, Ph.D.

Associate Professor, Department of Classical Studies
University of Pennsylvania

Jeremy McInerney received his Ph.D. from the University of California, Berkeley, in 1992. He was the Wheeler Fellow at the American School of Classical Studies at Athens and has excavated in Israel, at Corinth, and on Crete. Since 1992, he has been teaching Greek history at the University of Pennsylvania, where he held the Laura Jan Meyerson Term Chair in the Humanities from 1994 to 1998. He is currently an associate professor in the Department of Classical Studies and chair of the Graduate Group in the Art and Archaeology of the Mediterranean World. Professor McInerney also serves on the Managing Committee of the American School of Classical Studies at Athens.

Professor McInerney's research interests include topography, epigraphy, and historiography. He has published articles in a variety of academic journals including *Greek, Roman and Byzantine Studies*, the *American Journal of Archaeology*, *Hesperia*, and *California Studies in Classical Antiquity*. In 1997, he was an invited participant at a colloquium on ethnicity in the ancient world, hosted by the Center for Hellenic Studies in Washington. His book, *The Folds of Parnassos: Land and Ethnicity in Ancient Phokis*, is a study of state formation and ethnic identity in the Archaic and Classical periods, and it was published by the University of Texas Press in 1999.

Table of Contents
Alexander the Great and the Hellenistic Age
Part I

Alexander the Great and the Hellenistic Age

Scope:

This series of lectures examines a crucial but often neglected period in the history of the ancient world, the age ushered in by the extraordinary conquests of Alexander the Great. In the opening lectures, we explore the enigma of Alexander, son of a brilliant father, yet always at odds with the man whom he succeeded. We trace his early campaigns against the Persians and follow him to Egypt, where he was acclaimed as the son of god. We look at his career after this and find in him a blend of greatness and madness as he strove to replace the Persian empire of the Achaemenid dynasty with a new, mixed ruling class of Macedonians and Persians.

Alexander's death in 323 B.C. ushered in a period of catastrophic change as ambitious warlords carved up Alexander's realm into their own separate empires, especially Seleucid Syria and Ptolemaic Egypt. In a series of lectures, we look at how a small ruling class of Macedonian nobles established their rule from the eastern Mediterranean to the Hindu Kush. In the Nile valley, the Ptolemies played the role of pharaohs and were treated by their subjects as gods. At the same time, however, their capital, Alexandria, was cut off from Egypt and run by Greek bureaucrats. Greek culture flourished here in the museum and library, and the Ptolemies were great patrons of the arts.

In the Seleucid empire, the rulers also built Greek cities, such as Antioch, but in older regions, including Mesopotamia, they too were ready to be worshipped as living gods. On the edges of the Hellenistic world, in places as far away as Afghanistan and Pakistan, Greek cities grew up around trading posts and military settlements. Here, philosophy and literature from old Greece went hand in hand with gymnasiums and theatres to plant Greek culture far from the Mediterranean. By military and cultural conquest, then, much of central Asia was incorporated into the Greek world.

Despite the geographic extent of this civilization, we shall see that the heartland remained the eastern Mediterranean. It was here, in such new cities as Alexandria and Pergamum and such old ones as Athens, that Greek culture developed its distinctive Hellenistic appearance. Philosophy became more academic, as different schools of philosophy emerged. Stoicism, epicureanism, and skepticism all looked for ways to teach people to avoid the emotional upheavals of life in an age of anxiety. At the same time, art rejoiced in exploring the very same turmoil of the age. Hellenistic sculptors looked at the old, the young, the ugly, and the tortured instead of merely fashioning images of the perfect athlete. Novelists also played with themes of the reversal of fortune in the lives of their characters, because such tumult was part of the experiences of so many people. Piracy, brigandage, physical hardship, and the supreme power of great kings were all realities of the age and left their marks on ordinary people.

As we shall see, these conditions helped spawn a vital interest in magic, spells, and incantations and in religions that offered people the promise of redemption and salvation. The cults of Isis, Serapis, and Cybele all grew in popularity throughout the Hellenistic world. This was the climate of the world in which Christianity was born.

Although the Hellenistic Age would result in some of the greatest accomplishments in Greek culture, especially in the poetry of Callimachus, Theocritus, and Apollonius, the political power of the age was overshadowed by the growth of Rome. Hence, we conclude the lectures with a study of the growth of Roman power, its expansion into the eastern Mediterranean, and the inevitable clash of Greek and Roman civilizations. As we shall see, Rome conquered, but Rome would be forever changed by the contact with Greek culture. In the words of the Roman poet Horace, "Captured Greece took captive her captor."

Lecture One
Greeks and Macedonians

Scope:

In this lecture, we examine the relations between Philip II of Macedon and the Greeks. We will look at the earlier history of Macedon and chart the region's growth up to the battle of Chaeroneia in 338 B.C. and Philip's assassination two years later. In particular we will pay attention to Macedon's position on the margins of the Greek world.

Outline

I. Alexander the Great is the watershed figure between the Hellenistic Age and what preceded it.

  A. According to conventional formulations, the Hellenistic Age followed the Archaic and Classical stages of Greek civilization. It was, in other words, a "decadent" phase.

  B. But the Hellenistic Age is a dynamic period, one in which the Greek world was vibrant and vast.

II. The relationship between Macedon and Greece is historically complex. Although the Greek city-states were primarily democracies or oligarchies, Macedonia was a kingdom composed of separate cantons ruled by powerful local chieftains. We can use Herodotus's criteria to judge whether the Macedonians were Greek: genealogy, language, religion, and custom.

  A. Even in the heroic genealogies of the Greeks, the Macedonians were seen as on the very border of being Greek.

  B. Inscriptions and many personal names from Macedon are primarily Greek, and it is a safe, but not watertight, conclusion that Macedonian is a part of the family of northwest Greek dialects.

  C. Good evidence exists to show the widespread worship of Zeus and Artemis, two clearly Greek gods. Evidence also exists of the popularity of Bendis, a Thracian goddess, and

Enodia, a goddess shown on horseback and holding a torch, who is without any close Greek parallels.

   D. The Greeks expected certain behaviors to demonstrate that you were Greek, including participation in the panhellenic games and consultation of the panhellenic oracles. Macedonians took part in these events, but it was usually the Macedonian kings who asserted that they were Greek.

III. Philip II was seen as the man who transformed Macedonia and made the Macedonians fully Greek.

   A. Philip probably never even expected to become king of Macedon. Although his father, Amyntas III (393–370 B.C.), was king, Philip had two older brothers who preceded him to the throne: Alexander II (370–368 B.C.), who was murdered by his brother-in-law, and Perdiccas III, who ruled in 360–359.

   B. The early history of Macedon is one of territorial expansion under powerful kings acting on the threat of invasion from neighboring tribes, including the Illyrians, the Triballi, and the Paeones, and internal discord between powerful clans vying for power.
   1. At times, the inland mountain regions were under central authority.
   2. At other times, these regions were relatively independent. This combination of internal discord and external threat kept Macedon a peripheral power in the Greek world for 300 years.

   C. When his brother, Perdiccas III, died, Philip took over as regent for his nephew before killing him and establishing his own dynasty.
   1. His early reign was taken up with border wars involving various northern tribes, whom he pacified using the three techniques that were the hallmark of his success: diplomacy, bribery, and military alliance.
   2. Some tribes he conquered in battle through deploying the infantry phalanx; some he bought off with huge indemnities; and some he mollified by marriage alliances.

   D. After securing the western and northern borders of his kingdom, Philip's ambitions moved south and east.

1. Once he had captured the gold mines of Mt. Pangaion, the next step was to deal with the cities of the Chalcidice: Torone, Olynthus, and Amphipolis. This move brought him into conflict with Athens, which regarded Amphipolis as its own colony.
2. His thirst for expansion was endless, taking him eventually all the way across the Thracian coast to the Hellespont and south into Thessaly, where he intervened in a civil war before becoming the commander-in-chief of the Thessalians.

IV. Philip moved into southern Greece as a result of the Sacred War (357–346 B.C.), when Delphi was seized by the neighboring people of Phocis.

A. Philip marched south to liberate Delphi in 350.
1. The Athenians were alarmed and sent a force to Thermopylae (where the Spartans had headed off the Persians 130 years before) to block his way. Philip retreated, as he said, like a battering ram in order to strike harder the second time. This second attempt came in 346, when he seized Thermopylae and Delphi at the same time.
2. Aware that they had been outmaneuvered, the Athenians under Demosthenes began frantically trying to raise an alliance against Philip. But Philip withdrew from Delphi, and most Greek states believed that he had kept his word: he had only come south to liberate Delphi.

B. When war at Delphi broke out again in 338 B.C., Philip again marched south, but this time, after he had passed through Thermopylae, he turned southeast.
1. Hurriedly, an Athenian army marched north, joined the Thebans, and continued west to Chaironeia.
2. There, in 338, the last free army of Greeks was destroyed by the Macedonians, with Philip commanding the right wing and his 16-year-old son, Alexander, the heir designate, holding the left.

C. At Corinth, Philip established a Hellenic league without claiming royal authority. Because the Greeks were unified in their hatred of Persians, Philip proposed an invasion of Persia.

D. Two years later, in 336, Philip was assassinated in Macedon and succeeded by his son, Alexander.

V. The Macedonian victory would initiate a new era, during which Alexander's armies would take Greek culture from Athens to Afghanistan, but not until the war of independence against the Turks, 2,100 years later, would the Greeks be free.

    A. The Hellenistic Age began with an irony: as Greece lost its independence, its culture was exported far and wide.

    B. This culture, however, was little more than a thin veneer in the lands to be conquered.

    C. Even so, new cities would be planted by the Greeks and ruled by urban elites steeped in Hellenism.

Suggested Reading:

E. N. Borza, *In the Shadow of Olympus: The Emergence of Macedon.*

R. M. Errington, *A History of Macedonia.*

N. G. L. Hammond, *Philip of Macedon.*

Questions to Consider:

1. What motivated Philip's relentless campaigns of expansion?

2. Why were the Greeks unable to resist the advance of Macedonian power?

Lecture One—Transcript
Greeks and Macedonians

Hello and welcome to our series of lectures on the Hellenistic Age. Historians usually like to think of history as occurring in neat and distinct periods, where they can divide up time and look at separate societies as they exist during that period. But of course, history really isn't that neat. But in this case, the case of the Hellenistic Age, there really is a definite distinction, a clear marker that separates the Greek world of before 330 B.C. and the Greek world after that time. The distinction is: Alexander the Great.

Rarely has there been a period in human history that relied more on the genius of one man, to distinguish his reign and the entire period that came after him from everything that came before. In the 19th century, when historians looked at the periods of Greek history, they liked to think of three periods as marking the development of any culture: an archaic period, during which that culture began to grow and develop; a classical period when that society reached its maturation; and then a period of decadence, when things began to fall apart. It was applying that system to Greek history that led the German historian Droysen to coin the phrase "Hellenistic," because in his model of Greek history, which divided Greek history up into three periods, that period of initial growth, that period during which the Greeks were first developing their distinctive culture, was the archaic period. It was the period when they colonized the Mediterranean, when they made the first steps toward democracy, when they acquired their alphabet from the eastern Mediterranean, and so forth. And then, according to Droysen, in the Classical Age, the Greeks reached the height of their civilization. This was the Age of Pericles. The Age of Socrates. The Age of the Athenian Empire, of the Parthenon, of Greek philosophy, of Greek tragedy written by Aeschylus and Sophocles and Euripides. And in this model of three phases of civilization, according to Droysen, the last phase was the Hellenistic, deriving its name from the Greek word for Greece (in fact), "Hellas". This Hellenistic phase was supposedly the decadent phase, the period that came after the Classical Age, when the Greeks were at their height.

We still use these distinctions, as far as periods are concerned. We still talk about Archaic, and Classic and Hellenistic, but I'm hoping that this course of lectures will persuade you that it is entirely wrong to think of the Hellenistic Age as a period of decadence or decline. It isn't a period during which the Greeks lose their genius. Rather, it is the dynamic period of Greek history when, in fact, Greek civilization is spread over a much broader canvas than ever before.

This is the first thing I want to introduce in our study of the Hellenistic Age. It is a period during which the scale of Greek culture is unlike anything that has come before. Prior to this, the Greek world has been essentially mainland Greece, the Aegean, the western coast of Asia Minor (modern-day Turkey), and some Greek colonies further west, in, say, Sicily. But now, thanks to Alexander and his conquests, Greek civilization will be spread across an entirely new canvas, so that Greek armies following Alexander will march from Macedon all the way to the Hindu Kush, to the Indus Valley, and the Punjab plain of northwest India. This is dramatically new. If you think about the modern nation-states which during antiquity regions of which would have been part of the Hellenistic world, one finds an extraordinary list. One could include Turkey, Syria, Lebanon, Israel, Egypt, Libya, Arabia, Iraq, Iran (what was formerly known as Persia), and also Afghanistan. All these areas are areas which during the 3rd century B.C. down to the 1st century B.C. were brought into the Greek world. They received Greek culture as Greek colonists following Alexander came and settled here. So it is a period that is one of completely new scale to Greek culture.

As the scale increases, so does the presentation of power in the Greek world. Everything gets larger. It is like Greek culture on steroids. In the Classical world, the Greeks had used triremes, war boats that had three banks of oars. Now, in the Hellenistic period, we'll find naval battles where the ships have banks of five oars, or ten or fifteen banks of oars. Everything is getting larger and larger.

It will be a period also where we will see a great deal of anxiety as people begin to worry about their place in the world, because the old certainties have now been shattered. A world in which people will study the psychology of the individual in the Greek novel, and in Greek epic poems. In which the torment of the individual will be expressed in Greek art, as we're going to see later in these lectures. A period during which Greek philosophers will be concerned with the question of establishing inner harmony and peace, as they deal with the anxiety of this new age.

And, because it's an age of anxiety, also an age in which people turn more and more to astronomy and astrology and casting spells and using magic to control their lives and the lives of other people. So it's going to be a Greek world, or a Greek culture, that's unlike anything we've seen before in the Classical or Archaic periods. And looming over all of this is one man. Alexander. Alexander the Great.

Now, Alexander's accomplishments, which we're going to look at in the next couple of lectures, would not have been possible but for the fact that his father conquered Greece. So we have to begin even before Alexander in this, the first lecture of our series, with Philip (Philip II), the king of Macedon.

When we look at Macedon, we find that the relationship between Macedon and Greece is a highly complex one. It certainly remains that today. At the moment, there is a region of northern Greece, a province of the current Greek republic known as Macedon. And yet there is also a former Yugoslav republic that claims the name of Macedon. So it's still a vexed issue. What is the relationship between Macedon and Greece? You will still hear today Greeks defiantly proclaiming, "Macedon was, is, and ever will be, Greek!" But the reality is actually very complex, and more complicated than that.

Macedon was a part of Greece, but it was also somewhat distinct and different from the rest of Greece. The Greece of the Classical World, and of the south and central parts of the Greek peninsula, was an area made up primarily of city-states. *Poleis*, as the Greeks called them. Small areas centered around a particular city. Each governed by either a democracy, where virtually all the citizen men were members of the ruling group of that society, or oligarchies, where the franchise was restricted to a narrower group, say, the *aristoi*, the aristocrats, or the wealthy merchant class (in Corinth, for example).

Macedon was actually unlike either one of these models, because Macedon was a kingdom, located in the northern part of the Greek peninsula. It was a kingdom where power was not strongly centralized in the hands of the Argead dynasty, the family that provided the rulers of Macedon. There were, in fact, inland areas (we can call them cantons or fiefdoms, if you like) where local barons ruled sometimes almost independently. These were the barons, the ruling class, the aristocratic elite of Macedonian society.

You might like to think, I'd suggest, you might like to think of the relationship between Greece and Macedon as being something like the relationship between Scotland and England. Geographically connected. Culturally overlapping. And yet, in some fundamental ways, also quite distinct and different. The Greeks themselves were interested in the question of "what makes a Greek a Greek?" And, "were the Macedonians Greek?" Fortunately, we have a guide to the way the Greeks understood their own ethnicity. Herodotus tells us in a celebrated passage that there were four ways of determining who was a Greek. In Herodotus's formulation, the elements that made up your ethnic identity were your blood (expressed in genealogy—who was your father, and who was his father), the language that you spoke, the religion that you followed, and the customs that you used in your daily life. So let's use these Greek criteria to look at the Macedonians.

First of all, on the question of blood. The Greeks expressed their Greekness through a series of heroic genealogies, so that every Greek could claim descent from a heroic forefather. Eventually, above all of these, at the very beginning of all of these genealogies was Hellas, the man from whom the Hellenes (the Greeks) took their name. The Macedonians were a part of the heroic genealogy of the Greeks, but they were out on the very edge of this genealogy, as if the Greeks of, say, Athens and Thebes and Argos and Sparta thought of the Macedonians as being distant cousins. Greek, but Greek with a question mark, perhaps.

What about language? Our best evidence here is from the inscriptions and the many personal names that we know of individual Macedonians themselves. Here we can state fairly safely that the Macedonians appear to have spoken Greek. That's certainly the language that they used for their inscriptions, and the names of individual Macedonians are Greek names. So it looks as if, from the point of language, that the Macedonians spoke a dialect of Greek. It may have sounded a little odd to people down in Athens, but it would have been intelligible and understood.

What about from the point of view of religion? Once again, we find the same mixture of both Greekness and non-Greekness contributing to the Macedonian identity. For example, there's good evidence in Macedon that Zeus ("the father of gods and men", as he's called by Hesiod) and Artemis (the virgin goddess who was the hunter and the goddess associated with wild places) both were worshiped in Macedon. These are clearly Greek gods. But on the other hand, there's also evidence for the popularity of a goddess called Bendis, who's a Thracian goddess. In other words, the Greeks would have thought of her as being vaguely foreign. Not quite the same as the Olympian gods. And there's another goddess named Enodia, a goddess who's normally shown riding on a horse and carrying a torch. She really has no close parallels in the southern Greek world. So the Macedonians betray their relationship to the Greeks of the south and also to the peoples further north of them, the Thracians, a so-called barbarian people, in the eyes of the southern Greeks.

And what about custom? Here we have an anecdote that perfectly expresses the relationship between the Greeks and the Macedonians. The best way that you could show that you were Greek, in the eyes of other Greeks, was to participate in the Olympic Games. The Olympic Games were one set of what were called the Pan-Hellenic Games. Games that were held every four years, but were only open to Greeks for participation. So if you could participate there, it meant that the judges of the Games (who were, in fact, known as the "Greek Judges"—the *Hellanodikai*) it meant that you were, in their eyes, a Greek. A Macedonian king, Alexander I, wanted to participate in the Olympic Games. When he went to Olympia, on his first try, he was rejected by the *Hellanodikai*, the "Judges of the Greeks". Why? Presumably because they didn't believe that he was really Greek. So what he had to produce was a family tree, that showed that his family (the ruling family of Macedonia) was, in fact, related to the Argeads, so it had a good Greek pedigree.

I think this perfectly expresses the relationship of Greeks and Macedonians. The ruling class likes to see itself as Greek, but in the eyes of the southern Greeks, the civilized Greeks, the men from Macedon were really somewhat suspect.

What transformed the relation between these two sides was the career of one man: Philip II, because it was Philip who united the Macedonians and eventually conquered the Greeks, making the distinction between the two almost meaningless.

Ironically, Philip probably never expected to become the king of Macedon. The reason for that is that even though he was a prince (his father Amyntas ruled from 390 to 370 B.C.), Philip had two older brothers, and both of them preceded him to the throne.

Alexander II was the king of Macedon briefly in 370-368. He was killed by his brother-in-law. Then later, in 360, Philip's older brother Perdiccas III ruled from 360-359, before dying in battle, fighting against the Illyrians. So Philip probably didn't expect to become the king of Macedon, but death cleared the path for him.

The early history of Macedon is a fluctuating story. It's one of territorial expansion when the kingdom is strong and when the kingdom is united. But then there is always the threat of invasion from the tribes that lie on the outskirts of the Macedonian realm. The Illyrians to the northwest, the Tribaldi and the Paeones to the north and the northeast. And, as you can already see in Philip's own family, there is always the threat of internal discord, as different groups are vying for power. So at times, the inland regions of Macedon, these fiefdoms or these areas ruled by barons, if you will, were under central authority, and at other times they were relatively independent. It's this combination of internal discord and internal weakness and external threat that prevents Macedon from playing a more considerable role in the affairs of the Greeks during the Classical period.

Back in the 5th century, most Greeks would have thought of Macedon as nothing more than a good place where you could get timber for ships. It was marginal to the concerns of the Greeks.

When Perdiccas III, Philip's older brother, died in 359 B.C., Philip still did not technically come to the throne. Rather, he served as regent for Perdiccas's son, who reigned now as the child king Amyntas IV. Philip soon killed his nephew, though, and took over, establishing his own family as the ruling family of Macedon. His early reign was taken up with establishing his authority by making firm the borders of Macedon. He was involved in warfare with the three major tribes on the outskirts of Macedon that threatened their security.

The three techniques that he used in order to establish his authority and to end these wars are hallmarks of his success. He uses them repeatedly throughout his career. The three are: diplomacy, bribery and alliance. In the case of warfare, at which he was very good, Philip had been trained in the techniques of *hoplite* warfare when, as a child and as a young man, he had lived in Thebes. Here he learned the techniques which he applied to the heavily armed battalion of Macedonian soldiers known as the *phalanx*. This *phalanx*, made up of thousands of men, tightly packed, each holding an 18-foot-long pike, required extraordinary attention to detail and drilling constantly. But it was an almost impossible task to face the *phalanx* and to resist its attack, if it hit on open ground. It was by training this national army that Philip really established his later successes.

At the same time, in some instances, he found that it was easier simply to buy off his opponents. So his reign began with him going massively into debt, as he spent vast amounts of money to buy peace with the northern tribes. And when conquering them in war, or buying them off with a bribe didn't work, he married their daughters. So we find that Philip, during his career, ended up with something like nine wives. Not consecutively, like Liz Taylor, but rather all at once, establishing a great deal of peace and harmony, no doubt.

After securing the western and northern borders of his kingdom, Philip's ambitions turned south and east. This was an ominous development for the Greeks, because south of Macedon lies mainland Greece. Once he had captured the gold mines of Mount Pangaion, which lie just on the eastern edge of Macedon, he found himself equipped with an extraordinarily rich supply of gold and silver, with which he could pay for the training and equipping of a large national army. And it was with this army that he was able to embark on a series of campaigns in the first region of Greece, the three-pronged peninsula that sticks out into the Aegean on its northwestern corner, known as Chalcidice. Here he came up against Greek towns such as Torone, Olynthus and Amphipolis. Olynthus, for example, he leveled to the ground after he had captured it.

His attack on Amphipolis brought him into conflict with the Athenians, because the Athenians regarded Amphipolis as their own colony. So it was now, for the first time, that the Athenians began to pay close attention to Philip's ambitions in the Aegean and in Greece in general. His thirst for expansion was endless. People have sometimes asked me what I think Philip was aiming at, and historians often wonder what exactly was his goal. I don't believe that Philip had a concrete goal. He really simply wanted to get more and more power and territory. That is all that is needed to explain the endless campaigning of Philip II and his Macedonians.

His expansion was relentless. Eventually it took him across the northern coast of the Aegean, across through Thrace, all the way to the Hellespont, the Dardanelles (the strip of water that separates

Europe from Asia). And, as well, campaigning not only east of Macedon, but south, he marched into Thessaly, where he intervened in a civil war, and, after establishing peace in Thessaly was able to take over as commander-in-chief of the Thessalian forces, the *Tagus*, as the Thessalians called it.

Philip's move into southern Greece, bringing him against Athens and the states of southern Greece, came as a result of the Sacred War, a war that lasted from 357 to 346, and which was precipitated by the attack on Delphi (the holiest shrine of Greece) when it was seized by the people of Phocis, the neighboring tribe that lived around Delphi. Philip marched south. He used the capture of Delphi as a pretext, proclaiming himself a liberator, who, as head of the Thessalian forces, rather than as Macedonian king, would march south and set free the gods' sanctuary. This march south came in 350 B.C.

The Athenians were mightily alarmed. They knew that a large army of a Macedonian phalanx and Thessalian cavalry marching into central Greece could keep on marching all the way to Athens and into the Peloponnesus. So, heroically, they sent a force to Thermopylae, that hallowed spot where, 130 years earlier, the forces of the Spartans had held up the advance of the Persians. At this bottleneck at Thermopylae, the Athenians set up a garrison and prevented Philip from marching any farther south.

He, this time, retreated. He did not give battle. But he retreated, as he said, like a battering ram, to strike all the harder the next time he came. This second occasion came in 346 B.C., when he marched south and seized both Thermopylae and Delphi at the same time. The Athenians recognized that they had been outmaneuvered, and Demosthenes began frantically trying to raise an alliance of the various Greek states against Philip. Once again, he outfoxed everyone's expectations and withdrew, leaving Delphi, as he had said, liberated.

So we go into a period of a kind of hiatus, from about 346 for the next eight years, as Philip campaigns further in the north and in the east. But then, in 338 a war broke out. The Fourth Sacred War broke out around Delphi. Once again, Philip marched south. Once again, he came to Thermopylae. But this time he didn't march on to Delphi. He marched into the plain of Chaeroneia, heading towards Athens. It was here that the Athenians, joined by their Theban allies, marched to the plain on the western side of Thebes, at Chaeroneia, and in 338, in a battle between the forces of the Athenians and the Thebans on one side and the Macedonian phalanx on the other, the Greeks were defeated, and Philip and the Macedonians were victorious. The battle of Chaeroneia, the last day on which the Greeks would be free until the war of independence against Turkey in the 1820s A.D. A long period of subjugation coming up.

On this day at Chaeroneia, when Philip was victorious, he commanded the right wing. On the left wing was his sixteen-year-old son, Alexander. Clearly, the heir-designate, the man who would take over from Philip after his death.

What came next for Philip was an attempt to pacify the Greeks whom he had just conquered. Rather than rubbing their nose in his victory and proclaiming himself King of Greece, instead he convened a convention of the Greeks at Corinth. Here he established a new league, a Hellenic League. So very carefully, he was trying to position himself as the leading man of Greece, but he did not claim royal authority. Instead, he proclaimed himself the Captain-General of the Greek forces. Greek forces for what? For a campaign against Persia.

For 130 years, the Greeks had hated the Persians, because of the Persian sack of Athens and because of the invasion of Greece. For 130 years, Greek intellectuals had recognized that in the world of Greece, where every state was out for itself and where warfare continued year after year, the one thing that united the Greeks was their hatred of Persia. A Greek intellectual named Isocrates wrote to Philip and actually invited him to take on the role of Captain-General of the Greeks. Other Greek philosophers, such as Plato, had tried to make men like King Dionysius of Syracuse think of themselves as philosopher-kings, who would lead the Greeks to a new age of unification. So Philip had learned his lesson well, recognizing that he should not try to conquer the Greeks and force them to his will, but rather appeal to them. Appeal to the one thing that would unite them, and would take them off on a new grand quest. This time what he proposed was nothing less than an invasion of Persia.

So after 338, we actually find the Macedonians continuing their preparations for war, even though they've pacified all of Greece. But these preparations for war take place on the other side of the Hellespont, as the advanced forces of Philip's army actually claim a portion of Asia Minor as the beachhead for what is coming: the invasion of Persia by the Macedonian forces.

And yet, when that invasion is just on the brink of occurring, when Philip is about to change everything, and to go from being a Macedonian king and the conqueror of the Greeks, to being Captain-General of this invasion army, he's cut down.

He's celebrating a festival back in Macedon. He's just had twelve statues of the Olympian gods brought in to the theater, with a thirteenth statue following, a statue of Philip himself, as if he is claiming some sort of semi-divine status. And now, at the very peak of his glory, just as he is ready to embark on the next great stage of his military career, he is assassinated.

People would love to know by whom. We have the name of the actual assassin, but the assassin and his accomplices were cut down virtually straight away, leaving people to speculate a great deal afterwards about who it was that assassinated Philip and exactly why. I'll give you a clue: many people think that the person who gained the most from this was Alexander. So it's quite possible that Alexander's career, which would take up exactly where his father's had left off, was the result, in fact, of yet another one of the internecine disputes or one of the feuds within the Macedonian royal family.

From such inglorious beginnings, however, would erupt the campaign of Alexander, which would take a Macedonian and Greek army across into the realm of Asia Minor before heading farther south and east, as far as Egypt and through the Persian Empire, conquering the great king of Persia, and eventually establishing Greek culture as far away as India.

It would take Greek culture from Athens, to Afghanistan. And yet, it would be built on the lack of independence back in Greece itself. So we begin the Hellenistic Age, then, with an irony. It is a world built on the glories of Greek culture, at the very time when Greece itself is losing its political independence. It is going to be a story in which the same kinds of ambiguities exist throughout.

Will Greek culture reach all levels of the world it conquers? No. Instead, I'm going to be arguing that there is very little fusion between the Greek culture brought by Alexander's armies and the native cultures that already existed. In fact, I'm going to suggest to you that there is no fusion at all in this world, but rather a thin overlay of Greek culture at the very top. Quite frankly, if you were a Syrian peasant under the Persians or a Syrian peasant under Alexander or a Syrian peasant under Alexander's successors the Seleucids, it wouldn't matter. You spoke the same language and you thought the same way and you were still oppressed by the overlords that ruled above you.

But what would be different is that cities would be planted throughout the Middle East, Egypt, Asia Minor, and these cities would be ruled by urban elites. These urban elites would become Greek. Whether they were born in Greece, whether they were colonists, didn't matter. But rather, they would acquire Greek culture and they would speak Greek. It would be this urban elite, ruling the entire Near East and Middle East, that would bring Hellenism from Greece to the whole world, from the Mediterranean to the Indus Valley. In our next lecture, we'll begin the story in detail, with the story of Alexander the Great.

Lecture Two
Alexander the Divine?

Scope:

Alexander's path was prepared by his father, Philip, but few could predict how the son would eclipse the father. After only two battles, Alexander would command more territory than any Greek before him and would demand that the Persian king address him as an equal. At the height of his power, he would visit Egypt, where he would not only assume the role of pharaoh but would be greeted as the son of god.

Outline

I. Philip's murder in 336 B.C. came at an opportune moment for Alexander, because Philip's most recent marriage was to a young Macedonian woman, named Cleopatra, daughter of a powerful general named Attalus.

   A. At the betrothal feast in 337, Attalus had toasted the couple, wishing them a fruitful marriage that would produce a legitimate Macedonian heir.
      1. Alexander, then 17 years of age, interpreted this as a slight: because his mother, Olympias, was from Epirus, he could be said to be only half-Macedonian.
      2. When he flew into a rage and cried out, "So what does that make me, a bastard, you villain?" Philip drew his sword and the two very nearly cut each other to pieces.
      3. Olympias withdrew from Macedon, and Philip and Alexander were temporarily estranged, though later reconciled.

   B. In 336, Philip celebrated the marriage with a festival at which his own statue was carried behind the statues of the 12 Olympian Gods. As Philip entered the theatre, he was stabbed in the chest and died.

   C. The circumstances of Philip's death have resulted in the theory that Alexander plotted his father's death to get to the throne. Some believed this in antiquity, but the charge cannot be proved. Nonetheless, Alexander profited greatly from the timing of his father's death.

II. At the time of his death, Philip had been preparing for the invasion of Persia. He would lead a combined army of Greeks and Macedonians in a quest to avenge the sack of Greece by the Persians 150 years earlier. Alexander continued with this plan, crossing into Asia Minor in 334 B.C.

   A. At the Granicus River in northwestern Asia Minor, Alexander defeated an army assembled by the various satraps of Asia Minor.

   1. The ancient sources put the victory down to the reckless courage of Alexander, who led his cavalry across the river, forcing the infantry to follow them.

   2. Alexander's tactics represent an innovation in Greek warfare. Until then, Greeks had fought either massed hoplite engagements or had relied on skirmishing troops with light arms. Cavalry had remained a neglected tactical weapon, used primarily to sweep up after the hoplite army had broken the opponent.

   3. Alexander appreciated the potential of the cavalry to function as a wedge, capable of splitting the enemy and turning the tide of battle.

   B. Alexander presented his expedition as a new Trojan War, with himself as the new Achilles.

   1. His campaign was compared with the labors of Heracles and the epic journey of the god Dionysos. He was a superhuman hero.

   2. Alexander cultivated these comparisons, wandering as he did far and wide like Heracles, casting his conquest of the East as divinely inspired.

   C. The victory at the Granicus left Alexander in control of much of Asia Minor. This was followed the next year by Alexander's victory at Issus (333 B.C.), just beyond the point where the pass through the Taurus Mountains leads down into the Syrian plain.

   1. On this occasion, the Persians were led by the Great King himself, Darius III. The armies passed each other while jockeying for position and, when they eventually met, the narrow coastal strip prevented Darius from employing his superior numbers.

   2. The result was a second overwhelming victory that left Alexander in command of all the former Persian

possessions from the Aegean to the headwaters of the Euphrates.

III. The rapid and massive success of Alexander posed some interesting problems for the 21-year-old king. How should he behave toward the Greeks and the Persians? What was the basis of his authority?

    A. To the Greeks, he addressed himself still as King Alexander, that is, as King of the Macedonians.

        1. A decree from 334 B.C.—revealing democratic concerns while announcing a military levy—shows Alexander's mix of idealism and pragmatism.

        2. He arranged affairs in the Greek cities now under his control but encouraged the Greeks to submit conflicts to arbitration by a Hellenic council.

        3. Alexander saw that he could not afford disruptions and endemic warfare behind him, because he needed the resources of the Greek cities—either their manpower or their navies.

    B. But to the Persians, Alexander was much more.

        1. He had captured the Great King's family, his possessions, and his gold and had conquered his army and even driven Darius from the field. Not surprisingly, then, Alexander presented a very different face to the Persians, styling himself "Lord of Asia."

        2. This is the key to understanding Alexander: he was caught between two cultures that could not be reconciled. You cannot be both first among equals, as a Greek, and semi-divine, as a Persian.

    C. After the battle of Issus, Alexander turned south to secure the coastal cities of Tyre and Sidon. From here, before pursuing Darius inland, Alexander headed for Egypt, anxious not to leave a large Persian presence in his rear.

        1. The Egyptian campaign included a march across the Libyan desert to the oracle of Zeus Ammon at Siwah, where Alexander, in one account, was greeted by the oracle as the son of Zeus Ammon. Another possibility is that he was called "son of Amun," or pharaoh, a ritual recognition of his new position.

2. Did Alexander believe in his own divinity? Did the event give shape to incipient delusions? Some have tried to psychoanalyze him 2,500 years after the fact to ascertain whether he actually considered himself a god.
3. But the event does highlight the dilemma facing Alexander: his Greek and non-Greek subjects expected him to play very different, perhaps irreconcilable, roles. None of his generals would attempt to bridge this difficult gap.

Suggested Reading:

R. L. Fox, *Alexander the Great.*

J. Roisman, *Alexander the Great: Ancient and Modern Perspectives.*

Questions to Consider:

1. How were Alexander's claims to divinity received by the Greeks?
2. What does the episode at Siwah reveal about the attitudes of the conquered toward Alexander?

Lecture Two—Transcript
Alexander the Divine?

In 338 B.C., Macedonians defeated the Greeks at the Battle of Chaeroneia. Philip II was victorious after a career spent planning to extend his reign and his territory. He defeated the Athenians and the Thebans. But he proved to be magnanimous in victory. He sent Alexander, his sixteen-year-old son, who had commanded the left wing at Chaeroneia, to bring back the ashes of the Athenian war dead to the city of Athens, as a mark of respect and of honor for fallen foes. So at the age of sixteen, Alexander was clearly marked for greatness by his father. He had been given the highest military command in Macedon, other than that of commanding the right wing of the phalanx, which Philip had done. And he had now acted as an ambassador on behalf of the king to the most prestigious of the southern Greek states. Clearly, Alexander, at sixteen, was the heir designate to his father Philip II.

And yet, as we saw in the lecture last time, affairs in Macedon could change very rapidly. The conflicts within the royal family were sometimes hard to fathom, and could certainly be dangerous to the people who ended up on the wrong side. A year later, by 337, Alexander had fallen out of Philip's good graces. The reason for this (and this probably ended up contributing to Philip's murder in 336) was that late in his life, Philip had taken yet another bride. But the difference was that, whereas we've seen that his earlier brides tended to be from regions around Macedon, and they were brides that he married because of alliances that he needed with outlying tribes, on this occasion, Philip had betrothed himself to a young Macedonian girl named Cleopatra. Her father, Attalus, was one of the Macedonian nobles who formed the officer corps of Philip's army. At the betrothal feast, celebrating the upcoming wedding of Philip and Cleopatra, Attalus proposed a toast, drinking the good health of the bride and wishing the happy couple a fruitful marriage that would produce a legitimate Macedonian heir.

One can imagine Alexander's reaction. Was he not the Macedonian heir? Well, perhaps. But he was certainly not in the eyes of some of the other Macedonians a legitimate Macedonian, because his mother, Olympias, was actually a princess from Epirus, the kingdom located immediately to the west of Macedon. So that, from one point of view, Alexander was only half a Macedonian. The toast of Attalus was clearly a slight at Alexander. But more than that, it also raised the possibility that if Philip, who was still a strong man, were to father a child with this young girl, Cleopatra, that child might be or might become the heir designate, if the child grew to be, say, twenty years of age while Philip was still alive.

So Alexander's rage was prompted both by the immediate insult and by the sudden specter of his being shunted out of power. He flew into a rage at the wedding feast. He drew his sword and stood up to Attalus and said, "What does that make me? A bastard, you villain?" At which point, not Attalus, but Philip drew his sword, and the two men, the father and son, nearly cut each other to pieces until they were separated by the other men and soldiers at the feast. It was a dramatic rupture in what otherwise appeared to be a smooth motion towards power by Alexander.

His mother withdrew from Macedon, estranged from her husband Philip. Alexander temporarily left as well, until he was persuaded that Philip would accept him back again, and that they should resolve their differences.

But in 336, in the following year, when Philip marched into a festival behind the statues of the Olympian gods and a statue of himself, as well, on that occasion, when Philip was cut down, there was still bad blood between him and his son, despite the fact that only two years earlier they had celebrated the most glorious military victory of Macedon's history.

Philip entered the theater and was stabbed in the chest. His assassin was shortly afterwards cut down as well. There were many theories in antiquity about the death of Philip. There were stories that Philip had failed to intervene when his later-assassin had been dishonored, and that the man had held a grudge against Philip. But there were also those who claimed that Alexander had engineered the whole thing, and that the death of the assassins rather conveniently covered the trail, so that Alexander came to power unhindered. We'll never know the truth.

Some modern scholars have believed that Alexander was implicated, but there's simply not enough evidence, and you cannot hold a man in court 2500 years after events like this have passed. The charge can't be proved.

But it is certainly true that Alexander profited mightily by the timing of Philip's death in 336. As we saw last time, at the time of his death, Philip was actually planning the invasion of Persia. He was going to lead a combined army, not as the conqueror of Greece, but rather as the Captain-General of all the Greek forces, in a war that would avenge the Greeks for what had been done to them by the Persians 130 years earlier.

Alexander simply took over the plans that his father had already laid. In 334, he crossed the Hellespont, and in good Macedonian fashion he hurled his spear into the ground. The claim that Asia Minor was "spear one" territory was the claim that began the campaign of conquest against the Persians.

The first of Alexander's three great victories over the Persians came early in his campaign. It was shortly after crossing over into Asia Minor that Alexander was brought to battle by the local satraps or provincial governors left in charge of the area by the Persian king. This took place at the Granicus River in northwestern Asia Minor. Alexander was entirely successful.

I'm not going to spend a great deal of time in this series of lectures on the details of military history, although it's a fascinating topic. But there is one aspect of the victory at the Granicus River that deserves to be mentioned. The ancient sources put the victory down to the reckless courage of Alexander. And it is true that throughout his career, Alexander led from the front. Always putting himself in danger before endangering the lives of any of his men. The effect of this, I think, was to make his army feel astonishingly devoted to the personality of that one man. He was a very, very successful commander because his men loved him. But it's actually not that point that I want to make about the Battle of the Granicus.

It's this: Up until this time, the major battles fought by the Greeks, either amongst themselves or against the Persians, had been battles won by the forces of their infantry—*hoplites*, heavily armed soldiers wearing a shield that protected them from the neck to the knee. And then a bronze helmet and bronze greaves below meant that the individual heavily armed Greek infantryman was wearing 60 pounds of bronze armor. These men would stand in close formation with their shields protecting both themselves and also the body of the man next to them as well. It had been the mass of these men that had won the victories in great battles up until now. People have sometimes

©2000 The Teaching Company.

observed that Greek battles were often like tugs of war, with the two sides pushing against each other until one side broke and the other side followed.

But Alexander introduced a change in tactics. A dramatic change. Prior 'til now, the cavalry had only been used either on the wings to skirmish at the edges of the *hoplite* battalion. Or, once one line had broken, the cavalry would pour into the gap that had been created and would cut down the forces of the enemy as they fled. Cavalry had not really been used as a tactical weapon. But now, Alexander appreciated the potential of the cavalry to break the enemy's forces. That an attack of cavalry could shatter the line, create a weakness and a break into which his phalanx could then pour, splitting the enemy.

So, while the ancient sources emphasize Alexander's bravery, and it certainly had its effect, I'd like to emphasize his military intelligence. His keen understanding as a tactician of the potential of both infantry and cavalry. Once the cavalry had broken and once the heavily armed Macedonians then hit the opposite line, the battle turned into a rout. You have to imagine that most forces in the Persian army would be made up of lightly armed infantrymen. Men carrying either wicker shields or leather shields. They were no match for the heavily armed Greeks and Macedonians. In fact, in most of the battles between Greeks and Persians, when it was a close-fought fight, it was because the Persians were using Greek mercenaries. So it was the Greek army versus the Greek mercenaries in the Persian army that usually proved to be the essence of the battle.

So Alexander, already in 334, has begun his campaign. He's still a young man, in his early twenties, and he's won a victory over the "Great King", the forces of the Persian king. He now begins to think about how he's going to present this entire campaign. How it will be "packaged," both to his Greek audience and also to the Persians. Naturally what he does is to think in terms of epic and mythic events in earlier Greek history. He begins to think of this as a new Trojan War, with the forces of the Greeks coming east into, in this case, Persia. He begins to think of himself as a new Achilles, a character straight out of Greek myth. A character who is the son of a goddess. Something more than just human, but rather of heroic status.

Now, when we use the term "hero", we usually mean somebody who has simply done something courageous. To the Greeks, the word "hero" means something else. A hero is a man who, either by his descent or particularly by his actions, has actually achieved a semi-divine status. He may be the son of a god or the son of a goddess, or he may be someone who, like Heracles, has done such wonderful deeds (the labors of Heracles were famous) that he's actually been taken up into heaven. These men are not human like you and me. They are superhuman. And the Greeks think of this as a separate category of being.

Alexander already, I think, in his early twenties, is propagating that image, and may even be believing it himself, as well. Plutarch tells us that he used to sleep at night with a dagger under his pillow and a copy of Homer's *Iliad*, as if he could imbibe overnight, in his dreams, the very essence of being a Homeric hero.

And so it wasn't long before people began to compare his campaign, which had already broken out of the confines of the Greek world, and had marched into Asia Minor, as a campaign that was like the labors of Heracles. Heracles himself had wandered far and wide away from the Greek world. Remember that even Gibraltar was known to the Greeks as the "Pillars of Heracles," because he had gone that far west. And the Greeks also worshipped a god, Dionysos, known for having come from far in the east. So the notion of an epic journey, a journey that went far beyond the normal confines of the Greek world, was something that the Greeks were already attuned to thinking of as the work of a god or a hero. That's what Alexander was plugging into, making these comparisons between himself and these characters, casting his conquest to the east, therefore, not merely as a campaign of vengeance against the Persians, but as a divinely-sanctioned campaign with himself in the role of either hero or god.

The victory at the Granicus River left Alexander in control of much of Asia Minor, the area that corresponds to what we would now call western and central Turkey. It was followed a year later by another victory of Alexander's at the Battle of Issus, as it's called, in 333 B.C. Southern Asia Minor (southern Turkey) has running along it a range of mountains, known as the Taurus Mountains. Between the Taurus Mountains, with Turkey on one side and (now) Syria on the other, there is a narrow pass, the only pass that allows you to conveniently march an army from what would now be Turkey into Syria. (From Asia Minor into Syria.) It was through that pass that

Alexander marched his troops, and strangely enough, the Persian army and the Greek army (or the Macedonian army) actually passed each other in the night. So it ended up that the Persian forces were closer up to the mountains, and it was the Greeks who occupied the more open territory.

This was a fortuitous turn of events for Alexander, because the Persians had a vastly larger army, but were not able to deploy it on great open ground where they could use their numbers to their advantage.

The Persian army at this stage was led, in fact, by the Great King himself, Darius. So this was a momentous event in 333 B.C., as the great king, the king of kings, the one anointed by Ahura Mazda, came all the way across to the western provinces of his empire to face this Macedonian interloper. Here, at the Battle of Issus in 333, Alexander, once again, was stunningly victorious, vanquishing completely the Persian army.

So now, in only two years of campaigning, and with only two battles, Alexander had extended the possessions of the Macedonians and the Greeks from the Aegean, their original homeland, all the way to the headwaters of the Euphrates River. If you look at that on a map, you will find that that essentially doubles the landmass under the control of the Greeks, in two years and two battles.

I talked in the first lecture about the scale of the Hellenistic world, and we get some taste of it here. The scale of these victories could not be measured by the Greeks. It was so much larger than anything that had ever happened before. Because it was off the scale of what the Greeks could comprehend, it raises some very interesting questions for Alexander. No Greek and no Macedonian had ever faced the issue before of how to deal with the Greeks and how to deal with the Persians, both as subjects within the same empire. What is the basis of his authority? He's not the ancestral king of Persia. He wasn't born the son of the Persian king. So how should Alexander behave toward the Greeks and the Persians?

We're fortunate, in that we actually have documentary evidence to give us a clear idea of what Alexander thought of his authority at this stage of his career. To the Greeks, he simply styled himself as "King Alexander." He doesn't say, "Alexander, King of Greece" nor does he say "Alexander, King of the Macedonians," but I think that that is probably what he implies. Simply "King Alexander." Something greater than they've ever seen before.

We have a wonderful document that comes to us from around 334 B.C. I want to read you some of it, because it is a document that contains a decree of Alexander's. A decree written to the people of the island of Chios. These are Greeks who are now behind the line of advance, and they've written to Alexander to ask him to settle their internal affairs. What you'll see in this document is a good illustration of how Alexander is dealing with his Greek subjects.

A letter from King Alexander to the Chian people:

> All those who have been in exile from Chios shall return home.
>
> The constitution that exists in Chios shall be democratic. Law-writers shall be chosen to write and correct the laws in order that nothing opposed to the democracy or the return of exiles shall be in the laws. Whatever has been corrected or written, shall be referred to Alexander.
>
> The Chians shall provide twenty manned *triremes* at their own expense, and these *triremes* shall sail as long as the rest of the fleet of the Greeks sails with us.

And so it goes on with a few more stipulations.

What is very significant about this is that we see a combination of interesting idealism and practicality. The practical stipulation in here is that the people of Chios have to provide twenty boats for Alexander. He's still marching, with a Greek navy following closely along the coastline in support of him, and to make sure that a Persian fleet doesn't come in behind Alexander and either destroy his lines of communication or attack him from the rear. So that's a practical stipulation.

But at the same time we find that it is Alexander who is guaranteeing that the Chians shall be a democracy. In other words, they're not going to be ruled by a Macedonian garrison or a Macedonian commander. They'll be free, or, in the words of the Greeks, *autonomous*, to govern their own affairs. So Alexander's genius expresses itself here. He recognizes that the best way to get the Greeks on his side was in fact to rule with a very light hand. Unlike many of his successors, who would impose their rule directly on the

Greeks? Alexander essentially left the Greeks to rule themselves, with the proviso that when they redrafted their laws they would send them to him for ratification. He's acting as a kind of supreme court, if you will, to make sure that everything is exactly as he wants it to be.

So here we have King Alexander, the Macedonian king, the legal expert, ruling very lightly, and encouraging the autonomy of the Greeks. But to the Persians, a completely different story. To them, Alexander presented himself quite differently, because he now had defeated the Persians twice in battle, and he had demonstrated that he was the equal of the Great King. So to the Persians, Alexander presented himself as a character every bit on a par with Darius. We have a letter that Alexander apparently wrote to Darius, and here I think you'll find that the tone of his communication to the Persians is very different from what he had to say to the Greeks. I want you to listen to what he says about his own authority. He writes to Darius:

> Your ancestors invaded Macedonia and Greece and caused havoc in our country, although we had done nothing to provoke them. As Supreme Commander of all Greece, I invaded Asia because I wish to punish Persia for this act. I took the field against you, although it was you who began the quarrel. First I defeated in battle your generals and satraps. Now I have defeated yourself and the army you led. By god's help I have mastered your country, and have made myself responsible for the survivors of your force. Come to me, therefore [orders King Alexander], as you would come to the Lord of the Continent of Asia. Should you fear to suffer any indignity, I will give you the proper guarantees. Come, then, and ask me for your mother [who Alexander had captured in this battle] and ask me for your wife [whom he also had captured] and your children and anything else you please. For you shall have them, and whatever besides you can persuade me to give you. And in future [he says, and now we hear the king talking to his fellow king], let any communication you wish to make with me be addressed to 'The King of All Asia.'

So Alexander to the Greeks is something very different from what he is to the Persians.

You may wonder why I'm belaboring this point. Clearly, the way you deal with your own people and the way you deal with an enemy is always going to be somewhat different. That's fairly obvious, yes. But what I want to do here is to establish an important point. I think a fundamental point in the interpretation of Alexander. Alexander was caught between two cultures that had very different ways of viewing the world. Two cultures that had very different ways of understanding authority and power. What I'm going to be suggesting is that Alexander couldn't reconcile the difference between these. That, in fact, you cannot be the first among equals, as you would be as a Macedonian, with being a semi-divine, supreme autocrat, as you must be amongst the Persians.

So the beginnings, I think, of a deep conflict between the cultures is to be found right here, in Alexander's correspondence both to the Greeks and to Darius.

After the Battle of Issus, Alexander turned south, to secure the coastal cities of Tyre and Sidon. And from here, before pursuing Darius inland, which would be the last phase of his victory over the Persians, Alexander instead headed for Egypt.

I want to talk about this episode for a moment, because this is really quite a critical moment in Alexander's career. First of all, why did he go there? Well, we will be talking in a moment about the oracle of Zeus at Siwah, which Alexander went to visit, and that's going to be an important part of his reign. But we shouldn't neglect something far more basic, and that is that there is a tactical and strategic reason for going to Egypt. You do not want to leave a large Persian province, as Egypt was at this point, in your rear as you march inland, east, across towards Iraq and Iran. You don't want to do that, because Persian forces back there may invade Greece, send a navy towards Macedon, and you'll find yourself having to scurry back again. So he is establishing his conquest in an orderly fashion to make it possible later to march further east.

This explains his campaign in Egypt in general, but (as I'm sure you're all aware) that the kingdom of Egypt, which was now a Persian province, is essentially just the Nile valley and the delta of the River Nile. But when Alexander marched into Egypt, he didn't stay just in the delta and just on the river. He didn't merely go to Memphis. He marched further west, even further, going across the coastline of the Mediterranean as far as the modern-day location of

Mersa Matruh and then turning south and marching into the desert, until he came to the oracle of the god known as Zeus Ammon, located at Siwah (the oasis of Siwah). What happened here is a story that has bedeviled historical analysis for many, many years. Because it appears as if Alexander was greeted as the son of a god. And it also appears as though he entertained that belief quite seriously thereafter.

Now, there are many conflicting stories about this, and I won't go through all of them in detail. In some stories, when he arrived at Siwah, he wanted to find out about his father, and so he asked about Philip. And the oracle said, "You shouldn't assume that Philip is your father." Which made Alexander think, "Ahh! Perhaps it's a god, rather than Philip." Such double parentage, with a human father and a divine father is very much in the Greek tradition, and that may be what happened.

Another story is that as he walked toward the temple, the priests came out to visit him, and they meant to say "Oh, *Paidion*, my little boy, my young one", but their Greek wasn't so good, and when they said it, it came out sounding like "Oh my *Paidios*, son of Zeus," so perhaps Alexander's belief in his own divinity was based on simply a rather poor pronunciation of Greek.

But I'd like to suggest another interpretation, and that is this: By conquering Egypt, Alexander became pharaoh. That's a simple given. If you conquered Egypt, you were, once again, pharaoh. And the Memphite priesthood, the priestly group that ruled in Memphis, and gave continuity to Egyptian culture for so many centuries, would have recognized Alexander as the new pharaoh, and one of the titles of pharaohs in late Egyptian history, during the Persian period and now in this period, was "Son of Ammon." So it is quite likely that in his visit to Egypt, Alexander, in taking on the role, now, of the pharaoh, in proclaiming himself the inheritor of that royal authority, was ritually recognized with the title, "Son of Ammon." When he went to Siwah, that same title was bestowed on him by the priests there, in recognition of the fact that it was not merely a Greek or a Macedonian who was visiting their oracle, but rather it was the pharaoh of Egypt.

hat makes sense of the events, and it's an explanation of how he came to be known as the "Son of the God", but what's much more important is what Alexander himself did with this. I've suggested already that he sees himself as another incarnation of the heroic character, like Heracles and Dionysos. Being greeted as the son of a god may strike us as being incredibly arrogant, but in fact it fits in with the model of Greek thinking, already before Alexander. That the great man might be able to accomplish a higher status and become "godly" as the Greeks would call it. The *theos aner*, the godly man.

So it's quite possible that Alexander was not merely going through the motions of taking on an Egyptian title, but that he actually was coming to believe this, as well, and that, in the latter part of his career, Alexander wanted to present himself as a god, as a divine man, as the two together. I somewhat hesitate at advancing that particular view, for the simple reason that to give it real credence, we have to psychoanalyze Alexander. And we can't do that. As we're going to see in a later lecture, so much of what we know about Alexander is a result of the way different sources in antiquity wrote about him. There was so much romance, and there were so many popular stories that getting back to the original is very hard to fathom.

But what I think we have seen so far, is a man who is very aware of the need to package himself to an audience. Both to the Greeks and to the conquered people, as well, whether to the Persians, writing to the Great King as the Lord of Asia, or, in this instance, to the Egyptians, taking on the role of the pharaoh. And what we find here, I think, is the key to Alexander. He is a man who is trying, always, throughout his career, to reconcile the irreconcilable. To reconcile the demands of Greek culture with the demands of the cultures of the conquered peoples in the Hellenistic world. He makes attempts to reconcile those, by presenting himself to his different audiences in different ways, but finally (I'm going to be arguing) he's unsuccessful in those attempts.

The best proof of that will be that in the generation after Alexander, none of his successors will try to do the same thing that he did. The great tragedy of Alexander, to my mind, is going to be that none of his generals will attempt to be both Macedonian and pharaoh in the same way as did Alexander, the blazing star.

Lecture Three
The Blazing Star

Scope:

The visit to Siwah may have convinced Alexander he was a god, or he may have recognized the value of blurring the lines between human and divine. Whatever his motives, he still faced the matter of bringing the Great King Darius to battle. The second half of his campaign would be spent pushing further east.

Outline

I. Leaving Egypt after installing Macedonian garrisons and a Macedonian governor, Alexander marched north, following the caravan trails across northern Syria and into Mesopotamia. He had left the Mediterranean and was headed toward the heartland of Persia.

   A. Descending into Mesopotamia, Alexander made his way toward the headwaters of the Tigris River.

   B. Here, at Gaugamela, in 331 B.C., he met and destroyed the army of Darius, who fled north and east. Alexander was now Lord of Asia in deed as much as in title.

   C. Babylon surrendered to him, as did the royal capital of Susa, and the wealth that fell into Alexander's hands vastly outweighed anything previously known to the Greek world.

   D. A comparison demonstrates the scale of this wealth: the revenues of the Athenian empire in about 480 B.C. amounted to 460 talents. At Susa, Alexander captured 40,000 talents of coined money, along with such riches as 5,000 talents worth of purple cloth.

II. Now began the pursuit of Darius.

   A. The Achaemenid king had been retreating into the wild northern regions of Hyrcania and Media in northern Iran and near the region bordering modern Turkmenistan.

   B. Once Alexander's army closed in on Darius, however, the Persian king's own men turned on him and he was assassinated by a Persian nobleman named Bessos.

C. This was an anticlimax to the great personal rivalry between Alexander and Darius (descended from the Darius who had invaded Greece 150 years before), but Alexander brilliantly turned it into an opportunity to refashion himself as both the Lord of Asia and the legitimate successor of Darius.

D. Alexander continued his pursuit of Bessos until he was captured and executed, torn in two.

III. Alexander was now king of Macedon, Lord of Asia, and heir to the Achaemenid throne. Could these be reconciled? Could he be all things to all men?

A. Alexander's veterans grew unhappy with the king's adoption of Persian practices and announced a litany of complaints against their leader. In a tense face-off, Alexander won back their loyalty.

B. At a banquet at Opis, near Babylon, in 324 B.C., Alexander initiated a policy of reconciliation between Greeks and Persians, praying for harmony between the two peoples.

1. He and thousands of his men took Persian wives, and plans were made for training their children as the new, mixed ruling class of the empire.

2. Persian nobles were integrated into the army, and new battalions were created to blend the skills of both groups. Overnight, the long-standing enemy, the Persians, became close allies.

C. Alexander also introduced the rituals of the Persian court and began dressing in Persian garb. These actions failed to reconcile the conflicting demands of Macedonians and Persians and prompted misgivings about Alexander's "orientalism."

D. The Persian court ritual of obeisance, or prostration, was disdained by the Greeks.

E. None of Alexander's successors embraced his attempt at cultural fusion.

IV. Even after his conquest of Darius, Alexander's campaigns continued. He pushed the Macedonian army into the mountain passes of the Hindu Kush, into Pakistan, and on toward India in an effort to supersede the mythical exploits of Heracles.

A. In each of these regions, he conquered enemies whom he then befriended, such as Taxiles, and made allies of men like Porus, whom he would never see again, because his armies had had enough. By the Indus River they mutinied, refusing to follow Alexander any further.

B. The return from India has sometimes been interpreted by Alexander's critics as evidence for his megalomania. The march across the Gedrosian desert looks like punishment inflicted on the Macedonians by a spoiled boy-king, though now he was close to 30 and had nothing left to prove.

C. His disastrous return from the east was followed shortly after by his death in Babylon in 323 B.C.
    1. Because he had known only conquest, it is difficult to evaluate Alexander as a ruler.
    2. His policy of administration appears to be more of the same as the Persian system. Sometimes, Greeks were left in charge of newly acquired territories but just as often, Persians were, too.

D. At the time of his death, Alexander may have been planning further campaigns to the west. Like many other conquerors, he found it easier to wage war than to rule a stable domain.

Suggested Reading:

R. L. Fox, *Alexander the Great*.

Questions to Consider:

1. What motivated Alexander to pursue conquest so relentlessly?
2. How durable were the administrative arrangements made by Alexander?

Lecture Three—Transcript
The Blazing Star

In our last lecture we looked at the first half of the meteoric career of Alexander the Great. We saw that from the foundations established by his father, Philip II, Alexander initiated a campaign of conquest which would demolish the power of Achaemenid Persia, and would establish Greek culture as the elite culture of the entire Near and Middle East.

During that lecture, I pointed out that it seemed to me that Alexander was faced with a dilemma: How to be both the Macedonian king and a beneficent and gentle king in the eyes of the Greeks, whom he wanted to leave essentially ruling themselves, and how to be the king equal in status to the Great King of Persia, a role, in fact, he would come now to take on when he defeated Darius III.

I suggested that the turning point for him in his attempt to reconcile these two competing demands probably came as a result of his visit to the oracle of Zeus-Ammon at Siwah in the Libyan Desert, west of the Nile Valley and Memphis. Here, I suggested, Alexander found a way to present himself as something that the Greeks would understand; as more than just a mortal man. A hero. A character that was godly or semi-divine, if you will. Something that he learned both because that notion was a part of Greek culture, but also because here he was greeted by the priests as the son of Zeus-Ammon, a title modeled on his now official title as pharaoh, the son of Ammon.

So the visit to Siwah certainly gave Alexander an idea of how to present his kingship. It may also have convinced him that he was, in fact, a god, by blurring the division between the human and the divine. But whatever it did to his psyche (and we'll never know exactly what the truth is there), there was still a much more pressing matter, and that was finally defeating Darius III , the Great King of Persia. He had already defeated his forces once at the Battle of the Granicus River, shortly after crossing into Asia Minor in 334, and a year later, just south of the Taurus Mountains, he had defeated Darius himself at the Battle of Issus.

But now it was time for Alexander to begin in a serious way, a campaign that would take his forces way away from the Aegean and the Mediterranean, the heartland areas of Greek culture. So, after leaving a Macedonian garrison and a Macedonian governor in control of Egypt, Alexander began marching north, back through the modern-day regions of Israel, Lebanon and Syria, before crossing the caravan trails that headed from northern Syria eastward towards the headwaters of the Tigris and Euphrates, the region known to the Greeks as Mesopotamia, "the land between the rivers."

He had left the Mediterranean behind, and he was headed toward the heartland of Persia. Moving into Mesopotamia then, Alexander made his way towards the headwaters of the Tigris River. Here, at the Battle of Gaugamela in 331 B.C., he met, and destroyed convincingly the army of Darius, who fled the scene of battle and ran away, fleeing to the north and to the east. Some of you may have seen the well-known mosaic depicting this battle, which is now located in the national museum in Naples. The mosaic shows the very moment at which Alexander is breaking through and Darius, in his chariot, has turned and is fleeing. People in antiquity recognized that that very moment was a turning point in history, because it marked the beginning of the end for Persia and the final stage of the ascent of Macedon. Alexander was now Lord of Asia, in deed, as much as in title. He continued his victorious march eastwards, descending on Babylon. Here, the city surrendered to him, as did the royal capital of Darius at Susa.

It's easy to pass over these events as merely further steps in the continual progression of Alexander's inexorable Eastern campaign. But what we should stop and recognize is the astonishing degree of wealth that fell into Alexander's lap as a result of this victory. The wealth that Alexander now had at his disposal vastly outweighed anything that any Greek, and probably all of the Greeks combined, had ever known in their history previous to this. Once again, this theme I introduced a lecture or two ago, of the massive scale of Hellenism. A whole new scale even now, of wealth.

Consider this fact—a simple comparison that I think illustrates the point nicely. In 480 B.C., when the Athenians defeated the Persians and established their empire, the states of the Aegean sent them tribute. The Athenian Empire's tribute in 480-479 B.C. amounted to 460 talents. 460 talents. At Susa alone, Alexander captured 40,000 talents of coined money, as well as uncoined bullion, and even 5,000 talents worth of just purple cloth (the cloth used by kings) because its color is made from tiny sea creatures that are crushed to create purple dye. Massively expensive. Ten times more value just in royal cloth than the entire revenue of the Athenian Empire in the early part of the 5th century. So this gives us an idea of the astonishing scale of the wealth that would now begin to move from the Persian Empire towards the Mediterranean. This wealth would eventually find its way back to Macedon and the Hellenistic kingdoms of Seleucus in Syria and to Ptolemaic Egypt. Finally this wealth would make its way even into Rome. This gold and silver can be melted down and reused time and again.

But before Alexander had an opportunity to enjoy this new-found wealth, he had to pursue Darius. Though the king had been beaten in battle, he was still alive. The Achaemenid king, the last ruler of the Achaemenid dynasty, began retreating away from his royal capitals of Susa and Babylon and moving into the upland country. Moving into the area beyond Media, towards the Caspian Sea, towards the area known in antiquity as Hyrcania, and across into the regions that would correspond in our geography now, to northern Iran, right up to the border of modern-day Turkmenistan.

However, just as Alexander's army was closing in finally on Darius, the king's own men turned on him and he was assassinated, cut down by a Persian nobleman named Bessus.

This was a terrible anti-climax. The entire movement of Macedon into the Persian Empire; this epoch-making campaign that was going to change history forever, had been framed as a personal rivalry between Alexander, representing the vengeance of the Greeks, and Darius, the sitting Achaemenid king, the descendant of the Darius and the Xerxes who had invaded Greece 150 years earlier. So it was a terrible anticlimax that Alexander did not get the opportunity to defeat Darius in battle, capture and execute him.

But, and here we see another example, I think, of the genius of Alexander, he took this disappointment and he refashioned it now, using it as a brilliant opportunity to change the way that he presented his own authority and power. Because instantly, he went from being the force of Greek vengeance over the Persians, to refashioning himself as the Lord of Asia and the legitimate successor of Darius, who would now pursue Darius' assassin in order to bring him to justice. Alexander and his men did this, in a forced march, gradually, day after day, catching up to Bessus, capturing him, and eventually having him mutilated, sent back to Babylon, and executed. Torn in two.

Alexander was now the King of Macedon, King Alexander to the Greeks, the Lord of Asia and the heir to the Achaemenid throne. The question that really we must pay attention to now is, "Could these things be reconciled? Could he be all things to all men?" My answer to that is: "No, he couldn't, though he tried mighty hard."

The key event, the seminal event that illustrates the kinds of tensions that Alexander was dealing with here, comes in 324, at Opis, near Babylon. A town where the Macedonian army briefly mutinied against Alexander. Alexander, in dealing with this mutiny tried to establish a reconciliation between Greeks and Persians. The events that surround this mutiny and the banquet of reconciliation, I think give us a very clear idea of what was going on in Alexander's kingdom, and the relations between the various factions and ethnic groups. Let me read you a part of the description that we have:

> On arriving at Opis, Alexander called together the Macedonians, and he declared that he was discharging from campaign and sending back to their country all those who were unfit for service. [He was instantly allowing to leave all of his veterans, going back to Macedon.] The presents he would give them would make them the object of even greater envy at home, and would encourage the other Macedonians to take part in the same dangers. [So the old guard, the men who had been campaigning now for about ten years, are allowed to go home and a fresh group will be brought in.] Many of the Macedonians, however, were displeased by this, and they felt that Alexander despised them. It was not unreasonable for them to take exception to Alexander's words, and they had many grievances throughout the expedition. [And now what will spill out is a whole litany of the grievances that these men feel about Alexander.] There was the recurring annoyance of Alexander's Persian dress. [He had now begun to dress like the Persian king. We'll talk about the significance of that in a moment.] They hated the fact that he was training barbarian successors. [*Epigonoi*, as they were called in Greek. His "successors," or "inheritors." Persians who would be trained in the Macedonian style of warfare.] And the introduction of foreign cavalry into the squadrons of the Companion Cavalry.

Now try to imagine for a moment the attitude of Alexander's veterans. These are men who, for ten years, have marched way beyond the Greek world, have defeated the Persians in three major battles, and now find that their glorious king is dressing like a Persian, is dismissing the Macedonian veterans, is raising young Persians and teaching them Macedonian styles of warfare, and, worst of all, is actually including Persian battalions in the Macedonian army. Now if any of you are veterans, I'm sure that you'll be able to recognize the kind of ill will that was brewing in Alexander's army as a result of this. Why was he doing this?

I think it must be that he was planning for the future. That to rule this entire empire, which stretched from Macedon to India, he would need to have a ruling caste that included more than simply the Macedonians who had fought with him. His response to this mutiny, his immediate response, was to go into a sulk and to retire for three days into his tent. Until, after he had worn down his men, and his men had come to him and said that they were sorry about this. When they said to him that they simply wanted to be recognized as his kinsmen, then he came out of his tent, and he saw his men, these beloved soldiers who had marched with him. And now look at the moment of reconciliation. This passage is very, very interesting.

> Alexander came forward to speak, but his men remained there imploring him. One of them, whose age and command of the cavalry made him a chief officer, spoke as follows, and he says: 'Sire, what grieves us [the Macedonians] is that you have already made some Persians your kinsmen. Persians are called the kinsmen of Alexander and are allowed to kiss you. [To come up to him and kiss him on the cheek.] While not one of the Macedonians has been granted this honor.'

And Alexander, understanding the power of the moment, said, "I make all of you my kinsmen." All of the Macedonians now are ennobled. Are the equals, if you like, of the king.

"And at this, Callisthenes stepped forward and kissed him, and so did everyone else who wished." So there is a great moment of reconciliation between them. What Alexander does then, after making a sacrifice, is to order a great banquet to be held. The banquet begins with this description:

He and those around him drew wine from the same bowl and poured the same libation, beginning with the Greek seers and the magi [the Persian priests]. He prayed for other blessings and for harmony [note this] harmony and unity in rule between Macedonians and Persians.

It is said that there were 9,000 guests at the banquet. Now, what is happening, I think, very clearly at the banquet at Opis, is that Alexander is trying to fashion a policy that will reconcile these former enemies, so that the kingdom will have a new ruling elite. He's not asking for the unity of all mankind. He's not behaving like some religious leader who simply says, "Can't we bury our differences and all unite together?" No. It is a very specific political gesture. Harmony between Greeks and Persians, to create a new ruling elite.

And I would support that contention that he's actually trying to engineer a new ruling class, by noting that he also forced all of his major officers (80 of them, in total) and thousands of his men (possibly as many as ten thousand) to take Persian wives. I think that dramatically and graphically illustrates exactly what Alexander was trying to do. Because the simple fact is that those couples would have children who would be bicultural and bilingual. Both Greek and Persian. Now of course, many of his men had already taken Persian wives, or at least concubines, camp followers. These too, he tried to recognize, by taking these children who'd been born to the marriage of Greeks and foreigners, and by training them now, as Macedonian soldiers for the future. Alexander the Great was one of the first leaders in history to practice eugenics. He is trying to manufacture a new ruling caste.

The description of the marriage of his men to their Persian wives is a fascinating one. Alexander goes through each of the officers, and he tries to find a woman who comes from a corresponding family on the Persian side, of equal status. So that he specifically gives to Craterus, Amastrine, the daughter of Oxyartes, who is the brother of Darius. So she's the niece of the Great King. Alexander sat down and charted this very carefully, matching specific women of Persian background to corresponding Greek men. Then, as for the Macedonian men who had already married Asian women, we're told, Alexander ordered a list of names to be drawn up (it numbered over ten thousand), and Alexander gave them wedding gifts.

So what we've got here is a very clear attempt, I think, to create a new ruling class. The integration of Persian soldiers, both those who had been trained and those who were now brought in as new cavalry battalions, was an attempt to blend the skills of the two groups, and it, of course, recognized the authority of the Persians as equals in empire. This may strike us as merely good sense, but I'd suggest to you that it shows a kind of generosity of spirit and perhaps a view or a look towards the future on the part of Alexander that is dramatically different. The Greeks have thought of the Persians for 150 years as the enemy. And virtually overnight, the Greek who finally conquers those Persians is inviting them to join in rule.

Alexander may have recognized the need for this, forbearing the differences. But his men certainly did not. His introduction of the rituals of the Persian court, his wearing of the gowns of the Persian king, simply infuriated his men. I think that Alexander finally was unable to reconcile the differences in view between the two. Let me try to illustrate this with one specific example that shows you how far apart these two cultures were.

In the Persian system, the Great King, who was anointed by Ahura Mazda, is the supreme commander of a hierarchically organized society. Throughout that society, every person has a station. When you meet someone of a higher station (if you're a serf and you meet the bailiff; if you're a bailiff and you meet the landowner; if you're a landowner and you meet the regional governor; and so on and so on, all the way up), when you meet that person, you perform an act of obeisance. You prostrate yourself before your superior. Now, Darius is gone. Bessus is executed. Alexander's the Great King. What will his Persians do? They must, of course, prostrate themselves in front of him. And Alexander accepts this as the Persian way of recognizing their king.

Alexander then attempted to introduce the same practice at the court for his Greek and Macedonian subjects. In the Macedonian and the Greek system, you greet a powerful man with a kiss, because there is an egalitarian spirit amongst the Greeks and the Macedonians, particularly among the leading Macedonians. Many of these were generals who had fought with Philip. They were even older than Alexander. To them, he was a successful younger man, but they weren't going to prostrate themselves. Because in the Greek and the

Macedonian view of things, that act of obeisance is what you do before a god.

So even at the level of court gesture and ritual, Greeks and Persians speak a different language. As a result, Alexander, by attempting to introduce this Persian practice, only managed to infuriate the people of his court. I'd like to give you the description here of Alexander's attempt to introduce this practice, known as *proskynesis* or prostration, because I think it dramatically illustrates the kinds of misgivings that his followers felt. And also, I might add, the way in which he himself is trying to engineer court ritual. There is a story told on the question of obeisance, and it goes as follows:

> It had been agreed between Alexander and the sophists [the university professors in his retinue] and the most distinguished of the Persians and the Medes at his court that the subject should be raised during a drinking party. [So they've engineered this. They're setting the seeds for this occasion.] Anaxarchus launched the topic, saying that Alexander had much better claims to be regarded as a god than Dionysos and Heracles. Not so much because of the number and magnitude of his achievements, as because Dionysos was a Theban and not related to the Macedonians and Heracles was an Argaed, and only distantly related. The Macedonians would have better reason to honor their king with divine honors.

So Alexander and his inner circle had decided to engineer a conversation at a dinner party to raise the topic of divine honors for Alexander.

There was no doubt that once Alexander departed from men, that he would be a god. How much more justifiable it would be, therefore, to honor him now, while he was still present among them as a man. After Anaxarchus had spoken to this effect, those who were privy to the plan praised his words and they wanted to begin prostrating themselves before Alexander. But the majority of the Macedonians were displeased with this and kept quiet.

This is a fascinating incident. We've got an eyewitness here of the Macedonians standing back and thinking, "What the hell is going on here? Does this man seriously think we're going to treat him the way the Persians treat their gods?"

And so, Callisthenes intervened and said, "I declare that there is no honor befitting a man that Alexander does not deserve. But a distinction has been drawn by men between honors fit for mortals and honors fit for the gods."

This is crossing the line from the point of view of many of the Greeks. So Callisthenes then goes forward and he tries to resist this notion of Alexander receiving obeisance. And then some of the Persians actually come forward to perform the act of prostration. The Greeks actually laugh at them. They think that this is comic. The idea of actually performing prostration before Alexander. So they burst out laughing. And Alexander once again becomes angry at the whole matter.

Alexander now engineers an episode so that if the Greeks give him a kiss, they will then perform the obeisance to him. It's his way of saying, "Look. We're Greeks. Just give me a kiss and we'll carry on as usual. But this way, the Persian subjects will be pleased."

Callisthenes apparently went forward to get the kiss and failed to make the obeisance, so Alexander refused him the kiss, at which he said, "Then I depart the poorer for a kiss." What these incidents, I think, reveal to us are that Alexander is trying to manipulate every aspect of court ritual in an attempt to fashion himself as someone higher than either the Greeks or the Persians. But all he succeeded in doing was aggravating the Greeks' misgivings about what they called his "orientalism."

In fact, after Alexander's death, most of his successors would simply put aside these women. Divorce them and ignore these marriages. The *epigonoi*, these Persians trained as Macedonians were disbanded, and none of the successors made any attempt to reconcile or to fuse Greeks and Persians. They simply imposed Hellenism, Greek culture, on their subject areas. So the dream of a kind of fusion between the two cultures really dies with Alexander. That may be unfortunate or it may be inevitable. It's hard to say.

Even after his conquest of Darius, though, Alexander's campaigns continued. We resume the story as he pushes his Macedonian army even further east. Now, what is left to gain, one has to ask here. The Great King is dead. Alexander has taken over. He's won all of the great capitals of the Persian kings: Babylon, Susa, Persepolis and so forth. And yet, Alexander keeps campaigning, driving his army further and further east. He takes them into the mountain passes of the Hindu Kush. He takes them up into Pakistan. He tries to attack a mountain ridge 7,000 feet above the Indus River, the area known to the Greeks as Aornos. The principle reason that he does it, according to our ancient sources, is that Heracles had failed to do it.

I've tried to resist psychoanalyzing Alexander up to this point, but it does seem to me that in the final phase of his campaign, after he's won all that he can legitimately expect to win, in conquering the Persians, we have to entertain the idea that Alexander has really taken on the notion seriously that he is a god, and that he will now perform accomplishments and deeds that not only no man has ever accomplished before, but not even a god has accomplished.

So he keeps marching, right into the Hindu Kush. And then he comes back down towards the Indus. And there he overtakes and conquers most of the local governors, men such as Taxiles, and he even conquers the most powerful king of northwest India at the time, the king known as Porus. And, frankly, he would have kept on going even further, across northern India, probably across Tibet and even into China, but for the fact that his army had had enough.

The popular story told of Alexander that he wept because there were no more empires to conquer is actually nonsense. Alexander didn't weep. He knew that there were more empires to conquer, and he wanted to go after them. But now I think we are really talking about a man driven by a kind of madness. To the Greeks, it was a *pathos*, as they called it. A yearning. A desire to go ever further, beyond every pass and every mountain, into every new territory.

But his army wouldn't go any further. They had had enough. They had had enough of seeing him become more like the Persian king they had conquered. They had had enough of seeing Persians brought into their army. They had had enough of the training of young Persians. They had had enough of prostration. And most of all, they had had enough of marching east. Because by now, they had been on the road for eleven years, had conquered the empire, and simply wanted to return and to enjoy the fruits of their victory.

It is in the return from India that I think we really see the best evidence for what, frankly, we can call Alexander's megalomania. He had a fleet built, which was commanded by his general Nearchus, which sailed along the northern coast of the Persian Gulf. How easy it would have been to have transported his army back that way, and to bring them quickly, and safe and sound, back to Babylon. But instead, he marched his army through the harshest desert regions he ever crossed at any time in his campaigns. At a time when there were no more enemies to conquer, except isolated towns in the southern Iranian desert. The area known as Gedrosia, in antiquity.

It really looks to me as though a spoiled man, who has been cheated out of his chance of further eastern conquests by his army, is now, in fact, punishing them by marching them through the desert. So that there are men going mad with thirst, and even dying. And his disastrous return from the east then is only finally capped off by his own death, of a fever, in Babylon, in 323 B.C. A pathetic end, frankly, to what had been a great military career.

But on the other hand, perhaps it's better that it did end at that point. Because, though Alexander was a great general, we have little evidence that he was a great commander or king of a region. His policy of administration was essentially a duplication of the Persian system. Often, he simply left the same men in charge of a region that he conquered, who had been there before him. He may have wanted to go further west and take on the Carthaginians. We'll never know, because he died before any of these plans could be put into operation.

But I think the final lesson from Alexander is that, for a great general such as him, it was much easier to wage war than it was to rule a kingdom.

Lecture Four
Alexander—Myth and Reality

Scope:

Alexander had an astonishing effect on the political development of the eastern Mediterranean, yet opinions remain deeply divided about him. This was true in antiquity and remains true now. The man is lost inside the mythmaking, leaving the historical Alexander only a shadow of the fantastic Alexander of romance and folklore.

Outline

I. The career and accomplishments of Alexander have always been the subject of widely different interpretations.

    A. To some, he was an idealist, attempting to create a new world in which Greeks and non-Greeks would live in peace and harmony.

    B. To others, he appears a drunken despot unable to envisage anything more than ever-greater feats of conquest. History gives us two very different Alexanders: the altruist and the megalomaniac.

    C. The most positive interpretation of Alexander was offered by W. W. Tarn, a historian writing in the aftermath of World War I at the time of the League of Nations. Influenced by contemporary ideas concerning international harmony, Tarn imagined Alexander's empire as an ancient forerunner of the 20th century's experiment in international cooperation. He even likened Alexander to St. Paul.

    D. At the other extreme are the views of such scholars as Ernst Badian, for whom Alexander is a paranoid tyrant, continually engaged in conspiracies against real and imagined enemies and relentlessly driving his troops forward in his maniacal and bloody quest for personal glory, no matter what the cost to his innocent victims, including his own men. Indeed, we know of summary executions committed during his reign, sometimes proceeding on flimsy evidence.

        1. At one banquet, Cleitus, a Macedonian general, objected to Alexander's being compared to a deity.

      2. Alexander, in a drunken rage, killed him on the spot.

II. These conflicting views of Alexander were already in place in antiquity and can be traced to two quite separate traditions.

    A. Alexander was accompanied by a historian, Callisthenes, who appears to have recorded the great man's deeds even as the campaigns were in progress.

        1. Although Callisthenes was eventually executed by Alexander, he lived long enough to produce a highly eulogistic account that compared Alexander to the Homeric heroes and Dionysos. He established a "court tradition," in which Alexander was heroic, semi-divine, and always right, inspired by an unidentified yearning.

        2. Other accounts, written soon after Alexander's death by men who had marched with him, such as Ptolemy and Aristoboulus, also depicted a sanitized, godlike figure.

    B. A more popular tradition also developed that emphasized the passion, drama, and bloodshed of Alexander's reign.

        1. The first author associated with this tradition was Cleitarchus and, although his work was hated by the critics, it was immensely popular with the public. Here was an Alexander who flew into rages—then became extravagantly remorseful. This was the Alexander who killed Black Cleitus in a drunken brawl and was prostrate with grief afterwards.

        2. This colorful tradition survives in the work of Diodorus Siculus and Justin.

    C. Eventually, both traditions would be combined in the works of later historians, such as Plutarch, who had to sift between two very different approaches.

        1. The court tradition lived on in the theme of Alexander's *pothos* or yearning, the semi-divine quality that leads him onward to his destiny.

        2. The vulgate lived on in fantastic stories that Alexander had been visited by the Queen of the Amazons, a story soundly rejected by those who followed the court tradition.

III. Alexander continued to influence the Mediterranean and Near East long after his death, both because of his accomplishments and because of his legend.

A. We will examine the changes wrought by the Greek and Macedonian control of the eastern Mediterranean up to the time of the Romans. It is worth remembering, however, that as a figure of legend, Alexander, like King Arthur, exerted an enormous influence over a vast area for even longer than the duration of the Hellenistic *oecumene,* or commonwealth, ruled by Alexander and his successors.

B. The Alexander legend, beginning about the 3rd century A.D., is a collection of stories from different lands and shows Alexander's mythic status even among later peoples.

    1. The *Ishkandanamah*, for example, makes Alexander a good Muslim who is actually the son of Darab, the Persian King, and falsely presented as the son or brother of the Caesar of Rum, Filqus. This story appropriates Alexander and makes him Persian and Muslim, despite the fact that Islam did not even come into existence until 1,000 years after his death. In this work, Alexander is frequently referred to as "the two-horned one," a reference to attributes of Zeus Ammon in his official graven image.

    2. The Alexander legend would eventually reach from Britain to Yemen and Sri Lanka.

    3. In a later medieval Christian story, Alexander is depicted as ascending into heaven before being rebuffed by an angel.

IV. We may glimpse why Alexander became even more important as a figure in myth than in real life if we consider the Greek tale of Alexander's sister.

A. Alexander gave his sister the water of immortality to guard, but she foolishly lost it, went mad, and was turned into the *gorgona,* or mermaid.

B. Now the mother of storms, she stops passing ships and asks, "Does Alexander live?" Sailors must answer, "Yes, Alexander lives and rules the world," otherwise Alexander's sister will destroy their ship.

V. Alexander may be dead, but so mighty is his power that he is still a cosmic force who must be honored by the living.

A. The story of the Gorgon illustrates the place of Alexander in myth.

B. But Alexander is in many ways a normal man, somewhere between the two extremes favored by historians.
  1. He is much like his father, Philip, extending the territorial claims of his people.
  2. Though a great general, he was only mortal. The reason he failed to create a lasting, united empire was that he died so young.

Suggested Reading:

L. Pearson, *The Lost Histories of Alexander the Great.*

R. Stoneman, ed., *The Alexander Romance.*

Questions to Consider:

1. Is it possible to reconstruct the character of Alexander with any accuracy?
2. Why does Alexander's legend continue to fascinate us?

Lecture Four—Transcript
Alexander—Myth and Reality

Welcome back to our series of lectures on the Hellenistic Age. We've been looking at the career of Alexander the Great, the blazing star, who, in the course of eleven years, totally transformed the size and area of Greek culture and introduced Greek culture to a region that extended as far east as the Hindu Kush and northwest India, ushering in this three hundred years of political change, as Greeks ruled through much of the Middle East, and a cultural epoch that lasted even longer, following the Roman subjugation of the eastern Mediterranean. We've observed that this entire epoch, really, is the creation of one man, in a single eleven-year campaign.

And yet, curiously, the Alexander we've been examining in some respects is an ambiguous character. Almost schizophrenic. Because on the one hand we've been looking at an Alexander who seems to dream of fusing Greeks and Persians together to create a new ruling elite. We've seen a man who engages in these banquets of reconciliation. Of trying to get his men to marry Persian women, and to create even physically a new ruling mixed group of Greeks and Persians. And on the other hand, we seem to have someone not so much a visionary, so much as a megalomaniac. A man so intoxicated with his own power that he even came to believe the stories of his divinity. Stories which may have grown up in the realm of court titles, such as "Son of Ammon," but which were taken up seriously by Alexander.

Did he promote these ideas merely as a way of fusing his two ruling groups, as seems to be the case when he introduced prostration? Or did he really believe it? So that he grew increasingly (frankly) insane? So that by the end of his career, he was punishing his men by pushing them over the Gedrosian desert when they could have sailed back to Babylon.

The career and the accomplishments of Alexander have always been subject to widely different interpretations because the data that we have seem so contradictory. To some, he has appeared as an idealist. As someone (frankly) attempting to create a new world order, in which Greeks and non-Greeks would live together in harmony. To others, he's a drunk. A despot. An autocrat. Someone whose unbridled power corrupted a weak character, and who was driven by nothing more than an endless appetite for further and further conquest. Much, in fact, as his father had been before him. So history gives us, really, two very different Alexanders. Alexander the megalomaniac. Alexander the altruist. I'd like to explore these two interpretations a little further for a moment.

The most positive interpretation of Alexander, the notion that Alexander is really trying to create something new, comes from a British historian, W.W. Tarn, who, writing in the aftermath of World War I and at the time of the League of Nations—a time, in other words, when internationally we were playing with the idea of finishing war and living together in unity and harmony together—Tarn introduced the notion, based (I think) on these contemporary ideas, that Alexander's empire was an ancient forerunner, if you will, of the 20th century's experiment in international cooperation. So for Tarn, the banquet at Opis, which we've been talking about, where Greeks and Persians sat together and drank from the same cup, and offered a toast to unity and harmony, becomes the unity and harmony of all mankind. Tarn speaks about Alexander actually seeking to transcend national differences. And quite explicitly, Tarn likens Alexander to someone like Saint Paul, who famously remarked on one occasion, "there are no Greeks and barbarians". In other words, there are no distinctions between different national groups. Between different ethnicities. So that's the highly altruistic view of Alexander that we get in the work of some 20th century historians, particularly Tarn.

But at the other end of the scale, you will find other interpretations of Alexander, particularly in the work of Ernst Badian, an ancient historian at Harvard, for whom Alexander is, frankly, nothing more than yet another example of the paranoid, power- hungry tyrant who has afflicted us throughout history. An ancient Napoleon or an ancient Hitler, cast in exactly the same way. In exactly the same mold. In Badian's view, Alexander, the paranoid tyrant, is continually engaged in conspiracies, finding conspiracies against him, which he then weeds out, leading to assassinations and executions. Relentlessly driving his troops forward, in his maniacal and bloody quest for personal glory, no matter what the cost to innocent victims, including his own men.

And frankly, there is a certain amount of material in the sources about Alexander that really does confirm this line of interpretation. We know of leading Macedonian nobles, such as Philotas, and

Parmenio, who were summarily executed by Alexander. The hallmark of a tyrant—afraid that some other power grouping might emerge in his court, to challenge his own supreme power. We know, in another instance, of someone exposing what they called the "pages' plot," a group of young boys at the court, the wine-bearers and cup-bearers, who were supposedly engaged in a plot to assassinate Alexander. All of them are executed on the basis of very flimsy evidence.

So we seem to have some evidence for this kind of maniacal character at work in Alexander. Probably the best-known instance, and one that I'd like to share with you, is a story told by the historian Arryan, that involves a character from Alexander's court named Cleitus. There are two Macedonian officers of this name. This one is called Cleitus the Black. He was a general who had served with Alexander. He'd been through all the campaigns. He wasn't particularly impressed with the kind of orientalizing style of the new Macedonian court. So we read of a feast in honor of the god Dionysos. It was Alexander's custom to offer sacrifice at this feast of Dionysos every year on the sacred day of the festival.

On this particular occasion, the Macedonians, as usual, end up having a drinking party afterwards. On this occasion, Alexander, for some reason best known to himself, sacrificed not to Dionysos, but to Castor and Pollux, the so-called Dioscuri. Two somewhat lesser Greek gods. There had been some pretty heavy drinking. Another innovation, says Arryan. In drink, too, he now tended to barbaric excess. He seems to be drinking more as the campaigns go on. And in the course of talk, the subject of the Dioscuri came up, together with the common attribution of their parentage to Zeus, instead of Tyndareus. Here's an interesting topic of conversation while the Macedonians are drinking. These semi-divine figures. They weren't really the sons of a human, they were the sons of a god.

Do we hear a theme here? Yes. The theme of the great man who may become a god. This is probably why Alexander introduces this topic of conversation. Now we know already (we've seen in earlier lectures) that Alexander is sometimes surrounded by men who are all too willing to play the sycophant. To play up to him. Some of the company, the sort of people whose sycophantic tongues always have been and always will be the bane of kings, declared with gross flattery, that in their opinion, Castor and Pollux were not to be compared with Alexander and his accomplishments. Others, being thoroughly drunk, extended the invidious comparison to Heracles himself. So we have yet another one of these set pieces, where the Macedonians are drinking, and instead of the conversation following its normal turn, someone introduces the idea of Alexander being greater than the heroes and gods that have gone before. And as people drink and the whole thing starts to get more inflamed, the Macedonians who resist this idea get more and more angry. And so we read:

> Now Cleitus, for some time past had obviously deprecated the change in Alexander. He didn't like what Alexander was becoming. He liked neither his move toward the manners of the East, nor the sycophantic expressions of his courtiers. When, therefore, he heard what was said on this occasion (he too had been drinking heavily), he angrily intervened.

So a major Macedonian general stands up and says, "this is nonsense!" It was intolerable, he declared, to offer such an insult to divine beings. And he would not allow any one to pay Alexander a compliment at the expense of the mighty ones of long ago.

This is good, traditional Greek piety saying, "Come on! Hold up!" In any case, he continued. Alexander was deeply hurt by this. What happens next is that Alexander grabs a sword and he runs Cleitus through, killing him on the spot, in a drunken rage.

We've had echoes of this right back to the very beginning of Alexander's reign when he drew his sword on Philip as well, at the moment of the wedding feast involving the daughter of Attalus. So we seem to have this recurring theme of the drunkard. In fact, one interpretation of Alexander has simply suggested that he was an alcoholic. But we have this version of Alexander increasingly getting into drink and increasingly getting into these fantasies of divine power, and eventually even killing in cold blood, in manslaughter, there at the court, one of his senior generals.

Now how on earth are we to reconcile these two competing views of Alexander? It's very difficult. It's very difficult because these views of Alexander go right back to antiquity and the different and separate traditions about him. The first tradition, we'll call "The Court Tradition." This is the sanitized view of Alexander. Alexander as "the Great Man." The man, as Aristotle would say, of *megala*

©2000 The Teaching Company.

psyche, "great spirit." This is the version of Alexander that was written out for him by the official court historian. Alexander, like Napoleon, had a whole retinue of intellectuals along with him, and one of them kept a daily record of events and then wrote them up in the grand inflated style of contemporary history writing. His name was Callisthenes. He was a student of Aristotle. He reported on the campaign day by day as it progressed. Callisthenes eventually would fall out with Alexander, and would be executed. But he lived long enough to produce a highly eulogistic account of the great man. And it is to that tradition, close to the court itself, that we owe the stories of Alexander presenting himself as a Homeric hero, like Achilles, and being compared with Dionysos and Heracles.

So in this court tradition, Alexander was heroic, he was semi-divine, and he was always right. And of course, other writers followed this tradition, as well. Two of the men who marched with Alexander, Ptolemy, who eventually would establish his kingdom in Egypt, and Aristobulus, who was one of the engineers who was along with Alexander, both wrote memoirs. And of course, it was in the interests of men who had marched with Alexander, who probably loved Alexander dearly, to also present him as this larger-than-life figure who would transform the world with his godlike campaign.

It is to this tradition that we owe the thing that we see in so much of the sources about Alexander of his yearning. *Pathos*, as the Greeks called it. He conceives a desire to go to Siwah. He conceives a desire to capture the rock of Aornos. He conceives a desire to campaign against King Porus. Alexander in this tradition is being led on by some vague and unidentifiable yearning, which seems to come from heaven, as if some spirit is actually ordaining his campaigns.

But, on the other side, there was, even in antiquity, this very negative tradition about Alexander as well. And it is this tradition that emphasizes the passion that drove and motivated Alexander. The bloodshed of Alexander's reign, as he increasingly resorts to executions. The first author who is associated with this view of Alexander is called Cleitarchus. And although his work was hated by the critics, it was loved by the general populace. It became immensely popular reading during the Hellenistic period and even later, into the Roman Empire, as well. The Alexander that Cleitarchus portrayed in his work was an Alexander who flew into rages. Would kill someone in a drunken brawl, and then would be remorseful for three days, lying prostrate on his back in his tent, hidden from view.

It's this tradition that gives us the Alexander who killed Cleitus the Black in the episode I just read. It's this colorful tradition that continues and comes down to us in the works of historians such as Diodorus Siculus, and Justin, the Roman historian.

Eventually, these two traditions would become merged, in later antiquity, in the 1st century B.C. and the 1st and 2nd centuries A.D. Historians were reading whatever they could about Alexander's work, seeing whatever was in the library. So we find that the later historians, men like Plutarch, and men like Arrian, who give us some of our fullest accounts of Alexander's reign, are actually trying to marry two traditions together. The court tradition, which gives us Alexander's *pathos*, his semi-divine yearning for further conquests; and the *vulgate*, or the popular tradition, which gives us stories such as Alexander being visited by the queen of the Amazons.

So these later historians were often confronted with a choice. They would read these stories and have to say, "Is this reliable? Or is this popular fiction? Is this romantic nonsense?" Fortunately, some of the better historians would actually evaluate these stories and say, "This story is probably not true." Though they would ususally tell you anyway, since it made interesting reading. These conflicting traditions of Alexander are never fully reconciled.

In fact, Alexander finally becomes much greater than the record of his original campaign. He continues to influence the Middle East, the Mediterranean world, the Near East, long after his death because his accomplishments are simply so monumental, so off-the-scale, that no ordinary history can do them justice. We're going to be examining the changes that are wrought in the Mediterranean world by the Greeks and by the Macedonian control of the Hellenistic world, but before we go into the details of those changes in history, we should leave Alexander as the figure of romance and myth, greater even than the story of his accomplishments.

Because Alexander becomes, for the ancient world, and even for the Middle Ages, a figure like King Arthur, exerting an enormous influence over an entire culture and over a vast area, even longer than the duration of the Hellenistic commonwealth, or the *oecumene*, as the Greeks called it. Even longer than that, Alexander as a figure of myth and story survived. These stories, both based on the historians' accounts and the court tradition, and also in the vulgate tradition, and then, increasingly, stories added from local traditions, are all brought together in a work known as *The Alexander Legend*. This dates probably to about the 3rd century A.D. It's verse written in Greek.

It's attributed (incorrectly) to Callisthenes. It's not actually by him, it's by a later author, so it's sometimes called the work of Pseudo-Callisthenes. Fairly shortly after it's produced in the 3rd century A.D., it's then translated into Latin, and in Greek and Latin, it is distributed throughout all regions of the Roman Empire. In the Greek-speaking East, it makes its way to Byzantium. It is never forgotten in the Greek tradition. The Greeks today will tell you stories about Alexander the Great. In the West, it is translated into Latin, and from there it makes its way to France and to Germany and to England. So we find Alexander turning up all around both Europe and Central Asia, as well.

One version of this, for example, is the *Ishkandanamah*, the saga or epic of Ishkander, or Alexander, as he's known in the East. Some details of that will illustrate for you, I think, the magical quality of Alexander. Because in the *Ishkandanamah*, Alexander actually becomes a Muslim, despite the fact that Islam is not established until about 900 years after the death of the historical Alexander. Nevertheless, he is a good Muslim. He's actually the son of Darab, obviously the Persian king's name Darius now transformed. And according to this version of events, Alexander's not really the son or the king from the West, who in this version is known as Filqus, clearly Philip, transformed, who was known as the Caesar of Rum, which is the generic term used in the East for the entire Greek and Roman world of the Mediterranean. So in this version of the story, virtually every detail that you can imagine about Alexander has either been ignored or inverted. He's not a Greek. He comes from a thousand years later. And he's actually really the son of a good Muslim king. Persian and Muslim. It's an extraordinary appropriation of the historical Alexander. That is what is going to continue with the story of Alexander, ever afterwards.

One of the interesting details of the *Ishkandanamah* that I want to draw to your attention, is that throughout that work of the epic of Alexander, he's often referred to by an expression which translates into English as the "Two-horned one". Historians, I think, have reliably explained this term, because on the coins of Alexander, his picture, his portrait was shown in profile. And in that profile, we're shown not just his head and his royal diadem and his curly hair, but also a horn coming out of his forehead, representing Zeus-Ammon. So that, on his coins, Alexander was minting images of himself to look like Zeus-Ammon. That image survived long after Alexander was dead and gone. Those coins remained in circulation for hundreds of years. People would hoard coins and keep them. Gold was really valuable. So these coins survived for hundreds of years.

We have to imagine a point later on where some Persian poet, in telling the story of Ishkander (Alexander) sees one of these coins, and, wondering about those coins, calls him "the double-horned one," as though it's some mark of his kingship and his divinity. Probably not even aware of the fact that these horns had originated with Zeus-Ammon, and with a particular moment in Alexander's self-presentation and ideology during his own career.

Eventually, this story of Alexander, this romantic figure, will reach as far away as Britain in the west and Yemen, Sri Lanka and even northwest India in the east. In various versions of the Alexander legend or the Alexander romance (as it really should be called), Alexander will be a Russian; he will be a Serbian prince; he will be a Goth; and he will be a Saxon. So any ethnic group, essentially, from about 300 B.C. through to the Renaissance, at some point is likely to claim Alexander for themselves.

Alexander's accomplishments had been so astonishing that he himself came to stand for some kind of superhuman status that took him beyond the realm of the normal. It's for this reason that Alexander, in the medieval West, at least, and in some of the Greek stories, as well, becomes associated with two particular episodes that you should know about.

The first is the story of Alexander ascending into heaven. Alexander in these versions of the Alexander romance is a good Christian. But he is also so powerful and so wondrous that he is able to do what no man before him has done, and to approach heaven. How? Well, very cunningly he grabs a couple of griffins, that is, flying eagle-headed lions. He chains them up and starves them for a couple of days until they become so hungry that they will eat anything. He then chains them to a basket and he holds above the basket a stick that contains the liver of a dead beast. The griffins, in their eagerness to get to the liver and to eat, start flapping their wings and fly up. Thus does Alexander ascend into the heavens, only to be greeted by an angel, who points out to him that it would be arrogant and wrong for a good Christian king to try to make himself the equal of heaven. Alexander acquiesces and peacefully returns to earth.

So Alexander here, the scale of his accomplishments to the east is being transformed into accomplishments going up, literally out of this world, into the heavens.

The other area, where humans in antiquity would like to have gone, but weren't able to explore, was, of course, the deep sea. You probably didn't know that Alexander invented the first diving bell. According to medieval traditions in the Alexander romance, it was Alexander who created a glass sphere, in which he put various animals. A cock so that its crowing would tell him when it was daytime, even in the depths, when it was too dark to see. And a cat, whose breathing, it was believed, would purify the air. And a dog, which he took with him because if he ran into trouble and had to escape, he would kill the dog, knowing that the sea will not maintain dead bodies within it, but will spew them out. So Alexander in this way, and because he was actually betrayed and was left at the bottom of the sea, was able to get back to the seashore once again.

These stories give you some idea of what Alexander means to people. He represents what cannot be accomplished by normal human beings. He comes to stand for the superhuman in every age after the Hellenistic period. It's not surprising, therefore, that leaders—real men, seeking to present themselves as great commanders—would always present themselves in the style of Alexander. Julius Caesar would do it. Augustus would do it. Later kings would do it as well.

One of the most telling, I think, examples of this use of the Alexander story—the image of Alexander—comes with Pope Paul III, who, before he was elevated to the pontificate, was actually known as Alexander. This was his given name. And while most of his opponents were decorating their Roman villas with stories taken from the glories of Rome's past, he decorated the Pauline chamber, his inner sanctum, with pictures showing Alexander the Great. In other words, this was the heroic figure of the past that this Alexander, Pope Paul, wanted to liken himself to. So Alexander has become a mythical figure, much greater than even his original accomplishments.

There's one last story from the Alexander romance that I want to leave you with, because I think it once again conveys this idea of Alexander representing the unattainable in human life. If Alexander went further, higher and deeper than any other human being, he very nearly also succeeded where no other man has succeeded, and that is in capturing immortality. He actually did find the plant of immortal life. You perhaps didn't know this. He entrusted it to his sister, but she lost it. In her remorse, she threw herself overboard and dropped to the bottom of the sea, where she was transformed into a mermaid. What the Greeks call the *gorgona*. Whenever you find yourself sailing at sea and a storm arises, you must recognize that the reason for that storm is that the *gorgona*, Alexander's sister, is in turmoil. Invariably, at some point during that storm, she's going to appear out of the water, holding the boat in her hand. She's going to give you an opportunity either to sail on safely to harbor, or else she's going to destroy you. The question she's going to ask you is, "Does Alexander still live and rule the world?" You better know what the answer is, because if you say the wrong thing, she's going to shipwreck you. The answer, of course, is, "Yes. Alexander the Great lives and rules the world still today."

The story of the *gorgon* demonstrates, I think, rather beautifully the way in which Alexander has ascended to the realm of myth. He has become a figure so much larger than life because of his unparalleled accomplishments that he came to stand in later ages for all those quests for what could never be attained, such as immortality.

It's true that the distance that he covered opened up a new world to the Greeks. Though he would not live to see it, thousands of Greeks would pour out of mainland Greece, moving east. First into Asia Minor, and then later into Syria and right across into what is modern-day Iran and Afghanistan. So he changed the face of the world, but I don't want to leave you with Alexander the figure of myth, the superhuman Alexander.

I think we need to try to summarize this man as more of a mere mortal. For me, charting a course between Alexander the magalomaniac and Alexander the altruist, Alexander emerges in some ways as a normal man. Oh yes, he was a genius as a military strategist. He was a great general. No doubt. But when he set out at the beginning of his career, did he have any other aim rather than simply to repeat what his father had done? Namely, to fight as many wars as he could, and to conquer as much territory as he could. He's very much like Philip, expressing the same Macedonian notion of conquering wherever one can, filling the vacuum and extending one's own territorial conquest. That's a very limited aim to begin with.

Because of his own successes, and the rapidity with which he did overwhelm the Persians, he was therefore faced with a vastly greater challenge: that is, to find some way of ruling over an empire vastly bigger than anything the Greeks could ever have imagined. Now, to those people who think of him as a megalomaniac, the record shows nothing more than the loneliness of supreme power. A man who never came to grips with that task. I would suggest instead that what we see is a very mortal man. A great general, but a mortal man, trying to respond to the challenge of this new age by devising a new plan for the world that would follow. He failed, because his generals didn't repeat the plan. But it wasn't because of his madness, and it wasn't even because of unavoidable cultural differences between Greeks and Persians. I'd suggest to you that it was simply a matter of time.

Alexander campaigned for eleven years and died. Augustus ruled for forty years, and transformed the Roman Republic into the Roman Empire, with himself as the first emperor. So I'll leave you with this thought. It may well be that Alexander's failure was not that he didn't have a vision for the future or that he wasn't equipped to make that vision become reality. He simply ran out of time.

Lecture Five
The Formation of the Kingdoms

Scope:

A generation of warfare between Alexander's successors saw the end of his empire. Alexander's death created a crisis that would not be resolved until a series of wars had destroyed the possibility of a united empire. In the aftermath of the wars of the Diadochi, the major Hellenistic kingdoms would emerge under the control of Alexander's former generals and staff officers.

Outline

I. Alexander died having attempted to reconcile two irreconcilable systems: the hierarchical Persian system, which demanded an absolute monarchy, and a Macedonian system, with its emphasis on performance, achievement, and the leadership of the best and the bravest.

A. The dream of a new, mixed Macedonian and Persian nobility died with Alexander. Instead, Alexander's officers would plunge the eastern Mediterranean into continuous war for a generation, until the emergence of separate Hellenistic kingdoms extending from Macedon to Egypt, through Asia Minor and Syria.

B. To understand the resistance of Alexander's officers to the prospect of sharing power with the Persians, we must remember that the Macedonian nobles were not just subjects of the king; they were also his *philoi*, his companions.

1. Among the nobility, a strongly egalitarian ideology existed; the king was not king by divine right but because of his preeminence among men who were his peers.

2. Just as the king ate and drank among these equals, so too they fought as equals. The elite battalions of the army were labeled "the Companion Cavalry" or, in the infantry, the *Pezetairoi*, "the Foot-Companions."

C. For men who had proved their valor by defeating the Great King and his armies, Persia was not a noble adversary to be treated as an equal but a conquered empire to be divided up like the carcass of a beast that they had hunted down and slaughtered.

II. Alexander was the glue that kept the Macedonian enterprise together, and his death created a void, especially given that he had no clear successor. The issue of succession was complicated by two factors.

   A. The first was that Alexander left a wife, Roxane, who was pregnant. The complication this presented was obvious.

      1. In a matter of months, she might bear a son, Alexander's heir, who would have an obvious claim to the throne.

      2. On the other hand, she might bear a girl, and the Macedonians had never been ruled by a queen. Even if she bore a son, the child would be in no position to assert himself as the legitimate Macedonian king for at least another 16 years.

      3. Nor was there any guarantee that the Macedonians would recognize a son born not to a Greek or Macedonian, but to the daughter of a mountain chieftain from Bactria.

   B. The second complication was that all the negotiations conducted by Alexander's successors were done in the belief that the army officers would have the final say.

      1. As Perdiccas, Ptolemy, Lysimachus, Seleucus, and the rest bargained with each other, they failed to reckon on another factor in the equation of power: the Macedonian army, the Macedonian state under arms.

      2. The Macedonian infantry in Babylon wanted a king of the blood of Alexander. In the midst of the deliberations being held by the cavalry officers, the infantry went into revolt and insisted that Alexander's half brother, Arrhidaeus, be acknowledged as king.

      3. Perdiccas and the other power brokers had no choice but to accept. Alexander was succeeded by a half-witted brother and an unborn child.

III. The early Hellenistic Age, from 323–301 B.C., can largely be told as the quarter century during which two men fought to reclaim the unity of Alexander's empire and failed. At the same time, it was the quarter century in which Alexander's successors moved from thinking of themselves as Macedonian officers to considering themselves as kings in their own right.

A. The first of the two men to try to reunify the kingdom was Perdiccas.

    1. After the decision at Babylon, he found himself in a powerful position. He had control of Alexander's army, and he possessed the two kings in his entourage, acting as their guardian.

    2. But Perdiccas's power evaporated in his first campaign to Egypt, where Ptolemy, one of Alexander's bodyguards, had established himself nominally as satrap but really as an independent ruler. It is fairly certain that Ptolemy managed to infiltrate Perdiccas's army and engineered his assassination.

B. With Perdiccas dead, in 321 B.C., a second round of negotiations took place in Syria at Triparadeisus.

    1. The two kings, Philip Arrhidaeus and Alexander IV, were escorted home by the regent of Macedonia, Antipater.

    2. Ptolemy retained Egypt and Seleucus received Babylon, but the most powerful figure to emerge, and perhaps the last man to dream of uniting Alexander's empire once again, was Antigonus, the satrap of Asia.

C. From 320–311 B.C., Antigonus was opposed by an alliance of Ptolemy, Seleucus, Lysimachus, and Cassander. When these men reached a peace settlement in 311 B.C., the terms reflected the status quo that had operated for the last decade but had also been marked by continuous warfare.

IV. This was to be the legacy of Alexander's successors: intermittent yet virtually continuous warfare between great dynastic and regional blocks.

A. The issue of ruling an empire was always subordinate to the more pressing issue of acquiring or securing an empire.

B. Because external warfare and foreign policy were the driving concerns of these men, internal questions of defining the relationship of ruler to ruled were worked out only in the most haphazard fashion, without much planning.

C. For the first generation, at least, the new rulers of the Hellenistic world were uninterested in marrying Greek and non-Greek cultures. They were too busy trying to kill each other.

V. By 310, the political landscape of Alexander's empire had assumed the shape of the new Hellenistic kingdoms. The Ptolemies controlled Egypt; the Seleucids held Syria and Babylon; Macedon remained a separate region, now ruled by Antipater's son, Cassander; and the Antigonids controlled most of Asia Minor.

VI. Even so, all these rulers still ruled nominally as governors of territory conquered by Alexander.

  A. In 310 B.C., Cassander, aware that Alexander's son was approaching adolescence, executed Alexander's widow, Roxane, and his 12-year-old son, Alexander IV.

  B. Philip Arrhidaeus had been killed 7 years earlier, leaving no legitimate heir of Alexander's blood.

VII. The final stage in the dissolution of Alexander's empire came only 4 years later when, after a naval victory off Cyprus, Antigonus and his son Demetrius were hailed by their men as kings.

  A. Kings of what? It didn't matter. This new notion of kingship was not tied to a particular territory but to a man.

  B. Ptolemy's men, it is said, didn't want him to be downhearted because of the defeat of his navy, so they, too, acclaimed him as king.

  C. The origins of his kingship, therefore, lay not in his control of a particular territory—in this case Egypt—but in his men's acclamation.

VIII. No constitutional guidelines existed for the formation of the Hellenistic kingdoms, only charismatic leadership and the need of people, Greek and non-Greek, to give the authority that ruled their lives a shape and a form that they could understand.

  A. The philosophers of the Hellenistic Age describe the ability to handle the army and administer competently as justification for kingship.

  B. Syria, Egypt, and Macedon, born of this void, will be major dynastic blocks until the rise of the Roman Empire, 300 years in the future.

Suggested Reading:

P. Green, *From Alexander to Actium*.

Questions to Consider:

1. When did the idea of a single empire of Alexander die?

2. What prevented Alexander's successors from taking the title of king until 17 years after his death?

Lecture Five—Transcript
The Formation of the Kingdoms

When Alexander died in Babylon in 323 B.C., there also died with him the dream of a united empire of Greeks and Persians. We've already seen that Alexander had been trying to reconcile two systems that fundamentally could not be reconciled. On the one hand, there was the Persian system, which was hierarchically organized, and required, at its apex, a king ordained by heaven. A great king, to whom you prostrated yourself. On the other hand, there was a Macedonian system, in which the king was the leader of a band of essentially equal nobles.

Alexander's officers were utterly uninterested in trying to continue the experiment in fusion that he had initiated. I've suggested that Alexander's failure was probably not due to any irreparable difference between the cultures, but quite simply to the fact that he died after campaigning for eleven years, but before being allowed to rule that empire for any length of time. I compared him, for example, to Augustus, who effected a transformation in the Roman world, largely because he continued to rule for forty years.

But instead of there being a united Greco-Persian monarchy or ruling elite running the empire, instead the generation after Alexander's death saw the entire Eastern Mediterranean and much of the Near East plunged into a paralyzingly difficult-to-follow round of civil wars. Wars fought by one Macedonian general against another, extending for thirty years and embracing all of the region that Alexander had just conquered and annexed for the Macedonians. It is, in fact, the most depressing coda to the brilliant career of Alexander that one can imagine. As his generals clustered around his dead body in Babylon, and carved up his empire, like jackals around a carcass.

What I want to look at today is the issue of how that round of warfare worked itself out and what kind of political order emerged from that, since it was clearly not going to be anything like the earlier Macedonian kingship or the dream that Alexander had had for his empire.

First of all, I think we need to understand why it is that his officers resisted so strongly the kind of dream, the kind of vision of the future that Alexander had offered, by trying to merge Greeks and Persians.

Why were they so resistant to the notion of power-sharing? Or of creating a new elite?

The reason, I think, is that his generals were not merely subjects. They called themselves his *philoi*, in other words, his friends. That is, they regarded themselves as being, in many ways, his equals, even though, of course, they had not led the campaign that he had. But you must remember that many of the generals and many of the leading soldiers in that army, were men, in fact, of Philip II's generation. Men who were twenty or thirty years older than Alexander. These men were uninterested in the idea of sharing power with the Persians. Among the nobility in Macedon, there existed a strongly egalitarian ideology. The king was king, not be divine right, but because of his pre-eminence. That is why Alexander had always had to be the first man over the wall, the first man into the breach, the first man on the attack. Because he was the first among peers.

Just as the king ate and drank among his peers (we've seen many of the stories already, of Alexander drinking with his other generals), so too they fought as equals. This notion of equality is evoked even by the names of the battalions within the Macedonian army. So that the elite cavalry is called the Companion Cavalry. Companions of the king. Companions of each other. Equals in the game of war. And the elite battalion in the infantry was known technically as the *Pezetairoi*, which means the "foot companions." Again, men who proclaimed that they could stand shoulder to shoulder in battle with the Macedonian king.

For these men who had proved their valor by defeating the Great King and his armies, Persia was not a noble adversary to be treated as an equal, but rather a conquered empire. It was booty, to be carved up the way a carcass is carved up after it has been hunted down and slaughtered.

Alexander was the glue that kept the Macedonian world together. This entire enterprise of taking Macedonian power out way beyond anywhere the Greeks had ever gone before. It was he who was at the very center of all this. With his death, the Macedonians were confronted by a paralyzing void. In fact, you go so far as to say that just about every bad condition or circumstance imaginable conspired to occur upon the death of Alexander.

Consider these factors, for example. When Alexander died, his queen, his wife Roxane, was pregnant. The complication here is obvious. It is not clear, for a start, that she is going to bring the child to term, and that the child will be born. It could be still-born. Or it could die in the womb. If she does bear a child, there is no guarantee that it's going to be a boy, who will have a claim to the throne. It could have been a girl. No one could predict, at Alexander's death, whether the pregnant Roxane would have a girl. The Macedonians had never put a queen on the throne. So that was left in doubt.

And, quite frankly, even if at some future point she were to give birth to a boy, there is no way that he would be in a position to assert his authority (and that's what makes a Macedonian king a king—not his blood, but his authority), he wouldn't be able to assert it for at least another 16 years. So Alexander's death had left the Macedonians in limbo, without any clear indication of who was going to be the next king, and who would have legitimate authority. And even if, quite frankly, the child were born and grew up and eventually were to be recognized as a stout commander and a good general, he wouldn't even be a purely born Macedonian or even a Greco-Macedonian, because his mother, Roxane, was from Bactria, out in the eastern satrapies of the former Persian Empire.

Who knows? In twenty years' time, the Macedonians might be saying, "We don't want a posthumous bastard ruling over us, if he's not even Macedonian and Greek." So that was massively complicated, and it really paralyzed the negotiations upon Alexander's death.

There was a second great complication. During all the negotiations between the Macedonian generals, the jockeying for power that took place after Alexander's death, the common belief, the assumption that every general made, was that it was they, the Macedonian elite, the generals of Alexander's army, who would have the final say. So that we hear of negotiations involving Perdiccas, Ptolemy I, Lysimachus, Seleucus, these great men who had led the Macedonians in battle. They bargained with each other. They negotiated with each other. And they completely ignored one other important factor in the negotiations. That is, that the Macedonian king was to be acclaimed by the Macedonian state.

The Macedonian state here in Babylon was the army. Not the generals and the officers. But the ordinary men who had fought for

Alexander. Now, these men were committed, not only to Alexander, but they were committed to the blood line of his family. They wanted someone related to Alexander to be on the throne. And they had a candidate, and they put him forward.

The candidate's name was Arrhidaeus. He was the older half-brother of Alexander. According to all accounts (and it's hard to test this, but according to all accounts) there was something wrong with him. He may have been mentally defective. He may have had some debilitating disease, some dreadful form of epilepsy. We don't really know what it was. Of course there were stories in antiquity that Olympias had poisoned him when he was a child, to clear the way to the throne for her son Alexander. But we don't know. But what we can say is this: Alexander had carefully ensured that no competitors to the throne who had royal blood stayed alive, when he himself (Alexander) became king.

The fact that Philip Arrhidaeus (Arrhidaeus now as king was called Philip) was still alive must suggest that he was regarded by the rest of the Macedonian nobility as physically incapable of serving as king. Now exactly what the nature of the disability was, we don't know. But while all the negotiations were going on between Perdiccas and Ptolemy and Seleucus and the rest of these generals, there in the tent, right next to them, was Arrhidaeus, whom they had ignored and overlooked. It was he who the Macedonian soldiers said, we want as king.

The army threatened to go into revolt and to rebel completely from the entire officer corps. All of these high-ranking generals were forced, simply, to accept the fact that Alexander the Great was now going to be succeeded by an unborn fetus and a half-wit older half-brother. That's what the Macedonian Empire was put into the hands of.

The period that follows Alexander's death and the elevation of Philip Arrhidaeus and finally the birth of Alexander's son, who would be called Alexander IV—the period after this, from 323 down to the end of the century, virtually the last quarter of the 4th century B.C., is essentially a period during which the various great generals of Alexander's army jockeyed for position in relation to each other. Forming alliances, fighting against common enemies, in an attempt to secure their own power and in two cases, in an attempt to re-establish the unity of Alexander's empire. So what I want to look at now is the record of these campaigns, despite the fact that the detail is often difficult to follow. Because I want to chart the course by which the two men who had a chance of unifying Alexander's empire failed, and how, out of the void of that failure was created a new political order, namely the political order of the Hellenistic Age.

The first of the men to try to unify the empire of Alexander was Perdiccas. Perdiccas had served as his vizier, as his prime minister, if you like, after the death of Alexander's close friend Hephaestion. He was the natural person to take over the reins of power. While negotiations were going on at Babylon, it was Perdiccas who had made sure that in the tent where the generals did their trading, Alexander's ring and scepter were there, on a throne, looming over all of these negotiations.

At Babylon, in the first round of negotiations between the Hellenistic generals, he found himself in a very powerful position, because he had commanded Alexander's army, and he possessed the two new kings in his entourage. It was he who took over as guardian for Philip Arrhideus, and for the now infant child Alexander IV. So he had a shot, he had a real shot, at keeping Alexander's dream alive. Of keeping the empire in the control of this family, with himself as the power behind the throne, or, perhaps (who knows?) even asserting himself as the new king of Alexander's empire.

But Perdiccas's power evaporated almost immediately, because in the very first year, after the generals had divided up Alexander's empire, as each of them went off to their various provinces, their satrapies, as they were called, to take over, Perdiccas made the decision to attack Egypt. Egypt was the province that had been taken over by Ptolemy. Ptolemy, one of Alexander's bodyguards, one of his generals, now one of his most successful followers, had had himself appointed as satrap of Egypt. Satrap (provincial governor)— in effect he was the independent ruler. He continued to put up monuments and issue decrees "in the name of " Philip Arrhideus and Alexander IV, the Macedonian kings. But the true power was certainly in Ptolemy's hands.

And Egypt had been a cunning choice, because it was an area that was virtually self-contained. It was hard to attack from the east because of desert. Hard to attack from the west because of desert. Hard to attack from the north because of the Delta, and hard to attack from the south because of the river and because of the cataracts of the Nile. So he'd cut off a hunk of Alexander's empire that he could hang on to on his own. But Perdiccas wanted to dislodge him. Why? Perdiccas, with the Macedonian kings in tow, was heading back to Macedon. He couldn't afford to leave this powerful, independent ruler behind him, ready to attack.

So he headed to Egypt. But just as he was on the point of crossing over the Nile, his army went into revolt against him, and Perdiccas was cut down by his own men. Almost certainly, the men who cut him down had been bribed by Ptolemy. So the round of warfare between these Macedonian generals had moved into its next phase.

With Perdiccas dead—with the one man who had control of the army and control of the kings dead—the various generals of Alexander's army met again, this time in Syria at a site called Triparadeisus, and we have an account of the meeting between these various generals. I'll read you a short segment of it, because I think it gives a very graphic illustration of the mindset of these men, and how they were treating Alexander's domains.

> Antipater [who was the regent of Macedon] in his turn carried out a distribution of provinces [so he's divvying up the empire], partly confirming the previous arrangements of Bablyon in 323, and partly modifying them.

Now listen to just some of the names. These names are going to run throughout the rest of this course. These are going to be the founders of the great dynasties of the Hellenistic world. They begin here, as Alexander's generals being awarded satrapies or provinces, which will mutate into kingdoms.

Ptolemy was to control Egypt, Libya and all the expanse of territory beyond it. Syria was entrusted to Laomedon. Philoxenus he appointed to Cilicia. Of the upper satrapies, he assigned Mesopotamia to Amphimachus. To Seleucus, he gave Babylon. That's going to be an important name. And then, here's an interesting detail: Antigenes who had been the first to attack Perdiccas, and who commanded the Macedonian Silver Shields, was granted the rule over the whole of Susiana.

What's happening here is that these men have quite literally sat down with a map of the old Persian Empire. These maps existed, specifying particular satrapies. And they simply traded with each other. "OK, you get Egypt. You get Babylon, You get Susa." Jackals

©2000 The Teaching Company.

'round a carcass. According to this arrangement at Triparadeisus in 321, the two kings, Philip Arrhideus and Alexander IV, were escorted home, back to Macedon, by Antipater, who remained regent. Ptolemy kept control, as we saw, of Egypt; Selecus getting Babylon. But the most important character, the most powerful man to emerge in this round of warfare between the various forces, was a man by the name of Antigonus, who is made satrap of Asia.

Antigonus is one of the most romantic figures in the Hellenistic period. He was from Philip's generation, older than Alexander, so while Alexander dies as a young man, around thirty, Antigonus here we have to imagine as a man of about 50 or 60, and he continued to campaign for the next ten years or so, even though he had lost one ey and was known as Antigonus the One-Eyed. A tremendously vigorous campaigner. Between 320 and 311 B.C., after Triparadeisus, and for the next decade, Antigonus' power was so great that he was immediately opposed by an alliance of the other Hellenistic kings: Ptolemy in Egypt, Seleucus in Babylon, Lysimachus in Thrace, and Cassander, who had taken over in Macedon after the death of his father Antipater.

These men would reach a peace settlement in 311 B.C., and the terms of the settlement reflect the status quo, which had emerged over the course of that last decade, a decade that had been marked by virtually continuous warfare. This status quo of great power blocs competing with each other, always aligning whenever one ruler became more powerful then the others, was to be, really, the legacy of Alexander's successors. Intermittent, yet virtually continuous warfare between great dynastic and regional blocs.

The issue of ruling an empire in the early Hellenistic Age was always going to be subordinated to the more pressing issue of acquiring or securing the empire. External warfare, foreign policy, dealing with the other successors of Alexander, these other generals—these would be the driving concerns of a generation of Macedonian generals. So, for them, the question of the internal organization of their kingdoms (for example, the relation between ruler and ruled) would be worked out in a completely haphazard fashion. They had no plan for rule at all, because they were always more concerned with the others.

For the first generation, at least, the new rulers of the Hellenistic world were uninterested in any questions of Greek culture and its fusion with non-Greek culture, because they were too busy trying to kill each other.

By 310 B.C., the political landscape of Alexander's empire had assumed the shape that it would keep throughout the rest of the Hellenistic era. That is to say, major kingdoms were emerging, though the title was not yet used. The Ptolemies controlled Egypt. The Seleucids held Syria and Babylon. Macedon remained a separate region, which would be ruled first by Antipater's son Cassander, and later would be controlled by another dynasty, while the Antigonids controlled most of Asia Minor. So these four or five major power blocs will be the essential political shape of the early Hellenistic period.

Even so, the rulers here—these great men—were still ruling nominally as governors of territory conquered by Alexander. The decisive step in the final transformation of these territories into kingdoms came in 310 B.C. It was in that year that the last blood of Alexander finally died. His son, Alexander IV, was killed. That event cleared the way for these generals to assert their independent authority as kings.

We have a description of this in Diodorus, and clearly we see, if you consider the dates (310). Alexander had died in 323. His child is now about 13 years of age. He's getting close to the age. In about three years he'll be 16, the same age as Alexander was when he fought on the left wing at Chaeronea. This child is just at the point of entering adolescence and becoming a man. That's a problem, because now we'll have a real and viable successor to Alexander.

So here are the circumstances. In that peace treaty of the various Hellenistic rulers in 311:

> … Ptolemy, Cassander, and Lysimachus put an end to the war against Antigonus, and they concluded a treaty. It was specified in it that Cassander should be general of Europe, until Alexander, Roxane's son, would come of age. Lysimachus should be master of Thrace and Ptolemy master of Egypt and the neighboring cities of Libya and Arabia. Antigonus would have command of Asia, while the Greeks would be autonomous. [So this is the usual Hellenistic division of power that we've already seen on at least two earlier occasions.]

> Nevertheless, they failed to abide by this agreement [says Diodorus], and each of them put forward fair pretexts and sought to increase their power. [And now we get to the important clause] Cassander [Antipater's son] saw that Alexander [IV, the son of Roxane and Alexander the Great] was growing up and there were some who were spreading the word in Macedon that one ought to release the boy from custody and hand over to him his father's kingdom. [So the critical moment has come. That posthumous heir is now ready to become king.]
>
> Afraid for his own safety, Cassander instructed Glaucias, who was in charge of the boy's custody, to assassinate Roxane and the king and to conceal their bodies...

Though eventually news did creep out of what had happened. Philip Arrhidaeus, the older imbecile, had been killed in another round of these wars some seven years earlier. So that, from 310 B.C., there was now no longer anyone of the blood of Alexander to sit on the throne of Macedon.

So we're facing a void. There is no king of Macedon of that blood, when it is that kingship which had defined all of these emerging territories. The final stage really will come almost as an anticlimax only four years later. I must read you the description of this, because the anticlimax is itself quite amusing. This is how Ptolemy, Seleucus and the other generals became kings. Listen to this. It's from Plutarch's life of one of these generals, named Demetrius.

> The multitude then, for the first time proclaimed Antigonus and Demetrius kings. They had just won a battle off the coast of Cyprus, against the navy of Ptolemy. Antigonus' friends tied at once a diadem around his head, while Demetrius was sent a diadem by his father and addressed as king in a letter he wrote. [Now, listen to this, this is really astonishing.] When the news was reported, Ptolemy's followers in Egypt also proclaimed Ptolemy king, to dispel any impression that his defeat had humbled his pride. [There, there, Ptolemy, don't feel badly. Oh, by the way, now you're a king. This is how he's acclaimed.] And so emulation spread the practice like a contagion among the successors. Lysimachus began to wear the diadem, Seleucus began to

style himself as king. And Cassander wrote to the others and said that they should address him as king, as well.

So it's a slightly pathetic expression, if you will, of what's happened at the end of the 4th century. Because of a naval victory, two guys call themselves king, and the rest of them follow suit so that nobody will be too depressed. Perhaps they had issues of self-esteem.

Kings. Kings of what? They're not kings of Macedon. Ptolemy's not in Macedon. Seleucus is in Babylon. So what are they kings of? The answer, finally, doesn't matter. The idea that you were a king of a specific kingdom no longer even made any sense to the Greeks of this period. Instead, this notion of kingship was not associated with a territory, but only with the personality of a man. *He* was king, because of his accomplishments. Ptolemy's men said they didn't want him to be disheartened because of the defeat of his navy, so they, too, acclaimed him king. Not because he had control of Egypt. Simply because of himself.

So the origins of this kingship don't lie in the control of a particular territory, but rather in the acclamation of a king by his people. So there were no constitutional guidelines for the formation of these Hellenistic kingdoms. They'd emerged piecemeal from the wars between Alexander's successors. The only qualification that one needed to be a king in this new age was charismatic leadership. Success in battle. Being able to rally your troops.

It is this new notion of kingship which comes to attract the attention of the philosophers and the writers of the Hellenistic Age. They become fascinated about the question of "What makes a king a king?" So, for example, one definition of monarchy in the Hellenistic Age reads as follows:

It is neither descent nor legitimacy which gives monarchies to men, but the ability to command an army and to handle affairs competently. Such was the case with Philip and the successors of Alexander. For Alexander's natural son was in no way helped by his kinship with him, because of his weakness of spirit, while those who had no connection with Alexander became kings of almost the whole inhabited world.

So we've established here the notion that these kings are not kings because they're descended from royal families. They're not. They are bodyguards and generals. Nor even by legitimacy, or as, in fact, it really says in the Greek, "justice." It's not that they have some right to be king. It's certainly not a question of divine right. They have the right to be king simply because they are competent. They are able to supply their men, to command an army and to handle affairs. The justification for this kingship lies in the expression itself of being a great king.

Other thinkers also were fascinated by this question of where kingship comes from, and what makes a king a king. In one extraordinary document, recorded by Diodorus, it becomes clear that some people were playing with the idea that kings and gods were really two sides of the same coin. Let me read to you from the *Doctrines of Euhemeris*, who says that, "Uranus [*Uranos*, to the Greeks] was the first king. An honorable man, beneficent and versed in the movement of the stars, and who was the first to honor the heavenly gods with sacrifices."

That's why he was called Uranus. His wife Hestia had two sons. They reined in a place off somewhere near the perimeter of the Greek world, Panchaia, a kind of fantasy land, and after his death, he then becomes a god. He's taken up into heaven.

So the Hellenistic Age begins with a very fascinating conception of kingship. In a void created by Alexander's death, first we have them playing with the idea of the succession by blood of Alexander. But that doesn't work, because we have a child, who was a threat to them, and a half-wit. So then we begin playing with the idea of kingship based on valor. That is why these men must fight these wars for a generation against each other, until they have finally established their Hellenistic kingdoms.

What then emerges is the political pattern that is going to dominate the next three hundred years, from, essentially, the death of Alexander until the Roman conquest of the Hellenistic world. During that three hundred years, as we're going to see in the coming lectures, we will have one kingdom in Egypt, controlled by the Ptolemies. Another in Syria, controlled by Seleucus. And yet another in Macedon. It is going to be these great dynastic regional kingdoms, born out of the void created by Alexander's death, that will be the major dynastic blocs of the Hellenistic world. It will be they who rule independently, until, finally, by 31 B.C., we find the Romans establishing their authority in the Hellenistic world.

Lecture Six
Egypt Under the Early Ptolemies

Scope:

Ptolemaic Egypt is probably the most familiar and best documented of the Hellenistic kingdoms. In Egypt, Ptolemy, one of Alexander's companions and bodyguards, transformed himself into a new pharaoh, even as he remained separate from the conquered Egyptians. We investigate the Ptolemaic kingdom and examine how the Ptolemies blended pharaonic and Macedonian practices to create a new kingdom.

Outline

I.   In Egypt, the Macedonian conquerors encountered conditions such as they experienced nowhere else in the areas of the old Persian empire.

   A. Geographic unity, historic unity, and ethnic unity created a system of immense stability.

      1. Egyptian society was arranged like a pyramid. It was a hierarchical system in which the mass of peasants was dominated by a priestly, scribal class and topped by a pharaoh.

      2. The Graeco-Macedonian elite replaced the upper echelons of this hierarchy but continued to rule over the Egyptians as a foreign power. Locals who couldn't speak Greek were considered barbarians.

   B. Little intermarriage took place between the Macedonians and Egyptians, and few Egyptians served in the upper ranks of the massive Ptolemaic bureaucracy.

   C. The firm division of Egypt into two ethnic groups is mirrored in the distinction between Alexandria and the rest of Egypt. Alexandria was said to lie "next to Egypt," and ordinary Egyptians needed permission to enter the city.

   D. This split between the two cultures resulted in Ptolemaic rule being almost schizophrenic. The monarch was a pharaoh to the Egyptians and a Macedonian king to Greeks. Unlike Alexander's approach, the Ptolemaic solution was to keep the two realms strictly separate.

E. In the great temples of Egypt, the Ptolemies are depicted on stone reliefs as pharaohs, while in Alexandria, their court was filled with Greek advisors, scholars, and generals.

II. The Ptolemaic system abandoned Alexander's notion of a fusion. Instead the entire system was arranged with a view to the most thorough exploitation of Egypt's natural wealth, especially land.

A. Egypt is cut off from the outside world by seas, deserts, and cataracts. It was possible, therefore, to minimize outside influence and to concentrate on keeping the economy hermetically sealed.

B. Mediterranean merchants had to conduct their commerce directly with the king's agents. Such international transactions were made with silver and gold coinage, but trade within Egypt was conducted in worthless copper, making it impossible for any private commerce to challenge the control exercised by the crown.

C. The Ptolemies enjoyed monopolies in oil and grain, staples produced in abundance by the fertile Nile valley and exported throughout the eastern Mediterranean.

    1. The monopolies were not confined to the sale of produce but extended into every aspect of production as well.

    2. The king's agents determined how much land was to be planted, distributed seed, monitored the use of tools, announced the time of harvest, and arranged for storage and transportation to Alexandria.

    3. Every aspect of production was overseen by a Greek bureaucracy that reached from the court in Alexandria all the way to the local village officials.

    4. Such micromanagement incurred local resistance, and petitions proliferated. Ultimately, the system was more concerned with exploitation than justice.

D. This controlled economy relied on treating the *laoi* (peasants) just as the pharaohs had done and required the complicity of temple estates or the priestly class.

    1. The Egyptian priestly class was, for the most part, protected by the Ptolemies. Their rights and privileges, including their ownership of large parcels of land, were acknowledged by successive Ptolemies. This situation was especially true from the late 3rd century B.C., after which Ptolemaic control grew weaker.

2. The famous Rosetta stone, the inscription that allowed modern scholars to read hieroglyphics for the first time, dates to 196 B.C., in the reign of Ptolemy V, The inscription gives details of a series of tax breaks and remittances, reflecting the young king's desire to win the backing of the powerful Memphite priesthood.

III. Despite the coercive and top-heavy control of Egypt by the Graeco-Macedonian elite, the Ptolemies did attempt to make their power more acceptable to their Egyptian subjects.

A. Perhaps the most curious action of the Ptolemies to gain legitimacy in the eyes of their Egyptian subjects was the marriage of Ptolemy II in 275 B.C. to Arsinoe, his sister.

1. Some Greek gods, such as Zeus and Hera, enjoyed incestuous marriages.

2. Still, the Ptolemaic practice was offensive to Greek sensibilities and was probably designed to evoke parallels with the Egyptian pantheon, especially Isis and Osiris.

B. The other attempt to blend the two cultures was the creation of an entirely new religious cult to Serapis.

1. Figures from Egyptian religion, such as Osiris and Apis, were syncretized with Greek gods, such as Zeus, to create this new god Serapis, whose cult was meant to be a fusion of the two religious cultures.

2. Strangely, this and the cult of Isis became two of Egypt's principal contributions to the Hellenistic world, although they were much more popular outside of Egypt than amongst the Egyptians.

Suggested Reading:

A. Bowman, *Egypt after the Pharaohs, 323 B.C.–A.D. 642.*

D. Thompson, *Memphis under the Ptolemies.*

Questions to Consider:

1. How important was the pharaonic system of absolute rule to the later success of the Ptolemies?

2. What role did the priestly class play in the Ptolemaic control of Egypt?

Lecture Six—Transcript
Egypt Under the Early Ptolemies

Welcome back to our sixth lecture now on the Hellenistic Age. So far our story has involved Alexander and his conquests, but we've seen that with his death in 323, the Hellenistic world, the empire that he had conquered, which extended across the Near East all the way to India, was really plunged into turmoil. None of Alexander's successors was capable of maintaining the kind of unified empire that he had created, partly because, as we saw, none of them were interested in the kind of policy of cultural fusion which Alexander had promoted (at least in the upper echelons of his empire) between Greeks and Persians.

Instead, we've seen emerging in the void after his death, and after a generation of civil wars, a new political landscape in which the Hellenistic world is broken up into great regional and dynastic blocs. It's those that we're now going to start to examine a little more closely.

The first of these, the one about which we have the most information, and probably the most famous, then, is that of Ptolemaic Egypt. We've seen that Ptolemy was one of Alexander's bodyguards. We've seen that Ptolemy very cunningly realized upon Alexander's death, that Egypt was the one province or satrapy of the Persian Empire which could be most easily maintained on her own. Hermetically sealed off, if you like, from the rest of the Mediterranean and the rest of the world. So it was to Egypt that Ptolemy took himself, transforming himself in the course of his career from bodyguard and general of the Macedonians to satrap of the now dead and departed Alexander, until, finally, by the end of his career, he was a pharaoh. Once again, the manifestation of the power of god on earth, at least as far as his Egyptian audience was concerned.

In this lecture, then, let's look at the ways that the Ptolemies administered Egypt and how their dynasty rules that country for 300 years.

I've pointed out that Egypt is cut off from the rest of the Mediterranean by desert on two sides, cataracts to the south, and the delta to the north. It also has a kind of ethnic and historical unity that goes back thousands of years, to the age of the pyramids, at least. So all together, these factors created in Egypt conditions for an immensely stable society. Egyptian society was essentially structured like a pyramid. That is to say, the pharaoh was on top, supported underneath by a priestly/scribal class, which relied on the pharaoh for their power. In turn, the pharaoh and his family and the scribal class (the priestly class) then depended upon the work of the vast majority of peasants living in the Nile Valley.

What I'm going to suggest is that Egypt is a good place for examining how Hellenism really works. What we're going to find (I think) is that the Greeks and Macedonians only replace the top level of that pyramidically, hierarchically organized society. Ptolemy will replace the pharaoh or the Persian provincial governor. And a Graeco-Macedonian elite will supply the upper echelons of the hierarchy that rules this country. But the priests will continue to offer a great deal of stability. They will cooperate with these new Macedonian overlords. Together, those two groups will continue to rule over the vast Egyptian peasantry, for whom pharaoh, Ptolemy, Persian governor—the differences were negligible. Their lives continued in much the same pattern year after year.

So what we find is that the Greeks and the Macedonians are not really interested at all in any kind of cultural fusion between Egyptians and Greeks. In fact, one of the most heart-breaking documents to come out of the sands of Egypt is a petition written by a man in the Hellenistic period to one of the local officials complaining about the treatment that he's received. I want to read you the details of this, and then I want you to pay attention to exactly what it is that is the nub of the problem. This fellow, whose name we don't know (the beginning of the letter is broken), writes to Xenon and says:

> I hope you are healthy. I, too, am well. You know that you left me with Crotas [that's a good Greek name] and I did everything that was ordered in respect to the camels and was blameless towards you. [We don't know what his job was, but perhaps he was a camel driver.] When you sent an order to give me pay, he gave me nothing of what you ordered. When I asked repeatedly that he give me what you ordered and Crotas gave me nothing, but kept telling me to remove myself, I held out for a long time, waiting for you. But then I was eventually compelled to run away, although I did

everything that was ordered. For nine months now, all he's given me is no oil, no grain, except for two month periods when he also paid for the clothing. [This is some sort of allowance. So our poor complainant says:] I am in difficulties both summer and winter, and he orders me to accept ordinary wine for salary. They have treated me with scorn because I don't speak Greek.

"I don't speak Greek." This poor man is a native Egyptian. He's dealing with some of the Greeks that have come into Egypt. And because he does not speak their language, they regard him as a barbarian. So in this instance, they're trying to screw him out of the salary that he deserves. The two groups kept very separate from each other. There was very little intermarriage between the two groups. We have very full records for Ptolemaic Egypt, of documents with both Greek names and Egyptian names. And in the few instances where we do have intermarriages, invariably between Greek men, new colonists and officials who were pouring into Egypt, and Egyptian women. There are virtually no instances of Egyptian men marrying Greek wives.

Most of the Greeks and the Macedonians who pour into Egypt at this time come in to serve in the Ptolemaic bureaucracy. They remain separate from the Egyptians over whom they exercise power. This distinction between the two ethnic groups is also mirrored in the relationship between the city of Alexandria and the rest of Egypt. Alexandria, according to its foundation myth (and this is probably vastly exaggerated), had been laid out it was said, by Alexander himself. Now the fact was that Alexander had planted seventy cities across the Near East. Most of them were probably originally garrisons or trading stations. It is just a matter of historical change that some of them grew into great cities. Samarkand, and so forth. This Alexandria probably began the same way. Probably as a trading port, on the very tip of Egypt. Right up there on the delta, close to the Mediterranean Sea. But it was turned into the capital of the Ptolemaic realm. But it was essentially a Greek city on the outskirts of Egypt. Ptolemies chose not to rule from Memphis or from Thebes or from any of the traditional capitals of the pharaohs that had come before them. Even in the Roman period, when the Romans talked about Alexandria, the called it *Alexandria ad Egyptum*, "Alexandria next to Egypt."

So these Ptolemaic rulers are almost ruling Egypt, *almost* as absentee landlords. On the very edges. Because as good Macedonian Greeks, they're more interested in what's going on in the Mediterranean. That's their realm. That's the realm where their navies operate and their armies operate. Egypt is behind them. As long as it is a well-organized and well-run system, that's all that they care about. In fact, the peasants, the Egyptians living in Egypt, needed permission from their local authorities to enter the city. Almost an internal passport, if you will.

So there is a split, I think, in Ptolemaic Egypt. There's a split almost in the way the Ptolemies see themselves in relation to Egypt. It's a kind of schizophrenia. The monarch, the Ptolemy, has to be a pharaoh to the Egyptians. He must be a pharaoh to maintain all those traditional Egyptian values of *maat*, of justice and good order. But to his Greek audience, up in Alexandria, he has to be a Macedonian king. So in this respect, the Ptolemies are negotiating (I would argue) the same kind of difficulty and dilemma that Alexander faced. Only their solution is to keep the two separate and to really behave as almost two separate dynasties. A pharaonic dynasty in Egypt and a Macedonian dynasty in Alexandria.

On the great temples of Egypt, such as at Karnak, if you go and look at the presentations of these figures of the great pharaohs of Egyptian history, I defy you to distinguish Ptolemy I from Thutmoses III, who reigned hundreds of years earlier. In both cases, the pharaoh will be three times larger than life. He will be seen striding manfully forward to attack his enemies. He will have a war club in one hand and he will be holding his enemies by the hair in the other hand, ready to smash their brains. And whether it is 2300 B.C. or 1300 B.C. or 300 B.C., the same imagery is being used. Frankly, if the audience looking at this was illiterate, as invariably most of the peasants were, they were seeing continuity. Ptolemy was pharaoh to them. But not to the Greeks. So the Ptolemaic system completely abandoned, I think, Alexander's notion of a policy of fusion.

One other element that helped to contribute to the Greek occupation of territory here, and to the split between them, was simply the annexation of land. In many parts of Egypt, Greek colonists poured in and simply took over the choice land. We happen to have, fortunately, the records of one Egyptian village from the Hellenistic Period. A place called Kerkeosiris, where we have quite specific details of how the land was owned. We know that in this small village, 52% of the land was owned by Ptolemy himself. If that's true across all of Egypt, and it probably is, it means that literally half of Egypt is the king's own private domain. Right? Then the next largest category, 33%, belongs to the Greek colonists. Clerics, as they're called. They are simply handed over this land, and as we've seen from our letter to Xenon earlier, we can understand how they treated their Egyptian neighbors. That comprises 85% of the land of Egypt. (Or, at least, of Kerkeosiris, and I would suggest, of the country as well.) And of the remaining 15%, 6% of that belongs to the temple. So Ptolemy, the Greek colonists and the Egyptian priests own over 90% of the land around and in this village. The final nine percent? That's the land that is actually owned and run by the Egyptian peasants. In other words, that's the land that they live off. That has to supply all their needs.

So what we're finding, dramatically in this evidence from Kerkeosiris, is that the Ptolemaic system is not about fusing Greek and Egyptian. It is about the more thorough and the more complete exploitation of Egypt's resources.

Egypt, as I've said, is cut off from the outside world by deserts and cataracts. Therefore, it's possible to minimize the outside influence on Egypt. As a result of that, it is a perfect place to be hermetically sealed and to be treated, as it was by the Ptolemies, as a cash cow. They took their exploitation of Egypt to phenomenal lengths. I want to chart some of these for you, to give you an idea of exactly how Ptolemaic rule operates in Egypt.

First of all, Mediterranean merchants, who wanted to come to Egypt because it was so fertile and because it supplied so much grain to the Mediterranean basin, had to conduct all their commerce with the king's agents. So anything being exported from Egypt essentially went through the king's warehouses, and he took a cut at every level. On the contracts. On the storage costs. On the produce itself. On stamp duties. On everything. Every bit of money that could be extracted from this system was.

One of the ways that the Ptolemies controlled this trade was in this way: international transactions around the Mediterranean involving merchants moving goods backwards and forward, were conducted in silver and gold coinage. The real weight of that coin attested to the value of the Ptolemaic economy. It was a sign of good faith, because they had real bullion that they could use for their trade. But within Egypt itself, gold and silver did not circulate. Peasants never got to see any of that coinage. They got to use copper coinage, which was worthless outside of Egypt. So even in their monetary economy, no Egyptian would ever be able to make any money out of trade. All he could do was barter with other Egyptians and maybe the king's agents.

So private commerce could never really develop in Egypt. The Ptolemaic economy is really like a Stalinist planned economy, with complete control exercised by the crown. The Ptolemies enjoyed monopolies in all the major export-producing crops. So various kinds of oil (olive oil, linseed oil), various grains that were produced, staples that could be grown in abundance through the Nile Valley, and exported through the Delta to the eastern Mediterranean, were all tightly controlled by the central monopoly under the authority of the Ptolemy.

The monopolies were, therefore, not confined just to the sale of produce, but to every aspect of its production. This is really well-documented as a result of many papyri found in the sands of Egypt. We know from these papyri that the king's agents determined everything from when the land was to be sown. They distributed the seed that was to be sown. They monitored closely the actual use of tools to be used in the production of any of this produce. They announced the time of harvest. It was they who arranged for the storage and transportation of all of this produce back to Alexandria. They stamped everything to show that they had recorded it, and it was all copied out in triplicate.

We have astonishingly detailed instructions involving this. I'd like to read you just a few details of this. They get to be pretty boring after a while, so I won't read you too much. But I want you to pay attention to the astonishing detail of the control of the economy by the Ptolemies. This is from a series of documents dating to the middle of the 3rd century. They involve the revenue laws, as they're called. These are the instructions issued by Ptolemy Philadelphus, in relation to various monopolies that I've been talking about. This is quite amazing. We read in this document (in this papyrus):

> Those who own implements for making wine shall register with the manager of the farm when … [and then there is a gap.] When they are about to make wine, they shall exhibit

the seal placed on them, to show it is intact. [So they have to produce a seal to show that all the vessels that they've been given and what they produce is still intact.] Anyone who fails to register or to produce his implements in accordance with the law or to bring them for sealing when the farmer wishes to seal them [in other words, when they've finished with their wine-making implements, such as a press (for example, a wine-press); anyone who does that] shall pay forthwith to the tax farmers the amount of the loss they estimate they have made.

So even if you've got a little bit of land and you're growing just a few vines on it and you're going to produce some wine, you have to get your press (your wine-press) and the pruning shears from the king's agent. You have to sign for those, and there is a seal put on them, and you've got to have that seal when you come back. Otherwise, you get charged for it as well.

This is really what we would call micro-management. Down to the very last detail of the economy. The whole thing is being handled by the Ptolemies. Every aspect of production, therefore, was overseen by this Greek bureaucracy that reached all the way from the court in Alexandria down to a slew of local officials.

We have, for example, a letter which comes from the chief economic official up in Alexandria, known as the *dioiketes*. He's sending this regulation or this letter down to the local governor, further south. He says to him, "You must inspect the canals and the water conduits which run through the fields and from which the peasants are accustomed to take water to the land cultivated by each of them. You have to see whether the water intakes into them have the prescribed depth."

This is incredible. In the little canals running from the Nile out into the fields, these Greek officials have to go and measure the depth of the canal to make sure it's deep enough for the water into the fields.

In your tours of inspection, try, in going from place to place, to cheer everybody up and put them in better heart. I'll bet people loved hearing that. And not only should you do this by words, but also, if any of them complain to the local officials about any matter touching it, you should make inquiry and put a stop to such things, as far as possible.

What this note puts us in mind of is the fact that the Ptolemaic system was so thoroughly exploitative and so carefully managed that it necessarily resulted in a great deal of resistance. The most common category of document that we get from Ptolemaic Egypt is the petition. The complaint. By some poor peasant who is being hard put-upon by people who are oppressing him. Here's an example of one such document. It's a complaint about the owner of a lodging. The complainant writes directly to Ptolemy. Go to the top. I doubt that Ptolemy ever read this, and I'll explain why in a minute. But the letter reads:

> To King Ptolemy: Greetings from Biffus, one of the veterans of Cardenus. You gave us, O King, a lodging with the other colonists, so we might not be wronged by anyone or have to pay for lodging. But Hellenicus has forcibly entered the house. He's demolished the wall of the courtyard, and moved in. I earlier submitted a petition to you, O King, about these matters, which was transmitted to the general. But the man is still unwilling to give it to me, and continues to insult me. I beg you, therefore, O King, if it seems right to you, to right and to fix this matter. May I attain justice.

So every little complaint. Imagine if you had a tenant in your house and you were trying to get rid of him. Would you write to the President of the United States? This is what is going on in Egypt. The reason why I think that Ptolemy never got the letter is because, at the bottom of the document, written in another hand, is the note, put down by the scribe who finally received this petition. "Aginor to Timoxanus, Greeting! I sent you a copy of the petition that came to me from this fellow. If it was assigned to him, assign to them their shares in accordance."

In other words, the Ptolemaic bureaucratic system is wonderfully devised to allow people at the bottom to write to the top, so that people at the top could write back down to the local officials to say, "Look into it." We quite literally have archives, in which over the space of more than a generation or two, people write dozens of letters and clearly get no redress whatsoever. The system isn't concerned with justice. It's concerned with an efficient exploitation of all the economic resources.

Every aspect of production, then, is overseen by a Greek bureaucracy. We know of local officials. We know of local mayors.

We know of local policemen. We know of local scribes and virtually all of these are Greek. In fact, these petitions are all written in Greek, which means that those that came from the Egyptian peasants were not being written by them directly. They were going to the local scribe and paying to have their petition put into the language of the Greeks. This controlled economy relied on treating the *laoi*, as the Greeks called the peasants, just as the pharaohs had done, in exactly the same way.

But it also required the complicity of the temple estates. The great priestly families, particularly those of Memphis. The Egyptian priestly class was for the most part protected by the Ptolemies. Clearly here the Ptolemies thought about what it was that was needed to make the system run smoothly. The priestly class (the scribes and the priests who ran the old religion) were given the same rights and privileges that they had had during the earlier pharaonic period. They were given large parcels of land, and they were able to live freely off its produce.

In turn, and this is really a contractual arrangement, what they then did was to acknowledge successive pharaohs just as their rights were acknowledged by successive pharaohs. Particularly in the 2nd and 1st centuries, as the Ptolemies grew weaker and weaker, we find that some of the most remarkable and some of the lengthiest inscriptions to come to us from the Ptolemaic world are inscriptions that show negotiations between the priests and the central authority.

Because, of course, every time a Ptolemy was weak, the priests would gouge more land, more prerogatives, and more rights out of him, in return for their support. In fact, probably the most famous document in all of Egyptian history, the Rosetta Stone, a trilingual inscription, which was the first inscription that allowed us to actually translate Egyptian hieroglyphs, is, in fact, a Ptolemaic document. It dates to 196 B.C. It comes from the reign of Ptolemy V. What that document contains is a series of tax breaks. It's an excruciatingly long document. I wouldn't begin to read you the details of it. But what it shows is that this young, weak king was relying on the support of the Memphite priesthood in order to maintain his authority in his kingdom.

I've painted a fairly bleak picture of the Ptolemaic control of Egypt so far. Intentionally so. It was a top-heavy control exercised by a Graeco-Macedonian elite, to be sure. But there are a couple of other elements that we should probably throw into the mix here, because the Ptolemies did, in some ways, attempt to make their power more acceptable or more palatable to their Egyptian subjects. Probably the most curious practice in this regard, a practice which seems to be designed to gain legitimacy for the Ptolemies in the eyes of their Egyptian subjects, is the practice of incestuous marriage within the Ptolemaic dynasty.

Ptolemy II, the son of the founder of the dynasty, in 275 B.C. married his sister, Asinoe. They were known throughout the rest of their joint reign as the *theoi philadelphoi*, that is to say, the brother- and sister-loving gods. They'd already claimed this status for themselves. But what does this marriage mean, and how would it work with its different audiences? Some Greek gods had been regarded as living in incestuous relations. The father of gods and men, Zeus, was married to his sister Hera, yes. But in ordinary Greek practice the idea of marrying your sister was certainly regarded as disgusting. In fact, we have some amazingly disgusting poems written at the time, about Ptolemy marrying his sister and presumably having sexual relations with her. This offended most of the Greeks.

But it probably was designed to play to an Egyptian audience. In the Egyptian pantheon, at least in late Egyptian religion, two of the most important gods had been Isis and Osiris. These were regarded as both husband and wife and brother and sister. So this practice of marrying one's sister, which took place among the Ptolemies and was continued by later members of the dynasty, was probably an attempt on their part to cast themselves in the role of the living embodiment of Isis and Osiris, the chief mother and father god within the Egyptian pantheon.

That may have been their intention. It certainly offended the Greeks, and I don't know that it ever persuaded any of the Egyptians. Nevertheless, the practice continued for, essentially three hundred years. Even Cleopatra VII, the famous Cleopatra, who we'll be talking about at the end of these lectures, was, for a time, married to her own brother, Ptolemy XIII.

The other attempt that was made by the Ptolemies to try to bridge some of the gap between Egyptian culture, the culture of the conquered, and their own culture, was in the creation of a new religious cult. This is really a bizarre story. It was a religious cult that was based on the figure of Serapis. Serapis himself is a figure who is a synthesis of Osiris from the Egyptian pantheon, and the Apis bull, which had gained in respect in later Egyptian history. So these two figures have already been put together. Osiris and Apis. And they're treated now, by the Greeks, as a new god, called Serapis. But this god is really un-Egyptian in appearance. We have statues and busts of this god, Serapis, and he looks really, very much like Zeus and Asclepius, and even, to some extent, Apollo. So it looks as if we have the figure, which is, in some ways, recalling Egyptian religion, but is also geared towards Greek religion.

In fact, we even know that Ptolemy II, who was responsible for the creation of this cult, actually imported Greek priests from Greek cities to come to Egypt and to write a liturgy. In other words, to write the hymns and the poems to be recited in honor of this god. So it represents a very curious fusion, because all the trappings, and all the external appearance of it is really Greek. And yet the central figure is borrowed from the Egyptians. Some have argued that because of this packaging, if you will, it's not really designed for an Egyptian audience at all, but rather it's designed for those Greeks who were fascinated by everything Egyptian. And that may well be true. Because the fact of the matter is that in the Ptolemaic period, even though the worship of the Apis bull remained quite a powerful religious presence in the Egyptian world, the cult of Serapis, and the cult that went with it, that of Isis, now presented as a Greek goddess, these two cults were actually much more popular outside of Egypt. In fact, they were really the most successful export of the Ptolemaic Egyptian dynasty. A cult that was a repackaged version of pseudo-Egyptian religion designed for a Greek audience.

The Greek world in the Hellenistic Period was as fascinated by Egypt as we are still today. They also looked at the pyramids and thought that these were strange and wonderful monuments. The Greeks had, for hundreds of years, thought that Egypt was the ancient fountain of all wisdom. So it may be that what the Ptolemies were doing in this cult of Serapis and the cult of Isis was tapping into that awe, that respect, that veneration that the Greeks felt for the Egyptians. Tapping into that, and now appropriating it for themselves, so that what had been Egyptian, now became Ptolemaic.

Lecture Seven
Alexandria and the Library

Scope:

Alexandria, the capital of Ptolemaic Egypt, was the jewel of the Hellenistic world. Not only was it the seat of Ptolemy's court, but its library and museum were the two premier cultural institutions of the Hellenistic world. We examine the city and its institutions and ask whether they represent a blending of Greek and Egyptian elements or the imposition of one culture over the other.

Outline

I. Located at the west end of the Nile delta, Alexandria's very location evoked its ambiguous nature.

    A. It is not in the Nile valley, as were the great pharaonic cities and temples, but in the region bordering Egypt on one side and the Mediterranean on the other. An important Greek emporium had existed in the same region at Naukratis as early as the 6th century, so the notion of keeping the Greek presence on the edge of Egypt already had a precedent.

    B. Alexander was responsible for the city's foundation, a fact remembered with pride to this day. According to Plutarch, he laid out a city plan in the shape of a Macedonian military cloak, a story that recalls the Macedonian notion that conquered lands were "spear-won" territory.

        1. Alexander did not live to see the building of the city, and it is entirely likely that the city was originally planned to be nothing more than one of the many garrisons that Alexander left throughout his empire.

        2. It was the first Ptolemies who brought the city into existence. They ennobled the city and themselves by making it "Alexander's city," a fact that they advertised by hijacking Alexander's corpse and making his mausoleum, the Soma, the central attraction in the city.

    C. Alexandria is the quintessential Hellenistic creation: a city that bears Alexander's name and evokes the magic of his physical being. In many ways, however, the city is more truly that of the Ptolemies, because they developed it and made it into the Greek capital of a Hellenistic kingdom.

II. Alexandria was different from the rest of Egypt.

   A. Here, the population was not composed of what the Greeks called the *laoi*, the Egyptian peasants, but was primarily Greek and Macedonian.

   B. Even those who came to the city from other regions, such as North Africa, Judaea, or Bablyon, tended to be Hellenized; they spoke and read Greek and had adopted Greek manners. One such group was the large Jewish community that lived in the northeastern quarter of the city.

   C. Many of these non-Egyptians were connected directly or indirectly to the court, the *aulos*, which in some estimates physically occupied one-quarter of the entire space of Alexandria.

   D. Craftsmen, such as silversmiths, goldsmiths and jewelers, sculptors and painters, and mosaic makers, made the city an artistic capital. Dyers, weavers, merchants, teachers, and doctors came from all parts of the Greek world. Soldiers came to enroll in Ptolemy's army.

   E. At the same time, because Egypt was a massive producer of oil and grain, Alexandria was also a mercantile center through which Egypt's produce was exported to the rest of the Mediterranean.

   F. The confluence of these factors—dynastic power, phenomenal wealth, and the exclusivity of Greek culture—arguably made Alexandria the most creative center of Hellenistic culture.

III. The heart of Hellenistic culture was the museum, the temple of the Muses.

   A. It was founded by Ptolemy I Soter and modeled on the Athenian institution of the same name that housed the library of Aristotle. The library and museum went hand in hand; the entire institution revolved around the library.

   B. Ptolemy Soter appointed Demetrius of Phaleron, a pro-Macedonian Athenian philosopher, to organize the collection of texts that eventually grew to 500,000 books. The post of librarian, which also covered the running of the museum, was one of the most influential at the Ptolemaic court.

C. Throughout most of the 19th and 20th centuries, modern scholars have been fascinated by the library, but no physical remains of it exist and even its exact location is disputed.

    1. Scholars usually assume that the entire institution of library and museum represented an attempt by the Ptolemies to connect themselves with the great history of Athenian philosophy, especially the Aristotelian tradition.

    2. This desire to replicate Athenian culture, it seems to some, represents the typical apathy of the Hellenistic Greeks toward native and indigenous cultures.

D. It is possible, however, that a pharaonic antecedent to the Library of Alexandria may have existed.

    1. Descriptions of the library and museum suggest that the complex may have resembled the funerary temple of Ramses at Thebes.

    2. At the back of the temple was a set of banquet chambers with depictions of the king doing homage to Osiris. In this area were shelves housing scrolls, probably sacred texts.

    3. Like the Ramasseum, the library had communal dining rooms for the scholars and priests who worked there.

    4. It, too, housed books, including the sacred texts of foreign cults.

    5. The buildings of the library and museum were probably built abutting the tomb of Alexander, just as the Ramasseum included the tomb of the pharaoh. This quintessentially Hellenistic Greek institution may owe more to pharaonic practice than has generally been perceived.

IV. Inside the museum and library, scholars, poets, and scientists toiled away producing some of the most innovative thought and art of the Hellenistic Age.

A. Callimachus, Theocritus, and Apollonius represent the new directions of Hellenistic poetry, to be discussed in more detail in Lecture Twelve.

1. Pastoral poetry, which purports to concern the life of shepherds, is actually a carefully wrought and highly artificial genre destined for an elite, courtly audience.
2. Poems dense with allusion to mythology also supposed an audience that was well educated in Greek culture.
3. Epic poetry was still being composed as well, but it was now infused with a spirit of uncertainty and psychological drama that would have a deep impact on Virgil's Latin epic, the *Aeneid*.

B. Scientific inquiry begun in Alexandria produced remarkable results.
1. Eratosthenes, for example, observed that at Assouan, in upper Egypt, a vertical pole in mid-summer cast no shadow.
2. By measuring the shadow of a similar pole on the same day in Alexandria, he calculated that the distance between the two sites was 7 1/5 degrees, or one-fiftieth of a circle.
3. Because the actual distance between the two is 500 miles, the total circumference of the globe calculated by Eratosthenes was 25,000 miles with a diameter of 7,850 miles, an error of only 50 miles.

C. Other scientific advancements included the work of Euclid, whose theorems remained the basis of Western mathematics for another 2,000 years. Less well known is Hypsikles, who divided the circle into 360 degrees.

D. Although the library was not concerned with applied science, the speculative brilliance of Greek thinking continued to flourish under royal patronage.

E. Also in Alexandria, scholars first began the systematic study of texts, especially that of Homer. Studies in textual analysis, philology, etymology, and grammar all flourished as never before. In many ways, the library and museum were the ancient forerunners of the modern research university.

Suggested Reading:

L. Canfora, *The Library of Alexandria: A Wonder of the Ancient World*.

G. Lloyd, *Greek Science after Aristotle*.

Questions to Consider:

1. Why was Greek science so uninterested in the practical applications of scientific principles?

2. Was the scientific work of the library compatible with royal patronage and the authority of the Ptolemies?

Lecture Seven—Transcript
Alexandria and the Library

Hello and welcome back to our series of lectures on the Hellenistic Age. Last time we were looking at the Ptolemies and the Hellenistic dynasty that ruled Egypt for three hundred years following the conquest of the Persian Empire by Alexander. At that time, Egypt had been a province of the Persian Empire, and following Alexander's death the whole area of Egypt was taken over by Ptolemy, who established a dynasty that ruled successfully for three hundred years, its last independent ruler being Cleopatra VII, the famous Cleopatra, mistress of Julius Casesar and Marc Antony. It was upon her death in 31 [sic 30] B.C. that Egypt finally lost its independence and became another province of the Roman Empire.

We talked about the system of government in Ptolemaic Egypt last time. We saw that the Ptolemies presented themselves as Pharaohs to their Egyptian subjects, but as Greek kings to their subjects in Alexandria. And it is to Alexandria that I want to turn today, because Alexandria, in antiquity, as in the early part of the 20th century, was probably the most glorious, sophisticated, and cosmopolitan city of the eastern Mediterranean.

Certainly, in recent literature, it has played that same role, if one reads the poems of Constantine Cavafy, the Greek poet who was born and grew up in Alexandria, or the novels of Lawrence Durrell, one finds a city which, in the early part of this [20th] century, could boast of many families of different backgrounds. Where people would grow up speaking five languages. Where Jewish bankers and British naval officers and Italian merchants rubbed shoulders with each other in an environment of absolute tolerance. A truly glorious and cosmopolitan city. A true example of the idea of the melting pot.

So it was in the Hellenistic world, as well. It was the jewel of the Hellenistic world. It was not only the seat of the court of the Ptolemies, but also its library and its museum were the two premier cultural institutions of the Hellenistic age. So today what I want to do is to look a bit more at Alexandria, and to look at these institutions, and to try to recreate in some sense what life was like in this glittering jewel in the crown of the Ptolemies.

Located at the western end of the Nile delta, Alexandria's very location evokes its somewhat ambiguous nature. The pharaohs, you will recall, had ruled in cities like Memphis, and Thebes and Luxor, where there were great temples, advertising their relationship to the gods, and where their dead ancestors were buried and worshiped.

But the Ptolemies chose not to build along the Nile valley, but rather to situate themselves at a remove. At a point where the Nile spews out into the Mediterranean. This idea of being next to Egypt, rather than in Egypt, as such, is something that does not begin with the Ptolemies, and doesn't even begin with the founding of Alexandria. There had been Greek traders living on the area on the edge of the delta going back at least to the 6th century B.C., at the city of Naukratis, a city where Greek traders and merchants would come from around the entire eastern Mediterranean, to do their business with the pharaohs and the king's agents. That pattern was exactly copied once again by Ptolemy.

It is also an area that was well-known to the Greeks, not only by the foundation of Naukratis, but also because Homer had mentioned this area. He talks about an island called Pharos, which lies just off the coast of Egypt. That island of Pharos, which came to be connected to the mainland, was the point at which Alexandria was physically located. It was on that island, or the tip of that peninsula, that the great lighthouse of Alexandria was built. In fact, that lighthouse was known to the Greeks as Pharos, taking its name from the very island.

Alexander was supposed to be responsible for the city's foundation. We have a detailed account of the foundation myth. It comes from Alexandria. The foundation story recorded in Plutarch gives us some idea of what the Alexandrians, and particularly the Ptolemies, wanted to project about their city's foundation. Let me read you a section of it. As you listen to this, I think you'll find that the Alexandrians are not really interested at all in anything to do with Egypt. They are seeing their city as a sort of divine foundation of the Greeks. So Plutarch tells us that once Alexander had come to Egypt, he then left behind him a large and populous Greek city which would bear his name. Alexandria.

On the advice of his architects, he was about to measure out and enclose a certain size, when during the night, as he was sleeping, he saw a remarkable vision. This is a good Greek foundation legend, that a god or some divine character appears to the founder during his sleep. So he has this remarkable vision, and listen to what happens in this vision:

He thought he saw a man with very white hair and a venerable appearance standing beside him and speaking these lines. 'Then there is an island in a stormy sea in front of Egypt. They call it Pharos.'

Now, this isn't a god. This isn't Asclepius the healer-god. It isn't Zeus, and it isn't Apollo. It's a venerable old man. No Greek god is described in those terms. I'd strongly suggest that this was Homer appearing to him. So Homer, whom Alexander read every night (remember he had the *Iliad* under his pillow), appears to him and recites to him two lines from the *Odyssey*, describing the location of Pharos. It's there that Alexander decides to found his city.

He rose at once and went to Pharos, which at that time was still an island a little above the Canopic mouth of the Nile, but which has now been joined to the mainland by a causeway. When he saw that the site was eminently suitable (it is a strip of land similar to a fairly broad isthmus, running between a large lagoon and the sea, which terminates in the great harbor), he exclaimed that Homer, who was admirable in other respects, was also an excellent architect.

So he follows the guidance that comes in the dream, the divine inspiration. He goes to Pharos. Then he actually has to lay out the external circumference of the city, which is what the founder of a city will always do. Since there was no chalk available, he used barley meal to describe a rounded area on the dark soil, to whose inner arc straight lines succeeded.

So he's laying out the grid plan of the city. And it produced a figure which is called in Greek a *chlamys*, which is to say, a Macedonian military cloak. A trapezoidal shape, if you like.

The king was delighted with the plan, when suddenly a vast multitude of birds of every kind and size flew from the river and lagoon onto the site like clouds. Nothing was left of the barley meal as these birds came down and picked it up. Even Alexander was much troubled by the omen. But his seers advised him [and this is when you need your seers to give you a good interpretation] there was nothing to fear. In their view the city he was founding would abound in resources and would sustain men from every nation. He therefore instructed his overseers to press on with the work.

So the city is founded thanks to a dream. It is laid out by Alexander himself and then there is an omen from the gods to suggest that it is

©2000 The Teaching Company.

going to be a prosperous city. These are the stories that the Macedonians liked to tell. Some of these elements are quite straightforward: the divine inspiration, the birds promising the future prosperity of the city. I think even the shape of the city, likened to a Macedonian war-cloak, the cloak worn by a Macedonian soldier, is meant, in a way, to evoke this notion that the Macedonians promulgated that their land, their empire was spear-won territory, was won by the might of their soldiery. So the city of Alexander was meant, in some respects, to be an evocation of this conquest by Alexander and also by his Macedonian successors.

Alexander didn't live to see the building of the city. It's entirely likely that the original city was there primarily to act as a garrison on the edge of Egypt and looking towards Syrianca and also to act like Naukratis, as a trade emporium. To encourage trade between Egypt and the Mediterranean. But whether it was intended only for those simple purposes or whether it was designed as something more, what we know is that its location proved to give it a brilliant advantage. The Greeks themselves understood this. We have a short description that I want to give you from Strabo, written in the second century, when he comments on the advantages of the site.

> The advantages of the site are many [he says], for, first, the place is washed by two seas. [You have to imagine a coastline with the Mediterranean above, and then a lake to the south. So it's in the strip of land between two seas.] In the north, by the so-called Egyptian Sea [which we would call the eastern Mediterranean] and in the south by Lake Mareotis. Many canals from the Nile fill it [so there are canals running from the Nile and through the delta, down to Lake Mareotis] from above and on the sides, and through these [this is interesting] far more goods are imported than from the sea. [In other words, there's more produce coming into Alexandria from the Nile Valley than coming from outside.] With the result that the harbor on the lake was much wealthier than the one on the sea. Here the exports from Alexandria are greater than the imports.

So this trade emporium was brilliantly located to allow all the material coming from southern Egypt, from Upper Egypt to be brought towards the Mediterranean and then from there exported out. As we know from the lecture last time, all of that trade was controlled by the Ptolemies. It was their agents that stored and traded all these goods. So its brilliant location added to the prosperity of the Ptolemaic dynasty.

It was really the first Ptolemies who brought this city into existence. They ennobled the city by making it Alexander's city. They were helped in this quest of calling this city the City of Alexander by the fact that the body of Alexander was there in Alexandria. How could that be? Surely Alexander would be buried either in Babylon where he died, or back in Macedonia, where the Macedonian kings came from. The answer is that after his death, his generals spent a number of months preparing a glorious funeral cortege, which would bring his body in state, across Asia and back to Macedon. But once it got halfway, it was hijacked by Ptolemy.

Brought back to Alexandria, it was installed in the center of the city. It became the center (like the mausoleum of Lenin in Moscow). Let me read you the description here.

> The so-called Soma or tomb is also part of the royal palaces. This was an enclosure, in which were the tombs of the kings and of Alexander. [So the royal mausoleum is right in the middle of town.] For Ptolemy son of Lagos [that's Ptolemy I] got in ahead of Perdiccas and took the body from him when he was bringing it down from Babylon. [He hijacked it in Syria. We've got another account that speaks of the flying column of men being sent up to grab this and spirit it back down to Alexandria.] He gave it burial in Alexandria where it now lies, though not in the same sarcophagus. The present one is made of glass, while Ptolemy placed it in one made of gold.

So in Strabo's time, you could actually go to Alexandria and you could see the embalmed body of Alexander inside his glass coffin. This hijacking, I think, makes Alexander the central attraction of the city. It gives us an idea what role Alexander played in this Hellenistic world. Alexandria is the quintessential Hellenistic creation. It carries the name of Alexander. Its foundation myth says that it was brought into being by Alexander through his inspiration and through his actual laying out of the city.

And yet it is in some ways more truly a city of the Ptolemies, who are evoking the Alexandrian connection, since it was they who developed it and made it into the Greek capital of their Hellenistic kingdom.

Alexandria was different from the rest of Egypt. Here, the population was not composed of what the Greeks would call the *laoi*, the peasants. Rather, the population was primarily Greek and Macedonian. But there were also others who came into the city to add to its cosmopolitan flavor. There would have been (we know of) Italian merchants coming there. We know that there were Phoenician merchants from Tyre and Sidon coming there. And probably Berbers from North Africa.

One such group which came to the city, and which, like most of the other groups, eventually adopted Greek speech and wrote Greek and behaved with Greek manners, one such important group in the city was the Jewish community, which lived in the northeastern quarter of the city. It was very important for this community of Jews living in Alexandria to maintain that the Ptolemies and the high priests in Jerusalem maintained friendly relations. This was a way of confirming their own status as a privileged community. We have a document going back to the 2nd century, probably fictitious, but interesting nonetheless, which purports to be a letter from King Ptolemy to Eleazar the High Priest in Jerusalem. While it may be fictitious, I think it does give us an idea of what the Alexandrian Jewish community wished to project of its relations with the Ptolemies.

> King Ptolemy, to Eleazar the High Priest, greetings and good health. Since it happens that many Jews have been settled in our country, some of whom were transplanted from Jerusalem by the Persians during their period of rule, and others came as captives to Egypt in our father's day, we have given their freedom to over 100,000 prisoners [of war], paying their own as the proper value in money, and putting right any harm done through the impulses of the crowd.

An interesting suggestion that perhaps not everything was calm in Alexandria. Later on we do know of race riots and ethnically divided hostilities in the city. But what follows is particularly interesting.

> It was our intention [says Ptolemy in his letter] to perform a pious deed and to dedicate a thank-offering to the greatest god [Notice that he doesn't say which god. So, in deference

possibly to the monotheism of the Jews, he doesn't say who.] who has kept our kingdom in peace and in the greatest renown throughout the whole inhabited world. We've enrolled in the army those in the prime of age and those capable of being in our service who are deserving of trust at the court, and we have appointed them to official positions.

In fact, we do know of Hellenized Jews serving throughout Egypt. We know of Hellenized Jews who were acting as tax farmers, as bureaucrats for the Ptolemaic civil service. We know of some of them acting as mercenaries and holding a garrison down at Elephantine, for example. And military settlers in the countryside. So there were many Hellenized Jews, Jews who had taken on Greek language and practice, living throughout the kingdom. But look at what Ptolemy asks of the High Priest in Jerusalem. He says:

Now, as we wish to show favor to them, to all the Jews in the inhabited world, and to those of future generations, we have decided to have your law translated from the Hebrew language you use into Greek, so that they, too, may be available in our library, together with the other royal books.

He actually then commissions Eleazar to appoint a series of elders who are versed both in Hebrew and in Greek to provide a translation of the Hebrew Torah. This will eventually come to us as the Greek Old Testament, the Septuagint.

So this was a city where, it seems as if many different groups lived cheek by jowl and managed to get on with each other. Many of these non-Egyptians were connected directly or indirectly to the court (the court of the king), known as the *aulos*, which in some estimates physically occupied one-quarter of the entire space of the city. So we have to imagine a city where much of the city is actually built up using the great buildings of the palace, the museum, the library, the body of Alexander. And many people living around the palace earning their daily bread from working for the Ptolemaic palace.

There were craftsmen in Alexandria such as silversmiths, goldsmiths and jewelers. Clearly, they're producing material for consumption by the Ptolemies. There are painters, and there are mosaic makers responsible for the glorious decoration of the palace. These men made the city into an artistic capital that people came from all around the Mediterranean to see. Dyers, weavers, merchants, teachers, doctors—all of these people flocked from around the Greek world to come to Alexandria. We have poems written by Greek poets, saying, for example, if you're really poor, and you need some cash, go to Ptolemy. He pays the most for a good mercenary. So everyone felt that they could get a job if they went to Alexandria.

Alexandria must have been very much like New York in the 20th century. And it existed not only in reality, but in the minds of people in much the same way, as well. At the same time, since Egypt was a massive producer of oil and grain (we've already seen that in previous lectures), Alexandria was also a mercantile capital. It was a center through which all of Egypt's produce was filtered as it was exported out to the rest of the Mediterranean.

It's this confluence of factors, of the strong central authority of the Ptolemies, the dynastic power, the phenomenal wealth of Egypt, all being filtered through here. And the exclusivity of Greek culture—their desire to remain separate from the rest of Egypt, these all, I think, contribute to making Alexandria probably the most glorious, the richest and the most creative center of Hellenistic culture.

The heart of this Hellenistic culture was the museum, named for the Muses. *Mouseion* in Greek simply means the temple of the Muses. It was founded by Ptolemy I, who was known as Ptolemy Soter (Ptolemy the Savior). It was modeled on an Athenian institution of the same name. In the museum (or the *mouseion*) back in Athens, the library of Aristotle was housed. So the library in Alexandria was also considered to be a part of the museum. They went hand in hand, the two institutions.

Ptolemy I appointed an Athenian by the name of Demetrius of Phaleron, an Athenian philosopher, to organize a collection of texts, which eventually grew to 500,000 volumes. The largest library in the ancient world. The post of librarian was not merely that of a glorified cataloguer. Rather, the librarian who was in charge of this institution and also in charge of the *Mouseion*, was one of the most influential men at the court of the Ptolemies. He was really like a minister of culture, if you will, and even served as the tutor of the children of Ptolemy. So it was a very prestigious institution, and it was honored by the official dynasty.

Throughout most of the 19th and 20th centuries, modern scholars have been fascinated by the Library, but there are no physical remains that we have to give us an idea of its exact location or its exact lay-out and size. Because there was no physical evidence, people relying on literary descriptions have nearly always assumed that the whole institution of the Library and the Museum together represented an attempt by the Ptolemies to connect themselves with the older Athenian culture. So we have the museum at Athens and now we have a new one in Alexandria. And particularly to put themselves in the Aristotelian tradition. For many people, this desire to replicate Athenian culture (older Classical culture) and to make it grander in this Hellenistic setting, is typical of the way the Hellenistic Greeks were really uninterested in learning anything from their contacts with indigenous cultures.

But there's a new analysis of the Library that I want to share with you, because if it's correct, it may be that there was a much greater degree of fusion between the two cultures than we've previously expected. Descriptions of the Library and the Museum suggest that the complex may have resembled a funerary temple, the funerary temple of Ramses at Thebes. In other words, it may have been based on a ground plan copied from an Egyptian prototype. At the back of the temple of Ramses (called the Ramesseum) was a set of banquet chambers, decorated with depictions of the king paying homage to Osiris. In this area there were shelves housing scrolls, which were probably sacred texts. Books of the dead, and so forth. Like the Ramesseum, the *Mouseion*, or the Musuem and Library in Alexandria also had a communal dining room, where the various scholars and priests at work in the museum came to eat. It, too, housed books, and not just any books, but sometimes sacred volumes such as the ones that we've heard Ptolemy commissioning from the High Priest in Jerusalem. Jewish sacred texts. Babylonian sacred texts would have been stored here, as well.

And not only that. The building of the Library and the Museum, the entire complex, probably abutted the *Soma*, the mausoleum of Alexander the Great. So that, just as at the Ramesseum, one has the tomb of the pharaoh next to this complex, so too, in the Library/Museum, one has the tomb of the great and heroic Alexander. This can't be proved conclusively, but it's really worth considering; that this institution, which people regarded as quintessentially Hellenistic Greek, may, in fact, have owed a great deal to an Egyptian prototype. I think that's a wonderful idea.

There's a short description of some of the layout of the Library and the Museum in Strabo. He's been talking here in his description of Alexandria about the way that most of the city is occupied by the palaces. He talks about their location close to the harbor. He says that the Museum also forms part of the royal palaces. It has a covered walk. An arcade with recesses and seats, and a large house in which is the dining room of the learned members of the museum.

> This association of men [he says] shares common property and has a priest of the Muses, who used to be appointed by the kings, but is now appointed by Caesar.

Strabo was writing during the Roman period. The so-called *Soma* is also part of the royal palaces and he goes on to describe that. (We've already looked at that description.) So it was a wonderful institution. It would have been a glorious place to work. I think that any university professor who reads that description is green with envy, particularly because you got to do pure research and no teaching. But it may have had an Egyptian model.

Inside the Museum and the Library, scholars and poets and scientists toiled away, producing some of the most innovative thought and the most innovative art of the Hellenistic Age. For example, the three greatest poets of the Hellenistic period (and once again we have this tendency to think in terms of threes: the three periods in Greek history; later on we're going to see the three great sculptors; now we're going to see the three great poets) all end up at one time or another working at the Museum.

I'm not going to go into great detail about them right now, because we'll have another lecture on poetry later, but briefly, their names are Callimachus, Theocritas and Apollonius. Each of them represents a new direction in Hellenistic poetry. Pastoral poetry, set in an idealized countryside, dealing with the lives of shepherds, is in fact a very carefully wrought and highly artificial genre of poetry. It's not cowboy poetry, at all. It's actually poetry written for a court. For an elite. So it was clearly appropriate for the Ptolemies. Poems dense with allusion to mythology are also produced at the time. To understand these poems you really have to know Greek mythology inside out. That's clearly not written for an Egyptian audience. It's written for Greeks. Well-educated Greeks, who can share "in" jokes about references to events in Greek myth.

Epic poetry is still being composed, as well, but the epic poetry that we find being composed in the Hellenistic period is very different from Homer's epic. It is much more an epic that is concerned with the interior life. The psychological drives of the hero. We'll look more at that later on. This plays a very important role in the Western European tradition of epic, because the poet most influenced by this is Virgil, who produces Rome's great epic, the *Aeneid*. Aeneas, the hero of that poem, is really (though the poem is written in Latin) a Hellenistic hero. His interior concerns are really those that are shown in Hellenistic poetry.

The Museum, of course, was also known for scientific inquiry. One can mention here, in particular, one of the librarians, a man known as Eratosthenes. His nickname was "Beta". "Beta," because, as we would say, he was jack of all trades, master of none, He was never alpha, but he was always very good as the number two man, in a range of fields. He wrote histories. He wrote chronicles. He did geography. He did mathematics. It is one of his scientific experiments, that, in a way, best sums up the spirit of science in the Hellenistic Age.

Eratosthenes observed that if you are at Assouan, in Upper Egypt (to the south)—if you were there, and you held a vertical pole of a particular length at midsummer on a particular day, it cast no shadow, because the sun was directly overhead. If you held a pole of exactly the same size, on exactly the same day, at exactly the same time in Alexandria, by measuring the length of the shadow that was cast, he was able to calculate that the distance between the two sites represented seven and a fifth degrees, or one fiftieth of a circle. Since he knew the relative value of that distance and he knew the absolute value, namely five hundred miles (because the distance was measurable) he was able to calculate the circumference of the globe (which he calculated at 25,000 miles) and the diameter of the globe (which he calculated at 7,850 miles). An error (so I'm told—I'm not a scientist) of only fifty miles.

That (I always find) is a pretty astonishing bit of scientific reasoning, because it is essentially working out the size of this planet using two sticks. That, I think, is quite an accomplishment.

Other scientific advances included the work of Euclid, and of course Euclid's theorems remain the basis of Western geometry and mathematics for another two thousand years. Lesser known, but probably just as important in the long run is the work of Hypsikles, who divided the circle into 360 degrees.

So many of the approaches to mathematics that we take for granted today really derive from research during the Hellenistic Period.

The Library was not concerned with applied science, at all. It was really speculative brilliance that was the hallmark of Greek scientific thinking, both before and during the Hellenistic Period as well, as it continued to flourish under royal patronage.

The last area that we will mention, one that many people don't pay much attention to, but it's important to historians like me. Alexandria is the first place in the West where people are engaged in the systematic study of text. It is in Alexandria that scholars take all the different versions of Homer that people are reading, and they try to work out which is the proper, authoritative text of Homer. So the next time you pick up a book that has been edited (say, *Moby Dick*, or some other classic), if you can rely on that text as being an authoritative text, as opposed to just some bogus knock-off copy, then you should think of one of the scientists or one of the grammarians working in the Library and the Museum in Alexandria, because that is the legacy of their scholarship.

Lecture Eight
The Seleucid Realm

Scope:

The second great Hellenistic kingdom was ruled by the Seleucid dynasty, which built cities from Syria to Iran. We examine their ways of ruling a kingdom that stretched across all of Central Asia. Like the Ptolemies, the Seleucids would not create a fusion of Greek and eastern cultures but would impose Hellenism. Even so, on the eastern edges of their realm, a hybrid culture would emerge in the Greek kingdoms of Bactria.

Outline

I. Seleucus was assigned the satrapy of Babylon upon Alexander's death.

    A. Although this was a potentially rich power base, Seleucus was left to assert control of his territory and fend for himself when Antigonus marched east in 316 B.C. From this unpromising start, Seleucus went on to assert control over a greater expanse of territory than that governed by any of Alexander's successors.

    B. In fact, so considerable was his success in reclaiming control of the upper satrapies in eastern Asia that many historians have seen the entire flow of Seleucid history as a gradual decline from a high point coinciding with its first ruler. Instead of emphasizing decline, we should rather ask how Seleucus and his descendents managed to rule and control a territory that was everything Ptolemaic Egypt was not—geographically vast and ethnically diverse.

II. Intelligently, Seleucus adopted a range of different strategies to establish his power, depending on the particular circumstances of each region.

    A. In the far east, Seleucus confirmed his hold on territory by giving up territory.

        1. In 306 B.C., Seleucus established the eastern border of his domain, ceding the Indus valley and adjoining desert regions to the Mauryan king, Chandragupta.

    2. In return for renouncing claims to any lands further east, Seleucus was given 500 elephants, the heavy armor of Hellenistic warfare.

B. In the remote upper satrapies of central Asia, Bactria and Sogdiana, Seleucus and his son Antiochus founded dozens of cities with Macedonian veterans and Greek settlers.

C. These swelled to become thriving emporiums on the trade routes that cross central Asia. Antioch Persis, Antioch Margiana near Merv, Soteira, Ai Khanum, and the island city of Falaika off Kuwait were all Seleucid foundations or thrived under the Seleucids.

    1. Margaiana is a typical example of Seleucid urbanization. It is located in an oasis of fertile territory surrounded by mountains and high desert. An Achaemenid citadel was here, captured by Alexander, but archaeology has shown rapid expansion at the time of Seleucus, with pottery dating from the same time as the expansion of Ai Khanum and Samarkhand.

    2. With the erection of inner and outer walls, the garrison was transformed into the acropolis of a much larger settlement capable of supporting a large population and protecting the caravan routes bringing silk, spices, and other precious commodities into the Seleucid realm. The presence of canals also attests to the greater exploitation of land.

    3. This occupation was essentially Greek, with little sign of intermarriage or ethnic mixing.

D. Greek colonization was stressed in more remote areas, because there was no lack of poor Greeks hungry for opportunity on the borders of the empire.

III. A second region that was heavily colonized was Syria.

A. From the Mediterranean across the Fertile Crescent stretched a network of Seleucid cities: Laodicea by the Sea, Apamea on the Orontes, Seleucia Pieria, Antioch on the Orontes, and Seleucia on the Tigris.

B. These show a heavy concentration on the western end of the empire and reveal the continuing concern of the Seleucid kings to be participants in the Mediterranean world.

C. In addition, Greek cities were already established in Asia Minor that fell under Seleucid control through much of the 3rd century, and here we find the typical pattern of a reciprocal patron-client relationship. This relationship is well attested in many long "formulaic" letters and petitions in which the people offer honors in return for royal favors, such as tax exemptions.

IV. Between the Mediterranean and the upper satrapies lay Babylon, the heart of the ancient culture first taken over by Persians and now Greeks.

A. Here, the Seleucids could not hope to impress an ancient culture with their Greek manners any more than the Ptolemies could impose Hellenism on the priests of Memphis. Instead, the Seleucids presented themselves as pious successors of the Achaemenids and as legitimate Babylonian rulers.

B. At Borsippa and in Babylon, we have building inscriptions in which Antiochus presents himself as the anointed priest-king who built the very bricks of the temple.

C. What lay behind this utterly non-Greek approach was a sensible policy of confirming, rather than stripping, the rights of temple estates. As focal points of power and social organization, the temples remained central to the stability of the region and were, therefore, protected by the Seleucids.

V. Nevertheless, it would be wrong to think that this was simply a world of Greek cities ruled by a distant, benevolent Hellenistic king.

A. A good deal of the best territory and many of its people would have felt Seleucid rule quite directly. The administration reached to every corner of the kingdom, which borrowed the Persian system of satrapies and included a slew of minor officials, such as *dioiketes* (manager) and *logistes* (accountant).

B. Large swathes of land were owned by the king. The people of these regions, the *basilikoi laoi*, were tied to the land. They paid either a tithe or a fixed tax each year and these revenues, along with the land and the people, could be apportioned out or sold by the crown, as is attested in the divorce documents of King Antiochus.

C. The chief beneficiaries were the king's friends, the *philoi*—the commanders, officers, and bureaucrats who served as the administration of the empire. These men were reinforced by the soldiers and military contingents that were settled on land holdings around the empire and remained liable for military service.

D. Only the nomads of the mountains or the deserts remained free of active interference. With these people, the Seleucids carried on the Achaemenid practice of gift-exchange.

    1. They confirmed desert chiefs as independent potentates as long as they provided contingents in the great musters of troops for the royal army.

    2. The camel corps from the Arabian dessert and cavalry from Armenia were both contributed to the Seleucid army in this way.

VI. The Seleucid realm presents an approach to the problem of Hellenistic rule that may be called "polyvalent kingship."

    A. The Seleucid kings would play different roles and use different institutions, depending on which audience they were playing to and which subjects they were dealing with.

    B. The one true innovation of the Seleucids was a system of shared kingship, whereby the senior king held the western domains and his son, as junior partner, held the east. The size of the empire required some such arrangement, and it is not coincidental that the Ottoman Empire followed the same practice centuries later.

    C. The Seleucid Empire, then, can be thought of as a complex mixture.

        1. It was influenced by the history of Persian control.

        2. The Seleucids also practiced sensible policies of noninterference, in which territorial control was out of the question. Religious respect was also maintained in situations in which cooperation was as strategically profitable as confrontation.

    D. As was the case in all the realms of the Hellenistic world, the institutions of the Seleucid empire were not designed to create harmony or fuse races but to establish order and royal control of a vast geographic area dominated by a small Graeco-Macedonian elite.

Suggested Reading:

S. Sherwin-White and A. Kuhrt, *From Sardis to Samarkhand.*

Questions to Consider:

1. In what ways did the geography of the Seleucid Empire shape the nature of Seleucid kingship?

2. In what sense could the urbanization encouraged by the Seleucids be termed imperialistic?

Lecture Eight—Transcript
The Seleucid Realm

Hello and welcome back to our series of lectures on the Hellenistic Age. We've now had an opportunity to look in depth at one of the most famous of the Hellenistic kingdoms, namely the Egypt acquired by Ptolemy after the death of Alexander, and ruled by his descendants for the next three hundred years. We saw that at Alexandria, we were able to find evidence for a Greek city that showed little attempt to fuse the cultures of the Greeks and the Egyptians, although in the case of the Library and the Museum, I suggested that it may be possible that an Egyptian template or model provided the outline for that particular institution. But most of the culture and the scientific research that we found going on at the Library and the Museum we saw as continuations of earlier Greek culture. Exclusive. Not designed to fuse the two races at all.

The second Hellenistic kingdom that we should include in our survey is one which is a little less known to people. It made not such an impact, in the way that the Ptolemaic kingdom did. And yet it is an area that embraced a far greater amount of sheer territory than did Ptolemaic Egypt. In some respects, the Seleucid realm, with its heartland of Syria, but its outlying provinces, as well, was, in a way, the nearest thing to a continuation of Alexander's empire. At its greatest extent, the Seleucid realm, named after its founder Seleucus, another one of Alexander's officers—at its greatest extent this realm included all the territory of Asia Minor, all of Syria, much of the area of Arabia and Mesopotamia, and way across through modern-day Iraq and Iran, all the way to the eastern end of Alexander's empire.

So in sheer geographic scope, we're looking at something that resembles what Alexander's empire would have been, had he continued alive for another thirty or forty years. What we're going to find when we examine this empire (that of the Seleucids) is that, once again, we don't see a fusion of cultures such as earlier historians had argued. But here, we're going to have even better evidence for the imposition of Greek culture over native populations, except at the very eastern edges. There, we're going to find a hybrid culture in the region of Bactria, an area where Gaeco-Bactrian kingdoms will eventually emerge. We're going to look at that in another lecture, because it's very interesting material.

Let's first begin with an outline of how the empire of the Seleucids takes shape. Seleucus was assigned the satrapy of Babylon upon Alexander's death. This was a potentially very rich power base. He, however, was left to assert control of the territory by himself. None of the other Hellenistic generals, none of the other officers of Alexander's army went to his assistance. When Antigonus marched east in 316 (Antigonus, you remember, being one of the few men who had a real shot at uniting Alexander's empire in the next generation), Seleucus temporarily had to flee. From this very unpromising start, Seleucus then rebounded and went on to exert control over a vaster domain and a larger territory than any other of Alexander's successors.

So considerable, in fact, was his success in reclaiming the upper satrapies, as they're called (these are the satrapies of modern-day Turkmenistan, and Uzbekistan—the region that we used to call the Central Asian Soviet republics) this area to the far east of Alexander's march—so successful was he in claiming control in here, that many historians have argued that the Seleucid Empire reached its high point during the reign of its founder, Seleucus I. The prevailing view that you'll read in textbooks about the Seleucid Empire, is that the next three hundred years presents a gradual falling away, a decline of power, as the entire empire begins to sink into decrepitude.

I don't want to emphasize decline here. That reminds me too much of the whole notion of the Hellenistic period as a period of decadence after the glory of the classical age. Instead, what I'd like to do is to ask, "How did Seleucus and his descendants manage to rule and to control so vast a territory. Their territory is really the exact opposite of Ptolemaic Egypt. Ptolemaic Egypt, as we saw, was an ethnic, historic, geographic unity. The Seleucid Empire is the exact reverse. It is geographically vast. It is ethnically varied. Everything about it is dispersed in a way that isn't in Egypt.

The answer is that, in fact, intelligently, Seleucus and his descendants adopted a range of different strategies. They did not attempt to impose a single style of rule across the entire empire. In fact, their strategies of rule are really dictated by the different regions in which they found themselves as the new ruling power. First of all, we can begin at the far eastern end of the empire, right over toward the Hindu Kush, the area, you remember, where Alexander had stopped, only because his army had said, "No more," and had gone into revolt.

In this area, Alexander had established alliances with such kings a Porus and Taxiles. Seleucus found that the easiest way to maintain his hold on any territory at the far eastern end, was to give up the border zone. By 306 B.C., Seleucus had established an eastern border. He had done this by ceding the territory of the Indus Valley and the adjoining desert regions, to the Mauryan king Chandragupta (Sandrocottus, as the Greeks called him). So establishing a fixed border between the Mauryan Empire of northwestern India and the Seleucid domain, he was now able to concentrate on the west. He no longer had to worry about those far eastern domains. In return for renouncing his claims to these territories (really only nominal claims—the Greeks had never controlled this area well, but in return for renouncing his claims, and establishing this border, Seleucus was given 500 war elephants.

War elephants are the Panzer tanks of Hellenistic warfare. So it was actually a pretty good deal. By giving up a nominal claim to a region he never really controlled, he was able to beef up his heavy armor quite considerably. Most of the battles of the Hellenistic period are between Greek mercenary armies employed by one Hellenistic king against Greek mercenary armies employed by another, with the heavy impact as their two lines joined being given by the elephants. So 500 war elephants was a considerable advantage.

In the upper satrapies of Central Asia, a little further west of that eastern border, a region far away, though, from the Mediterranean—a region where Alexander had tried to conquer the mountain of Aornos and where he had found his wife Roxane—in these so-called upper satrapies of Bactria and Sogdiana, Seleucus and his son founded dozens of cities, with Macedonian veterans and Greek settlers. This is the hallmark of Hellenization,. That you found a city by establishing a garrison and by encouraging trade. You give much of the land to Greek veterans and Greek settlers, so that you pour a Greek population into that region. There, the local people continue to serve as the peasants operating at the behest of their Greek overlords.

These foundations by Seleucus and his son swelled to become thriving emporia. Cities that dominated the trade routes running across Central Asia. The so-called "Silk Route," for example. We have dozens, literally dozens of cities founded at this time: Antioch

Persis, Antioch Margiana (which eventually will mutate into the name Merv), Soteira, Ai Khanum (excavated by the French up in Afghanistan), and the island city of Falaika (located just off the coast of Kuwait). These were all either Seleucid foundations or settlements which may have existed before the Seleucids, but which were now made much larger, and which thrived as a result of the trade going on under the Seleucids.

A good example of this process is to be seen at Antioch Margiana, the city of Merv. It's located in an oasis of fertile territory surrounded by mountains and high desert. So any people crossing these deserts and taking their goods (their silks, their spices from the East to the west) are going to gravitate to this area, going through the oasis. There had been already an Achaemenid citadel here, a small Achaemenid garrison to watch over the trade running through. The area was captured by Alexander, but what archaeology has shown is that the rapid expansion of Margiana dates to the time of Seleucus. The pottery here dates from his time, as does the pottery from Iconium and Samarkand. Some of these cities are named for Alexander (Samarkand recalls Alexander's name), but they are actually either foundations of the Seleucids or they really grow to prominence under the Seleucids.

Here at Margiana, with the erection of outer and inner walls, we have protected a much larger area. The garrison is transformed into an acropolis located right in the center of town. Then a much larger settlement is laid out in the area below this acropolis. A settlement capable of supporting a large population. An area where caravans can be brought in, as well. Protecting, therefore, the caravans that bring spices and silk and other precious commodities into the Seleucid realm.

The land is also being worked, as well. A series of canals have been excavated there, showing that the Seleucids paid a great deal of attention to exploiting the land so that they could feed that local population.

This was, essentially, a Greek occupation. It is Greek settlers, Greek soldiers and Greek veterans who populate this site. There is little sign of any intermarriage between these Greeks and Macedonians or the local population. There is very little sign of any kind of ethnic mixing. So we've seen in two regions so far two quite separate policies: In the east, cede the territory and establish the border. In the northeast, establish cities and trade posts at strategic points. Garrison them with veterans. Give land to the veterans so that you encourage a Greek population to move east. In fact, surveys back in mainland Greece have demonstrated that about this time, the population was declining. The reason for that is not that the Greeks are dying off or there is starvation. It's because a lot of Greeks are engaging in this Greek Diaspora. This movement away from the mainland, out to a land of new opportunity, to the provinces of these new Hellenistic kingdoms.

Why be a poor Greek farming five acres of rocky soil, when you could be a princeling with an estate of 500 acres in Afghanistan? It was a bargain that many people took.

A second region that we should look at, that also involved heavy colonization, was Syria, the far northeastern corner at the eastern edge of the Mediterranean Sea. From the Mediterranean, across the Fertile Crescent, so this one fertile stretch, linking the Mediterranean with the beginning of Central Asia, there stretched a network of Seleucid cities: Laodicea-by-the-Sea, Apamea (on the Orontes River), Seleucia Pieriea, Antioch on the Orontes, and Seleucia on the Tigris. So five major cities (five capitals, really) clustered in this area of Syria, which becomes the absolute heartland of the Seleucid kings.

It's very interesting, if you look at a map, and see the layout of this empire, and see where the Seleucids choose to stay. They are not interested in moving inland at all. They are not interested in moving to the geographic center of their empire. They don't spend most of their time in Babylon or in Susa. They're not like the Achaemenids, who live essentially in the middle of their empire. Why is this?

I think it's because the emphasis in Hellenistic culture, even amongst these Hellenistic kings, is dealing with the rest of the Hellenistic world around the Mediterranean. They are from Macedon. They never wish to lose sight of the Mediterranean. It's by the Mediterranean that you have contact with Egypt, with Asia Minor, and with Macedon and Greece. So there's a heavy concentration then, of Greek cities in Syria.

In addition, there were also Greek cities there in Asia Minor, which fell under Seleucid control during the course of the 3rd century. We're fortunate, because here, in the relations between the Seleucids and the Greek cities, we have a good deal of documentation, and it gives us a good idea of how the Seleucids were presenting themselves as kings. What I think we're going to find here—well, I'll read it first, and you can see what you make of it. This is King Antiochus writing to the city of Erythrae. Erythrae is a Greek city that had been founded hundreds of years earlier. It was located on what we would call the very western coast of Turkey. That is to say, it was in the region that the Greeks called Ionia. That coastal strip of Turkey, still considered part of the Greek world, because it's on the Aegean coast. King Antiochus says:

> To the people and the council of Erythrae, greetings.
>
> Tharsynon, Pythes and Bottas, your envoys, handed over the decree to us, in which you voted us honors and brought the crown with which you crowned us, and likewise the gold offered as a present.

So the ambassadors have arrived, and they've said, "Hello, king. We've voted you these honors. Here is this crown and here is this gold."

> They themselves spoke about the goodwill which you have constantly felt towards our house, and in general about the gratitude felt by the people towards old benefactors.

So the ambassadors have clearly come with a message of goodwill. They're treating the king, not as their supreme overlord—they're not performing obeisance or prostration before him—they're saying we have voted you honors because you're a benefactor of ours. This is going to be very potent language in the Hellenistic Age, so pay close attention. Now look at what happens when King Antiochus responds to these overtures from the ambassadors. He says:

> Since your ambassadors declared that, under Alexander and under Antigonus, your city was autonomous, and free from tribute, and our ancestors were constantly zealous on its behalf; and since we see that their decision was just, and we ourselves wish not to fall short in our benefactions, we shall preserve your autonomy, and we grant you exemption from tribute.

So the nub of the matter was that a Greek city was trying to have its taxes canceled. But the way in which this is processed, or dealt with, in the Hellenistic Age is that a Greek city will petition its king by offering it honors. They will declare him to be their savior, their *soter*. They will call him a benefactor (*euergetes*). Sometimes they will set up a festival in honor of his dead father and mother. A *soteria*, a festival in honor of the savior gods. Or they might even recognize the king himself as a living god (*epiphanes*). These are all the terms that turn up in this diplomatic language of the Hellenistic Age.

People have wondered about why you get these excruciatingly long documents, with this tedious honorific language. The reason is that this is the way that underlings in the Greek world speak to their superiors. They turn the relationship from subjugation into a contract. "We'll give you these honors if you'll give us these rights." What they get in return is something of concrete value to them. A tax exemption. That year, they didn't have to pay money into the Seleucid treasury.

So we see the kings here being actually quite concerned with their prestige and with their relationship with the Greeks. But when it came to other regions, they behaved very differently. Because, of course, in a place like Babylon, there were no Greek cities for them to indulge in this reciprocal relationship. So let's look what happens there.

Right between the Mediterranean and the upper satrapies that we've talked about is the heart of what used to be the Persian Empire. Here the Seleucids could not hope to impress an ancient culture with their Greek manners. They weren't going to convince anybody in Babylon that being Greek was superior, any more than the Ptolemies could impose their Hellenistic manners on the priests at Memphis. We've seen how the Ptolemies there behaved as if they were pharaohs. So what did the Seleucids do in Babylon?

Well, instead of dealing as Greek kings dealing with their cities, instead, they behave as Achaemenid kings. As if they were Persian kings. As if they were the legitimate successors of the kings who had ruled in Babylon. This emerges from a most astonishing letter that we have—this one is absolutely genuine—which is from King Antiochus. He is speaking of his position as King of Babylon. Remember, a moment ago we heard Antiochus writing to the people of Erythrae, saying, "We're concerned for your justice. Our ancestors were concerned for your justice. We wish to be a benefactor as well." Everything was placatory. The group's being mollified. Now listen to the rhetoric King Antiochus uses in Babylon.

> I am Antiochus, the Great King. The legitimate King. The King of the World. King of Babylon. King of All Countries. The caretaker of the temples Esagila and Ezida. The firstborn son of King Seleucus the Macedonian, King of Babylon."

So even in his opening rhetoric, he's adopting all of the pomp and all of the grandeur of an Achaemenid king, just like Darius calling himself the King of Kings, the anointed of Ahura Mazda. Not only that. Now, in what follows, listen to the way he presents himself. What a true king in Babylon would do.

> When I conceived the idea of reconstructing the temples Esagila and Ezida, I formed with my august hands when I was still in the country the first brick for Esagila and Ezida, with the finest oil and brought it with me for the laying of the foundation of Esagila and Ezida.

And he goes on. He actually says, "I made the first brick." You know, like a good Babylonian king, showing his piety towards these gods, who, as a Greek, he probably didn't even recognize. He goes on:

> O Nebo, lofty son, most wise among the gods, splendid and worthy of all praise, firstborn son of Marduk, child of Aru'a, the queen who fashioned all creation, do look friendly upon me, and may upon your lofty command which is never revoked, the overthrow of the country of my enemies, the fulfillment of all my wishes against my foes. Constant predominance. A kingdom ruled in justice and orderly government. Years of happiness. Enough progeny to be your permanent gift to the joint kingship of Antiochus and his son King Seleucus.

It's an extraordinary document. There is nothing Greek in it at all. There is no way in which you would even know that this man was a Greek, but for his name. So what we find here, is that there is a very sensible policy at work in the Seleucid realm. Here, in an area like Babylon, which in some ways is just like the Nile (where there are great temple estates along the river), we find that there is a policy of recognizing the rights of the temple estates. As focal points of power and as social organization, the temples remained central to the authority of the region, and were therefore protected by the Seleucids.

What we're finding here is that there are different styles of Seleucid kingship. Different treatments of different populations depending upon the part of the kingdom that we're talking about. Nevertheless, we need to modify the view that I've been advocating, somewhat. It would be wrong to think that this was simply a world of Greek cities imposed on native populations ruled by a distant and benevolent Hellenistic king.

In fact, in the Seleucid realm, a great deal of the very best territory and many of its people would have felt Seleucid rule quite directly. The administration reached into every corner of the kingdom. It borrowed the Persian system of satrapies that had existed even before the Greeks were here. We know from the documentation that there was a slew of minor officials, in fact, often carrying the same Greek names as the officials in Egypt: the *dioiketes* (the manager), the *logistes* (the accountant). So there is an imperial apparatus in the Seleucid realm, just as there is in the Ptolemaic realm.

Even more than that, we find in this Seleucid kingdom large swathes of land owned directly by the king. When I say that the land is owned by the king, I mean that every building on it, every village on that land, and the people living in the villages are owned by the king as well. So these peasants in the villages are called the *basilikoi laoi*, "the king's people." They are tied to the land. They pay a tithe or else a fixed tax every year. The revenues, the land, the villages, the buildings and the people, could all be bought and sold by the king.

This we know from what I think is truly one of the most astonishing documents from the Hellenistic Age. We know this from a contract between King Antiochus and the woman, Laodice, his queen, who he was divorcing. This is a divorce settlement. These are some of the terms in the divorce settlement of a Seleucid king.

> In the month of Decius, King Antiochus writes to Metrophanes, greetings. We have sold to Laodice, [the village of] Pannucome, the manor house, the land which is attached to the village [it is bounded by the territory of Seilia and Zizichus, and the ancient road which is above

Pannucome, but has been plowed up by the peasants nearby so that they might appropriate the place. The road which now exists for Pannucome was constructed later.] Together with any hamlets which are found in the region, the peasants who live there with all their household and belongings, with the revenues of the 59th year, at a price of 30 talents of silver. And also any of the peasants of this village who have moved to other places. On the condition that she pays no taxes to the royal treasury, and that she will have the right to attach the land to any city that she wishes.

In other words, the whole thing, lock, stock and barrel, was handed over to his divorced wife. And if you happened to be a peasant who for one reason or another had actually managed to move away, five miles down the road to the next village, but you'd been born here, then you also were sold in that transaction, as well. It's quite an astonishing document, illustrating the absolute power of the rule of the Seleucids.

The chief beneficiaries in this type of system, apart from the king himself, of course, were the king's friends. His so-called *philoi*. Throughout both the documents of Ptolemaic Egypt and in the documents from Seleucid Syria, as well, we find reference to these men, who, in a petition will call themselves the *philos*, the friend, of the king. This is a term which, as we know, had originated back in Macedon. We've already seen that the elite battalions of the Macedonian army were known as the Companion Cavalry or the Companion Infantry. But that idea, that sort of egalitarian ethos that, in a way, we're really comrades with the king, men in arms with him, had now been extended. In the Hellenistic world, the term *philos* really comes to mean a member of the imperial bureaucracy. If you're in the civil service, one of these Greeks or Macedonians (very rarely are local), but if you're one of these Greeks or Macedonians, the benefit from this exploitative system, you're known as the king's *philos*.

These men were the military commanders of garrisons. They were the provincial commanders and regional governors. They were the officers in the villages. Sometimes even down to the level of policemen or of scribes, who served as the administration for the entire empire. And though reinforced, of course, by soldiers and by military contingents, who were settled on the land holdings around the empire.

So you had garrisons strategically placed. There would be soldiers on active services. Then around them there would be a Greek settlement that would grow up, and most of the men in that settlement would be veterans, who could be called up once again, if the need arose.

So we've got a very clear occupation and exploitation of the territory going on. The only people who remained free of this very direct exploitation were the nomads in the mountains, or the nomads in the deserts. The Bedouins, who remained free of active interference. Here, the Seleucids had learned well from the Achaemenids, that you could keep them on side, as well. This is yet another way of dealing with the native population: through the practice of gift exchange. Desert chiefs would be confirmed as independent potentates. They would recognize the power of some desert chief, provided that that chief would then send troops to the great musters of the Seleucid army. That's why we read about camel corps serving with the Seleucid army, and why the cavalry from Armenia, which was famous, both served regularly in times of war with the Seleucid army.

So the Seleucid Empire presents an approach to the problem of kingship and rule in the Hellenistic world (because, remember, we've been talking about how people from the small Greek kingdom of Macedon adapt to the requirements of ruling this vast empire. The Seleucid approach represents a style of kingship that I would call polyvalent. That is to say, the Seleucid kings play different roles and they use different institutions depending upon which audience they're dealing with. There is no single coherent notion of Seleucid kingship. You can be a latter-day Alexander, as Antiochus III tried to be, or you can be a great Babylonian King, who builds temples with his bare hands, as Antiochus I did. It depends upon who you are dealing with.

The one innovation that I think the Seleucids do come up with is a system of shared kingship. This is an intelligent adaptation, whereby the senior man (the father, usually) will hold the western domains, and his son will be made a co-king and will be given the eastern realms of the empire, where he gets his training, if you will. The size of the empire required such an arrangement. It means that you've got someone from the dynastic family in both the west and the east at any given time. It's a system that worked so well that the Ottomans replicate it later on. Ottoman princes are almost always sent to the eastern side of their empire for their training before they rule at the sublime court in Istanbul.

So the Seleucid Empire can be thought of as a complex mixture. It was influenced by the prior history of Persian control in these regions. The Seleucids also practiced a sensible policy of non-interference where territorial control was out of the question in the far east or in the deserts or in the mountains. And they practiced religious toleration in the well-established and ancient areas of Babylon and Mesopotamia. As was the case, then, in all the realms of the Hellenistic world, the institutions of the Seleucid Empire were really designed, not so much to create harmony and to fuse races, but rather to establish good order, to make it easier for a vast geographic area to be ruled by what, in our terms, would be a miniscule bureaucracy, but a bureaucracy which, in the Hellenistic period, was exclusively Graeco-Macedonian.

Lecture Nine
Pergamum

Scope:

Our survey of the Hellenistic kingdoms continues with the Attalid dynasty of Pergamum, whose dominion rose from a simple garrison to embrace all of Asia Minor and whose cultural influence rivaled that of Alexandria.

Outline

I. The Attalid kingdom of Pergamum, in present-day Turkey, was born in the chaos of the wars of the Diadochi, Alexander's successors.

    A. One of the successors, Lysimachus, seized control of Thrace and territory between Macedon and Asia Minor.

        1. During the 290s and 280s B.C., while embroiled in various campaigns, Lysimachus entrusted the fortress of Pergamum to a eunuch, Philetaerus.

        2. The site was located high on a crag and was virtually impregnable, giving Lysimachus a powerful base for controlling the Asian side of the Hellespont.

        3. Lysimachus died at the Battle of Corupedium (281 B.C.), and much of his territory fell to the victor, Seleucus I.

    B. Philetaerus, however, remained firmly in control of Pergamum, its fortress, and the royal treasure of 9,000 talents.

    C. Upon his death in 263 B.C., Philetaerus left his power and money to his nephew, Eumenes I, who ruled until 241 B.C., having defeated Antiochus I and put an end to the Seleucid claim to Pergamum.

    D. From the reign of Philetaerus until the death of the last king of the dynasty, Attalus III, in 133 B.C., the Attalid dynasty ruled over much of Asia Minor.

II. The success of the dynasty is remarkable, considering that no kingdom existed here before the Attalids, and they had no claim to the control of Pergamum based on inheritance, territory, or ancestral right.

A. We should ask, then, how the Attalids legitimized their rule and how they organized their kingdom.

B. Attalid rule relied on generosity.

    1. Rulers showered their subjects with gifts. These gifts were made not just to individuals, but also to entire cities.

    2. They might include gifts of money to pay for mercenaries, horses for territorial defense, tax exemptions during time of hardship, and supplies of olive oil and wheat, given either during famine or to hold public feasts.

III. The Attalids did not confine their generosity to the cities of Asia Minor.

    A. Entire buildings, such as *stoas,* or theatres, were also given by the Attalids to sanctuaries at Pessinus, near the Black Sea Coast; on Delos, at Delphi; and in Athens. In return, these sanctuaries gave the dynasty respect in the eyes of the Greeks.

    B. At Delphi, a generous gift of 21,000 drachmas from Attalus II paid for the salaries of teachers, supported an annual festival called the Attaleia, and provided a surplus that the sanctuary was able to lend out at 6.6 percent interest. Every Greek who went to Delphi saw the generosity of Attalus.

    C. The Stoa of Attalos, rebuilt in the 1950s, is a remarkable example of the Attalids' concern for public opinion. Built in Athens, the *stoa* physically links Athens and Pergamum, the cultural centers of the Hellenistic world.

IV. In their dealings with the Greek cities of their domain, the Attalids maintained the fiction that the cities were independent and autonomous.

    A. This was true insofar as the cities continued to appoint minor officials in charge of waterworks, streets, sewers, and so forth, but it is clear that real power was in the hands of the ruler.

    B. Eumenes I, for example, wrote to the city of Pergamum to commend the performance of its generals, who had balanced their budget.

1. He notifies the city of his decision to award the generals honorific crowns and advises the city whether it might wish to honor them as well.

2. Only in the city's response (written to the man who lived in a palace above the city) do we discover that the generals were appointed by Eumenes. Nor were these generals real commanders of Pergamene armies, but city magistrates responsible for administering revenues.

3. Pergamum's autonomy, then, was a polite fiction that existed only in the language of diplomacy between king and subject.

V. The real power of the Attalids rested on the judicious use of military force, especially mercenaries, who both provided a standing army that was loyal to the monarch and served as the administrators of the kingdom.

   A. Rather than relying on a national army, which might then agitate for some voice in affairs, Eumenes I entered into an elaborate contract with Greek mercenaries.

   B. In the contract, Eumenes set out pay scales, agreed to a 10-month campaign year, made arrangements for the care of orphans, offered tax concessions, and agreed to back payments.

   C. In return, the mercenaries swore to serve Eumenes and his descendants to the death.

   D. The mercenaries also swore to guard any cities, fortresses, fleets, or money entrusted to them.

   E. The contract reveals an elaborate system not of civil bureaucracy, but of military commands. The focus of this system is not a state or kingdom, but a single man, Eumenes.

VI. The transformation of Attalid power from simple, autocratic rule to legitimate kingship was brought about in the reign of the third ruler of the dynasty, Attalus I (241–197 B.C.).

   A. Early in the reign of Attalus I, Asia Minor was invaded by the Gauls, a Celtic people whose periodic migrations west included an invasion of Greece and the sacking of Rome.

B. Attalus defeated two branches of these Gallic tribes, the Tolistoagian and Tectosagian Gauls, in the 230s, at the same time as he defeated his Seleucid rivals, Antiochus Hierax and Seleucus III.

C. On the victory dedications made by Attalus, he styles himself "king" for the first time. The monument dates to the 220s, and King Attalus would go on to rule for another 20 years.

D. For nearly a century, then, Pergamum was ruled by only three men from one dynasty. By the end of that time, these rulers could claim to be kings, based primarily on their defense of Pergamum from a foreign foe.

E. These victories were a lynchpin of their propaganda. Both at home and abroad, Attalus celebrated these victories in sculptures that treated the Gauls as noble and heroic opponents. Greek order had once again triumphed over barbarian chaos, and the Attalid king could claim to be the savior of Greek culture.

VII. By 133 B.C., even the power of Pergamum and its kings was unable to withstand the inexorable rise of Roman power.

    A. Greece and the Hellenistic kingdoms would alternate between alliances with and rebellions against Rome, but Pergamum remained Rome's most steadfast ally in the east.

        1. This alliance meant that when Rome confronted the power of the Seleucid king Antiochus III early in the 2nd century, Pergamum was well placed to benefit.

        2. Antiochus was defeated in 189 B.C. at the battle of Magnesia, and he lost most of his holdings in Asia Minor the following year in the Treaty of Apamea.

    B. Uninterested in acquiring more overseas provinces, Rome handed much of the land over to Eumenes II, under whom Pergamene territorial holdings were at their greatest.

    C. Pergamum remained allied to Rome under Attalus II (160–139 B.C.), but Attalus III died without a successor in 133 B.C. and bequeathed his entire kingdom to the Romans.

    D. In this way, Pergamum was at one stroke changed from a Hellenistic kingdom into the Roman province of Asia Minor.

E. The great altar of Pergamum illustrates how the city proclaimed itself both an embodiment of the Greek legacy and the way of the future. The rulers proclaimed that the city was Greek in spite of Pergamum's garrison heritage.

Suggested Reading:

E. V. Hansen, *The Attalids of Pergamon*.

Questions to Consider:

1. In what ways did Pergamum differ from the other major Hellenistic kingdoms?
2. Why was acceptance from the other Greeks so important to the Attalid kings?

Lecture Nine—Transcript
Pergamum

Hello and welcome to our ninth lecture in our series on Alexander and the Hellenistic world. So far we've had an opportunity after looking at Alexander's career and its aftermath, the wars of the *Diadochi*, the wars of the successors, to examine in closer detail two of the kingdoms that came out of the void of a generation of warfare following Alexander's death. We've had a chance to examine the Ptolemaic rule in Egypt, where we've seen a combination of playing Pharaoh to the Egyptians and being a Greek king in his separate Greek capital of Alexandria. Then we've looked also at the Seleucid realm, where the Seleucids were faced by very different problems, that is to say, a large empire with a scattered population. We've seen that in this realm the Seleucids presented themselves in very different ways, both as legitimate Babylonian kings and as Greek kings to their Greek audience, and sometimes just ceding territory where necessary. So we've seen different patterns of Hellenistic kingship as the different Hellenistic kingdoms develop.

I want to continue a survey of these Hellenistic kingdoms by looking today at one of the most interesting of the Hellenistic kingdoms, that of Pergamum, a city located in what we would now call northwestern Turkey. Pergamum was originally a simple garrison. It does not have an earlier history like that of Egypt. It does not have an earlier history like that of the Seleucid realm, which was essentially the same as the Achaemenid Empire that had come before. Rather, we have a simple dominion based on a single garrison, which will come, during the Hellenistic Period, to embrace all of Asia Minor (the entire region that we would now call western and central Turkey). Not only would it come to govern a great deal of territory, in the Hellenistic world, it would also exert a cultural influence throughout the Hellenistic period that would rival that of Alexandria.

So let's begin by looking at how the kingdom of Pergamum came into existence. The story is a very interesting one. The kingdom is sometimes called the Attalid Kingdom, because, as in the case of many of these Hellenistic kingdoms, it takes its name from the ruling dynasty, that of Attalus. The Attalid kingdom of Pergamum was born in the chaos of the wars of the *Diadochi*, the successors of Alexander. One of these successors, a general by the name of Lysimachus, had seized control of the region of Thrace, that is to say, the northern Aegean. He held the territory, in other words, that lay between Macedon to the west, and Asia Minor to the east. During the 290s and the 280s, while he was embroiled in various campaigns involving Macedon and Asia Minor, he was able to establish his power across the Hellespont, in the territory of Asia Minor by developing and building up a fortress located on a crag at Pergamum.

Here, he entrusted his garrison to a eunuch by the name of Philetaerus. The site of Pergamum was well chosen, because it was high and virtually impregnable. If you go there today and visit the theater, for example, built on the side of the hill, you'll almost get a nosebleed trying to walk from the bottom at the stage to the top of the seats, because it is built on a very steep slope. Virtually impregnable. It gave Lysimachus a very powerful base there for controlling the Asian side of the Hellespont. That's what it was there for.

But Lysimachus died in battle, at the Battle of Corupedium in 281 B.C. Much of his territory fell to the victor in that battle, Seleucus, the victorious founder of the Seleucid dynasty, the king of the Hellenistic kingdom based in Syria. But despite the fact that Lysimachus had fallen in battle, and most of his territory went to Seleucus, Philetaerus remained in control of Pergamum, locked up in his mountain fortress, where he just happened to have a treasure of 9,000 talents of silver. Literally, a king's ransom. So Philetaerus held out against Seleucus, and Seleucus was never able to capture the city. So that, in these events, we have the beginning of what will become a kingdom based in Asia Minor.

When he died in 263, Philetaerus of course had been a eunuch and therefore had no children to succeed him. He left his power and his money to his nephew Eumenes I. Eumenes managed to rule in Pergamum for the next twenty years, having defeated in battle Antiochus I, the Seleucid king. So the Seleucid claim to Pergamum lapsed by the middle of the 3rd century. Before the Attalids declared themselves kings, they had actually ruled independently for at least a generation.

From the reign of Philetaerus, back in the 260s, down till the death of the last king of this dynasty, Attalus III in 133 B.C., the Attalid dynasty managed to rule over much of Asia Minor. Their success is particularly remarkable if one considers the fact that there was no kingdom here before them. They had no claim to the control of

Pergamum based on inheritance. It hadn't been left to them by an earlier king. There was no territorial integrity here. It didn't correspond to a single satrapy in the Persian Empire, which they could claim to have conquered. It did not come to them by ancestral right. They had not been among Alexander's successors. So they were, in terms of the Hellenistic kingdoms, if you like, upstarts.

I think we should ask, then: How did these Attalids, who had no legitimacy behind them, who had not conquered territory or inherited it, how did they legitimize their rule? How did they convince the people of Asia Minor to accept them as their kings? And, how did they organize that kingdom? These are questions that deserve to be looked at.

Attalid rule was based on generosity. The rulers showered their subjects with gifts. These gifts were made, not just to individuals, but to entire cities. We have dozens of documents attesting to this. Gifts given to include pay for mercenaries, if a city had been having trouble with marauders and needed a mercenary force to help it, they could appeal to the Attalid king and they would often receive a subvention to pay for this. They might be given horses for territorial defense. They were often given tax exemptions during times of hardship. If there were a famine, they might be given direct supplies of oil or of wheat. Even during times of feasting, they might appeal to the king and be given some kind of subvention to hold public festivals.

We have one document that I'll read you in relation to Attalid generosity. This dates from the reign of King Eumenes II, from 181 B.C. You'll notice as I read through this that we're not talking here about the dealings of a Greek king and a Greek city. This is just a little local village. But they have petitioned the king. King Eumenes writes to Artemidorus:

> I have read the comments you appended to the petition submitted by the settlers in the village of Cardaces [probably in southwestern Turkey]. Since after investigating you find that their private affairs are in a weak condition, as their trees are not yielding much fruit and their land is of a poor quality, give instructions that they may keep the piece of land that they bought from Ptolemy.

It turns out that they hadn't paid off the purchase price entirely, and he remits the remaining amount of money and pays it himself. Then he goes on to say that he's going to remit their tax burden because they apparently missed their last two years of taxes. (I wish the IRS were as generous as this.) So he grants them a tax exemption for the next couple of years as well, and if anyone who has fled from the area agrees to return, he also gives them a tax exemption for a couple of years.

Then he says, "See to it that they provide for repairing the fort that they previously held." Notice again this typical Hellenistic practice of getting the locals to erect a garrison. But here they've let it lapse into disrepair. "I myself will pay for skilled craftsmen who will go and repair the fort."

So they were very generous throughout their kingdom. The Attalids did not confine their generosity just to the cities and the villages in Asia Minor. Entire buildings, such as *stoas*, or theaters, were also given by the Attalids to sanctuaries such as Pessinus (up on the Black Sea coast), Delos, which was not a part of their realm (it was not a territory that they actually controlled), and, of course, Delphi and Athens. So this dynasty appears to have desired to celebrate its own power and authority by endowing gifts to celebrated Greek cities and sanctuaries back in the islands and in the homeland.

In return, these sanctuaries, by erecting monuments with the names of these kings on them, were giving the dynasty the respect that it craved in the eyes of the Greeks and of the other Hellenistic kingdoms. You can still go to Athens and to Delos and see buildings that will have the name of Attalus written in huge letters across the top. At Delphi, for example, we have a long inscription that records a generous gift when the Attalid king Attalus II gave the city of Delphi and the sanctuary of Apollo 21,000 drachmas. This money was to be invested in two funds. One fund was to be an investment of 18,000 drachmas. The interest that that fund gave every year was to be used to pay for public teachers. Public education at Delphi, in the middle of Greece, being paid for by a king in Asia Minor. The other 3,000 drachmas was to be invested, and the interest that it accrued every year was to be used for the holding of an annual festival. This festival was to celebrate the Attalid dynasty, so it was called the *Attaleia*, the festival in honor of the Attalids.

So every Greek who went to Delphi (and every Greek would want to go to Delphi sometime in his life, since it was the most important oracle in the Greek world) would see there the evidence of Attalid generosity, and might even be there at the time when a festival was being held where everyone would get to participate in eating the great barbecue that took place (the great feast) that was held after a sacrifice.

If any money were left over, Attalus made provision for this money to be lent out by the priests at Delphi, who could become money lenders, accruing about 6.6% interest per year. So this was a generous endowment by the Attalid king, but quite typical.

If you want to see a really graphic example of Attalid benefaction and generosity, go to Athens. Because in Athens today, you will see fully re-erected, a *stoa* that was given to the Athenians in the 2nd century. This building was rebuilt in the 1950s by the American School of Classical Studies. If you have ever seen any pictures of the *agora* of ancient Athens, and if you've ever wondered how is it that there is one building which seems to be is pristine and brand new, while everything else is broken down, the reason is that it is brand new. It was built only 40 years ago. Built in Athens, this *stoa* physically links Athens and Pergamum, the cultural centers of the Hellenistic world. So when Hellenistic kings came to Athens, they were, of course, greeted as if they were heroes, benefactors, coming back, in a way, to a city that was as much theirs as was Pergamum.

We have, in fact, a long description in Polybius, the historian, of the visit by King Attalus I to Athens in the year 200 B.C. We have Attalus arriving, and then we get a description of him actually walking downtown. This is how the description runs.

> When he entered the Dipylon Gate [which is located on the northwestern side of the city of Athens and is the gate leading into the *agora,* the major meeting place, the marketplace of Athens], they placed the priestesses and priests on each side of the street. They then opened all the temples, placed victims on all the altars and asked him to offer sacrifice.

So there's a day of celebration, with sacrifices going on throughout the city. Finally, they voted him honors greater than they had readily bestowed on any other of their previous benefactors. So a king from

Pergamum now honored as the greatest benefactor of Athenian history. This is really quite remarkable; something that's never done previously in Athenian history. In addition to other distinctions, they called a tribe after Attalus and enrolled him among the eponymous tribal heroes.

The Athenian city body was divided into ten tribes. But one of them will now be named for Attalus. It's as if, retroactively, he were being made one of the founding heroes of the city of Athens.

This is a remarkable insight into the relationship between the Attalid dynasty and the rest of the Greek world. They wished to portray themselves as, in a way, the embodiment of Athenian culture. The very acropolis at Pergamum was really modeled to look like the acropolis of Athens. It is as if old Athens is looking at new Athens. The two talking to each other. The links between the two made more concrete by the Attalids then sending masons and money to Athens to build buildings there, to make the cities even more similar to each other.

In their dealing with the Greek cities within their domain, the Attalids maintained the fiction that their cities were independent and autonomous, rather than cities within the realm of the Attalids. This was true to a certain degree. Local cities did continue, for example, to appoint their local magistrates and minor officials. We have long documents from these cities talking about officials who are in charge of the water works and the sewers and the street cleaning and so forth. So at the municipal level, life continued much as it had gone on before.

But it's quite clear that the real power in the Attalid realm lay in the hands of the ruler. This is dramatically illustrated in the documents that we have from the city of Pergamum itself. There's one famous inscription from Pergamum (I won't read you the whole thing, now, but I'll summarize it) where Eumenes writes to the city. He says that there are some generals who for the last year have been serving in office and have done a very fine job. They've managed to balance the budget. They've managed to pay off some debts and they did all of the sacred obligations quite well and piously. So what the king (Eumenes) does, is to say, "I've decided to award some honorific crowns to these generals." And he says, "Perhaps you might consider doing the same thing, as well." So it's phrased in terms of advice from a king to a city within his realm.

It's not until we read the response (that's on the same inscription) from the city, and the response is that "we will offer honors to these generals," that we find out that the generals being honored had been appointed by Eumenes in the first place. The whole thing was a farce. The whole thing was a charade. They weren't real commanders of the Pergamene army at all. They were local magistrates, who were responsible for running the city's revenues. They were the accountants of the city. They had been appointed by the king. And because they had done a good job, the king had rewarded them, and then he recommended that the city reward them, as well. But the entire thing is framed as if, as an outside benefactor, he's merely advising the city to honor these men for a job well done.

In other words, Pergamum's autonomy was a polite fiction that existed only in the diplomacy between king and subject. What makes this even more remarkable is to consider that what lay at the top of the acropolis at Pergamum, this city built on many tiers—what lay at the top were the palaces of the king himself. So this isn't a letter from some outside advisor to a distant city. It's a letter that has been sent down from the top of the hill to the bottom of the hill, saying, "They did a good job. Now say 'thank you' to them."

The real power of the Attalids rested on the judicious use of military force. I've talked about their generosity. That's the velvet glove. But now here's the iron fist. The judicious use of military force. As in many of the Hellenistic kingdoms, they rely particularly on mercenaries, rather than on local armies. Why? Because there was always a danger that a standing army, made up of local populations, would develop nationalistic tendencies, asserting its own authority, resisting the outside rule of the Graeco-Macedonian dynasty.

The Ptolemies in Egypt are at no time weaker than when, at the Battle of Raffia, they rely upon Egyptian troops to help them. This leads to a series of revolts in the years thereafter. So these Graeco-Macedonian monarchs are not stupid. They recognize that, generally speaking, you must not put arms into the hands of the local population. You must rely on mercenaries.

These mercenaries will be loyal to the monarch, and they will also serve as the administrators of the kingdom. So rather than rely on a national army, which may agitate, Eumenes enters into an elaborate contract with his mercenaries. We have the details of this particular contract, as well, which gives us an astonishing eyewitness account of how a Hellenistic king deals with his mercenary forces. In this contract that we have, Eumenes sets out the exact pay scale so that every man will know if he signs up how much he's going to get. There is an agreement that they will only have to campaign for ten months out of the year. So they're negotiating for their two months vacation, as well. He even makes arrangements for the care of orphans.

We're not talking here about a few hundred individual soldiers who had come from Greece. We're talking about men who have lived here for a long time and who have wives and have children. Entire families. Almost private armies, if you will. So we get the care of the orphans being taken care of. There are often tax concessions, so they'll be tax exempt while they are working for him. There is also an agreement about back pay, because apparently Eumenes had slipped in the payment of his mercenaries over the last few months.

In return for this, the mercenaries are expected to swear an oath of loyalty to Eumenes, and are prepared to fight to the death. The mercenaries also swear to guard any of the cities or the fortresses or any of the money that's been entrusted to them. The contract reveals an elaborate system, not so much of civil bureaucracy, but rather of military commands. The focus here is not on the state. It is not on the kingdom, or even the city of Pergamum. It is on the man, King Eumenes, so that his authority is recognized by this army, and he it is to whom they swear their loyalty. What we find then, is that in the early phase of Attalid kingship, there is a strong emphasis on the personal authority of the king. We could call this a kind of simple autocratic rule, which is obviously necessary since there was no prior legitimacy to account for their controlling this kingdom.

But in the latter part of the 3rd century and the early part of the 2nd century, the Attalids were able to transform their control of this kingdom into something new. Into a kind of legitimate kingship. It comes about during the reign of Attalus I, the Attalid king who visited Athens, and whose visit I read a moment ago. The precise circumstances involving this shift in Attalid kingship are that, early in his reign, in the 240s, King Attalus witnessed the invasion of Asia Minor by the Gauls, a Celtic people. Some of them would stay in Asia Minor, establishing a kingdom called Galatia. We know from the letters of Paul that some of his letters are written to the Galatians. There is also a Galicia in Spain, where some of the Gauls end up.

And of course they end up in the area we now call France. They were involved in periodic migrations during the course of the 5th, 4th, and 3rd century, which had led them to invade parts of Greece. At one stage they sacked Delphi. They even got to Rome before moving even further west and ending up in France and Spain. Two branches of these invasions by these Gallic tribes, one branch led by the Tolistoagian Celts and another led by the Tectosagian Celts or Gauls, arrived in Asia Minor in the 230s. In these battles, Attalus was completely victorious. It is around the same time he also defeated his Seleucid rivals. Antiochus Hierax (Antiochus the Hawk, as he was known) and Seleucus III.

As a result of these victories, Attalus was able to erect victory monuments, celebrating his glorious military successes. The monuments that he erected date to the 220s B.C. Here, King Attalus now styles himself "King," while downplaying the titles and authority of his opponents Antiochus and Seleucus. So it has taken quite some time. The Attalids have been in control of Pergamum since about the 280s. But now, after two generations of control, they are in a position to assert legitimate authority, proclaiming themselves "King." Why? Because they have saved Pergamum from the Gauls.

For nearly a century, Pergamum was ruled by only three men from one dynasty. By the end of that time, these rulers could claim to be "kings," based on the fact that they had defended Pergamum from a foreign foe. This victory over the Gauls, over the Celts, became a kind of lynchpin in the propaganda of the Attalid dynasty. It was in celebrating these victories that they presented themselves as the great defenders of Greek civilization.

We've already seen how Attalus wanted to make Pergamum the Asian equivalent of Athens, to, in effect, replicate the city over in Asia Minor. Now, thanks to his victory over the Gauls, he is able to maintain that he is the representative of Greek order against the threat of a foreign invasion, in much the same way as earlier, the Athenians had been able to maintain that their victory over the Persians had also been a victory of order over foreign invasion.

So barbarian chaos has been put to rout and an Attalid king can proclaim himself the savior of Greek culture. There is one irony to all of this, and that is that the statues which were made to celebrate these victories seem to glorify the defeated as much as the victors.

Some of you may have seen examples of these sculptures of the dying Gaul. There is one that shows the Gaul spread-eagled on the ground as he's about to expire from his wounds. Another where a Gallic chieftan has his wife crooked in his arm. She's already died as a result of the defeat, so he's now in the process of stabbing himself. In a way, the Attalids understood that you could make your victory even more poignant if you made your enemy into a noble enemy. An enemy, a victory over whom made you even more noble. By 133 B.C., even the power of Pergamum and its kings was unable to withstand the inexorable advance of Roman power. That we're going to be dealing with in a lecture later on in this series.

Greece and the Hellenistic kingdoms would alternate in the 2nd century between alliances with and rebellions against Rome. But throughout this period, which will be the swan song of Hellenism politically, the period when the Hellenistic states will eventually come under Roman control, Pergamum remained the most steadfast of Rome's allies in the East. This meant that when Rome confronted the power of the Seleucid king Antiochus III, early in the 3rd century, for example, Pergamum was well-placed to benefit from the superpower match-up between the Seleucid king from Syria and the power of Rome from the West. Antiochus was defeated, in 189 B.C. at the Battle of Magnesia. In that battle, he lost virtually all of his holdings in Asia Minor. He was forced to sign a peace treaty the following year with the Romans, the so-called treaty of Apamea. This treaty made him cede all of his territory north of the Taurus Mountains. Who received it? The Attalids. Their reward for being steadfast Roman allies was that they were given territories that embraced all of Asia Minor. Then, the remarkable ending of this story of their independent kingdom is that in 133 B.C., when Attalus III died without a successor, he bequeathed his entire kingdom to the Romans, rather than see it be torn apart by civil dissension. So that, dramatically, at one stroke, the Hellenistic Kingdom of Pergamum became the Roman province of Asia Minor.

There is one last aspect of Pergamum which I want to mention, although it's somewhat discrete from the elements we've been talking about earlier. That is a particular monument, which is still to be seen today, now in Berlin. That is to say, the great altar of Pergamum. People often wonder where does it fit in with this larger narrative of Pergamene history. The answer is that the monument is a graphic illustration of the way that, under the Attalids, Pergamum was proclaiming itself both a living embodiment of the Greek past, and a suggestion of the Greek future.

This great altar has on it a frieze running around all sides. This is the so-called Telephos frieze. The story that's told here in sculpture is that of the founding hero of Pergamum. The character derived from Greek myth who is supposed to have been brought to Pergamum and to have established the city. So by putting this on their frieze, what the Pergamenes are doing, and what the Attalids in particular are doing, is attempting to say, "We may have been founded by Philetaerus, and we may be a garrison from the Seleucid Empire that's become independent. But really, what we are is a good Greek city, with the same kind of foundation story as any other Greek city, whether it be Sparta or Corinth or Athens. So in a way, there was an attempt here to make them like the rest of the Greek world and the older Greek world by connecting with Greek mythology.

But what we'll find on the rest of this altar is a whole new approach to the representation of myth and of history, the like of which has never been seen before. Because in this altar, you actually walk up steps from the ground level to the top, to take part in any sacrifices going on. As you walk up the steps, on either side of you, you will find, cut in deep relief, sculptural figures showing the victory of the gods over various giants and beasts and monsters. These are cut in deep relief, so that they're almost completely free-standing sculptures. They are as large as the people walking up the steps.

So that, in Pergamum, you actually enter into history. It doesn't merely advertise history for you to look at from a distance, as though you were looking at the Parthenon in Athens. Now there is a whole new approach to the representation of identity and to inviting people into that history. As you walk into the monument and actually witness the battles—the great battles between chaos and order that characterize Greek history, going on right around you.

This is done vividly, to mark the fact that, in Pergamum, you are entering the place where once again, but most recently for the Hellenistic world, order has been established over chaos. That battle, which has been going on psychologically at the heart of Greek culture forever, is now being appropriated by Pergamum, to make itself both the embodiment of Greek culture and the latest expression of that Greek culture in a new and modified Hellenistic form.

Lecture Ten
Bactria, the Edge of the Hellenistic World

Scope:

Hellenism, the transplanted culture of the Greeks, flourished primarily around the eastern Mediterranean seaboard. Even so, the Greeks traveled further than the coast and left their imprint on areas far from the Mediterranean. In this lecture, we look at one region where Hellenism established itself far from its Mediterranean roots: Ai Khanum, in Afghanistan.

Outline

I. When Alexander turned back from the Indus River toward Babylon, he did not withdraw all his troops from the eastern portions of the newly conquered empire.

    A. In Bactria and Sogdiana, which correspond today to the high regions of northern Iran, Afghanistan, and the other republics of central Asia, Alexander left behind garrisons of Macedonian soldiers and Greek settlers, totaling around 23,000 men.

    B. Already by 325, some of these regions had gone into revolt; a further military occupation took place in 323 B.C., when Macedonian veterans were sent to settle the area once again.

    C. After Alexander's death, the region was assigned to a Cypriot Greek named Stasanor. That it was a Greek and not a Macedonian who received these territories may suggest that the region was not highly prized by Alexander's successors.

    D. Nevertheless, the first Seleucid kings, Seleucus I and his son Antiochus I, were unwilling to cede territory they considered part of their domain, and they campaigned vigorously to recapture control of the so-called Upper Satrapies.

II. Their policy was to pour settlers and troops into the region.

    A. This vigorous colonization can still be seen in the names of various famous cities of central Asia, such as Samarkhand and Kandahar, both originally Seleucid cities named Alexandria.

B. By 250 B.C., the region was under the control of a Greek satrap, or governor, named Diodotus, who profited from the vast distance between Bactria and the Mediterranean to establish an independent kingdom.

C. Over the next 300 years, 40 different kings from Greek dynasties would rule over the Indo-Greek kingdoms of Bactria and Gandhara.

III. Evidence concerning these Indo-Greek kingdoms is limited in comparison with the rich documentation of Ptolemaic Egypt or the archaeological record of Pergamum.

A. For a long time, scholars relied primarily on numismatic evidence.

   1. The coins of such kings as Euthydemus and Antimachus tell us how these kings wished to be understood.

   2. The message is simple: they were the successors of Alexander. Their coins show no hint of any local influence.

B. A second body of evidence has been furnished in the last generation by French excavations at the site of Ai Khanum on the banks of the Amu Darya River in northwestern Afghanistan.

   1. Ai Khanum sits on a fertile plain situated on a caravan crossroads. The buildings uncovered there include a palatial complex with peristyle courtyard; a cult shrine, or *heroon*; and a hypostyle hall adorned with lush Corinthian-column capitals.

   2. On the blocks of the *heroon* were inscribed philosophical maxims, such as the Delphic oracle's injunction "Know thyself"—3,000 miles from Delphi!

   3. Papyri have also been recovered showing that the transplanted Greek population enjoyed the same Greek philosophy and literature as was being read and discussed thousands of miles away.

   4. Just as at Alexandria or Athens, the Greeks here could exercise in a Greek-style *palaestra* at the gymnasium.

   5. Greek fountains with dolphin-head spouts and country villas adorned with mosaics outside the town center point to a transplanted Greek culture.

IV. Around 200 B.C., the Bactrian kingdom expanded east and annexed territory on the western side of the Indus Valley. Increasingly cut off from the west, the Indo-Greek kingdoms came to display a genuine fusion of Eastern and Western elements.

    A. A statue of the Greek character Marsyas found at Ai Khanum was dedicated to the god Oxus by a certain Atrosokes.

        1. Oxus was the local river god, and Atrosokes's name suggests his Iranian background; his name means "he who shines with sacred fire." He has been identified as a priest of the old Persian fire cult.

        2. In this dedication, we find a fusion of Greek, Iranian, and local elements, unlike anything found in the Mediterranean basin.

    B. A pillar dedicated to Garuda and Vishnu has been found in the Punjab district of India. Inscribed in Prakrit, an Indian language, the pillar copies Achaemenid Persian models, but was dedicated by a Greek ambassador named Heliodorus on the occasion of his visit to the court of the Indian king, Bhagabhadra. This syncretism, however, isn't typical of the Hellenistic world.

V. The Bactrian kingdoms were assaulted by invading tribes, known as the Saca, from the middle of the 2nd century, and the last Greek king, Heliokles, was replaced by the Saca chief Azes around 50 B.C.

    A. In trying to evaluate the significance of the Greek control of this region, historians have tended to look for evidence of Greek influence on local cultural traditions. The line of transmission, however, may have been from the East to the West.

    B. One of the Greek Bactrian kings who invaded northwestern India, named Menander, was well remembered in Indian tradition, not as a great conqueror but as a Greek who converted to Buddhism. He is still known in Buddhist writings as Milinda.

    C. Perhaps the most dramatic evidence for the relationship between the two great cultural traditions of Greece and India is to be found in the career of Asoka the Great, king of the Mauryan empire of northwestern India from c. 268–232 B.C.

1. Seleucid kings had had dealings with the Mauryans from as early as 305, when Seleucus I gave up claims to the eastern satrapies in return for 500 war elephants from Chandragupta, grandfather of Asoka.

2. Asoka had united virtually the entire Indian subcontinent.

3. A convert to Buddhism, he proselytized vigorously. Buddhist edicts were inscribed and erected throughout his empire.

4. He sent embassies to Hellenistic monarchs, such as Antiochus II, Ptolemy II, Antigonus Gonatas of Macedon, and Alexander of Epirus, introducing them to the tenets of his religion and trying to win their conversion.

5. At Kandahar, which lay outside his kingdom, he set up bilingual inscriptions using both Aramaic, the language of the Persian empire, and Greek to appeal to the Greek colonists and lead them toward Buddhism.

VI. The eventual disappearance of the Greeks of Bactria as a separate state and culture can probably be attributed to a complex set of factors.

A. First was the isolation of the Greeks from the cultural heartland of Hellenism, the Mediterranean.

B. Second was the pressure of outside populations, such as the nomads of central Asia, ever ready to plunder the riches of the Silk Route.

C. Finally, there was the presence on the very edges of this Hellenistic outpost of a complex and powerful empire, the Mauryan, itself gripped by the struggle between Vedic and Buddhist culture.

D. Against such a tumultuous background, the Greeks of Bactria gave way, eventually to be swallowed up by the world around them.

E. What if the Greek Bactrians had survived longer? As it is, the gulf between East and West eventually led India to be considered an exotic locale. The Greeks were in the world of the East but not of it.

Suggested Reading:

P. Bernard, "Ai Khanum on the Oxus," *Proceedings of the British Academy* 53, 71–95.

A. K. Narain, *The Indo-Greeks*.

Questions to Consider:

1. Can the culture of Greek Bactria be properly termed a fusion?

2. What other cultures, if any, have colonized foreign territory by importing a dominant culture, as the Greeks did in Ai Khanum?

Lecture Ten—Transcript
Bactria, the Edge of the Hellenistic World

Hello, and welcome back to our series of lectures on the Hellenistic Age. So far in our survey of the Hellenistic kingdoms, we've had an opportunity to look at kingdoms which are all primarily located around the Mediterranean. We've looked at Ptolemaic Egypt and we've seen that the Ptolemies tended to keep close to the Mediterranean at Alexandria, rather than having their capital in Memphis or anywhere down on the Nile. We've also looked at the Seleucid kingdom, and we saw that despite the fact that their kingdom ranged over a vast geographic area, they preferred to concentrate their cities and their imperial rule in Syria, right on the edge of the Mediterranean. Then the third of the kingdoms that we looked at was that of the Attalids, who reigned in Pergamum, and once again we found that, though their domain was in Asia Minor, they were still close to the Mediterranean. In fact, the Mediterranean forms the border on the west and the southern side of their kingdom.

So there is this tendency of the Hellenistic kingdoms to stay as close as possible to the Mediterranean, as if they want to stay in close physical contact with Greece itself. Certainly we saw, in the case of the Attalids, that there was a strong emphasis on connecting their culture with that of mainland Greece, celebrating the glories of Classical Greek culture, and trying to recreate those, whether it be on their acropolis, or even in their great altar, where they attempted to show their connection to old Greece.

This is quite typical of the Hellenistic world, where, somehow, Greek culture and the older Greek world remain the central focus of the attention of the Hellenistic world. And yet, there is one area that breaks the pattern. It's because it's so interesting and so anomalous, really, that we need to look at it. It is Bactria. The region which is located far away—5,000 kilometers or 3,000 miles away from the Mediterranean. In the area that we would now call Afghanistan and Pakistan and Turkmenistan. This area far to the east of anywhere most of the Greeks had ever gone. An exotic area. An area where, strangely, for about 300 years, there existed a transplanted culture of the Greeks, flourishing far away from the eastern seaboard. We'll be particularly looking at Ai Khanum, the farthest outpost, if you will, of Greek culture in the Far East.

When Alexander returned from the Indus River to Babylon, he didn't bring with him all of the troops that he'd had on his campaign. He left some behind in the provinces of the newly conquered empire to act as settlers and veterans, who would be the lynchpin of holding these eastern satrapies for the Greeks. In Bactria and in Sogdiana, which correspond today to the high northern regions of Iran and Afghanistan and the other republics of Central Asia, Alexander left behind Macedonian garrisons and Greek settlers. It appears as if, as early as 325, there were already about 23,000 men in the area. But they were not happy to be left behind, as they saw Alexander returning to the Greek world, back towards the beloved Mediterranean. Already, before Alexander was dead, in 325, there were revolts in these Upper Satrapies, as they were called.

So a further military occupation took place in 323 B.C., when Macedonian veterans were once again sent out to settle the area, and to increase the presence of Greeks, so they would not feel so isolated and so cut off. Nevertheless, the area remained at the very outskirts of the world known to the Greeks. I think we even get some suggestion of this when we look at the breakup of Alexander's empire. We've already looked in detail about how Babylon went to Seleucus and Egypt went to Ptolemy, and Antigonus received Asia Minor. Well, the area of Bactria was given to a Greek named Stasanor, who wasn't even Macedonian. He was a Greek from Cyprus. The inner circle of Alexander's officers had received the choice bits. The further one went to the east, the slimmer the pickings, from the point of view of the Greek officers. So Stasanor was a relatively low-grade officer.

Nevertheless, the first Seleucid king, Seleucus I, reigning in Babylon, and his son Antiochus, were unwilling to cede this territory. We don't know what finally happened to Stasanor, but we do know that Seleucus and Antiochus asserted their control of the region. They campaigned vigorously in the region to regain control of what they called the Upper Satrapies. As we saw last time, they had ceded the very eastern border of their empire, but their policy in the Upper Satrapies was to pour in settlers and troops to colonize the region. This was probably the most vigorous colonization ever witnessed in the Hellenistic world. The names of the various cities in Central Asia today, still evoke this Hellenistic layer of history: Samakand, Kandahar or Gandhara, originally Seleucid cities named after Alexander.

By 250 B.C. the region was under the control of a Greek satrap, that is to say, a provincial governor, using the title borrowed from the old Persian Empire, and ruling, often, almost independently, because he was so far away from the central authority of the Seleucid realm. His name was Diodotus. He profited from this vast distance between Bactria and the Mediterranean to declare himself an independent king. Over the course of the next 300 years, forty different kings from various Greek dynasties would rule over these Indo-Greek kingdoms of Bactria and Gandhara.

Evidence concerning the Indo-Greek kingdoms is, unfortunately, much more limited than the rich documentation that we've had so far, from Ptolemaic Egypt and from Seleucid Syria. We don't have dozens of Greek inscriptions, for example, petitions on papyri, letters to the king, responses from the imperial bureaucracy. We don't have this for the far east. So it's very difficult to reconstruct with absolute detail the history of this area. There are gaps in our knowledge, when, for even decades, we don't know the names of the kings ruling.

For a long time, the principal way that scholars reconstructed the history of the Upper Satrapies was through numismatic evidence. Here, the coins are very interesting. We have gold and silver coinage from the Upper Satrapies, just as we have in the Mediterranean world. The coins of these kings, bearing the names of men such as Euthydemus and Antimachus, both good, straight, solid Greek names—these coins show us how the kings advertised their kingship (how they wished to be seen). The message here was very simple: they wished to be seen as the Macedonian successors of Alexander.

In the coinage, there is absolutely no hint of local influence whatsoever. Think for a moment about the importance of coinage. The salaries, for example, of soldiers in the garrisons, and the money used for major transactions, is money that is being coined by the king, so it is a good propaganda tool for sending out a message to each person in that area as to what the king's authority is.

These kings are not Indo-Greek or Graeco-Indian, as we sometimes call them. In their eyes, they are Graeco-Macedonian. The fact that they are 5,000 kilometers away from Macedon is merely an accident of geography, as far as their self-representation is concerned.

But, more recently, and this is the work of the last generation, we now have some significant archaeological information coming from excavations conducted by the French at Ai Khanum. This material really has exploded completely our range of knowledge of what was going on in the Graeco-Bactrian kingdoms. Let's take a little look at this.

The excavations here were conducted during the 1970s, and have been well-published in the course of the 1980s and the 1990s. These are excavations conducted by a French team at a site known as Ai Khanum. We don't actually even know its Greek name, though presumably it had some sort of name like Alexandropolis or Seleucopolis or Euthydenopolis, but we don't know what it is, so we still call it Ai Khanum. It was located on the left bank of what the ancients called the Oxus River, known more recently as the Amu Darya, at the very northwestern edge of Afghanistan.

Here, we've uncovered traces of buildings, including a palace and shrines and a *heroon*, which illustrate the Greek presence here. Now, first of all, the Greeks back in Greece had not built many palaces, because kingship had died out in Greece hundreds of years earlier. So the pattern for the palace here is really borrowed from the Persians. It's a Persian style palace, built on a vast scale. At the front of the palace there is a peristyle hall, that is to say, four halls running around in a large square enclosing a courtyard. On each of these four sides, the hall is supported by 118 columns. So it's built on a massive scale. This has led the excavators to suggest, and I think they're probably right (it's certainly plausible), that this is a royal palace. We'd love to know the name of the king who built it, but I'll bet it was a Greek name.

Why here? What about this location? The location here is blessed. It sits along the trade routes running from east to west as part of the Silk Route. It is an area of high desert and mountains. But in the middle of this high desert and mountains, there is one oasis. One fertile plain, of ten by thirty-five kilometers, so about seven-and-a-half by about twenty-five miles. This is exactly where the city is located. So it's one fertile oasis that the caravans would come to as they were bringing goods across from the East.

The area had earlier been occupied, and we know that its fertility had been enhanced by a series of irrigation ditches. The Greeks in the

Hellenistic period increased this and made the land even more fertile. Obviously the Greek settlers here relied on the produce of this land.

They also defended themselves by building up a rampart around the city. Now, Greeks, as I'm sure you're aware, would normally build for preference stone walls for the walls of their city. They would have done that here had they had the opportunity, but in fact there is very little stone in the area, so they relied on mud brick. But the size of these mud brick walls gives you some idea of the wealth of the city. The mud brick walls were probably ten meters high, in the estimate of the excavators. That's about thirty feet. They would have been six to eight meters thick. So up to 24 feet in thickness. This was a city that clearly was wealthy, because it was trying to protect itself from the various nomads and invaders that pour through Central Asia at various times.

Within this wealthy city, in the middle of its oasis, up in the high plains of the desert, the Greeks established not only this royal palace, but a series of other buildings, as well, which advertise their wealth and their prestige. They had a cult shrine. They had a *heroon*, dedicated probably to some local founder hero. A hypostyle hall adorned with Corinthian columns. You could have been back in mainland Greece, looking at the columns of this building.

And the houses of the individuals who lived within the city (clearly the local elite) also advertised their great wealth. These houses often measure 65 by 35 meters. These are monumental villas built within the safety of these mud brick walls. The plan of the houses are very instructive because they look exactly like Greek houses, only on a larger scale. They have a lovely courtyard at the beginning, as you come in off the street. Then there is a small court that leads through into the back chambers of the house, where there is a living room. Often these will be adorned and decorated with glorious mosaics. As good as any mosaics that you'll see back in the Mediterranean world, and with bath complexes as well. People who enjoyed their luxury, in other words. The luxury of being a Greek settler.

The people who lived here have also, fortunately, left us some information about what they were reading and what they were learning, which gives us good evidence for the fact that these were Greeks who saw themselves very much as if they were still living back in the Mediterranean world. For example, if you go to Ai Khanum (in Afghanistan, now), you will find here the sayings from

Delphi inscribed on the blocks at Ai Khanum. Here's an inscription found there, that reads:

> These wise sayings of men of former times, the words of famous men, are consecrated at holy Pytho. [That means Delphi, back in the Greek mainland.] And from there, Cleochas copied them carefully and set them up, shining afar, in the precinct of Kineas. [Three thousand miles away from Delphi. This is an age before there are cars, planes, buses, trains–and people are inscribing Delphic maxims.] When a child, show yourself well-behaved. When a young man, self-controlled. In middle age, just. As an old man a good counselor. At the end of your life, free from sorrow. [Good aphorisms to live by, learnt from Delphi and now turning up almost in India.]

The papyri that we have from the area (we've actually found examples of the books that they were reading) show that the population was reading Aristotelian philosophy, and reading Greek poems, as well. A completely transplanted Greek culture. And, just as if you were in Alexandria on the seaboard of the Mediterranean, or back in Athens, you would do some of this reading in the public location of a gymnasium, the place where Greeks went to recreate themselves, to listen to university lectures, to do their reading, and of course, to do their exercise in the *palaestra*, the sandy area.

So the elite are living in houses. They're reading books. They're conforming to the social conventions of ordinary, everyday life in Greece, but they're doing it over here, in the Punjab. It's really quite extraordinary. It makes one suspect that Plutarch was right when he said that hundreds of years after Alexander's march to the East, the people of eastern Asia (what we would call Central Asia) were still reading Greek plays. The plays of Sophocles and Euripides. I doubt that the ordinary people working in the fields were reading this, but certainly the local elite was. Probably because that local elite was originally Greek.

Features of the decoration of the city are really quite astonishing. I remember the first time I was looking at some of the illustrations of the fountains that were found there, as in most Greek cities, the fountains will have a spout, which will be decorated, either to look like an animal or some other feature to make it slightly more interesting to look at. The water-spouts at Ai Khanum are shaped like dolphins. I don't think there are many dolphins in Afghanistan. So somebody was bringing the idea of the kind of decoration that you get back in the Aegean. Others, that you can see, represent theatrical masks. And it has to make one wonder, were people also going to drama performances? Watching plays by Euripides and Sophocles. If they were reading their texts, why not perform them, as well?

So we had people here living in country villas adorned with mosaics outside the city center, as well as living in. All pointing to a transplanted Greek culture in this small area far, far away. Around 200 B.C., this Bactrian kingdom situated around Ai Khanum expanded east, and it even annexed territory down on the western side of the Indus Valley. So we see some expansion going on here. Increasingly, this Bactrian kingdom was cut off from the west, and the Indo-Greek kingdom came to display probably the only example of genuine fusion between eastern and western elements that we can see in the Hellenistic age.

Let me try to give you some examples of the kind of fusion that goes on as a result of the increasing isolation of the Bactrian East. One good example is a statue that we have of a Greek character, a character called Marsyas, who is well-known in Greek myth. He's a character that challenged Apollo to a contest, but then you should never challenge a Greek god, because they always beat you. Marsyas ends up being flayed alive. The image of him with his hands tied and his skin being torn off is a well-known feature of Hellenistic art.

We have one such statue of this sort, of Marsyas, found at Ai Khanum. But it was dedicated to the local river god, Oxus, by a character named Atrosokes. As I said, Oxus was the local river god, so it's a Greek statue, but it's a local dedication. And Atrosokes' name is Iranian. So he's probably of a Persian background. His name means, "He who shines with sacred fire." He's being identified, very plausibly, as a priest of the old Persian sacred fire cult. So we've got this extraordinary dedication fusing Greek elements, Iranian elements, and local elements, as well. There's really nothing quite like that anywhere in the Mediterranean Basin. So it may well be that the very isolation of the Bactrian kingdom was the key to this very curious fusion of elements. A Greek statue, dedicated by a Persian priest to a local deity. A funny (to our eyes) mishmash of elements.

There's another example of blending. This curious blending of various elements. That is a pillar that was dedicated to the Hindu gods Garuda and Vishnu, which has been found in the Punjab district of northwestern India. It is inscribed in Prakrit, which is an Indian language. The pillar, in its style copies Achaemenid forms, so it's got a Persian influence. But it was dedicated by a man named Heliodorus. About as good a Greek name as you can get.

Heliodorus was an ambassador who dedicated this pillar on the occasion of his visit to the court of the Indian king Bhagabhadra. So we have this fusion of different elements going on here, as well, with a Greek making a dedication that honors Hindu gods, but uses Persian motifs. I find this kind of mixture, this *melange*, very exciting, but it's not typical at all of the Greek or the Hellenistic world. It's really on the exotic eastern corner, and to a lesser extent, in the area of Sudan, south of Egypt, where there is a similar blending of Hellenistic and African elements in the kingdom of Meroe. (But that's a whole nother area.)

The Bactrian kingdoms that we've been looking at were assaulted by invading tribes, known as the Saca, beginning around the middle of the 2nd century B.C. The last Greek king, Heliokles, was replaced by the Saca chief named Azes, in 50 B.C. So the kingdom really comes to dramatic end towards the end of the 1st century B.C.

In trying to evaluate the significance of the Greek control of this region, because we know basically when the Greek control here terminates, and people have wondered, "was there any longer-lasting influence in the East from this Greek layer?" Historians have tended to look for evidence of Greek influence on local traditions. In other words, did the Greeks leave any influence behind after they had gone? So that, for example, Greek historians will often point to the fact that monumental Greek sculpture, life-sized Greek sculpture, which is well-known in the Greek world, in the Classical age and in the Hellenistic period, is really not very well-known in India before this, but comes to be much more popular. So there is the suggestion that maybe the decoration of Indian temples, the use of sculpture of the human form, may be something that represents a Greek influence moving into India. That's certainly possible.

But the line of transmission may also have gone in the other direction, and this is rarely thought about. Is there any evidence, for example, of the eastern contact influencing western traditions as early as this stage? We can't be certain about this, but I'd like to throw out a couple of suggestions, anyway.

One of the Greek Bactrian kings who invaded northwestern India was known as Menander. It's a good Greek name. It's also the name of one of the playwrights of the Hellenistic period. He's actually well-remembered in Indian tradition. So we have an example of a Greek character from this period, who is remembered in Indian tradition. But he's actually remembered as a Greek who converted to Buddhism. His name in the Buddhist scriptures is not Menander, but Milinda. In other words, his name has been transformed by his contact with the East, rather than an easterner who's been transformed by contact with the West.

That's one interesting example. And Menander was a powerful king, who reigned over a large area, so the fact that he converted to Buddhism and became a Buddhist holy man is really quite dramatic. It may be evidence for the Greek Bactrian kingdom losing its Greek character and really assimilating local traditions. That, I find very interesting.

The other good example—dramatic evidence, really, for the relationship between the two cultural traditions of Greece and India is to be found in the career of the great king Asoka, the king of the Mauryan Empire, which controlled all of northwestern India in the 3rd century B.C. Asoka reigned from 268 to 232 B.C. We have some evidence for the relationship between Asoka and the Greek who lay on, what to him, would be his western border. You will remember that Seleucus already had dealings with the Mauryans back in 305 B.C., when he had given up the Seleucid claims to these eastern provinces in return for 500 war elephants. Those 500 war elephants were given to him by Chandragupta (Sandrocottus as the Greeks called him), who is the grandfather of Asoka. So Asoka is already used to the idea of dealing with kings from this far west. Men whom he may not have known personally, but he would have heard about them as he was growing up. Asoka had united just about the entire Indian sub-continent, and he'd converted to Buddhism, proselytizing vigorously. So here we have a very powerful monarch in India, aware that there is a world further to the west, quite different from him. As a Buddhist, and as a proselyte, he's interested in sending his ideas out into this new realm.

Buddhist edicts were inscribed or erected throughout his empire. But he went further than that, as well. He also sent embassies out to the Hellenistic kings. Embassies that came from India all the way back to Syria (to visit Antiochus II), to Egypt (to visit Ptolemy II)—ambassadors from India that made their way all the way to Macedon (to visit Antigonus Gonatas), and Alexander of Epirus, as well, located on the northwestern side of Greece. To each of these great potentates of the Hellenistic world, these ambassadors came bringing messages of good will from Asoka, and trying to explain the basic tenets of Buddhist religion to these men.

I think that this was the wrong audience to talk to. I don't think the Hellenistic rulers were particularly interested in the messages of Buddhism. So the attempts at conversion were unsuccessful. But it is in fact a much more deliberate attempt at conversion than anything the Greeks did in relation to the East. It is the East talking rather to the West.

At Kandahar, which, in fact, lay outside of his kingdom, and was really part of the Bactrian kingdom of the Greeks, he then set up bilingual inscriptions using both Aramaic, the language of the old Persian Empire, and Greek, as well, trying to appeal to the Greek colonists to lead them toward Buddhism. This is, I think, absolutely fascinating, because it means that the sort of religious fusion that's being proposed here, or the cultural influence—the direction is not West to East, but rather East to West. Again, men may have converted to this, but because the kingdoms eventually collapsed, there was no long-lasting influence on Greek culture, because really it was only an outpost of Greek culture that was in contact with Asoka. The eventual disappearance of the Greeks of Bactria as a separate state, as a separate kingdom, and a distinct culture, can probably be put down to a complex set of factors. There is the isolation of the Greeks from the cultural heartland of Hellenism. Geography is a major factor in history. They are simply so isolated.

There is the pressure of outside populations on them. The nomads of Central Asia, for example, who were ever ready to plunder the Silk Route. If you're going to have a major trade route with wealth running along it, you're going to have people ready to attack it. The presence on the very edges of this Hellenistic outpost of a complex and powerful empire, namely that of the Mauryans, itself gripped in a struggle between different religious and cultural forms, namely, Vedic culture and Buddhist culture.

It was against such a tumultuous background that the Greeks of Bactria gave way, eventually being swallowed up by the world around them, and really leaving very little impact on later history. I think that the Graeco-Bactrians of the Upper Satrapies allow us to indulge in something that historians are not supposed to do, and that is to ask, "What if?" What if these kingdoms had survived longer? What would have happened?

Certainly the relation between East and West would have been vastly different. But I rather suspect that the sheer geographic distance between these provinces and the Mediterranean meant that, in the long run, there was really very little possibility of these kingdoms acting as a kind of funnel for eastern thinking to the West and western thinking to the East.

Instead, what happened was that throughout the rest of Greek history and certainly in Roman history, as well, the people of the Mediterranean tended to think of India as being exotic and strange. A place with which they had had a peripheral and temporary contact, but where there was no chance of any long-lasting cultural contact, and certainly no chance for any kind of cultural fusion.

In a way, then, though the Bactrian kingdoms are unlike any other kingdom that we find in the Hellenistic world, the story that we end up finding is exactly the same as what we've seen elsewhere. That for a variety of reasons, both including the exclusive quality of Greek culture, and for a variety of other reasons, as we've seen, the prospect of cultural fusion in the Hellenistic world was really nil. The Greeks lived as foreigners in this territory. It was far enough from the Mediterranean that they wanted to recreate their Mediterranean world. They would be in this world, but they would never be a part of it.

Lecture Eleven
Sculpture

Scope:

The Greeks will always be associated with such masterpieces as the Parthenon, but Hellenistic art is very different from the Classical art that precedes it. Excessive, gargantuan, and emotional, Hellenistic art explores aspects of the human experience that were previously outside the concerns of the Greeks.

Outline

I.   Classical sculpture is a model of calm and repose—typically, it doesn't explore emotions or inner states. By the 4th century B.C., Greek art had enjoyed more than 200 years of sculpting in stone, but three masters dominated the field of sculpture in that century. They were Polyclitus, Scopas, and Lysippus.

   A.   The works of Polyclitus frequently concentrated on young male athletes, the living embodiment of manly excellence. The Spear-Bearer, or Doryphorus, was famous for establishing "the canon," the correct set of proportions and stances to capture the ideal figure in stone. But what comes after such an image of perfection?

   B.   Scopas was famous for a wide variety of statues of the gods and for sculptural representations of such concepts as *pothos*, or yearning, a favorite theme of the Hellenistic Age. He was the first to convey human emotion in stone.

   C.   Lysippus may have been the most influential of the 4th century sculptors, because Alexander preferred his portraits to those of any other sculptor. The Lysippan image of Alexander would be copied throughout the Hellenistic world on coins and gems and adapted by kings after Alexander.

II. Originally, the sculptors of the Hellenistic Age were fascinated by the great men of their time. Their patrons were kings, and they created statues of gods and kings for the new temples and palaces of their world.

A. Soon, however, sculpture was put to a new use.

    1. Intellectual heroes, such as Socrates, great orators, such as Demosthenes (who had opposed the Macedonians), and historians, such as Herodotus, were all treated as suitable subjects for sculpture.

    2. Clearly, earlier Greek culture was being packaged for the new age.

B. Eventually, busts of philosophers would become as common as those of kings.

    1. Many philosophers acted as the advisors of kings, but their status was especially enhanced by the Hellenistic view that philosophy offered an alternative avenue to power: self-mastery.

    2. Philosophers were the negative images of kings.

III. The human form doesn't have to be ideal in Hellenistic art. The artists' interest in people other than those in power led them to explore the poor, the disfigured, and the pathetic. Hellenistic art explores the extremities of human experience.

A. The statue known as the Old Fisherman demonstrates a fascination with the effects of age on the body. The stoic posture of the old man conveys a moral heroism, but there is nothing heroic in his physical body, as had always been the case before this.

B. Similarly, the Boxer shows a face to us that is battered and smashed. The position of hands and head suggest a terrible resignation and deep pain. Although the figure is heroic to our sensibilities because it evinces endurance and resignation, it is not heroic in the way that classical Greek art understood heroism. Also, the statue is intended to be looked at from various angles, not from a single perspective.

C. Similarly, such statues as that of the Old Drunken Woman or the Barbarini Faun represent a break from the earlier traditions, when the emphasis had been on poise and restrained power.

    1. The old woman is grotesquely hunched over her amphora so that the sculptor must render the body into a compact ball rather than the elongated, upright figure familiar from the Classical age.

2. The faun is shamelessly and provocatively posed in a way that violates all earlier canons in the same way that another faun's, Nijinsky's, would violate the canons of dance, both in terms of theme and technique.

IV. The entire sensibility of this sculpture is different. Where once Greek sculptures were either immobile or about to move, Hellenistic sculptures are caught right in the act of movement.

A. Laocoon wrestles with the serpents sent to punish him for warning the Trojans of the Greeks' gift. We watch as the snakes coil around his body and prepare to crush the life out of his children. This pathos in Greek sculpture is new.

B. The young jockey thrashes his horse on even as he turns back to see his competitors. There is nothing noble or Olympian about his pose.

C. Even when the figure is at rest, as is the Farnese Heracles, his rest is the rest of defeat, of endurance, of pain, not the immanent victory of a god.

D. Nudity is also treated differently. Whereas once only heroes and gods were naked and all females were clothed, a prurient fascination develops with showing Aphrodite stepping from her bath, exposing enough flesh to leave nothing to the imagination.

E. Ironically, so aware are the Hellenistic sculptors of the past that they also recreate it in an archaizing movement, producing statues that seem to date from the Classical period but are actually produced much later. A strange combination of nostalgia, taste, and historical sense combine as the Hellenistic Age packages its own glorious past for cultural consumption.

Suggested Reading:

J. J. Pollitt, *Art in the Hellenistic Age*.

Questions to Consider:

1. Can the term "baroque" be used to describe Hellenistic art?

2. Is it appropriate to judge Hellenistic art against Classical art and call it decadent?

Lecture Eleven—Transcript
Sculpture

Welcome back to our series of lectures on the Hellenistic world. So far the focus of our lectures has been primarily towards the political history of the Hellenistic Age. We have looked at the void created by the death of Alexander the Great, and we've investigated how the major Hellenistic kingdoms came into being. We've also looked a little at the administration and the structure of these Hellenistic kingdoms, ranging from Ptolemaic Egypt to the Seleucid realm, and also including the smaller Attalid Kingdom of Asia Minor and then finally considering the far eastern Bactrian Greek kingdoms, which were somewhat anomalous, because it was here that we found evidence for what might truly be called a fusion of Greek and local elements in the culture.

I want to move away in this next section of lectures from the political history and turn more to topics that we would sometimes call the social history of the age. But what I'm really trying to do is to investigate how the people of the Mediterranean world responded to the enormous changes that we've witnessed that they have undergone since the period of Alexander's conquests. We now find Greeks living in cities which, a hundred years earlier, were only ideas, or names to them. And new cities founded completely from scratch, where no Greeks had lived before.

We find the Greeks now living in a world which is dominated by these super-powerful kings. Men who had become the kings of the Hellenistic world, and who were often seen as the great benefactors, and (as we're going to see in a lecture later on) are often also portrayed as living gods. Saviors, benefactors and do-gooders dominating the political landscape. In this world, people were confronting a new uncertainty about the future. The old forms and institutions of Greek life were not well-adapted to a scale spread across the Hellenistic world.

So we're going to see real changes in the way people live their lives. The way artists respond to the conditions of the world in which they live. Nowhere can this change be better charted than in the sculpture of the age. In later lectures, we'll also look at philosophy and we'll look at literature, but I want to begin this set of lectures with the art of the Hellenistic period, and specifically the sculpture of the age. It's here that we see a dramatic difference between the earlier

Classical period and the age to come, the Hellenistic period, where human experience will be explored in a whole new way. Where the art will be dramatic. Where it will be emotional and, in the eyes of some, it will be excessive and gargantuan. It's this art which is sometimes described as baroque. It is this emotional art which, in the eyes of many critics in the 19th century, was excessive and was decadent when compared with the earlier period.

Before we go right into Hellenistic art, let's stop for a moment and consider what the Greeks had done up until this time in their sculpture. The Classical style of sculpture had tended to emphasize repose and calm. Classical sculpture, particularly the statues of gods and goddesses, had really derived from earlier Egyptian canons of sculpture. I'm sure you've seen Egyptian statues that show frontal figures, very stiffly arranged with their feet, one forward and one back and the arms held closely by their side. The Greeks had taken this style, and in the 6th century had begun to loosen it up somewhat, so that the figures of Classical sculpture tend to be somewhat more naturally posed than the Egyptian models they are based on. But the Greek artists of the Classical Age are usually not exploring emotions or the inner life of the individual. They're not really portraits in the sense that we know them. These are archetypal statues, expressing the Olympian calm of the gods.

If you consider, for example, the statue at Olympia, one of the pedimental sculptures from the temple there, showing a fight between the lapiths and the centaurs, in this great furious melee of combat going on, Apollo stands at the center of the scene, in the middle of the pediment, with his arm extended, and his face looking impassively over the action. Because he is a god removed from the realm of humans. Our world is chaos and disorder, as the Greeks see it, but the gods are somewhat beyond that. Removed. Distant. So the high point of Classical sculpture really comes, to my mind, at least, in this so-called severe style, where the face is impassive and immobile, and where very little human expression is allowed.

In the 4th century, the bridge between the Classical period and the Hellenistic Age, three masters emerged in the field of sculpture, whose careers really allow us to span the shift from Classical to Hellenistic. The first of these is Polyclitus, and I want to begin with him, because it's with Polyclitus that we really see, I think, the absolute apogee of Classical sculpture. His sculptures tend to be either of gods or young men (athletes) who are the living embodiment of manly excellence. The Spear-Carrier, for example, or, as it's known in Greek, the Doryphorus. Or another one, the Diadumenos, the athlete who has his hands up and is tying the ribbon around his head. These statues were famous for establishing what, in antiquity, was referred to as "the canon." In other words, this was the way that the male form should be represented, in its most ideal style.

There were very carefully worked out proportions in this sculpture, so that if you measured this sculpture you would find that the head would normally be one-sixth the size of the body. Very careful proportions. Not only that, but the stance of the figures, also, is carefully designed, and becomes canonical. It's the stance that's later borrowed in Renaissance art, the so-called *contrapposto* stance, where the weight is all on one foot, so that one leg is shown going straight to the ground, while the other, relaxed and easy, is bent at the knee. As a result of this stance, the hips, and the bottom of the rib cage, instead of forming parallel lines, form lines that meet and part at different angles. This is to impart to the body a more natural style. At the same time it's still an ideal figuration of the human form.

This is the human form represented in sculpture in perfection. I think it is what Classical sculpture has been moving towards. But it raises the question, If you reach perfection, what do you do next in your sculpture? It's all downhill from there. Well, not exactly. What the sculptors of the 4th century and increasingly of the Hellenistic period will do, is they move away from this Olympian calm, this absolute, awe-inspiring perfection of the Classical ideal, and they will start to explore much more human aspects of our experience through sculpture.

The first sculptor who really does this is Scopas. He's famous for a variety of statues of the gods, but also statues that represent human feelings. One such statue is the one known as yearning or *pothos*. It's another one you have in your dossier. This idea of *pothos* or yearning is a favorite theme of the Hellenistic world. In fact, you might recall that when we looked at Alexander's career, that some of the sources for Alexander's campaign constantly referred to his *pothos*, his desire, his yearning to go to Siwa to visit the oracle of Ammon, or his yearning to take the rock of Aeornos because Heracles had been unable to do it. This notion was caught in stone by Scopas in his statue of yearning, or *pothos*. He was trying to find a way of expressing human feelings in stone. That's a new development.

Then the third of the great Hellenistic sculptors is named Lysippus, and he also marks the final bridge, really, from Classical to Hellenistic, because it is Lysippus who is going to give to the world the image of Alexander. Lysippus was a sculptor whose image of Alexander the great king actually saw and admired, and he used it as the preferred portrait, which was then copied and spread throughout the Hellenistic world. The Lysippid image of Alexander would be copied, and it is very distinctive. You've probably seen various versions of it. There are some from Egypt. There are some from Macedonia.

But what they share in common is this: the king will always be shown as a young, beardless man. He's likened to the Athenian hero Theseus, who is also beardless, compared to Heracles, who's always a mature man. He will have a rather pouty face. He usually seems to have a bit of extra fat. In his expression, he always seems to be turning and looking up to heaven. There's a kind of dreamy look in his eyes and his mouth is open as if he's in a reverie. As if he's communicating, somehow, with the gods. You can always tell it's Alexander, because his hair, which is always beautifully curled, will also have a little part in the center, and the hair will bob up on either side. This is a style that is so distinctive that even in antiquity they recognized it and called it the anastole, and it makes him look as though he has a lion's mane around his head, or a halo.

This image would be very popular, and it would be copied throughout the Hellenistic world. It turns up on coins of Alexander. It turns up on engraved gems. The bust itself is copied numerous times throughout the Hellenistic period, so that people could have their own Alexander in their own court or in their own house.

What we see in the movement of these three sculptors is a move away from the old Classical ideal, where the sculpture is not really of an individual, but of a type, to a new interest in various forms of human expression, and particularly, thanks to Lysippus, an interest in the Great Man. It's hardly surprising that the sculptors of the time should be interested in this. Alexander the Great was an example of what Aristotle had talked about. The man of what he called *megalo psyche*, the great spirit. The man whose soul was so large that he became superhuman in his accomplishments.

Of course, to the men and women of the Hellenistic Age, they were surrounded by such men, because after Alexander came Ptolemy and Seleucus and Antigonus and Attalus and so forth. These great kings were the great men, the living embodiment of this principle. So there are statues of gods and statues of kings created to adorn their new temples and to adorn the palaces of this new Hellenistic world, that showed this interest in capturing the soul of the "great man."

To the extent that these sculptors are depicting the kings of the age, that's very understandable. But one of the first really interesting developments, I think, in Hellenistic sculpture, is that the artists begin to move beyond the king as great man, and they start looking at a range of other figures who also fit the bill, as well. Intellectual heroes, such as Socrates, come to be popularly portrayed in Hellenistic sculpture. Socrates is actually a very ugly type. He's a small, squat man, with a little pot belly and a little frog face, so he doesn't conform in any way to a canonical notion of male beauty. But there is something about him, and it's that he is a kind of moral hero that stood up to the Athenians. He had been prepared to die for his beliefs. In his *Apology*, his defense speech, instead of sniveling, and trying to get off scot-free, he challenged the Athenians by saying, "You ought to reward me, because I've been your moral educator." So this sort of moral heroism turns Socrates into a kind of intellectual hero, and he's widely depicted in the Hellenistic Age.

As, for example, are other figures, such as Demosthenes. It's in some ways an odd choice, if you think about it. Demosthenes was the great Athenian orator who had made his reputation (his immortal reputation, really) on the fact that he had opposed the Macedonians. And yet all the patrons of this great art were Macedonians, descended from the very people who had been opposed by Demosthenes. And yet, Demosthenes represented the high point of Greek oratory. Socrates, the high point of Greek philosophy, along with Plato and Aristotle. We also find many busts of them. Demosthenes the high point of Greek oratory.

We also find busts and full-length statues of men such as Herodotus and Thucydides. Why? Because they represent the high point of Greek history-writing. There's something very interesting going on here. What's happening is that in the Hellenistic Age, Greek culture is being packaged. The heroes of Greek culture are being given their own statues, and then these are popularly being exported throughout the Greek world and purchased by people and put up in civic squares or in people's own houses. It is as if the people of the Hellenistic Age are looking back with nostalgia to the Classical period, wanting to have some kind of contact, to suggest that they are the continuation of that, in the same way that people today might have a bust of Beethoven on their piano. They may not play like a concert pianist, but they want to suggest that they are still a part of that world of classical culture and classical music.

Eventually, and I think this is a very interesting development, busts of philosophers would become as common as those of kings. So if you go to, say, Aphrodisias today, a city in southern Turkey, a city that flourished in the Hellenistic and then in the Roman period—if you go to the museum there and look at the public statues that have been excavated there over the last 30 years, you will find that there are Roman caesars and emperors who have been recorded there, but there are also philosophers, as well.

This is the new development of the age. These philosophers, in real life, were often advisors of the Hellenistic kings. But I think that the reason that we find so many busts of the philosophers being made, and so many statues of them, is that, in the Hellenistic view, philosophy is a kind of alternative avenue to power. The Hellenistic kings, of course, represent supreme political power in this earthly realm. But there is another type of power. It's the control over your self. *Autarchy.*

If you can banish your appetite, so that you no longer really care about this world, so that you are untroubled, you have mastered yourself, and you are, in a sense, the perfect philosopher. And you are, in your own realm, your own Hellenistic king, as well. I can't help thinking that philosophers, in their popularity, represent the flip side of the power of the Hellenistic kings. And that, in some way, they represent a kind of negative image of kings. While the kings had to be mollified and respected and treated as benefactors, there are many people whose attitude was, "Ach! I prefer philosophy." That's one development that we find in the age, and already we're seeing something more interesting than we found in the Classical period, something new and vital and interesting in Hellenistic art.

But there's something more that goes on, as well. If we've really broken the Classical mold, as I think we have, after Polyclitus, then even the human form itself doesn't always have to be ideal. It means that the artist can begin to look at people as they truly are, rather than as they would like to be. What we find is that Hellenistic art, therefore, will begin to explore all the different shapes and sizes of the human body. It will explore the poor, the disfigured, the pathetic. Hellenistic art will go to the extremes of human experience in a way that Classical art had never done (in the period before). Of course it's exactly this interest in the extremes of human situations that led Hellenistic art to be disparaged in the 19th century as decadent. Because it wasn't Classical and ideal. Because it showed people, really, warts and all. And often with a lot more than just their warts, too.

A statue that illustrates this quite well, I think, is the statue of the "Old Fisherman," which we know from a Roman copy. In fact, it was so popular that we have a number of different Roman copies for this. I think that what they all share in common is that they illustrate that the artist, in making this figure, is not in any way or form trying to idealize the human body. The fisherman that we look at may be stoic, and he may be heroic, because he's putting up with the travails of life. But he is not physically beautiful. His body is shown in a cramped posture, with his knees bent. His arms are in a rather awkward position, with one stuck out on one side. And you can see, if you look at his body, that the skin is sagging on it, because he's a very old man.

This is absolutely new. He may be morally or stoically heroic, but he's not physically heroic in the Greek sense of that. This is very interesting, and very new, because up until now, the Greeks have shown everyone in their sculpture as being heroic, regardless of their real age. Even a statue such as the one we see here, showing Zeus preparing to throw his thunderbolt, shows the father of gods and men, so he's not a twenty-year-old. He's more like a fifty-year-old, but he has the body of a twenty-year-old athlete. This is common in the Greek world of the Classical period. But now we're going to start taking the blinkers off and showing old age as it really is.

Similarly, and even more dramatically, if you consider the sculpture known as the "Boxer," you find that we've got a character here whose face is battered and smashed. (He actually looks a little bit like Evander Holyfield, who's going to be fighting soon, again.) If you look in profile, you can see his nose has been pushed in. He is, in some ways, a very moving figure. In some ways he's even heroic.

But not heroic in the earlier Greek sense of the word. He's heroic in our sense and to our sensibilities because his body represents (through the position of his hands and the stooping of his head and back)—because it suggests a terrible resignation. It's as if the artist has caught him at the moment when the bell rings for the beginning of the new round, and the old man, tired and worn out, says, "Do I have to go out again?" And we know he's going to. He will get up and fight again, even though his body is exhausted. So there is a heroism in that sculpture, I think. It's a heroism of endurance, and a heroism of resignation. But it's certainly not heroic in the way that the Greeks had construed physical heroism prior to this time.

There's one other aspect of that sculpture that bears thinking about. That is, that if you look at it from the front, if you're right in front of the boxer, you can't see much of his face, because his face is completely turned away. On the other hand, if you go around to look at his face, you can't see much of his body, because his arms and his shoulders are blocking you. This sculpture is clearly designed for you to look at from a multitude of angles. It wasn't designed to be put high up on a pediment, where you couldn't see it. It wasn't designed to express some Olympian calm of a god. Rather, it's a living man, and it's going to be placed somewhere at a level where you can walk around it and investigate it, looking at the face, looking at the body, marveling at the musculature and sympathizing with his plight, as well.

So the whole way that we've been invited in, as it were, to look at this sculpture, I think represents a whole new attitude on the part of the artist. Not only to his material, but even also to us, his audience, as we come in to share the experience. In much the same way, as in an earlier lecture on Pergamum, I pointed out that as you go up the Great Altar, you see the figures around you. They're not high up on a temple above you. They are at the sides of the steps. And they tip out onto the steps, so that there will be a writhing beast and a figure in torment, with his knees right on the step that you're standing on. You are invited into this sculpture. A whole new attitude toward the audience.

Similarly, statues such as the well-known statue of the "Old Drunken Woman" or also the statue of the "Barberini Faun"—these represent a break from earlier traditions, where the emphasis had been on poise and on restrained power. The old woman that we see, the old drunken woman, as you can see, is clutching in her arms an *amphora*, a drinking jug. She's on the ground because she can't even stand up now. She's holding on desperately to this drinking jug, as if somebody said, "Come on, old lady, you've had enough. I'm going to take that away from you." It's a very dramatic moment. She's grotesquely hunched over the *amphora*, so that the sculptor must render the body, not as something standing upright and erect—there's no canon here of proportions of head to body—rather, it's a compact ball, with everything turned in on itself. It's a whole new way of representing the human body, and a whole new interest in what humans do. It's a graphic realism.

In the case of the "Barberini Faun," a figure who is reclining in the middle of the day, enjoying a reverie, with his hands up behind his head, and his legs, graphically, widely open, the faun is shamelessly provocative, in a way that violates all the earlier canons of Classical sculpture. Because, frankly, with the way his body is reclining, and with his legs open, the entire visual emphasis of the sculpture is on his genitals. These are not incidental, in the way that a naked male statue before has genitals, but you aren't asked to pay particular attention to it. Rather, this is taking you right to a creature of extraordinary sexuality, and it is inviting you to try to experience that same sexuality as well. So the sculpture violates all the earlier canons, in the same way that another faun (Nijinski's) later on would violate the canons of dance, in terms of both theme and technique. It's a very similar situation.

The entire sensibility of the sculpture that I've been talking about is quite different. Previously, Greek sculpture had been either immobile, or it had been just on the point of moving. In fact, in the example that we have over here of the Zeus statue that I mentioned a little earlier (Zeus who is holding a thunderbolt), if you could see his legs, you'd find that one leg shows that he's going forward and the other one is in balance with it. He couldn't actually stand in that position. His body is rocking forward, ready to shoot out his thunderbolt. But what we find now in the Hellenistic Age is not just something that is immobile or about to move. But we find writhing movement, such as in the statue of Laocoon.

In the case of Laocoon, who's being punished by the gods because he had tried to warn the Trojans that the Trojan Horse was a trap and that there were Greeks inside. In this instance, we know from literary accounts, the myth was widely known. But the serpents are sent out by the gods, and they capture the man and his sons, coil him up and kill him. We've known about this in mythology, but we don't see it depicted before the Hellenistic period. Whereas now, in the Hellenistic period, this becomes a very popular sculpture. It is widely copied. In it, the great emphasis is on the pain and the anguish felt by this character. The expression on the face of Laocoon, as he knows he's about to die, and his sons are about to die, is truly pathetic. So there's an extraordinary movement, and a drama in this sculpture that we don't find in earlier Classical sculpture. There's a terrible *pathos* and a drama to it, as we're taken into the very center of the action.

Similarly, if one considers another well-known Hellenistic sculpture, that of the "Jockey," who's riding on his horse, we find that there is nothing noble, nothing Olympian about this. It's a scene that people could have witnessed if they had gone to the races. So it's something taken out of daily life. Here we see the little boy sitting on his horse, the horse much too big for him, and he's thrashing it, as he turns around to see whether his competitors are catching up to him. As with so many other examples of Greek sculpture of the Hellenistic period, this sculpture is trying to capture a particular moment. A critical moment here, just as he turns away to see whether his opponents are coming. Similarly, in the Laocoon, as the snakes just grab hold of him, and now begin to crush him to death.

It's the same sort of thing that we find in that well-known mosaic from Naples that I mentioned on an earlier occasion. The one that shows Alexander defeating Darius, when, again, the artist's interest is in the moment. That critical moment when history's about to shift, and the Hellenistic world comes into the ascendant, as the Persian Empire passes into defeat.

Another well-known example of sculpture from the period that in some way sums up most of the tendencies of the age, is that of the "Farnese Heracles," again, known to us from Roman copies. This Heracles is utterly unlike the Heracles that you may have seen on Greek vases of the Classical period. This is not the triumphant Heracles who is defeating the Lernaean Hydra, or who is defeating the Nemean Lion. This, rather, is a Heracles who has accomplished his labors, but is exhausted by them. What we see, is a body, yes, of massive musculature, but something almost overgrown, almost on steroids, if you will, and at the same time, exhausted by the sheer effort of his labors. He's a Heracles who is triumphant and heroic if you like, but it's a triumph and a heroism that is based on endurance and on pain, not on the imminent victory of a god. This is a much more human Heracles than we find in earlier Greek art.

There are all sorts of interesting changes going on in the sculpture of this age. Nudity, for example, is another area where we find a very different treatment from earlier. Before, in the Classical Age, heroes and gods were depicted naked, and females were clothed. So that, for example, statues of Athena would show her completely dressed, and usually wearing her armor, as well. Nudity was something that was for men, because athletes exercised naked, and gods could be shown naked, as well. It was appropriate for them.

But now, in the Hellenistic Age, we begin to get a rather prurient fascination with the nudity of women. So we get statues of Aphrodite, and often she's climbing out of her bath, so that she must demurely cover her genitals so that the audience can't see it. Of course, in doing so, she's actually attracting the audience's attention right to that. These sculptures of the Hellenistic Age really leave nothing to the imagination. When one considers who the patrons for this may be—it's no longer just the state; it's private individuals and private drinking clubs and religious confederations that are commissioning these. Clearly the artists are responding to the tastes of the time. Moving away from the grand and the Olympian to something a little bit easier to grab hold of.

The last element of Hellenistic sculpture that we have time to mention is an ironic one, and that is that the sculptors of the Hellenistic Age were so acutely aware of the Classical period and what it had produced, that they were called upon sometimes to produce copies of what had been created in the earlier Classical Age. They produced *archaizing* statues. Not archaic. Not from the earlier period itself. But in the style of the earlier period. There is a whole market in the Hellenistic Age for buying these *archaizing* sculptures, so that people can make their house look as if they've got art treasures from 200 years earlier.

So what we find is a strange combination of nostalgia, taste, and historical sense combining, as the Hellenistic Age does something that the Greeks had not done before this. It packages its own glorious past for cultural consumption.

Lecture Twelve
Poetry

Scope:

Callimachus, Apollonius, and Theocritus are the three most well-known Hellenistic poets. The differences between them in temperament, style, and voice demonstrate the new directions of Hellenistic poetry. All, however, wrote for an audience that was expected to be immersed in Greek culture. Reflecting a complex world in which Greek was now an international culture, their poems also point to the concerns of the day: anxiety, nostalgia, and refinement all combine to make Hellenistic poetry quite unlike its classical antecedents.

Outline

I. Callimachus is well remembered for his remark that a big book is a big evil. He preferred shorter styles: epigrams, hymns, and brief lyric poems.

  A. Today, in an age that doesn't understand the artifice that goes into art, his poems can seem stylized and overwrought, but at times his work displays a depth of feeling that is powerfully moving.

  B. Consider the elegy written on the death of a friend:

> Someone told me, Heracleitus,
> that you were dead, and brought me
> close to tears, for I remembered
> how often in our talk we put
> the sun to bed. You, I suppose,
> my Halicarnassian friend,
> are ashes four times long ago,
> but your nightingales still live.
> On then Hades who snatches all
> away shall not cast his hand.

  C. The poem has the theme that later Roman poets would summarize as "Ars longa, vita brevis," (Art is long, life is short).

    1. It has the mood of resignation, of a gentle pervasive melancholy that would find its clearest voice, ironically, not in an Alexandrian poet but in one who had read the Alexandrian poets and was infused with their spirit, Virgil.

2. It was, after all, the Roman poet whose work expressed a view of the universe summed up in the line "*sunt lacrimae rerum,*" (the world is full of tears).

II. But Alexandrian poetry wasn't all gloom and shades of murky night. One Alexandrian, Apollonius, even tried his hand at epic, the great ancient tradition of singing the tales of heroes.

A. He chose as his hero not Achilles or Odysseus but Jason, whose expedition to the far side of the Black Sea in search of the Golden Fleece was a staple of Greek mythology.

1. Apollonius's audience knew the story; the challenge was to tell it in a new and original manner.

2. What he produced, in the *Argonautica*, was an extraordinary piece that in some ways is the first psychological novel, one with an anti-hero at the center.

B. Consider, for example, the following episode:

1. The Argonauts have landed on the coast of Mysia. One of them, Hylas, goes off into the bush, where he meets a water nymph who seduces him. He slides into her pool and she drowns him.

2. When Heracles gets the news, he slips into a blood-curdling rage and storms off in search of his young friend. He disappears, and the Argonauts don't see him again.

3. Next morning, the wind freshens, and one of the Argonauts urges them to set sail. They do so, but later realize that they have left without Heracles, the bravest and strongest of the Argonauts.

4. A terrible fight ensues among the Argonauts, as recriminations fly and the band almost disintegrates. The leader must come forward and impose his will. Instead, says Apollonius, "Jason, paralysed by an utter sense of helplessness, added no word to either side in the dispute. He sat and ate his heart out crushed by the calamity."

5. Ironically, in an age of supermen and god-kings, the hero has been reduced to the level of a wimp, literally speechless when faced with calamity. And this, in the age of Alexander!

C. Apollonius's work reveals the fascination felt by the people of the Hellenistic Age toward the inner workings of the human heart and mind.

    1. The emotional states that take us beyond our ordinary selves and those situations in which our actions are dictated by irrational feelings became key concerns of the poets.

    2. Rage is one such state, but even more common is passion, as when Medea falls in love with Jason.

D. Part of the complexity of the Hellenistic Age arises from the fact that artists and thinkers offered such different answers to human dilemmas.

    1. Philosophers were trying to teach people how to control their passions and appetites, while sculptors were exploring the human body as a vessel for these passions and emotions.

    2. The poets, too, were exploring in words the sensation of losing your wits to passion. Apollonius's description of Medea, for example, is the literary antecedent of both Juliet and Lady Macbeth. Apollonius, as much as Shakespeare, is fascinated by the inner turmoil we experience when our emotions are driven to fever pitch.

III. Alexandrian poetry could also explore aspects of life and art that strike us as much less significant. The psychological drama of a woman torn between lover and family resonates for us, but pastoral poetry and bucolic themes strike us as quaint and curiously affected. That is why the poetry of Theocritus is, in some ways, hardest for a modern audience to understand.

A. Pastoral poetry, which purports to concern the life of shepherds, is actually a carefully wrought and highly artificial genre destined for an elite, courtly audience.

B. Consider, for example, the singing competition of Daphnis and Menalcas in Theocritus's 37th idyll.

    1. No one would suggest that such an event is realistic, and the poet is not exploring the psychology of "cowboys."

    2. Instead, this poetry is largely about the artifice of art, the skill of finding sounds and words that go together to produce euphony. Tightly arranged, carefully conventional, these poems are the delight of an urbane society that enjoys the game of recreating the countryside, a countryside they have never set foot in, with this imaginary, purified, sanitized landscape.

3. Like Disney's Main Street, it does not reflect life so much as project an imaginary picture of how life might be if all the anxieties of crime, disease, and poverty were taken out—all that one is left with is pure art.

C. For this reason, pastoral poetry has rarely been produced by poets from the countryside, but by poets writing for a court that prefers the image of the country to its reality. In the world of a self-absorbed court, pastoral fiction was vastly more entertaining than reality.

D. Theocritus, however, was more than a dreamer. Some of his poems are written as if he had eavesdropped on the conversations going on around him in Alexandria.

1. He was able, for example, to catch the babble of two Alexandrian ladies hurrying to a recital.

2. Poems such as this chart new territory. They are not heroic, nor are they the laments of lovers, nor hymns to the gods. Instead, here is the speech of everyday life transformed just enough to make it literary.

IV. Whether writing for the court in epigrams or capturing the lives of ordinary people, all the poems share a common feature: their world is exclusively Greek.

A. Hellenism produces virtually nothing comparable to the modern literatures of the Caribbean, Africa, or India, where indigenous and colonial cultures collided but produced exhilarating new works.

B. Instead, these poets worked within the parameters of Greek culture alone, reacting to their own cultural heritage in the works of Homer, the lyric poets, and the dramatists of an earlier age.

Suggested Reading:

B. H. Fowler, *Hellenistic Poetry: An Anthology.*

Questions to Consider:

1. Does the lack of any non-Greek element in Hellenistic poetry suggest an active resistance on the part of the Greeks to any culture other than their own?

2. Should the *Argonautica* be read as mock-epic and, if so, what does this suggest about Hellenistic attitudes toward earlier Greek culture?

Lecture Twelve—Transcript
Poetry

Hello. We've now reached the twelfth lecture in our series on the Hellenistic world. In our last lecture we had an opportunity to move away from the political record of the age and to begin an examination of what we might call the spirit of the age. How did people react and respond to the massive changes that the Hellenistic Age had witnessed? In our first attempt to answer that question, we looked at Greek sculpture and Hellenistic sculpture. We tried to see the way in which Classical sculpture had reached a certain point in its development and it was ready, really, to break out of its mold and to explore whole new areas. To look at different ways of looking at the human form, different ways of exploring the human psyche, different ways of expressing through sculpture the human experience.

We observed that in Hellenistic sculpture there was a great deal of freedom in the way that people went about doing this. To such an extent, in fact, that some people even refer to Hellenistic sculpture as rococo or baroque, it seems to be so full, so elegant and so overblown at the same time.It's now time, I think, to look at another area of artistic development to see how the Hellenistic age differed from what had come before. This is in the realm of poetry. We've already seen in an earlier lecture on the topic of Alexandria, that three of the great poets of the age all ended up at one time or another working in Alexandria. As is so often the case, we can use the "Big Three," and we can examine their works to see how Hellenistic poetry charts new territory compared to what's come before.

The three men that we're going to look at are Callimachus, Theocritus and Apollonius. Though they produced bodies of very different work, the new directions of Hellenistic poetry will be summed up basically, in the work of these three men. All of them were writing for essentially a Greek audience, and not only an audience that spoke Greek, but an audience that understood Greek education and Greek mythology—in other words, an audience of educated Greeks. They reflect a complex world in which Greek is now an international culture, but at the same time it is also a kind of exclusive club. You have to speak the language, and you have to understand the references to earlier events in Greek history, but particularly to Greek mythology in order to understand this poetry.

We're also going to find that their poems are going to be unusual in that they're going to look at the daily lives of individual people. They're going to deal with themes like anxiety and nostalgia and also refinement. All of these, combining to make Hellenistic poetry quite unlike the Classical poetry that came before it.

Let's begin first with Callimachus. Callimachus is really best remembered for his remark that a big book is a big evil. In other words, what he was trying to say was, "I'm not going to be like Homer. I'm not going to write twenty-four books of epic." Instead, he preferred short, crisp poems. Epigrams. Often four line poems that quickly summed up a sentiment or an idea or feeling or an emotion. Brief lyric poems. He did write a couple of longer poems, running to a few hundred lines each. These are hymns, written in honor of the gods. But even here, the style of hymn that Callimachus wrote is very different from the style of hymn that had been produced by earlier Greeks, going back to, say, the 6th century.

Earlier hymns, which had told the story of the gods, had tended to be fairly serious works, because these were going to be recited in honor of a god, so even though you might talk about Hermes doing something like cattle stealing, which he did when he was a little boy, nevertheless, the essential tone of the poems was quite reverential. The hymns of Callimachus really move in a slightly new direction. For example, we'll have Artemis, as a little girl, beseeching her father Zeus, the father of gods and men, to give her a bow and arrow so that she can go out hunting. The scene is really comic, because she's a little girl, and she ends up a little girl's bow and arrow, to play with. It's really not in keeping with the earlier atmosphere of hymns written towards the gods.

Callimachus' poems are often very difficult for a modern audience to appreciate. His poems can seem stylized and overwrought. There are moments, nevertheless, in his poems when you will find moments of real emotion. A depth of feeling which is very powerful and very moving. I'd like to read you one such poem. It is an elegy written by Callimachus on the death of one of his close friends.

> Someone told me, Heracleitus,
> that you were dead,
> And brought me close to tears.
> For I remembered in our talk
> how often we put the sun to bed.

You, I suppose, my Halicarnassian friend,
are ashes four times long ago.
But your nightingales still live.
On them, Hades, who snatches all away,
shall not cast his hand.

It's a lovely poem. The notion that the nightingales, which are the songs, the poems of his friend, will live on is, in fact, the expression of a sentiment that we have long had in Western culture, summed up by the Latin tag, *Ars longa; vita brevis.* "Life is short, but art is long." It survives. This mood of gentle resignation, he's unhappy his friend is gone; this mood of a gentle, pervasive melancholy, that life is full of sadness, will go on to find an even clearer voice after Callimachus. Ironically, not in a Greek poet from Alexandria, but in a Latin poet from Rome, who, like the other good Latin poets, was thoroughly immersed in Greek poetry. Who had been infused with the very same spirit of gentle resignation and melancholy. Virgil.

It is in Virgil's work that this entire view of the universe will find its finest expression. *Sunt lacrimae rerum.* "There are tears in the world. The world is full of tears."

So that Alexandrian sentiment is very personal. The comment about the relationship between life and art is something that strikes us as being very recognizable. But its ground zero is here.

But Alexandrian poetry wasn't all gloom and shades of murky night. Not everything that Callimachus wrote was in honor of a dead friend. He had some very amusing poems, as well.

Also, the second of the Alexandrian poets that I want to discuss, Apollonius, tried his hand at the old genre of epic. That great ancient tradition of telling the tale of heroes such as Achilles and Odysseus, the heroes of Homer's epics, the *Illiad* and the *Odyssey*. But Apollonius went out on new ground. He followed a new direction. For a start, his epic is a great deal shorter than the Homeric epics. Not only that, but also he's chosen a different story to follow. He's decided to tell the story of *Jason and the Argonauts* and the trip that they undertook to the Black Sea, up to Colchis (to what we would call the Ukraine), in search of the Golden Fleece. This story was a well-known story in Greek mythology, it's certainly true. Apollonius' audience knew the story quite well. Like every other

Greek poet, he wasn't interested in finding a new story to tell. He was interested in finding a new way to tell an old story.

So the challenge that he faced was how to take this story that every Greek child had known for years, and to give it something new. What he came up with is quite novel and original. The *Argonautica*, the epic that he wrote, is really quite a typically Hellenistic document, in this sense. The hero is really not much of a hero at all. In a way he's almost an anti-hero. What Apollonius does is to take the old genre of epic and turn it quite on its head. What he also does for the first time, is to really spend a great deal of time examining the individual psychology of the hero. To take us into the interior.

What we're really getting, in a way, even though it's written in the epic form, just like Homer's work, and it's an epic poem, what we're really getting, in a way, is the first psychological novel. The first attempt to really get into the head of this man. Let me give you an example that I think will help to illustrate what I'm talking about. Again, as we're talking about this, I want you to think about the way that someone like Homer would have treated this story—this particular episode that I'm dealing with. The Argonauts, these heroes of ancient Greece, have assembled in their quest to go off to get the Golden Fleece and to help Jason, in his quest to become the lawful king of Thessaly. They've landed in the course of their trip on the coast of Mysia. While there, one of the Argonauts, a young hero named Hylas, has gone off into the bush, where he meets a water nymph, who seduces him. So he bends down to the pool. (You may have seen the glorious painting of Edward Burne-Jones that shows him about to be sucked down into the water by the nymph.) He slides into her pool and she drowns him. Nymphs are dangerous business.

When news comes back to Heracles, he slips into a blood-curdling rage, and he storms off in search of his friend. He can't believe that Hylas is gone. He disappears and the Argonauts don't see him again. The disappearance of the greatest hero amongst all of them. Next morning the wind freshens, and one of the Argonauts urges them to set sail. "Come on. We've got to cut our losses. Let's get out of here." So they set off.

They set off, but then realize that they left without Heracles. They knew that Hylas was left behind, but they didn't notice that Heracles was gone. So now, on board the boat there is a terrible argument as the recriminations begin to fly around. The entire band of heroes begins to disintegrate. It's clearly at this moment, when all the heroes are beginning to argue with each other, that we would expect, we would hope, that Jason, the leader of the expedition, would step forward to assert his authority and to impose his will. To restore unity. So we're getting a drum roll. This is it. We're waiting for the great hero to step forward. And this is what Apollonius says of Jason:

> Jason, paralyzed by an utter sense of helplessness,
> Added no word to either side in the dispute.
> He sat and ate out his heart, crushed by the calamity.

This is a hero who has no idea how to behave. This is Schwarzenegger finding out that the terrorists have run amok, saying, "Oh dear!. What do I do?" Not even saying that much. He can't find the words.

This, I think, is very interesting, not only because it's a new development in Greek literature. We've never had a hero like Jason before, that's for sure. But it's also ironic that the hero should be turning into a wimp at exactly the time in Greek history when the world is full of these super-human men. The successors of Alexander, who wish to see themselves portrayed as the Great Men of the Age. The men, who, I've said before, were worshiped as *Euergetes* (benefactor), *Soter* (savior), *Epiphanes* (god made manifest). So there are many more superheroes in the flesh in the Hellenistic world, and at the same time Apollonius is telling us that heroes are really not all that they're cracked up to be. I can't help wondering if there isn't something subversive in this, as well, as if the whole idea of the hero is being deconstructed by this poet.

Apollonius' work reveals the fascination felt by the people of the Hellenistic age towards the workings of the inner heart, the inner person, the emotional states that we experience as human beings, and particularly those emotional states that take us beyond our ordinary, everyday selves. Rage is certainly one of those states, but an even more common one is passion. You will not find, prior to the Hellenistic period, a description quite to match the description that we have in Apollonius' work, the *Argonautica*, when he comes to describe the passion that has taken hold in the breast of Medea, now that she's fallen in love with Jason.

Eros, meanwhile, went unseen through the gray mist,
distracting as the gadfly that attacks the heifers
and the cowherds call the breeze. Quickly beneath the lintel
  in the entrance he strung his bow and took
from his quiver an arrow, not shot before, to bring much
  pain.
With quick feet he slipped unseen across the threshold
and glanced sharply around. He crept, crouched low,
past Jason, and fitted his notched arrow end
into the middle of the string, stretched with both hands,
and shot Medea.

So far, this is something you could get in earlier Greek poetry, because love is being seen here as a little figure (Eros) who has a bow and arrow, and he shoots people, and they fall in love. That much is okay. But look now at what happens in the description of Medea's response.

She was struck utterly speechless.
(He himself darted away from the high route and laughed
  aloud)
but the shaft burned the girl's heart.
Deep down, like a flame.
She kept glancing at Jason with sparkling eyes.
And her breath came in panting gasps in her distress.
She forgot everything else
And her soul melted in sweet anguish,
As when a toiling woman piles dry sticks around a piece of
  burning wood,
That she may make a fire beneath her roof by night.
And if she has waked very early,
the flame from the small brand grows miraculously
And consumes all the kindling.
So, coiled beneath Medea's heart,
there burned in secret
destructive love.
The color of her tender cheeks turned
now to pale, now to red.
She was so distraught.

So we're getting this very graphic description, both of the physical symptoms, and also what it feels like. There's an attempt here by the poet to actually capture the experience—that gut-wrenching experience—of actually falling in love. This would be repeated by a number of other Hellenistic poets. It would become a staple, as the poets tried to deal with what it felt like to be in love, particularly to deal with that very human experience of being in love and acting stupidly. Let me read you one. This is from the poet Ruthenus. In his poem he says this:

> Melisias denies her love.
> But her body screams that it's been struck
> By a whole quiver of arrows.
> Her step is unsteady.
> She catches her breath in uneven gasps.
> There are dark, purple hollows beneath her eyes.
> But loves, by your fair wedded mother, Aphrodite,
> Burn the faithless girl until she cries aloud and says,
> "I burn!"

This is not just a love poem. It's a spell that's being cast by the poet, hoping to condemn the girl who, presumably, has not returned his love, so that she should burn and be consumed by this passion.

Part of the complexity of the Hellenistic Age arises from the fact that the artists and the thinkers of the age offered such different answers to the human dilemma. Philosophers were trying to teach people how to suppress their appetites. To control their passions. But sculptors, on the other hand, were interested in exploring these, particularly in exploring what the human body looked like when it was subjected to these. And the poets, too, were then exploring, through words, the sensation of losing your wits to passion.

So Apollonius' description of Medea, is really a kind of a literary antecedent of both Juliet and Lady Macbeth. This body overtaken. Apollonius, as much as Shakespeare, is fascinated by the inner turmoil we experience when our emotions are driven to fever pitch. In other words, when human experience is taken to the extreme.

The poem, the *Argonautica*, gave Apollonius a good opportunity to explore this particular problem. Because part of the story of Jason and Medea was that they were only able to escape successfully towards the end of their expedition by killing the brother of Medea. It's a gory episode, and it's going to allow the poet to think about or to explore what it is like when people have, in fact, become killers. That's the psychology he's exploring here.

I want to read you now the short episode that involves the death of Absyrtus, the brother of Medea. Then we'll look at the reaction that's described by Apollonius.

> Now when they had left Medea on Artemis' isle,
> In accord with the covenant,
> They separately beached their ships.
> Jason went to lie in ambush
> For Absyrtus.
> Then his companions, in turn.
> That he, deceived by these most dire promises
> Quickly crossed in his ship the swell of the sea.
> But in the gloom of night he stepped upon the sacred isle.
> Meeting her alone, he tested his sister with words,
> (Just as a tender child tests a stormy torrent
> Not even stalwart men can cross)
> To see if she had devised a seat for foreign men.
> The two of them agreed on every single thing.
> But then straightaway, Jason leapt from his dense ambush,
> Hefting his bared sword in his hand.

And now, follow this.

> Quickly the girl cast her eyes aside
> And covered them with her veil,
> That she not behold the brother's blood when he was struck.
> And Jason smote him
> Like a butcher that smites a mighty strong-horned bull,
> Sighting him near the temple,
> which the Breerye who dwell upon the opposite coast
> Had once built to Artemis.
>
> In its forecourt, he fell to his knees.
> At last, the hero, breathing his life away,
> Scooped up in his hands the black blood from the wound
> And crimsoned the silvery veil and robe of the girl,
> As she shrank away.
>
> With quick glance aslant,
> the implacable Fury saw the murderous deed they had done,
> and the hero, Jason, Aeson's son,

cut off the dead man's extremities
and thrice licked up his blood
and thrice spat the defilement from out his teeth,
just as a murderer might in rites to
expiate a slaying by treachery.
The clammy corpse, he hid in the earth.

There is nothing like that scene in epic prior to this time. Even though Greek plays had certainly been bloodthirsty, there's no doubt about that, most of the bloodthirsty action has taken place offstage. All we've had is a report on it. But here the description graphically brings it alive for us to witness in our mind's eye. So there is an interest here in a whole range of human experiences and emotions that Classical art, at least in the epic, has certainly not explored. Even so, we still haven't completed the full range of what the Alexandrian poets go after.

Epic we can follow fairly well. And Callimachus' poetry, too, we can find a lot in there that will resonate with us. The psychological drama of a woman torn between lover and family. We can understand a story like that. We've had stories like that in our own art. But there is a genre of Hellenistic poetry that is very difficult for us to follow. Very difficult for us to appreciate, because it's so unlike anything that we enjoy. That is pastoral poetry. Poetry set in the countryside. Poetry whose themes are bucolic, to do with shepherds and goatherds, and the singing competitions that they enjoy. The great master of this poetry was Theocritus. His poetry is, in fact, very difficult for us to fully appreciate.

First of all, we should begin by reading a little of it, just to get an idea of what it sounds like, at least in English. Then we'll try to talk about why it's difficult to follow. This is the *Sixth Idyll*, from Theocritus, involving two characters named Daphnis and Damoetis. The two of them are meant to be seen as cow-herds. So it's about a couple of cowboys out on the range. This, in Hellenistic poetry, is what two cowboys do when they meet. They sit down and they start to have a poetry competition. The first one's poem begins like this. (I won't read you the whole thing, because it gets a little hard to follow.) The first one pretends that his friend over here is Polyphemus, the old Cyclops, out of Greek myth. So he says:

Polyphemus!
Galatea with apples pelts your flocks and calls you cursed in
love.
And a goat-herd man.
And you don't look at her?
You wretch.
But sit and sweetly pipe.
But see again,
She pelts the bitch that guards your sheep.
And looks to see and barks.
The lovely waves that splash up on the sand reflect her
As she runs along the beach.

So this is an evocation of an earlier myth about Polyphemus and
Galatea, the nymph that he loved. That's the song sung by Daphnis.
Then his companion Demoetis sings back another song.

I saw her by Pan when she was pelting my flock.
With one sweet eye I saw her.
My only eye.
With which may I see forever,
To the end.

And he goes on about her being jealous and wasting away from the
sea, she's stung by love at my flocks and caves. And so forth. This is
very difficult poetry to understand. The Greek is literally easy to
understand, but it's certainly not realistic. We're not to imagine that
he's really accurately recording the words of two cowboys out on the
range. And the poet is certainly not psychological. It's not attempting
to explore the psychology of being a cowboy. It's not about the
isolation of taking care of your flocks and herds. No. This is poetry
that derives from a completely different tradition.

It is poetry that is largely concerned with the artifice of art. That is,
the artificiality of the poem. The skill of finding sounds and words,
literally syllable by syllable, that add up together to produce what the
Greeks would call *euphony*, a lovely sound. It is almost as if, when
we read that, what we're really reading is like the libretto of an
opera, but we're missing the music, so we can't really capture the
sound of it. Tightly arranged. Carefully conventional, these poems
are a delight, but they're a delight to an urbane society. A society
that enjoys the game of trying to recreate the countryside (and a

countryside, I might add, that they never set foot in), and populating it with an imaginary world. Making it a purified, sanitized landscape.

It bears the same relationship to the real world as Disney's Main Street does to a real town in the U.S.A. It doesn't reflect life, so much as project an imaginary picture of how life might be if all the anxieties of crime, disease and poverty were banished, and all one was left with was pure art.

For this reason, because it bears no relationship to the real countryside, pastoral poetry has rarely been produced by poets who actually came from the countryside. Rather, it is produced in the court. The court of King Ptolemy. It's produced in the most Hellenistic of institutions, the Museum and the Library. In this court, the *aulos*, the circle of Greeks and Macedonians who surrounded Ptolemy, it was considered enjoyable in this self-absorbed world, to create a pastoral fiction to replace the reality of the countryside, which was actually populated, not by Greek poets, but by Egyptian peasants.

It really is very similar, if you will, to imagining Marie Antoinette dressed up as a shepherdess, with three little sheep which she kept on the grounds of Versailles, pretending to be a shepherdess, but really having nothing to do with the lives of real peasants, who all lived outside the walls of Versailles.

So pastoral poetry is very difficult for us to appreciate, particularly because we don't listen to the Greek the way the Greeks would have, with that care and attention. However, there's more in Theocritus that's worth looking at. Some of his poems are really quite remarkable because they represent a new development in Hellenistic poetry and in Greek poetry in general, and that is, poems that are almost eavesdropping on the conversations of ordinary people. Now, once again, he will render this into art by writing the poems in verse. But what he captures here is the prattle of cosmopolitan daily life in Alexandria.

A very famous example of this is the poem which deals with two women, Gorgo and Praxinoa, who have a conversation. What we really get in this poem is something like a dramatic dialogue. You could almost have actors playing this out. It's almost like the script of a play. What happens in it is that you get two ordinary women, not figures from myth, not Medea, not the sorts of figures that Euripides and Sophocles would deal with, but rather ordinary ladies meeting. When for example, Gorgo comes to the house of a friend Praxinoa. She's come inside from a great hubbub outside, and she says:

> I was out of my mind to come,
> What with the crowd and the horses!
> I scarcely got to your place alive, Praxinoa.
> Soldiers' boots, men in military cloaks,
> Everywhere you looked.
> And the road went on forever.
> And your house was always further and further along.

It's like eavesdropping on a telephone conversation. The women then decide to go off to King Ptolemy's palace, where there's going to be a performance of a play, called the *Adonis*, or a recital, at least. So in this poem what we're getting is the preparation to go off to listen to this. So Praxinoa turns to her slave and this is like something taken right out of real life.

> Bring me my coat and my straw hat.
> Put them on properly.
> [then she turns to the baby]
> I'm not going to take you, baby.
> Oh boo. Horsey-bye.
> You cry all you like.
> No need for you to be maimed.
> Let's go Bridget,
> Take the little one, and play with him.
> Call in the dog.
> and lock the door.

This is a kind of realism that Greek poetry has never had before. It goes on with a wonderful description of them going through the streets, and being almost knocked over by the king's cavalry as they come charging through, and then gradually making their way into the palace, and getting tickets to go in. And then we actually get the singer singing this song, the *Adonis*, this recital. And of course, it's a perfect example of the kind of poetry that the court enjoyed. It's a story about Adonis, who's the lover of Aphrodite. No Egyptian would have had the faintest idea of what was going on. It's like an operatic recital.

So this interest in what's going on in everyday life, and then trying to transform that into something artistic, rather than going for what was grand and heroic, and something that had been found in myth—that represents the whole new spirit of the Hellenistic Age. There's one particular poem that I would like to then finish on, which I think sums this up. This is from the poet Philodemus. He says:

> I've been in love.
> Who hasn't?
> I went out and got drunk.
> Who hasn't?
> I was out of my mind.
> Who did it?
> Some god, no doubt.
> Well, let it go.
> White hairs come in place of the black.
> It's a sign of the age of sense.
> When it was time to play, I played.
> Now that it isn't, I'll try to put my mind
> To better things.

A whole new world being explored by the Greek poets, producing some poetry that is marvelous, some poetry that is almost impenetrable. What it all has in common is that it is Greek poetry written for Greeks. And exclusively Greek. If one compares the produce, say, of the French or the British colonies, where we now have a whole new literature, we find that in the Greek world, there is nothing comparable. There is nothing from the indigenous people. Instead, these poets are working entirely within the parameters of Greek culture, reacting to their own cultural heritage in the work of Homer, the lyric poets and the dramatists of an earlier age.

Timeline

359	Philip II comes to the Macedonian throne.
356	Birth of Alexander.
338	Philip and Alexander defeat the Greeks at Chaeroneia.
336	Assassination of Philip and accession of Alexander the Great.
334	Battle of the Granicus River.
333	Battle of Issus.
331	Alexander's visit to the oracle of Siwah; Battle of Gaugemala.
330	Death of Darius, King of Persia.
329	Alexander's Bactrian campaign.
326	Mutiny of Alexander's army at the Hyphasis River.
325	Alexander's return through the Gedrosian desert.
324	Mutiny and banquet of reconciliation at Opis.
323	Alexander dies in Babylon; beginning of the Wars of the Diadochi.
321	Death of Perdiccas during campaign against Ptolemy; division of Alexander's empire at Triparadeisus.
317	Murder of Philip Arrhidaeus by Olympias.
315	Coalition against Antigonus.
311	Peace treaty signed by Antigonus and the other Diadochi.

310	Cassander murders Alexander IV.
306	Ptolemy defeated off Cyprus; Diadochi assume the title of kings; Seleucus cedes eastern borders to Chandragupta in exchange for war elephants.
301	Death of Antigonus at Ipsus.
283	Death of Ptolemy I; death of Demetrius, son of Antigonus.
281	Death of Seleucus I; defeat and death of Lysimachus (Battle of Corupedium).
280	Pyrrhus of Epirus crosses to southern Italy.
274	Withdrawal of Pyrrhus from Italy.
272	Sack of Tarentum by Rome.
264–241	First Punic War.
263	Eumenes I succeeds Philetaerus (Pergamum).
246–241	Third Syrian War (Ptolemy III versus Seleucus II).
241–197	Reign of Attalus I (Pergamum).
240	Diodotus of Bactria assumes title of king.
238–227	Attalid victories against Celts (Galatians).
229	First Illyrian War.
219	Second Illyrian War.
218–202	Second Punic War.
217	Battle of Raphia.
215	Alliance of Philip V (Macedon) and Hannibal.

214	Roman alliance with Aetolia; First Macedonian War.
212–205	Eastern expedition of Antiochus III.
202	Battle of Zama (Roman victory over Hannibal).
199–196	Second Macedonian War.
197	Defeat of Philip V at Battle of Cynoscephalae.
196	Roman declaration of the freedom of the Greeks.
191	Defeat of Antiochus III by Rome at Thermopylae.
189	Defeat of Antiochus III by Rome at Magnesia.
188	Peace of Apamea.
168	Antiochus IV receives Roman ultimatum during campaign against Ptolemy; Battle of Pydna; partitioning of Macedon by Rome.
148	Macedon reduced to status of a Roman province.
146	Destruction of Corinth and Carthage by Rome.
133	Death of Attalus III of Pergamum; creation of province of Asia Minor.
96	Cyrenaica bequeathed to Rome.
75	Bithynia bequeathed to Rome.
66–62	Eastern campaigns of Pompey.
48	Defeat of Pompey at Pharsalus.
48–47	Caesar in Alexandria.
44	Assassination of Caesar.

31 ....Battle of Actium; defeat of Marc
Antony and Cleopatra.

Glossary

akatalepsia: Sceptic doctrine that holds that absolutely certain knowledge is impossible.

amicitia: Roman term for friendship; often applied to Rome's alliances with foreign kings and states.

Asclepieum: Any sanctuary of the healing god Asclepius, often including buildings for the diagnosis and treatment of disease.

asylia: Inviolability, especially the right of sanctuaries to be left unmolested, formally recognized by other states.

ataraxia: Imperturbability, a state of calm sought by many Hellenistic philosophical schools.

aulos: The court of a Hellenistic king, including his advisors, military officers, and officials.

basilikoi laoi: Royal peasants, i.e., peasants living on and tied to estates owned by the king.

catochi: Recluses. Individuals who withdrew from life in the world at large to live wholly within a temple precinct.

choregos: Citizen responsible for paying for a dramatic production at a religious festival.

dioiketes: A high-ranking government official responsible usually for taxation and financial affairs.

epiphanes: An epithet applied to Antiochus IV meaning "god made manifest."

epoche: A term from Sceptic philosophy asserting the need to suspend judgment because of the impossibility of absolute knowledge.

euergesia: Benefaction. The institution of public assistance offered by the wealthy to Greek states, especially in times of crisis.

euergetes: Benefactor. A term applied to wealthy citizens who assisted a city with gifts of food or money; often adopted as a royal title.

gymnasia: Cultural institutions, common in Greek cities, combining athletic training, poetic performances, and philosophy lectures.

gymnasiarch: Official in charge of the gymnasium, appointed by the city to oversee the training of young men.

heroon: A shrine dedicated to a man of heroic, i.e., semi-divine, status.

hoplite: Heavily armed Greek infantry soldier.

koine: "Common" Greek, the dialect of Greek based on the Attic (Athenian) dialect, common throughout the eastern Mediterranean.

laoi: The people, but usually used in Hellenistic times to refer to non-Greek peasants.

logistes: An official of the Hellenistic kings primarily concerned with record-keeping and accounts.

megalopsychus: An Aristotelian doctrine that identified the great man as the possessor of a "great soul."

oecumene: A general term referring to the sphere of Greek culture and language extending throughout the eastern Mediterranean.

palaestra: The wrestling ground of a gymnasium where young men took their exercise and underwent military training.

pezetairoi: Literally "foot companions." Elite infantry battalions of the Macedonian army.

phalanx: The massed formation of heavily armed infantrymen, equipped with pikes, forming the core of the Hellenistic armies.

philoi: Literally "friends." The noble companions of a Hellenistic king; the core of his military and administrative staff.

philoromaios: A term increasingly adopted from the 2nd century on, meaning "Rome lover," used by Rome's allies to advertise their friendship with Rome.

pothos: A popular expression in the ancient literature about Alexander meaning "yearning" or "desire," often linked to Alexander's divine status.

stoas: Open colonnaded buildings popular in the Greek world as public buildings for commerce, judicial hearings, and civic administration.

technitai: A general term for craftsmen but often used specifically for the guild of actors known as the technitai of Dionysos.

trierarchs: Citizens who undertook the task of manning and equipping a trireme or warship.

tyche: Fortune. A popular deity of the Hellenistic Age; often associated with either personal destiny or the fate of an entire community.

Bibliography

Badian, Ernst, *Foreign Clientelae (260–70 B.C.)* (Oxford, 1958).

Bernard, Paul, "Aï Khanum on the Oxus," *PBA* 53 (1967): 71–95.

Borza, Eugene N., *In the Shadow of Olympus: The Emergence of Macedon* (Princeton, 1990).

Bowman, Alan K., *Egypt after the Pharaohs, 323 B.C.–A.D. 642* (Berkeley, 1986).

Canfora, Luciano, *The Library of Alexandria: A Wonder of the Ancient World* (Berkeley, 1990).

Eddy, Samuel K., *The King Is Dead* (Lincoln, 1961).

Errington, R. Malcolm, *A History of Macedonia* (Berkeley, 1990).

Fowler, Barbara Hughes, *Hellenistic Poetry: An Anthology* (Madison, Wisconsin, 1990).

Fox, Robin Lane, *Alexander the Great* (London, 1973).

Grant, Michael, *Cleopatra* (London, 1972).

Green, Peter, *From Alexander to Actium* (Berkeley, 1991).

Gruen, Erich S., *Culture and National Identity in Republican Rome* (Cornell, 1992).

————, "Hellenism and Persecution: Antiochus IV and the Jews," in *Hellenistic History and Culture*, ed. P. Green. (Berkeley, 1993).

————, *The Hellenistic World and the Coming of Rome*, 2 vols. (Berkeley, 1984).

————, *Studies in Greek Culture and Roman Policy* (Berkeley, 1990).

Hägg, Thomas, *The Novel in Antiquity* (Berkeley, 1983).

Hammond, N. G. L., *Philip of Macedon* (Baltimore, 1994).

Hansen, E. V., *The Attalids of Pergamon* (Ithaca, 1971).

Harris, William V., *War and Imperialism in Republican Rome, 320–70 B.C.* (Oxford, 1979).

Herman, Gabriel, "The Court Society of the Hellenistic Age," in P. Cartledge et al. (eds.), *Hellenistic Constructs: Essays in Culture, History, and Historiography* (Berkeley, 1997).

Inwood, Brad, and L. P. Gerson, *Hellenistic Philosophy: Introductory Readings* (Indianapolis, 1988).

Lloyd, Geoffrey, *Greek Science after Aristotle* (New York, 1973).

Long, A. A., *Hellenistic Philosophy: Stoics, Epicurans, Sceptics* (Berkeley, 1986).

Narain, A. K., *The Indo-Greeks* (Oxford, 1957).

Pearson, Lionel, *The Lost Histories of Alexander the Great*, American Philological Association Philological Monographs 20, New York, 1960.

Piper, L. J., *Spartan Twilight* (New Rochelle, 1985).

Pollitt, J. J., *Art in the Hellenistic Age* (Cambridge, 1986).

Price, S. R. F., *Rituals and Power* (Cambridge, 1984).

Reardon, Brain P., ed., *Collected Ancient Greek Novels* (Berkeley, 1989).

Roisman, Joseph, *Alexander the Great: Ancient and Modern Perspectives* (Lexington, Mass., 1995).

Rostovtzeff, M. I., *The Social and Economic History of the Hellenistic World*, 3 vols. (Oxford, 1941).

Sherwin-White, Susan, and Amelie Kuhrt, *From Sardis to Samarkhand* (Berkeley, 1993).

Stoneman, Richard, ed., *The Greek Alexander Romance* (Harmondsworth, 1991).

Tcherikover, Viktor, *Hellenistic Civilization and the Jews* (New York, 1959).

Thompson, Dorothy, *Memphis under the Ptolemies* (Princeton, 1988).

Veyne, Paul, *Bread and Circuses: Historical Sociology and Political Pluralism* (London, 1976).

Walbank, F. W., *Polybius* (Berkeley, 1972).

Notes

Alexander the Great and the Hellenistic Age
Part II

Professor Jeremy McInerney

PUBLISHED BY:

THE TEACHING COMPANY
4840 Westfields Boulevard, Suite 500
Chantilly, Virginia 20151-2299
1-800-TEACH-12
Fax—703-378-3819
www.teach12.com

ISBN 1-56585-856-5

Jeremy McInerney, Ph.D.

Associate Professor, Department of Classical Studies
University of Pennsylvania

Jeremy McInerney received his Ph.D. from the University of California, Berkeley, in 1992. He was the Wheeler Fellow at the American School of Classical Studies at Athens and has excavated in Israel, at Corinth, and on Crete. Since 1992, he has been teaching Greek history at the University of Pennsylvania, where he held the Laura Jan Meyerson Term Chair in the Humanities from 1994 to 1998. He is currently an associate professor in the Department of Classical Studies and chair of the Graduate Group in the Art and Archaeology of the Mediterranean World. Professor McInerney also serves on the Managing Committee of the American School of Classical Studies at Athens.

Professor McInerney's research interests include topography, epigraphy, and historiography. He has published articles in a variety of academic journals including *Greek, Roman and Byzantine Studies*, the *American Journal of Archaeology*, *Hesperia*, and *California Studies in Classical Antiquity*. In 1997, he was an invited participant at a colloquium on ethnicity in the ancient world, hosted by the Center for Hellenic Studies in Washington. His book, *The Folds of Parnassos: Land and Ethnicity in Ancient Phokis*, is a study of state formation and ethnic identity in the Archaic and Classical periods, and it was published by the University of Texas Press in 1999.

Table of Contents
Alexander the Great and the Hellenistic Age
Part II

Alexander the Great and the Hellenistic Age

Scope:

This series of lectures examines a crucial but often neglected period in the history of the ancient world, the age ushered in by the extraordinary conquests of Alexander the Great. In the opening lectures, we explore the enigma of Alexander, son of a brilliant father, yet always at odds with the man whom he succeeded. We trace his early campaigns against the Persians and follow him to Egypt, where he was acclaimed as the son of god. We look at his career after this and find in him a blend of greatness and madness as he strove to replace the Persian empire of the Achaemenid dynasty with a new, mixed ruling class of Macedonians and Persians.

Alexander's death in 323 B.C. ushered in a period of catastrophic change as ambitious warlords carved up Alexander's realm into their own separate empires, especially Seleucid Syria and Ptolemaic Egypt. In a series of lectures, we look at how a small ruling class of Macedonian nobles established their rule from the eastern Mediterranean to the Hindu Kush. In the Nile valley, the Ptolemies played the role of pharaohs and were treated by their subjects as gods. At the same time, however, their capital, Alexandria, was cut off from Egypt and run by Greek bureaucrats. Greek culture flourished here in the museum and library, and the Ptolemies were great patrons of the arts.

In the Seleucid empire, the rulers also built Greek cities, such as Antioch, but in older regions, including Mesopotamia, they too were ready to be worshipped as living gods. On the edges of the Hellenistic world, in places as far away as Afghanistan and Pakistan, Greek cities grew up around trading posts and military settlements. Here, philosophy and literature from old Greece went hand in hand with gymnasiums and theatres to plant Greek culture far from the Mediterranean. By military and cultural conquest, then, much of central Asia was incorporated into the Greek world.

Despite the geographic extent of this civilization, we shall see that the heartland remained the eastern Mediterranean. It was here, in such new cities as Alexandria and Pergamum and such old ones as Athens, that Greek culture developed its distinctive Hellenistic appearance. Philosophy became more academic, as different schools of philosophy emerged. Stoicism, epicureanism, and skepticism all looked for ways to teach people to avoid the emotional upheavals of life in an age of anxiety. At the same time, art rejoiced in exploring the very same turmoil of the age. Hellenistic sculptors looked at the old, the young, the ugly, and the tortured instead of merely fashioning images of the perfect athlete. Novelists also played with themes of the reversal of fortune in the lives of their characters, because such tumult was part of the experiences of so many people. Piracy, brigandage, physical hardship, and the supreme power of great kings were all realities of the age and left their marks on ordinary people.

As we shall see, these conditions helped spawn a vital interest in magic, spells, and incantations and in religions that offered people the promise of redemption and salvation. The cults of Isis, Serapis, and Cybele all grew in popularity throughout the Hellenistic world. This was the climate of the world in which Christianity was born.

Although the Hellenistic Age would result in some of the greatest accomplishments in Greek culture, especially in the poetry of Callimachus, Theocritus, and Apollonius, the political power of the age was overshadowed by the growth of Rome. Hence, we conclude the lectures with a study of the growth of Roman power, its expansion into the eastern Mediterranean, and the inevitable clash of Greek and Roman civilizations. As we shall see, Rome conquered, but Rome would be forever changed by the contact with Greek culture. In the words of the Roman poet Horace, "Captured Greece took captive her captor."

Lecture Thirteen
The Greek Novel

Scope:

The late Hellenistic world witnessed the emergence of a new literary form that we take for granted: the novel. Written in prose and filled with adventures that take place in contemporary settings, these stories reflect many of the major concerns of the age and are an invaluable guide to the spirit of the Hellenistic world.

Outline

I. The surviving novels, or romances, as they are often called in English, actually date to the early period of the Roman Empire. In terms of culture, however, the eastern Mediterranean remained Hellenistic after the coming of Rome; it would be artificial to divorce the Greek novel from its Hellenistic setting.

II. Five novels survive.

   A. Chariton of Aphrodisias composed his love story, entitled *Callirhoe*, toward the end of the 1st century B.C. It is the first historical novel, set several centuries before it was written.

   B. Xenophon composed a tale entitled *Anthia and Habrocomes*, set in the region around Ephesus and Rhodes. It included many of the common elements of these tales: two young lovers, pirates, shipwreck, and the eventual triumph of the lovers are all found here.

   C. Achilles Tatius, according to tradition, eventually became a Christian and a bishop, but not before trying his hand at a similar story about a pair of lovers: Clitophon and Leucippe.

   D. By far the best known and most widely read in later periods is the novel by Longus, about whom we know nothing except that he wrote *Daphnis and Chloe*.
   1. This novel is remarkable for its treatment of the sexual awakening of the teenage lovers.
   2. Longus wrote for an audience that could recognize allusions to many other genres and writers, including Thucydidean history and Hellenistic pastoral poetry.

E. Heliodorus produced a work entitled *The Ethiopian Story*.

    1. Like the other novels, this work revolves around the story of a pair of star-crossed lovers.

    2. Digressions and subplots separate the lovers as the action moves from Ethiopia to Delphi and back to Egypt, reflecting the new geographic realities of the age in a kind of fictional travelogue.

III. The novels share many patterns and motifs, as well as a common outlook on the unpredictability of life. All the stories concern young lovers. All the stories could be termed adventures.

    A. Sex, in various forms, lurks beneath the surface. Sometimes it is in the sexual awakening of the couple, the threat of rape endured by the heroine, or the sexual initiation of the young man.

        1. Daphnis, after kissing Chloe, falls into a reverie, trying to understand what has happened to him.

        2. His interior monologue is reminiscent of the description of Medea's passion in the *Argonautica*. The novels display the Hellenistic world's fascination with art as a vehicle for expressing the inner life of a human being.

    B. Related to this theme is an interest in extreme states of mind. Just as Hellenistic sculpture emphasizes contortion and pain as natural states of the body, so too do the novels give us men and women pushed into emotional torment.

        1. When a Greek general named Charmides cannot contain his desire for Leucippe, she falls into an epileptic fit. With her bloodshot eyes and thrashing, she appears to have been possessed by some kind of madness.

        2. Traditionally, such possession is a religious state of ecstasy, but now it is treated as a human affliction.

    C. Another common theme of the novels is the unpredictability of life, which is often suggested by the sudden appearance of pirates.

        1. In Xenophon's *Ephesian Tale*, for example, Habracomes and Anthia are happily sailing from Rhodes to Ephesus when the hero has a dream in which a huge woman clothed in scarlet sets fire to his ship. She is, in fact, Tyche, or Fortune, and the dream portends a pirate attack the next day. As they are being led off amid a scene of carnage, one of the captives declares, "blessed are those who will happily die before they have become slaves to robbers."

2. Frequently, the human actors believe that the gods have acted capriciously, and that they, the humans, have no control over their lives. When Chaereas sees the tomb in which he expected to find Callirhoe empty, he cries, "which of the gods is my rival for Callirhoe, and has spirited her away and keeps her against her will, forced by a stronger fate?"

3. The novels reflect a world of uncertainty. The gods cannot be relied on. Although they communicate to us in oracles and dreams, their intentions are mysterious, and we are frequently the victims as much as the beneficiaries of their involvement in the world. The narrator of *Callirhoe* declares, "against Fortune alone, human reason is powerless. She is a spirit who likes to win!"

IV. The novels are linked in the way they reflect the contemporary world.

A. The novels are confined to the world of the eastern Mediterranean, from Syracuse in Sicily to Alexandria. Any places mentioned beyond this region are really fantasy realms.

B. Only in religion are non-Greek cultures a part of the world of the romances. Even in these instances, the novels portray a Hellenized religion in which such figures as Isis have been assimilated to Aphrodite.

C. Non-Greek cultures are seen as either inferior or a threat. Pirates may be Phoenician or Egyptian, but the heroes are clearly Greek.

D. When Clitophon is captured, he complains to the gods that he cannot even talk to his captors: "In what language should we implore them?"

E. Kings and courts do not figure in the romances. Instead, power is most often in the hands of pirate chiefs and brigands, many of whom style themselves "kings." Their world is an inversion of the Hellenistic court.

V. The novels present a view of the Hellenistic world from the bottom up. Power is capricious, law is a joke, and fate is ever ready to dump you. The community exists, but the world of the romance is one of scared and vulnerable individuals. An interest in individual psychology may be what makes the Hellenistic world seem so familiar to us.

Suggested Reading:

T. Hägg, *The Novel in Antiquity.*

B. P. Reardon, ed., *Collected Ancient Greek Novels.*

Questions to Consider:

1. Why do the Greek novels rely so heavily on coincidence and surprise to advance the plot?
2. How convincing are the principal characters in the novels?

Lecture Thirteen—Transcript
The Greek Novel

Welcome back to our thirteenth lecture, now, in the series on Alexander the Great and the Hellenistic World. We have had an opportunity in previous lectures to move away from the political history of the Hellenistic Age after Alexander the Great had conquered much of what had been the Persian Empire, and we've now had an opportunity to look at the cultural developments of the period. What we've been stressing is that the 19th century view of Hellenism (the Hellenistic Age) as a period of decadence, a culture that couldn't measure up to the heights of the Classical period, is really an incorrect way of seeing the age. What we've been trying to chart in the cultural history of the Hellenistic period is a great ferment and a great vitality in the work of artists working in different genres and different spheres. So, for example, in the realm of sculpture, we've been able to see how Hellenistic sculptors moved beyond the Classical ideal with its Olympian perfection and its figure of distant gods and heroes, and was able to grapple with real people and to show the old and the ugly and the infirm and the twisted. Exploring a kind of baroque mentality, vigorously interested in all aspects of life and expression.

We've also seen in the poetry of the age that similarly, the artists moved off in new directions, writing interesting works for the courts of the Hellenistic kings, such as their idyllic pastoral poetry, but also infusing the epic with a whole new sensibility, in the case of Apollonius, and exploring the interior life of individual men and women. Psychological works, if you will.

In the area of literature, the Hellenistic world is responsible for another remarkable innovation, and it's one I'd like to talk about today. It's the genre known as the Greek novel, or the Greek romance. Customarily, we think of novels as being a European art form that really developed from the Renaissance and later, into the Modern period. We might go back to, say, Cervantes' *Don Quixote*, or for the English novel we might read early novels such as *Moll Flanders*. It often comes as a surprise to people to find out that the Greeks, more than 1500 years before the modern European novel, had been writing works that really fit into the same genre.

When I say "novel," or in this instance, "romance," also, I'm referring to long works (hundreds of pages), written in prose. These are stories that are full of adventures. They are set in the contemporary world. They are particularly valuable for us to study because they give us a unique insight into the spirit of the Hellenistic Age.

The reason that I say that, is that these novels were widely read and immensely popular. The concerns that they express, the themes that crop up in these novels time and again, are the concerns and the themes of the age itself.

First of all, just a pedantic note I should add, is that most of these novels actually come to us from the Roman period, that is to say, after the end of the period B.C. and into the period we commonly term A.D. And yet, we can still refer to them as Hellenistic in the sense that the political transition at the end of the Hellenistic Age, with the coming of Rome and the establishment of Roman provinces in the East, did not end the Greek culture that had already been established there by Alexander and his successors. So even though chronologically I'm often referring to works that date from the 1st and 2nd century A.D., they are certainly Hellenistic in spirit. Hellenistic in feel, if you will. Hellenistic in setting, usually. And they are an insight into the culture of the Greek East, in both the Hellenistic and in the Roman periods.

There are five novels that people read most commonly. I'd like to begin by outlining just who wrote these, when they date to and what they deal with. Then we'll look in more detail at the themes and the substance of these various novels.

The first one that we have was written by an author named Chariton of Aphrodisias. Aphrodisias, a beautiful city in southern Asia Minor, which flourished under the Romans. He entitled his story *Callirhoe*, though like many of the Hellenistic romances, it really should be named for both Callirhoe and her lover, Chaereas. It's a story of star-crossed lovers, if you will. It was written toward the end of the 1st century B.C., as best we can tell. It's an interesting work, because it's actually set dramatically at the very end of the 5th and the beginning of the 4th century B.C. So it is, really, the first historical novel, as well as being a romance. It begins and ends at Syracuse, the Greek city located on Sicily. But in the course of their adventures, the lovers move as far east as Babylon. So it incorporates the geography of the entire eastern Mediterranean, as well as regions inland, too.

The second of the novels we have was written by an author called Xenophon, not to be confused with Xenophon the student of Socrates and the author of the *Anabasis (The March Up-Country),* but rather another Xenophon, whose tale is sometimes called *The Tale of Anthia and Habrocomes* and is also referred to quite often as *The Ephesian Tale,* because it is set around the city of Ephesus, again on the eastern side of the Aegean, and smack-bang in the middle of realm that we would regard as being the geographic center of the Hellenistic world, namely the Aegean and the eastern Mediterranean. It's a work that has many of the common elements that we find in the Hellenistic romances. It has two young lovers. They will be separated, and they will eventually be joined again. In their travails, they are often attacked by pirates. They're subjected to shipwrecks. Eventually true love will conquer.

This theme of young lovers being challenged, being torn apart and then being brought back together again, is probably the most common theme, the most common plot line, really, running through the Hellenistic romances.

The third novel that we have was written by an author named Achilles Tatius. He is particularly interesting because, after trying his hand at one of these Hellenistic romances, the story of another pair of star-crossed lovers, Clitophon and Leucippe, Achilles Tatius, according to tradition, after this then became a Christian, and finally, a bishop. So everyone in the Hellenistic world and then later in the Roman world was in on the act of writing these Hellenistic romances.

By far the best-known of all the Hellenistic romances, a work that exerted an enormous influence on later writers, particularly in France, and in England to a certain extent, is the novel written by Longus, known as *Daphnis and Chloe.* We know absolutely nothing about the author, aside from his name. But the novel really is one of the most remarkable works that one will read in any language. For a start, it's remarkable because of its interest in and its treatment of the sexual awakening of its young protagonists, Daphnis and Chloe.

The way in which the work deals with this is particularly interesting, because at times it is almost coy. At other times it is ironic. At certain times it is quite gentle. But at other times it's almost mocking and humorous. This was written for a sophisticated audience, despite its wide popularity. It was written for people who understood allusions to other works written by Greek authors at earlier periods of Greek history, and authors working in a range of different genres. So there are mock allusions to, for example, Thucydides' History, and there are certainly references to Hellenistic pastoral poetry. In fact, Daphnis and Chloe come together as a result of a kind of a competition between Daphnis and another shepherd, in just the same manner as we've seen competitions between shepherds in the Theocritean pastoral poems that we have looked at in other lectures. So it's a work that alludes to other genres, both of earlier Greek literature and of contemporary literature, as well. We'll return to it in a moment.

The fifth of the well-known Hellenistic romances is that of Heliodorus. It is a work entitled *The Ethiopian Story*. Like all the other novels, it again deals with a story of a pair of star-crossed lovers. And, like the other works, it has these digressions thrown in. Subplots, so that the lovers are separated at various points and the action then moves from different parts of the Hellenistic world such as Delphi and Egypt into areas like Ethiopia. The exotic outer margins of the Hellenistic world.

This common phenomenon of these works as, in a way, fictional travelogues, I think, suggests the fascination of the Hellenistic world with the new geographic realities of the age. That is that Hellenism and Greek settlers had moved way beyond the eastern Mediterranean. So there were many areas which the Greeks had known about for hundreds of years, but only really as romantic names. The Amazons. The Indians. The Ethiopians. But now we're having writers giving their audience a romantic story that includes these areas, partly to spice up the story, and to pique the interest of people who found the outer regions of the Hellenistic world exotic and fascinating.

The novels share many motifs and patterns. There is a common outlook that runs through each of them. That is, quite simply, the unpredictability of life. It's this theme which, I think, runs through Hellenistic culture, and is typified by these stories. The stories all concern young lovers, and the stories are all what we would term adventures. So they're there to entertain people. But they're also there to express an anxiety widely felt in the Hellenistic Age, that the scale of things was so large, that the geographic spread of things was so large that the old certainties were gone. That life was no longer simply a matter of a small city-state or a small village. That you could be abducted by pirates. That your life could change at a moment's notice. That you could end up living hundreds of miles—thousands of miles—away from the place you were actually born. People have said that the Hellenistic Age is a little like our age in that there is a greater sense of rootlessness, and people are not as connected as they had been generations earlier, to the same familiar places.

Sex, in various forms, lurks beneath the surface of many of the stories. Sometimes it's the sexual awakening of the couple, which can be treated quite gently or quite humorously. But at other times it's a much more violent expression. Often it's the threat of rape of the heroine. Or it may be the rough sexual initiation of the young man in the couple. I think in exploring this, what the Hellenistic novelists are doing is something that we've seen already in the work of Apollonius. They're trying to explore the human soul when it's in moments of great emotion. Heightened emotion. When human beings are facing experiences for the first time, that they've never faced before.

So, for example, in Longus' *Daphnis and Chloe*, much of the first book deals with the circumstances around the first kiss between the young lovers, and the response that they have to this. Here is what Daphnis has to say in an interior monologue after he's finally kissed his beautiful young girlfriend, who eventually he will marry (Chloe). He says:

> Whatever is Chloe's kiss doing to me? Her lips are softer than roses and her mouth is sweeter than honey. But her kiss hurts more than the sting of a bee. I've often kissed kids, and I've often kissed newborn puppies and the calf that Dorcon gave her. But this kiss is something quite new. My breath's coming in gasps. My heart's jumping up and down. My soul is melting away. But all the same, I want to kiss her again. Oh what an unlucky victory. And what a strange disease. I don't even know what to call it. Had Chloe drunk poison just before she kissed me? If so, how did she manage not to be killed? Hear how the nightingales are singing and my pipe is silent. Look how the kids are frisking about and I'm sitting still. Look how the flowers are blooming, and I'm not making any garlands. Yes, the violets and the hyacinths are

in flower, but Daphnis is withering away. Is Dorcon going to seem better-looking than I am, after all?

So he's emotionally overwhelmed by this experience of the first time of kissing a girl, trying to understand what's happened to him. It's this kind of interior monologue that's so reminiscent of the passage that we saw earlier in Apollonius' *Argonautica*, when he was describing the passion that Medea feels for Jason. So the novel, like Apollonius' epic poetry, displays the Hellenistic world's fascination with art being a vehicle now for expressing the interior emotional life of human beings. Of trying to chart that interior life and to explore it and to give artistic expression to it.

Related to this, as we've seen before, is an interest in extreme states of mind. We charted this particularly in the lecture on Hellenistic sculpture, where we saw the artists almost torturing some of their figures, as they are in contortion, and as they are feeling terrible pain. So, too, the novels give us men and women who are pushed to the brink of emotional torment. This is graphically expressed in Achilles Tatius' work, when at one point a Greek general by the name of Charmides, who has fallen in love with Leucippe, has been trying to press his claim on her. The reaction that she has is one that is so physically overwhelming that she actually is thrown into a fit. And in typical fashion for a Hellenistic novelist, Achilles Tatius will give a graphic description of this.

> We were still looking for a plan when a man rushed in, greatly disturbed, and told us that Leucippe, while walking abroad, had suddenly fallen down, her eyes rolling. So we jumped up and ran to her and found her lying on the ground. I went up to her and asked her what was the matter, but no sooner had she seen me, and her eyes, all bloodshot, she struck me in the face. And when Menelaus tried to constrain her, she kicked him. This made us understand that she was afflicted with some kind of madness. So we forcibly seized her and tried to hold her. She struggled against us, however, and cared nothing about what a woman doesn't want to be seen.

So she's thrashing around, and her clothes are coming up, and they can see her naked. As a result a great hubbub arose in the tent, so that the general hurried in and saw what was happening. At first he suspected that this illness of hers was but a pretence against his advances, and looked suspiciously at Menelaus. When he saw the truth, as he soon did, he too, grieved, and felt pity for her. And eventually, of course, she will recover from this.

So with her bloodshot eyes and with her thrashing, she appears to be possessed by a kind of madness. It's almost the language we would expect describing a priestess, who is being possessed by the god, at Delphi, for example. Traditionally, this kind of possession is a religious ecstasy. But now it's being presented here, not as an affliction from the gods, because the gods wish to speak through us, as an oracle, but a human condition. The reaction of a woman who is trying to resist the advances of a man who she doesn't like.

A common theme of the novels is the unpredictability of life. In the novels, this is often suggested by the plot device of having pirates suddenly appear out of nowhere. In Xenophon's *Ephesian Tale*, for example, the hero Harbracomes and his girlfriend Anthia are happily sailing along from Rhodes to Ephesus, when our hero has a dream in which a huge woman, clothed in scarlet, sets fire to the ship that he's sailing on. She, in fact, represents Tyche, or as the Romans would later call her, Fortuna. She is the spirit who has come to tell him that his life is about to take a drastic turn for the worse. What the dream portends, in fact, is a pirate attack the very next day. Just when things are going along well, you never know when change is going to happen.

This, of course, had been a theme in Greek literature for many years. There was the well-known story in Herodotus about Polycrates, the tyrant of Samos, who was so fortunate that he wanted to avert disaster by actually causing himself misfortune. He'd taken his gold ring off, thrown it into the water, only to find a fisherman bring a fish to table a few days later, with the gold ring inside. A sign from the gods that he couldn't avert the misfortune awaiting him by trying to create his own misfortune. So the Greeks have had, for a long time, the notion of the mutability of life, the unpredictability of life. In the Hellenistic Age, this becomes a veritable fixation.

People were clearly worried that, at any moment, their prosperous, stable lives could be overturned. They might be killed or carted off by pirates, sold at market and end their life as a slave in someone else's household. When one considers, in fact, the hundreds of thousands of people who did move from the eastern Mediterranean to Rome as a result of Rome's conquests, it's not an anxiety that was unreasonable. Many people did begin life happy, secure and prosperous, and ended up slaves, hundreds of miles away from where they had been born. During the scene of carnage as the pirates attack Habracomes and Anthia, one of the captives declares, "Blessed are those who will happily die before they become slaves to robbers."

That's not merely a literary line. I think that is an expression of a genuine anxiety of many, many people. Frequently the human actors in these stories believe that the gods have acted capriciously. The gods really don't care about them, at all. And that they, the humans, have no control over their lives whatsoever. This anxiety, again, is not merely a story device or a plot device. It's a real expression of anxiety. This was an age in which every household had a small shrine, and where people had charms that they carried with them to avert ill fortune. Where people tried to place curses on their opponents and their enemies. Little lead tablets, which they would wrap up and drop into a well. It is a suspicious age, and people don't know whether the old traditional gods are still on their side any more or not. When Chaereas sees the tomb of his beloved Callirhoe empty, he cries, "Which of the gods is my rival for Callirhoe, and has spirited her away and keeps her against her will? Forced by a stronger Fate."

"Forced by a stronger fate." That could be a tagline summarizing the Hellenistic Age and its attitude towards the gods and towards destiny. The novels reflect a world of terrible uncertainty. The gods cannot be relied upon. There's a very interesting moment parallel to this in the actual history of the age, not in the literary history, when Demetrius Polyorchetes, one of the great generals of the Hellenistic Age, arrives in Athens in the 290s. As he arrives, the Athenians greet him by saying, "You indeed are a god, because you are here, whereas the other gods either don't hear us or they've gone away or they don't exist."

So traditional faith was very much under threat at the time, as people felt the stability of an earlier age evaporating beneath them. The gods cannot be relied upon, although they do communicate to us in oracles and dreams. Their intentions are frequently mysterious. We can't be sure what these mean. So, often, we could be the victims, as much as the beneficiaries of their involvement in the world of humanity. The narrator of *Callirhoe* declares, for example, "Against Fortune alone, human reason is powerless. She is like a spirit who likes to win." So Fortune is not there to aid us, but manipulates our lives, and we can never tell whether we are going to have a good destiny or a bad one.

These novels that we've been looking at are linked in the way that they reflect their contemporary world. The novels are confined to the world of the eastern Mediterranean, from Syracuse in Sicily to Alexandria, and occasionally move beyond that. But the places that are beyond the Mediterranean realm still tend to be fantasy realms. In other words, the Greeks are still thinking of the Mediterranean as their world. Even though we've seen Greek colonies going as far east as Ai Khanum and we've seen these Bactrian kingdoms, in a way the Greeks never loses this sense that they are really tied to the Mediterranean. So any people who aren't a part of the Mediterranean world, are automatically fantastic, automatically exotic and weird.

The only area in which non-Greek cultures are represented in these romances at all, is in the area of religion. Even here, it's a Hellenized religion, in which figures like Isis have been assimilated to Aphrodite. We've already seen in our lecture on Ptolemaic Egypt, the way in which the Ptolemaic kings attempted to take a pre-existing cult, to give it a Greek packaging, and then to sell it, as it were, to the rest of the Mediterranean.

I think the novels give us an illustration of how successful this was. The Greeks did look at other religions, but they weren't interested in other religions for their foreignness, they were interested in these to the extent that they could understand them as Greek-like cults. So Isis in the Hellenistic Age, though originally an Egyptian goddess, is really, to all intents and purposes, a Greek goddess.

What I am suggesting here is that by looking at not only what is in the novels, but what is excluded from the novels, we get yet further evidence for the basic phenomenon of the Hellenistic world, and that is a lack of cultural fusion. These novels do not represent Greek and non-Greek cultures assimilating each other. Rather, they represent a Greek world which is fundamentally uninterested in anything outside the Mediterranean and anything which is non-Greek. So when non-Greeks do appear in these stories, they nearly always appear as characters who are either inferior or who are a threat. The pirates in the novels may be Phoenician or Egyptian, but the heroes speak and act Greek, all the way through, reminding us of the graffito that we came across in Ptolemaic Egypt, where a man complained in his petition that he was mistreated because he didn't speak Greek.

This is an exclusive world. When Clitophon is captured, he complains to the gods that he cannot even talk to his captors. "In what language should we implore them?" he says. So these novels reflect a world in which there is a clear linguistic barrier between Greeks and non-Greeks.

Kings and courts, interestingly enough, do not figure very much in the romances. This, I think, is a particularly interesting aspect of the novels. We've spent a great deal of time in this series talking about the various Hellenistic dynasties. We've seen how tight the control of city life and village life and country life was in the hands of these Hellenistic kings. And yet, in the novels, there is very little evidence for this. One doesn't come across Seleucus or Antiochus or Ptolemy or Attalus.

Instead, the power, the human power, not the divine power, but the human power that people run up against is usually that of pirate chiefs and brigands. In fact, many of these pirate chiefs and brigands, these robbers, actually refer to themselves as "kings." Their little pirate fleets and their robber bands are a kind of inversion of the world of the Hellenistic court. What are we to make of this?

For a start, I'm sure that it does mean that the vast majority of people in this world had no actual experience of the king. This was a super-human figure who lived hundreds of miles away and from whom they might receive decrees. But about him, they knew nothing practical. They didn't know the king at all. I think it suggests that, for many people, their resistance to authority, a phenomenon we understand well in this country, where people are often suspicious of government. This kind of suspicion in the Hellenistic world was often focused, not on the actual kings, but rather on their negative image. The kinglets, the princelings, the bandit chiefs, who modeled themselves on Hellenistic kings, but who really represented just more bald tyranny over the lives of ordinary people.

The novels, therefore, present a view of the Hellenistic world which I think is unique and valuable for us, because it's a view of the Hellenistic world as seen from the bottom up. That is to say from the point of view of the Greeks—not the most powerful people at court, but the Greeks who saw themselves above Egyptians and

Phoenicians and Babylonians, but beneath the power of their own kings. These are people who are caught in a world where power is capricious. They are caught in a world where law is a joke, which is enforced by the strong to the detriment of the weak, and where Fate (circumstances) are always ready to dump on you. You are the plaything of Fate.

So it raises some interesting questions about the nature of community. About the individual and his or her place in relation to the society around him. The community exists. But the world of the romance is one of scared and vulnerable individuals. These are people for whom life is a constant battle and a threat.

I think finally what we get in the Hellenistic novels is the nearest thing to something like sitcoms and TV dramas in our own world. That is to say, they give us an idea of the way life is, although it's not an exact replication of life. It's an artistic rendering of it. The concerns that we see in these novels—the interest in sex, which is often somewhat prurient (paralleled by sculptures that we've described on earlier occasions); the fear and the anxiety over fate; the contempt felt for anything that is non-Greek; and the suspicion that power is really coercive, and is not there to represent us, but to compel us—these are the kinds of things that emerge in the novels, and which give us, I think, a view into a world that was really quite familiar and remarkably like our own. A world in which the individual was not very secure, not very happy in his own position.

The lasting influence, then, of these novels is that they give us both a view of the world, and they also give us an idea of the individual psychology of people in the Hellenistic Age. For that reason, if you haven't read any of the Hellenistic novels, I would strongly urge you to go out and buy one.

Lecture Fourteen
Stoics, Epicureans, and Skeptics

Scope:

Hellenistic philosophy demonstrates a very different response to the anxieties of the new age. We examine the major schools of thought and relate them to the social setting of philosophy.

Outline

I. By the beginning of the Hellenistic period, the Greeks were well aware that their culture was heir to a long and rich tradition of philosophical inquiry. As early as the 6th century, the pre-Socratic philosophers of the Ionian enlightenment had speculated on questions ranging from the cosmological, "What is the essential substance of the cosmos?" to the ethical, "How should the good man live?" The Ionian philosophers were succeeded by the three men who were seen as the fountainheads of Greek philosophy: Socrates, Plato, and Aristotle.

   A. Socrates perfected the art of inquiry through methodical questioning. No assertion was so self-evident that it could not be scrutinized. In this way, Socrates tried to make the philosophical enterprise one of critical inquiry. For him, all virtues were, in essence, the same.

   B. Plato revered his master, Socrates, and made him the mouthpiece in a series of dramatic dialogues for a philosophy that blends the thinking of both men. The theory of Forms holds that this world is nothing but a poor copy of a more perfect realm and that permanence is an illusion, because at any given time objects are in the process of becoming something else.

   C. Aristotle brought deductive thinking to new levels by categorizing phenomena as widely different as weather conditions and political constitutions. By amassing as much evidence as possible regarding a phenomenon, Aristotle believed that one would be able to determine what its function or purpose was.

II. The Hellenistic Age continued these philosophical traditions but in a formal, institutional setting. Philosophers were no longer itinerant teachers but the heads of schools, offering regular courses of lectures and succeeded by specially chosen followers. Two institutions connected Hellenistic philosophy with the earlier age.

  A. The Academy took its name from the meeting place of the philosophical school that claimed descent from Plato and his followers.

   1. Influenced by Socratic and Platonic doubts regarding the certainty of knowledge, the Academy became most closely associated with skepticism.

   2. Skeptics attempted to demonstrate the impossibility of knowledge (*akatalepsia*) and argued for the suspension of judgment (*epoche*).

  B. Peripatetic philosophy was associated more closely with the followers of Aristotle, who met at the Lyceum.

   1. Here, as at the Academy, a garden and surrounding buildings provided the school setting in which the Aristotelian tradition of wide-ranging research continued.

   2. Peripatetic philosophy covered topics as different as physical science, geography, astronomy, and literary criticism.

III. In addition to the older schools, new schools sprang up early in the Hellenistic Age. The two most influential were Stoicism and Epicureanism. Both the older and the newer schools of Hellenistic philosophy divided the discipline into three distinct areas of inquiry: physics, logic, and ethics.

  A. Stoicism was founded by Zeno of Citium, who taught in Athens at the end of the 4th century B.C.

   1. Stoicism placed great emphasis on personal morality and was based on the belief that human reason is capable of grasping the nature of the world in which we live.

   2. The physical theory on which this line of thought was based maintained that everything in the world is composed of a universal world fire.

B. Epicureanism was the school of philosophy that derived from the teachings of Epicurus. Often reviled as a hedonist, even in antiquity, because of his dictum that the pleasurable is good, Epicurus in fact advocated an austere and ascetic existence.

    1. Epicureans held that sensual gratification only fueled desire and, therefore, did not contribute to true happiness. Denial and abstinence, however, suppressed desire and made true happiness attainable.

    2. In physical terms, Epicureanism was also based on earlier Greek atomic theory. The Roman poet Lucretius would praise Epicurus for freeing us from the fear of death.

IV. A common theme running through the philosophies of the Hellenistic Age is the search for inner harmony and peace, referred to as *ataraxia*, or freedom from disturbance. This theme led many to look to the philosophical life as an alternative to the turbulent political conditions of the age.

    A. The followers of Epicurus retreated to a compound referred to as the Garden and formed a quasi-religious brotherhood. Because they believed that life consisted of sense perception and rejected all superstitions concerning an afterlife, they regarded death as nothing to be feared. As Epicurus wrote to his friend, "get used to believing that death is nothing to us."

    B. The Stoics emphasized indifference toward material wealth. Why must the wise man make money, asked Zeno? Only virtue is worth pursuing for the sake of happiness, and virtue is indifferent to wealth.

    C. The most extreme expression of this indifference toward every aspect of social life was in the philosophy and behavior of the Cynics. Little of their writing survives and, in any case, Cynicism was never an organized philosophical school comparable to Stoicism or Epicureanism.

        1. Diogenes provided the model for Cynical behavior by living in a barrel and rejecting all social convention.

        2. The aim of the Cynic way of life was to live in accordance with nature. All human conventions, such as clothing, hygiene, and manners, were unnatural and, therefore, rejected.

V. Despite the tendency toward social withdrawal and the emphasis on purely individual and personal concerns, Hellenistic philosophy played an important role in the communal life of the age.

   A. At Athens, philosophers provided an alternative figure of charismatic leadership. Kings were figures of enormous and unpredictable power, often distant, but the philosophers were human and preached doctrines that emphasized the importance of the inner life.

   B. These doctrines and their proponents gained popularity throughout the Hellenistic world until it became commonplace for cities to erect statues to philosophers as readily as to their other benefactors. Philosophers, in fact, became both cultural and political ambassadors on behalf of the Greek states.

   C. As the living embodiment of Greek tradition, these men represented a human, individual Greek culture that was accessible to all in a way that the court of the Hellenistic king was not.

   D. The writings of the philosophers reflect this unusual pairing of the king and philosopher. When Zeno writes that the means of making money are ridiculous, which include receiving it from a king and therefore yielding to him, his rejection encompasses not just what we would call materialism, but also the contractual arrangement of social relations that was the foundation of Hellenistic social life.

   E. Other Stoics explicitly likened the virtuous or wise man to a king, claiming that both were self-sufficient and powerful. Often the wise and virtuous man is referred to as blessed. In later antiquity, the authority of the "holy man" would increasingly challenge secular authority. Here was an alternative model of power.

   F. The Hellenistic philosophers who rejected the material aspects of life are a link to later European history, setting the stage for the growth of the church as an alternative to the power of the state.

Suggested Reading:

B. Inwood and L. P. Gerson, *Hellenistic Philosophy: Introductory Readings*.

A. A. Long, *Hellenistic Philosophy: Stoics, Epicurans, Sceptics*.

Questions to Consider:

1. In what ways do the philosophies of the Hellenistic Age represent a different response to contemporary conditions from the responses of Hellenistic artists?

2. Why did such philosophies as Stoicism prove so popular, especially among such groups as the Roman aristocracy?

Lecture Fourteen—Transcript
Stoics, Epicureans, and Skeptics

Hello. This is our fourteenth lecture in the series on Alexander and the Hellenistic Age. Today we're going to turn our attention to philosophy. We've been looking at the culture of the Hellenistic Age, and we've been able to see how the artists, the sculptors, the poets, and the authors of the Greek romances, produced an art that was highly distinctive. Very different from the Classical Age that came before. We've been seeing the way the concerns of the age are expressed in this art. We've seen an age which is gripped by uncertainty. An age where people are very suspicious both of authority and deeply worried that Fate is a capricious entity that could overthrow their lives at any moment.

We would expect, of course, that the philosophers of the age would engage with some of these issues, to try to give people an idea of how life comes about, how the universe exists, and then also how ethically one should live in the world. These are the traditional concerns of philosophy. So what I'd like to do today is chart the ways in which the philosophical trends of the Hellenistic Age intersect with the major cultural trends that we've been seeing in other genres. We should begin, however, by observing that the Greeks of the Hellenistic Age came at the end of a long and fruitful tradition of philosophical inquiry. Philosophers did not spring up overnight in the Hellenistic Age.

In fact, as early as the 6th century B.C., long before the Hellenistic period, philosophers of the so-called Ionian Enlightenment, the philosophers often known collectively as the pre-Socratics, had already charted some of the trajectories that Greek philosophy would follow. These philosophers were interested in cosmology. In the essence of the universe. They had asked the question, "What is the essential substance out of which the cosmos (the universe) is made?" They had provided various answers to this. Some had maintained that it was water. Some had maintained that it was air. Others had said that the universe is made up of tiny, indivisible particles, an idea that seems strange, until you realize that they are talking about atoms. Atoms being, quite literally, the smallest particles that cannot be cut, according to the Greek philosophers, although we, of course, have shown that that's not exactly true.

The Ionian philosophers before Socrates, as well as being natural philosophers, observing nature and trying to understand the cosmos, had also been ethical philosophers. How should man live? What is the nature of justice? What is "the good"? These Ionian philosophers of the 6th and the 5th century were then succeeded by the three men who are traditionally seen as the fountainhead of Greek philosophy, and, in fact, of European philosophy in general. And though this is still before the Hellenistic Age, I should at least summarize their work so that we have some idea of how the Hellenistic philosophers had been trained, who their intellectual antecedents were, and what the tracks of Greek philosophy were.

Of course, the greatest of the three is Socrates. It is Socrates who perfected the art of inquiry through cross-examination, through methodical questioning. Socrates had been told by the oracle at Delphi that he was the wisest man in Greece. He thought this was a peculiar pronouncement, and set out to test it by asking other people what they knew. It was in the course of inquiring of other people about their opinions, that he came to the realization that while he knew that he wasn't the smartest man, other people, because they did think that they knew what they were talking about were actually less intelligent than he. So ironically and paradoxically, he did confirm the view that he was the wisest man of Greece.

His philosophy was one largely based on questioning. Let me give you an example of the way this works paradoxically. If you ask a group of undergraduates in college, "Should universities allow students to drink?" they will usually say, "Yes. Universities have to recognize that if a student is 21, and is an adult, then he or she has the right to drink and universities should acknowledge that and allow them to do so." Socrates (or the Socratic method) would approach this by saying, "Are those people who drink more healthy than those who do not?" And Socrates' interlocutor would say, "Of course not, Socrates. People who drink are less healthy than those who do not." And Socrates would say, "So drinking is not a healthy activity?" And the interlocutor would have to say, "That is correct." And Socrates would then say, "And should universities encourage healthy or unhealthy activities?" And the person would say, "This is obvious. Universities should encourage healthy activities. That's why they have gymnasia and sports teams and so forth." And Socrates would conclude, "Then if universities should encourage healthy activities, and if drinking is not a healthy activity, then surely universities

©2000 The Teaching Company.

should not allow drinking." And in this model dialogue, that I've just made up on the spot, Socrates' interlocutor would have to come back with a reply such as one does find in the Platonic dialogues, something along the lines of "It seems, Socrates, as if I didn't know what I was talking about."

The Socratic style that we have preserved in the Platonic dialogues usually illustrates Socrates' belief that all virtues are essentially the same. That justice, goodness, and piety are all really versions of the same essentially unified virtue.

Plato, the second of the great Greek philosophers of the Classical Age, revered his master Socrates, and he made him the mouthpiece in a series of dialogues (the Platonic dialogues) for a philosophy which seems to seamlessly blend the philosophy of the two individuals (Socrates and Plato). Plato, for example, takes the idea of virtue a step further, by arguing that there is, in fact, a more perfect realm beyond this, where forms exist in their most perfect type, and that what we have in this world is merely a set of imperfect reflections of that. So lights, sound, trees outside, cups, lecterns, cameras—these are all merely instances in this imperfect world of the more perfect versions of these in the realm of forms, or the realm of perfect ideas. So in this Platonic philosophy, permanence is really an illusion, because at any given time an object is in the process of becoming something else. A sapling grows to be a tree. A tree is then cut down and cut to become a plank. A plank is then used to make a deck, and a deck is part of a house. So the same substance is constantly undergoing change, that is, metamorphosing.

Aristotle, the third of the great Greek philosophers of the Classical Age approached phenomena slightly differently. Instead of looking for what is essential and perfect, which is then copied in this imperfect realm, he rather tried to deduce the essence of things by categorizing all the instances of phenomena. So, for example, if you wanted to understand what is a table in essence, Aristotle's approach would be to line up twenty or thirty or forty or fifty different tables side by side and say, "What is it that they each have in common?"

This approach proved to be highly influential in western philosophy because it could be applied in so many areas. If you want to understand politics, for example, in the Aristotelian model you would go to each one of the Greek city-states and you would copy down its constitution. You can find the best form of political constitution by comparing all of the known examples. Or you can find out about the weather by observing the weather every day in different parts of the Greek world or in different parts of the Mediterranean. So this scientific notion of observation leading to deduction is really the legacy of Aristotelian thought. By amassing as much evidence as possible regarding a phenomenon, whether it be plants or ethics or meteorology or constitutions, Aristotle believed that one would be able to determine what its proper function or purpose was.

So these are the tendencies—a mystical tendency in Plato and a deductive typological approach in Aristotle—that are inherited by the Hellenistic Age. The Hellenistic Age will continue these philosophical trends associated with Plato and with Aristotle. But the difference is that in the Hellenistic Age this will be done in a much more formal institutional setting. Instead of a single teacher and a group of dedicated students, we now can speak of philosophical schools. In a sense, the first European universities. Philosophers were no longer itinerant teachers moving from city to city, but rather were the heads of schools offering regular courses of lectures. When they retired or died they would be succeeded then by specifically chosen followers. So we're really talking about institutional philosophy.

The two institutions that are most connected with the earlier Platonic and Aristotelian traditions of Greek philosophy are the Academy and the Peripatetics. Let me explain who these are, briefly. The Academy took its name from the meeting place of the philosophical school that claimed descent from Plato and his followers. Influenced by Socratic and Platonic doubts regarding the certainty of knowledge. Socrates had already established that most of us, if questioned closely enough, can't really support most of the things that we believe as true knowledge. Influenced by this approach, the Academy became more and more closely associated with the point of view that says that you can never really know anything with absolute certainty. In other words, they were the original skeptics.

Skeptics attempted to demonstrate the impossibility of knowledge. As they called it, *akatelepsia*. They argued, therefore, that we should suspend judgment and base it merely upon the most likely of circumstances or opinions, but there was no absolute certainty. You can never say absolutely what was true.

Peripatetic philosophy, on the other hand, was associated much more closely with the followers of Aristotle, who met at another location in Athens, known as the Lyceum. Here, as at the Academy, there was a garden. There was a set of buildings around the garden. This provided the physical setting in downtown Athens, where the Aristotelian tradition continued, of wide-ranging research. This really is the origin of the modern research institute. The philosophers who met here were generally known as the peripatetics, deriving their name from the fact that some of the early lecturers would walk around (this is what *peripatetic* means), they would walk around as they were delivering their lectures. Like Aristotle, their founder, these peripatetic philosophers covered a range of topics in their philosophy: both physical science (geography, mathematics, astronomy and so forth) as well as literary criticism, too. So we find in the Hellenistic Age the traditions of the Classical world leading on into new directions.

In addition to these schools, which are really connected to the Classical period that came before, the Hellenistic Age also saw the development of new schools of philosophy that began now, really, for the first time. The two most influential that we should mention are Stoicism and Epicureanism. Both the older schools and the newer schools of Hellenistic philosophy treated philosophy as an area of inquiry that really had three distinct sub-areas, if you will. Physics, logic and ethics.

Stoicism was founded by Zeno of Citium, a Greek city on the island of Cyprus. He came to Athens towards the end of the 4th century, and for the rest of his life there he taught philosophy. He is supposed to have said that, "Fortune did me a favor by driving me to philosophy." Thereby expressing perfectly a Hellenistic sentiment that his entire life had really been dictated by fortune.

Stoicism placed a great emphasis on personal morality. It was based on the belief that human beings have the capacity through their human reason to grasp the true nature of the world in which we live. Of course, in this respect they were very different from the skeptics, who maintained that real and absolute knowledge was not possible. The physical theory on which the Stoics based their ethical point of view was that the world was made up of a universal fire. This was the substance that made up the entire cosmos.

Of course, each one of us, according to this theory, also has some spark of that universal, divine fire in us, so that it is a philosophy that had a kind of a theological overtone, if you will, and it really was very comforting to people who believed that we really do have something of the divine in us. It is a theory which became enormously popular in the Roman world. It stayed popular throughout the Greek East, but also, when the Romans became more familiar with the Greek world, it took off there, too. I think one of the reasons for this we can see when we read Cicero's interpretation of this philosophy, where he's talking here about the gods. He says:

> The Cosmos as a whole has been discussed. So have the heavenly bodies. We now have a pretty clear picture of a large number of gods who are not idle, but who do not have to carry out the tasks that they perform with laborious and unpleasant effort. For they are not held together by veins and nerves and bones, nor do they consume the sort of food and drink which would make their humors either too sharp or too dense. Nor do they have the sorts of bodies which would lead them to dread falls or blows or fear diseases produced by physical exhaustion. It was for fear of this sort of thing that Epicurus invented his insubstantial and idle gods. Endowed with that most beautiful of shapes, located in the purest region of the heavens, they move and steer their courses in such a way that they seem to have come to an agreement to preserve and protect everything. [And he says,] It remains to me to explain that the world is governed by the providence of the gods.

So this was a Greek philosophy that had clear connections with the earlier approaches of the cosmologists of the 6th century, trying to argue for an essence in the universe. But it didn't threaten traditional religion. Rather, it suggested that the gods are simply not quite as anthropomorphic as we may have considered them to be.

A much more radical break with traditional culture and with traditional philosophy, in some respects, was that of Epicureanism, the philosophy that takes its name from its founder, Epicurus. He's the one Hellenistic philosopher whose name is well known to many people, and his philosophy is completely misunderstood. So it behooves us to say a little about what Epicureanism truly is. Often reviled, both in antiquity and in modern times as a hedonist, because of his dictum that "the pleasurable is good," which seems to be a free license, Epicurus in fact was the exact opposite of this.

He advocated an austere and ascetic existence. The Epicureans held that since your gratification (that wonderfully rich meal that you had last night, that bottle of wine that's waiting for you at home tonight) only fuels desire, because you want another rich meal to match the one that you had. And you spend your life thinking of that next bottle of the perfect Chardonnay. Therefore, according to Epicurus, this didn't contribute to happiness at all, because you became a slave of your desires. On the other hand, he said, denial and abstinence suppress desire. You stop wanting it if you stop feeding those desires in your body. That makes true happiness attainable. Epicurus actually said that he would be as happy as Zeus if he merely had a barley cake and a cup of water.

Like the other philosophies, this moral philosophy was also based on a physical theory. Epicurus maintained that the world was made up of atoms, and that there was really nothing beyond this. When you die the atoms disperse. And that's all she wrote. There's nothing left, you would say. Later on this philosophy also became quite popular in the Roman world. A Roman poet named Lucretius praised Epicurus for having freed mankind from the fear of death, because of this notion that once we die, since there is nothing after death, we should have no reason to fear it beforehand.

A common theme running through the philosophies of the Hellenistic Age, both the traditional and the newer ones, is the search for inner harmony and peace. This makes good sense if you think back to the tortured sculpture that we've seen, and if you think back to the interest in heightened emotion, passion and rage, that we've seen in the novels and the poems of the Hellenistic Age. The philosophers' response to the uncertainty of the time was to turn inwards, and to look for inner harmony, a state that they called *ataraxia*, which literally means "freedom from disturbance." Not being upset, in other words. It led many people to find in the philosophical life, an alternative to the turbulent political conditions of the age. The followers of Epicurus, for example, retreated from active public life into a compound which was referred to as The Garden, where they formed a quasi-religious brotherhood. One of the great ironies of history is that though Epicurus believed that death is final, his followers actually revered him after his death as a kind of demi-god. Perhaps they didn't understand the professor's lectures very well.

Because the Epicureans believed that life consisted of sense perception, they regarded death as nothing to be feared since they rejected all superstitions concerning an afterlife. Epicurus actually wrote in a letter to one of his friends, "Get used to believing that death is nothing to us."

The Stoics emphasized indifference toward material wealth. Zeno asked, "Why must a wise man make money? Only virtue is worth pursuing for the sake of happiness. And virtue is indifferent to wealth. So why bother to be a merchant? Why bother to give money to the city or to build a larger house?"

The most extreme version of this disengagement from the contemporary world, if you will, is that of the cynics. Little of the writing of these men survives. And it's probably wrong to think of it as a philosophical school. The cynics really are more a way of life or an attitude. They model themselves on the first and the best-known of the cynics, Diogenes, who lived in a barrel and gave up all social convention. No clothes. Clothes aren't in nature. You don't see beasties running around at the zoo with clothes on. So why should humans? It's unnatural. We don't live in houses that are created by nature. We build them. Therefore they're unnatural. So you should live in something simple. Find yourself a large barrel. A cave. A hole in the ground.

The aim of this cynic way of life was to live in accordance with nature. And it therefore rejected all social convention as unnatural. This meant that not only was clothing was rejected, but so was personal hygiene, so were good manners, and various other practices. I'm not going to go into the gory details. I'll leave it to your imagination.

Despite the tendency towards social withdrawal and the emphasis on purely individual and personal concerns, Hellenistic philosophy actually played a very important role in the communal life of the age. At Athens, for example, philosophers provided an alternative figure of charismatic leadership. An alternative to what? An alternative to the real kings of the Hellenistic Age. We've already noticed in the Hellenistic novels that many of the pirates and the brigands are called "kings," almost as if people are seeing them as a scaled-down version of what the real kings are.

The other development of the age is that philosophers become, in a sense, the negative image of kings, as well. Kings were figures of enormous and unpredictable power. They are often distant. But the philosophers were intimately real. They were human. They preached where you could actually listen to them and see them. Their doctrines emphasized the importance of the inner life. In a sense, the thrust of their philosophy was to make every man a king, controlling his own destiny. These doctrines and their proponents gained popularity throughout the Hellenistic world, until it became commonplace, in fact, for cities to erect statues to philosophers, as readily as to their other benefactors.

So if you go today to a city like Aphrodisias, and if you look at the sculpture of a mid-level city of Asia Minor that flourished from the 1st century B.C. through to about the 3rd century A.D., yes, you'll see many statues of local magistrates and later of Roman emperors, but you'll also see dozens of statues showing philosophers. They are the intellectual heroes of the day.

Philosophers, in fact, even become the ambassadors of the Greek states, and when one of the first official embassies comes from the Greek world to Rome, this emerging superpower on the western edge of the Hellenistic Mediterranean, it is led by philosophers, like Carneades, who bamboozles the Roman Senate by arguing in favor of justice on one day and against justice on the next day. A typical example of a smart-aleck Greek philosophy professor, leading to a great deal of contempt on the part of his Roman hosts.

As the living embodiment of Greek tradition, these men represented a human, individual Greek culture that was accessible to all in a way that the court of the Hellenistic king was not. Political power was restricted to a very small echelon at the top of society. But philosophical power, self-control, freedom from disturbance, was as simple as stepping away from the world. Giving up public office and living in a garden, subsisting on a diet of beans and water.

The writings of these philosophers reflect this unusual pairing, this kind of inverse coupling, if you will, of the king and the philosopher. So, for example, in one instance, we find Plutarch commenting that the Stoics had said, "when they write, they write about politics to discourage us from practicing politics. And they write about rhetoric to discourage us from practicing rhetoric. And about kingship to discourage us from consorting with kings."

When Zeno writes that the means of making money are ridiculous, such as receiving money from a king, and therefore yielding to the influence of the king, the rejection that comes in those lines is not merely a rejection of materialism. He's not just saying that you shouldn't worry about money, because money isn't the road to virtue. What he's also doing is rejecting the entire contractual arrangement that makes up the Hellenistic world. The arrangement whereby you give honor to the king. You treat him as a god made manifest, and in return, he acts as a benefactor for you and for your community. So there is, in fact, something almost subversive, if you will, about these philosophies. Because, taken to their extreme, they would mean that people no longer lived as citizens in their state or kingdom.

One of them actually said, when asked of what state was he a citizen, replied, he was a citizen of the cosmos. In Greek, when you say that you're saying that you're cosmopolitan. He wasn't saying that he was sophisticated. He was saying "I reject your notion of this kingdom or of that state or of this city, and being citizens or subjects. I am a citizen of the universe. A cosmopolitan."

Other Stoics specifically likened the virtuous or the wise man to a king, claiming that both the virtuous man and the king were self-sufficient and therefore powerful. So, often the wise and the virtuous man is referred to as "blessed."

It's very important to recognize that this phenomenon goes back to the Hellenistic Age, because it would become tremendously influential in the Roman Empire, and would play a very important role in the future trajectory of both Judaism and of Christianity. Because many scholars have noted that it is under the Roman Empire that we find many people turning away from the power of Caesar or of the local governor, and instead investing the holy man with a different kind of authority. So in the Hellenistic world we find the roots of a powerful and important phenomenon: the creation of an alternative model of power. Not political power, but something which would challenge it. The power of philosophy and finally the power of the holy man.

Of course, the great irony of Christianity and later European history would be that that church, which grew up as an alternative to the power of the Roman state, would eventually, as a result of a rapprochement in the 4th century, become itself modeled on the Roman state, and would become as official an institution as the state that it copied. So there is a thread that connects the Hellenistic philosophers, who said, "I don't want anything to do with this life," and the later emergence of Christianity as an opposition to the Empire and the final transformation of that into a Church.

We see then, that, as in so many other ways, the Hellenistic world plays a hidden and unseen but extraordinarily influential role in the later development of European history.

Lecture Fifteen
Kingship and Legitimacy

Scope:

The monarchs of the Hellenistic world were not descended from Persian kings or local rulers. We examine the underpinnings of their power and the administrative arrangements of their realms.

Outline

I. The monarchs of the Hellenistic world were not descended from Persian kings or local rulers. Instead, they were Greeks and Macedonians who could offer no claim to rule based on descent, territory, or legitimacy, because the founders of their dynasties were soldiers and officials in the Macedonian army.

   A. What ideology, then, sustained the authority of the Hellenistic kings? By what right did they claim to rule, and how did they support their claim in practice?

   B. Often, answers to these questions have concentrated primarily on the phenomenon of Hellenization, as if the benefits of Greek culture were enough to justify the rule of these men and to make them acceptable to non-Greek subjects. A second aspect of Hellenistic kingship is that Hellenistic kings usually received cult honors and were worshipped as gods, either in their lifetimes or after their deaths. This has sometimes been seen as an ideological tool used to impress and pacify subject populations.

   C. In 307 B.C., the Athenian reaction to Antigonius and Demetrius was to call them kings and "savior gods."

   D. Ptolemy III was traced back to his dynastic beginnings and, even further, to the gods.

   E. For the Seleucids, the ultimate genealogy was similar.

II. In fact, the underpinnings of Hellenistic kingship are much more complex and included a variety of institutions, ideas, and methods to assert and maintain authority.

   A. In the first place, Hellenistic philosophers developed Aristotle's notion of the *megalopsychus*, "the man of great soul."

1. With his slow gait, deep voice, and contempt for anything except his own honor, Aristotle's "man of great soul" was a model for kings whose claims to kingship had to reside in their own qualities.

2. The "man of great soul" was also a model for Hellenistic philosophers, who often saw themselves as the intellectual equivalents of kings, as well as their actual advisers. Kingship, said the philosophers, was above review. One definition of kingship of the time frankly stated that it was neither descent nor legitimacy that gave monarchies to men, but the ability to command an army and handle affairs competently.

B. Military expenditure was an important part of the equation, not only because kings faced threats from their neighbors, but because great armies, vast fleets, and the latest weapons demonstrated to your own people and the rest of the world that you were powerful.

C. Spectacular festivals in honor of the gods gave rulers the opportunity to spend vast amounts of money in displays of their wealth.

1. The grand procession of Ptolemy Philadelphus lasted a full day. Floats up to 40 feet long pulled by 600 men carried gigantic tripods and statues.

2. These floats, which were between 15 and 18 feet tall, poured wine and included hundreds of gold and jewel-encrusted vessels and boxes and thousands of men, women, and children in costume, along with elephants and chariots drawn by antelope and ostriches. It was an early case of conspicuous consumption.

D. The king's generosity was not confined to displays of power but was also used to demonstrate his appreciation of Greek culture.

1. The Attalid kings of Pergamon were especially generous in giving entire buildings to Athens, but they and the Ptolemies also gave money to the Greeks to rebuild after earthquakes and sent grain fleets to Greece during times of famine.

2. In their own courts, the kings patronized Greek poets, musicians, painters, and sculptors, vying with each other

to transform their capitals, Alexandria, Pergamon, Antioch, and Pella, into cities comparable to Athens.

  3. Greek artists responded by eulogizing and glorifying their royal patrons, connecting them to the heroes of the glorious past.

 E. The cult of the ruler, either living or dead, also bolstered the kings' claims to legitimacy.

  1. Although modern scholarship is often skeptical about whether the subjects believed in the divinity of the Hellenistic dynasts, we now recognize that divine honors offered to a mighty king made royal power tangible to the people of the age.

  2. One might call this divinity the diplomatic language of the time.

III. Aside from these various forms of patronage, the Hellenistic kings also relied on administrative arrangements to confirm their power.

 A. In the 3rd century, administration was often in the hands of the king's friends, or *philoi*. Drawing on Macedonian traditions of companionship, the Hellenistic kings often relied on these informal close associates and advisers to run the kingdom.

 B. Gradually, in the 2nd century, this network of associates was complemented by an elaborate fixed hierarchy of officials with titles, grades, and specific duties.

 C. Together, the *philoi*, the family of the king, and the upper echelons of the bureaucracy constituted the court, a series of concentric circles with the king at the center.

Suggested Reading:

G. Herman, "The Court Society of the Hellenistic Age," in P. Cartledge et al., eds., *Hellenistic Constructs: Essays in Culture, History, and Historiography.*

Questions to Consider:

1. Why did Hellenistic kings compete with each other in their philanthropic spending?

2. In what ways did the Hellenistic concept of kingship go back to Alexander the Great?

Lecture Fifteen—Transcript
Kingship and Legitimacy

In our early lectures in this series on Alexander and the Hellenistic Age, we saw that Alexander's legacy was an empire that disintegrated after his death, in which a new series of kingdoms came into being as a result of the military victories of Alexander's successors. They established such dynasties as the Ptolemaic dynasty in Egypt and the Seleucid dynasty in Syria. We're going to be seeing toward the end of these lectures the way that these various kingdoms all finally came under the sway of Rome. But midway between these two, their birth and their death, I'd like to spend one lecture looking at how Hellenistic rulership operates. How do these kings rule? They are not descended from Persian kings, and they're not descended from local rulers, either. So the phenomenon of Hellenistic rulership is something absolutely new. It, as it were, creates itself. That is a very interesting phenomenon.

The Greeks and the Macedonians who ruled over the eastern Mediterranean and the lands connected to that area could not claim rule based on descent, or on territory, or on any ancestral legitimacy, since the founders of those dynasties were soldiers and officials and bodyguards of Alexander in the Macedonian army. So what was the ideology that sustained the authority of Hellenistic kingship? By what right did they claim to rule, and how did they support that claim in practice? These are the questions that I'd like to address today, because the answers to these questions, I think, take us right to the very heart of the nature of power in the Hellenistic world.

In the past, there have been two approaches to Hellenistic kingship that have tended to dominate scholarship. Scholars often point to the artistic and the literary traditions that cast the kings of the Hellenistic Age as the spiritual, if not the actual, heirs of Alexander. So, for example, the coins of Hellenistic kings show them often looking very much like Alexander. In fact, many of the Hellenistic kings actually put Alexander's head on their coinage, rather than their own. So this is a way of claiming that they are, in a sense, his heirs.

Many of the Hellenistic kings encouraged stories claiming that they had been personal favorites or friends of Alexander. Ptolemy, for example (the first Ptolemy), who had been one of Alexander's bodyguards, and who then founded the new ruling dynasty of Egypt, wrote a history of Alexander's campaign. It was one of the major sources for later writers such as Arrian. Fairly clearly, if one reads accounts like Arrian and Diodorus, one can see that what Ptolemy was doing here was advancing the notion that he had been an intimate of Alexander's. That, at crucial moments in Alexander's career, he (Ptolemy) had been dispatched with a particularly important mission, for example.

Many of the Hellenistic kings actually affected what we might call an Alexander style. So we read of some of the Hellenistic kings curling their hair, so that they would be able to imitate Alexander's distinctive anastole, the part in the middle of his forehead, with the hair rising up in two waves, making it look like a lion's mane. Some of them dressed like Alexander, as well, particularly one of the successors known as Leonidas.

But even more than these attempts to look like and to model yourself on Alexander, even more than this, a critical aspect of Hellenistic kingship is that the Hellenistic kings received cultic honors. They encouraged the idea that they were gods. Either after their death, or, increasingly during the Hellenistic Age, during their lifetime, as well. This ruler cult is really one of the most distinctive developments of the Hellenistic Age, because it had not been a feature of Greek culture prior to this time. Kings had largely passed out of Greek history before the Classical Age. The only part of Greece that still had kings on a regular basis was Sparta, and even there people understood very clearly that the Spartan kings were flesh and blood men.

So this notion that the Hellenistic kings (who were Greek and Macedonian) were gods, either in their lifetime or elevated afterwards, was something new. As a practice, it was something new. It has been seen at times, as a kind of ideological tool, as if it were a deliberate policy invented by the kings as a way of legitimizing their rule and, in fact, forcing people to treat them as something superhuman.

And yet, there are reasons for suspecting that that is not exactly the case. That the reality is somewhat more complex than that. Right back very early, at the beginning of the Hellenistic Age, we have an episode that occurs in 307 B.C., when, during the wars of Alexander's successors, two of the most successful of the next generation, Antigonus Monophthalmos (the One-Eyed) and his son Demetrius arrive in Athens. Here is a description from a later writer, talking about the way the Athenians react to these Hellenistic generals.

> The Athenians [says Plutarch], were the first to give the title of 'kings' to Demetrius and Antigonus, although they had otherwise avoided the name up 'til now, and it was the only royal prerogative still left to the descendants of Philip and Alexander which others could not touch or share in.

So, says Plutarch, these men arrive. They don't call themselves kings yet, because that's still something that you associate with Alexander's family. But the Athenians go ahead and call them kings. More than that, though, the Athenians were the first to call them "savior-gods." These men arrive. These are flesh-and-blood generals, and the Athenians are hailing them as gods.

The Athenians abolished the ancestral eponymous *archonship*, that is, the chief magistrate, who gives his name to the year, and they elected every year a priest of the saviors.

It is as if someone powerful were to arrive in Washington, and we would say, "No longer will we call this the eighth year of a particular presidency. We'll instead say that it's the first year of the priest of that particular god who has arrived."

They voted to weave the likeness, the face of Antigonus and Demetrius, into the robe of Athena, together with the other gods. This is the robe that is used for the statue of Athena up in the Parthenon. It is a holy garment. It is used for the most holy statue in Athens. It has embroidered on it, the faces of the other Olympian gods. Now it's going to have, also, the face of Antigonus and Demetrius.

They consecrated the place where Demetrius had first stepped down from his chariot. So the actual spot where he first steps out and touches the soil of Athens—they place there an altar, and they called it the Altar of Demetrius, the descending god. The same title that was used on other occasions for Zeus. They added two more tribes to the ten existing tribes. So there were ten tribes in Athens and now they add two more, and their names are Demetrias and Antigonis, named after Demetrius and Antiognus. And they raised the number on the Council from 500 to 600, because the two new tribes each provided 50 new counselors.

So this is very intriguing, because in this instance we see, very early in the Hellenistic Age, that the impetus for this comes, not from these Hellenistic rulers. It comes as something of a surprise to them. It is a set of honors given to them by the Athenians in an attempt to understand and to make manifest and real and tangible the power of these men, who can determine their fate.

Once the idea took root, of course, there was no stopping it, because it was such a useful tool for the developing Hellenistic kingship. It particularly took root in Egypt, because here, of course, there was a long tradition of treating the pharaohs as gods. I want to read to you just the beginning of a document from the Ptolemaic period. And I'm only going to read the very first part, where you'll hear the titles of Ptolemy, and you'll understand how, already in the 2nd century, we have a firmly embedded notion of the dynasty as a divine family.

> King Ptolemy the Great [this is Ptolemy III], son of King Ptolemy II and Queen Arsinoe, the brother-sister gods, children of King Ptolemy I and Queen Berenice, the savior-gods, descended on his father's side from Heracles, son of Zeus, and on his mother's side from Dionysos, son of Zeus.

And it goes on to explain the rest of the details of the inscription. But the point here is that this ancestry links them both back to traditional Greek gods and to heroes (Heracles, Dionysos, Zeus) and it figures each of the earlier generation as also being divine.

It also took root quite firmly in the Seleucid realm. We have a number of documents from there, as well. One interesting one is an inscription that details the various priesthoods that flourished in the city of Seleuceia, one of the key cities in the Seleucid heartland of Syria. In this document we hear of priests that are serving to Apollo, priests that are serving to Zeus, and then we hear of Seleucus Zeus Nikator (so Seleucus and Zeus are actually combined there), priests of Antiochus Apollo Soter (Antiochus and Apollo and the notion of the savior-god *soter* are all bound up together). And so on in the rest of this inscription, a good five members of the Seleucid dynasty are actually treated as gods. As either savior-gods or benefactor-gods; as gods made manifest. So the underpinning of Hellenistic kingship was far more complex than the simple matter of imposing ruler cult on an unwilling population. In fact, it often jibed very well with local traditions, and it was often something which grew out of the people as they approached these Hellenistic kings.

There are other concepts that also help to underpin this developing idea of the Hellenistic king. One of them was a traditional Greek notion, found in Aristotle, of the man who was known as the *megalopsychus*, the man of great spirit, the man of great soul. A kind of superman, if you will. Aristotle, in describing this man, actually gives us a notion of his physical presentation. The man of *megalopsychus*, the man of great spirit will walk slowly. He will have a deep voice. He will be moderate in his behavior. He will have contempt for all worldly honors. All that he will be concerned with is, of course, his own honor. This becomes a model for the Hellenistic kings. It offers them an opportunity to perform in the role of Hellenistic king, if you will.

We have an astonishing example of this in a description of one of the early Attalid kings. It's quite clear that both Attalus and the biographer writing about him were quite aware of Aristotle's notion, because you'll hear the term cropping up in this description. So here we have a description of King Attalus I. You'll remember, of course, that the Attalids had no claim to Pergamum based on legitimacy. They had simply inherited it from their uncle, Philetaerus, who had kept it when his overlord was killed in battle. But this is how the Attalids present themselves.

> Concerning King Attalus, who died at this time, it is right that I should say something appropriate, as has been my practice with others. Originally he had no other external advantage for royalty, except wealth [remember he had inherited 9,000 talents], which, when used with intelligence and boldness is indeed of great assistance in any undertaking, but without these qualities is usually the cause of disaster, and for most people, a total ruin. That is why one ought to admire this man's greatness of spirit. [His *megalo psyche*. His Aristotelian greatness of soul.] Because he never sought to use his advantages for anything except the acquisition of royalty. No greater fairer goal can be mentioned than that. Moreover, he took the first step in achieving this design not just by conferring benefactions and favors on his friends, but also by achievements in war.

There we have the essential ideas of Hellenistic kingship. That you have to be a great man, with a certain largeness of spirit, that you must be endlessly generous to the people around you, and you have to win wars. And if you've got that combination of qualities, you're on your way towards being a great Hellenistic king. The idea of *megalo psyche* or greatness of spirit was also a model for Hellenistic philosophers, who often saw themselves, as we've seen on previous occasions, as the intellectual equivalent of kings. Despite the fact that many of the Hellenistic philosophers advised their followers, "Steer clear of kings, don't be involved in that world," the actual practice was that many of them served as advisors to the kings. So there's a very close connection between this idea of largeness of soul on the part of the king, and largeness of soul on the part of the philosopher.

Kingship, said the philosophers, as they thought about what it meant to be a king in this new world, was above review. One definition of kingship at the time frankly stated that neither descent nor legitimacy gave monarchies to men, but the ability to command an army and to handle affairs competently. In other words, the justification for being a Hellenistic king was that you did a good job. That you were effective.

Military expenditure was an important part of this equation. You had to maintain a large army, preferably mercenaries rather than a native army. And you had to be effective in warfare, not only because kings faced threats from their neighbors, but because great armies, vast fleets and the latest weapons demonstrated to your own people and to the rest of the world that you were powerful. They were a living demonstration of your might. Here the Hellenistic world is absolutely similar to the modern world, where the arms race of the Cold War was a physical expression of our sense of our own power. Great parades, whether they be in Red Square or the Champs-Elysees, are meant to demonstrate to the people the military might of their own country. The Ptolemies and the Seleucids did exactly the same thing. Building ever larger and larger boats, with more and more rowers required to move them. And at the same time, inventing new and more deadly weapons. Various types of catapults and weapons designed to hurl spears at the ranks of the enemy. So there was a kind of arms race in the Hellenistic period very comparable to our own.

There's another element here, as well. Another way of impressing people is not just by showing them your cannons and your tanks, but by putting on vast displays of your wealth, to impress people. We have a most amazing description that occurs of a grand procession held in Alexandria by Ptolemy Philadelphus (Ptolemy II). This was a procession that lasted for an entire day. During that day, floats which were up to 40 feet long, and which were pulled by up to 600 men, were dragged through Alexandria. This was a kind of bloated version of what the Greeks had earlier had in Athens on the occasion of the pan-Athenaic procession. A procession that crossed downtown Athens, celebrating the unity of Athens, and gradually coming to celebrate the power of imperial Athens. But, as with so many other things, the original Greek model is vastly blown up onto a much greater scale, by the Ptolemies. The Hellenistic world is really like the Classical world on steroids.

These floats carried gigantic tripods adorned with statues of the gods, often statues between 15 and 18 feet tall. If you've seen statues of Greek gods from Olympia or in the museums in Athens, you will know that usually they are life-size. The idea of a statue that is three times life size is something quite new. Not only that. The statues are not the old fashioned statues that stand stiffly or in repose. Rather, these are now mechanical constructions that actually move. They are primitive robots, designed, for example, to pour wine. They're meant to be spectacular and to impress people because of their novelty and because of their size and because of their ingenuity. Novelty, size, ingenuity. Three features of the Hellenistic Age.

The procession was meant to impress also because of the sheer number of people involved. Thousands of men and women and children. But you don't just get anybody off the street, wearing their everyday clothes. You want them to be carrying boxes made of the most precious woods, or inlaid with gold and with silver and throwing out money to the crowd. Encrusted vessels. You want them to be dressed in costumes with outlandish fabrics and adorned by ostrich feathers and so forth.

These are going to be accompanied by the kind of creatures that you don't find in the Mediterranean, but which must be brought from beyond, in order, again, to demonstrate the enormous wealth and power of the Ptolemies. So you'll have vessels that are being dragged along by elephants and chariots that are being drawn by antelope and ostriches. Why? Because Ptolemy can do it. He can afford to do it. He's got the power to do it and the resources.

We know, in fact, that the Ptolemies maintained elephant hunting stations along the coast of the Red Sea so that troops of Ptolemy's army would be sent out every year, hunting these animals, either to bring them back for their ivory, or in the case of other animals, from sub-Saharan Africa, bringing them back live to put them on display. It's a kind of conspicuous consumption, if you will, that is designed to dazzle and impress everyone by the sheer amount of wealth on display. Let me read you a short part of the description. This is only a short part. It's a very long description. It really was a most amazing event.

130 Ethiopian sheep; 300 Arabian, 20 Nubian and 26 Indian oxen [notice these are coming from areas way beyond the Mediterranean] (all white); 8 Ethiopian, one large white she-bear; 14 leopards; 16 panthers; 4 lynxes; 3 young panthers; 1 giraffe; 1 Ethiopian rhinoceros. Next, on a four-wheeled carriage, a statue of Dionysos at the altar of Rhea, having taken refuge when pursued by Hera with a golden crown, and Priapus standing next to him wearing a golden ivy crown. [So figures from Greek mythology, little tableaux put on these floats.] Then, statues of Alexander [of course; it's the Ptolemies, but they're going to begin with the number one man, Alexander] and Ptolemy wearing ivy crowns made of gold. The statue of Virtue standing next to Ptolemy had an olive crown made of gold. Priapus stood next to them, with a golden ivy crown. [Priapus, this figure that represents the fertility of the Nile. The fertility of the Ptolemaic realm.] The city of Corinth standing next to Ptolemy was crowned with a golden diadem, [representing the connection between Old Greece and the Ptolemies.] Besides all these were placed a stand for drinking vessels, full of golden cups and a golden mixing bowl with a capacity of five measures (much larger than an ordinary one). This four-wheeled chariot was followed by women wearing expensive clothes and ornaments. They were given the names of cities. Some from Ionia and the rest of the Greek cities which were established in Asia and the islands that had been under Persian rule. They all wore golden crowns.

So we have a kind of beauty parade of lovely young women coming along, all representing particular countries or cities that have now come under the control of Ptolemy. On another four-wheeled cart was carried a Bacchic rod of gold, 90 cubits long. That's 135 feet long. This is the staff carried by Dionysos. But it's 135 feet long. A silver lance 90 feet long. We could go on, but you get the effect, I think, of just this massive glorification of excess in the wealth of the Ptolemies. What did you do with this? Apart from putting it on display, you spent it. You showed your generosity by giving the money back. The king's generosity was used to express his appreciation of Greek culture. The Attalid kings of Pergamum were especially generous, in building entire buildings in Athens. They and the Ptolemies also gave money to the Greeks to rebuild after earthquakes. This was the great power that you went to. They were the ones who sent grain fleets to Greece during times of famine. Again, if we think of the modern world, what are the organizations and what is the country to whom the rest of the world turns in times of crisis? Organizations like the World Bank and the United Nations and particularly the United States. People turn to these countries and organizations because of their power and their wealth and their prestige. This is what the Hellenistic kings are claiming for themselves as well.

In their courts, the Hellenistic kings patronized Greek poets, Greek musicians, painters, and sculptors. They vied with each other to turn each one of their capital cities (Alexandria, Pergamum, Antioch and Pella) into cities which were really comparable to Athens. Often, by giving buildings to the Athenians, they made even more concrete the connection between the two cities. So Greek culture is being transported out, and at the same time, Hellenistic cultures are being brought in to Athens. The old and the new are mixing.

Greek artists, who were patronized by these great kings, would then glorify them, by connecting them to the heroic figures of the past. So it's a kind of contractual arrangement, if you will, with the Hellenistic kings gaining as a result of their benefactions. We have a long poem by Theocritus (Idyll number 17). I won't read the entire poem, but it will give you an idea of the kind of language that's employed in this court poetry.

> Countless countries and countless nations
> Helped by the reign of Zeus,
> Caused their crops to grow.
> But none is as productive as the lowlands of Egypt,
> When the Nile in flood waters and breaks up the soil.
> Nor do any have as many towns of men skilled in work.
> Three hundred cities are built there,
> Then three thousand in addition to thirty thousand.

Over all these, mighty Ptolemy rules.
In addition, he cuts off for himself
a part of Phoenicia, Arabia, Syria, Libya,
and the dark-skinned Ethiopians.

So there's the traditional wealth of Egypt, but this man simply has "cut off", as if the whole thing were a piece of meat that he could hack away at, a portion of empire for himself.

He gives orders to all the Pamphyllians
and the Cilician spearmen,
To the Lycians and the warlike Carrians.
All the sea and the land and the roaring rivers
are ruled by Ptolemy.
About him gather a host of horsemen,
and a host of shielded warriors,
Equipped with glittering bronze.

It's not a surprise that, in the Egyptian sources, writers often refer to the Greeks as "the men who wear sword-belts", because the distinguishing feature of these men is that they are a military occupying force. The royal rulers wish to present themselves this way. So the cult of the ruler, either living or dead, also bolsters this claim to legitimacy.

Modern scholars have often been skeptical about whether those subjects really did believe this kind of overblown rhetoric that I've just been reading. Did they really believe in the divinity of these Hellenistic dynasts? Previous scholars have often argued that this was not really the case; that they didn't believe in it at all. But I think that we should now see this kind of language as the language of the two sides talking to each other. A kind of contractual arrangement. Why? Because the kings are seeking a way of making themselves legitimate, and because people are seeking a way of forming a concrete connection with their kings. With bringing the kings, if you will, on their side and winning their good will.

There's a good example of this that comes from the Aegean islands, which, for a short period, were dominated by Ptolemy. During that period, the islanders, who formed a small federation, wrote to Ptolemy. It's fairly clear that they're treating him as the one superpower who they wish to be connected to.

Resolved by the delegates of the islanders concerning the matter about which Philocles, king of the Sidonians and Bacchon, the leader of the islands wrote to the cities that they should send delegates to Samos to discuss the question of the sacrifice. The sacred envoys and the contest which King Ptolemy II is instituting in honor of his father in Alexandria, to be equal in rank with the Olympic Games. Philocles and Bacchon have now conversed with the delegates, who have now arrived from the cities.

So all of these cities have been worried about this particular set of games being set up by King Ptolemy. What they say is:

Be it resolved by the common body of these delegates of the islands: Since King Ptolemy the Savior has been responsible for many great blessings to the islanders and to the other Greeks, having liberated the cities, restored their laws, established to all their ancestral constitution, and remitted their taxes, and since now, King Ptolemy, having inherited the kingdom from his father continues to show the same good will and concern and is offering a sacrifice, [blah, blah, blah. It then continues:] Let us make these sacrifices in honor of Ptolemy and honor him.

I won't read you the rest of the inscription. What it shows us, though, is that this was the diplomatic language of the time. This was how you spoke to these great kings. You didn't simply send off ambassadors to say, "We would like you very kindly to remit our taxes." You go along and say, "We wish to have a sacrifice in honor of you and in honor of your father. We wish to recognize your godhead." Of course in return, you would incur the good will of the gods.

So Hellenistic kingship is one of performance, one of display, and it is a contract. Aside from all that, there are various practicalities to be taken into account as well. Hellenistic kingship also relies on administrative arrangements to actually keep the kingdoms running. Here, the model that the kings rely upon is purely taken from Macedonian tradition. In earlier Macedonian tradition, the king had been the first among equals. He had gone hunting with his comrades and he had gone to war with his comrades. So now, too, the kings of the Hellenistic kingdoms also have their comrades, who are known as their *philoi*. Technically, their friends. So it draws on a

Macedonian tradition of companionship, and this informal network of associates and advisors really acts as the upper echelon, running the entire kingdom. Gradually, during the course of the 2nd century, this comes to be complemented by a much more elaborate system. A fixed hierarchy of officials with titles, grades, and specific duties. Yet they will often refer to themselves as the *philos*, the "friend" of the king, even though they might be minor local magistrates.

Together, the *philoi*, the family of the king, and the upper echelons of the bureaucracy constituted the court, or, as the Greeks called it, the *aulos*. A series of concentric circles with the king at the center, and, notably, only Greeks around him. Hellenistic kingship, then, did a remarkably good job of adapting to the new conditions of the Hellenistic Age, by drawing both on Macedonian practices and local practices. Did the people of the age believe these men were gods? Finally, I don't know. But it certainly was to their advantage to say that they did.

Lecture Sixteen
Benefaction

Scope:

The Hellenistic Age would witness an increasing reliance on individual citizens, often of extraordinary wealth, to keep cities from starving or going bankrupt. Earlier city-state institutions provided a model for this, but in the Hellenistic Age, *euergetism* (voluntary gift giving) became critical to the survival of cities.

Outline

I. In the Classical period, such cities as Athens had relied on their wealthiest citizens to pay for many of the city's annual expenses. Cities benefited from the wealth of the elite, while the leading members of society enhanced their status in displays of wealth on behalf of the community.

  A. This system of expenditure on behalf of the public good was broken into different components, known as liturgies.

  B. There were two main types of liturgy.

   1. The *chorego*s, or producer, was responsible for producing a dramatic performance at the festival of Dionysus. He commissioned the playwright, paid the actors, and purchased all the costumes and scenery.

   2. *Trierarchs* were each responsible for the upkeep of a single trireme. They paid for tackle and equipment, guaranteeing the seaworthiness of the vessel for an entire year.

II. In the 5th century this system operated on a regular annual basis, but in the 4th century, it began to break down as states found it more and more difficult to fill the ranks of the liturgical class.

  A. In the Hellenistic period, the formal system of liturgies was replaced by ad hoc arrangements in which the super-rich and a narrowly defined elite emerged as the benefactors and sometimes saviors of the Hellenistic cities.

   1. The term for such behavior was *euergesia*, and the title of benefactor (*euergetes*) was adopted by many Hellenistic kings.

     2. The title was also conferred on many ambitious private citizens.

   B. Euergetism reflects the hierarchical arrangement of Hellenistic societies. It also points to a widening gap between the community as a whole and the few powerful men on whom the communities relied for their survival.

III. Benefactions could come in a wide variety of services and gifts. Public buildings, shipments of grain, and new fortifications were all regularly given to cities by their wealthy benefactors. Benefactors paid for *gymnasia*, public schools, acting companies, and public doctors. Two towns on the Black Sea, Istria and Olbia, have left us a rich legacy of public documents that show how benefactors were essential to the survival of the cities.

   A. In one inscription, the council and assembly of Istria record their gratitude to a certain Hephaestion.

     1. The city had taken out a loan of 300 gold pieces, but for nearly 20 years, it had repaid neither the loan nor the interest, which alone now amounted to 400 gold pieces.

     2. Hephaestion canceled the interest altogether, on the condition that the principal be repaid over 2 years.

   B. In another instance, the Istrians were suffering from raids by marauding Scythians, who had driven off their flocks. A benefactor, Agathocles, served as ambassador to the Scythians, paid them to leave the city alone, and led the Istrian forces into battle when the Scythians broke their word.

   C. The fullest account of a benefactor's career is that of Protogenes of Olbia, recorded in an inscription that is nearly 200 lines long.

     1. Three times, when the city had no money left, Protogenes gave sums of up to 900 gold pieces to a local chieftain to buy him off.

     2. He redeemed sacred vessels that the city had pawned to pay its debts.

     3. He twice gave the city interest-free loans to pay for grain when the inhabitants faced starvation and bought out the debts owed by the city, which he then forgave.

4. In time of war, he spent 1,500 gold pieces to rebuild the city's walls, towers, and gates.

5. Olbia finally owed Protogenes 6,000 gold pieces, a debt that he canceled completely.

IV. The decrees honoring the benefactors of the Hellenistic states provide some of our richest evidence for daily life in the Hellenistic Age. These documents point to a period of danger and turmoil in which many people must have faced terrifying uncertainty every day. The novels we have discussed also reflect this quality of the age.

    A. A decree from the island of Amorgos in the Aegean recounts a hair-raising episode in which pirates came ashore and kidnapped more than 30 people, including women and girls, both slave and free.

        1. Two of the prisoners were brothers named Hegesippus and Antipappus, who successfully negotiated the release of most of the prisoners and offered themselves as hostages.

        2. They were subsequently honored for their bravery.

    B. In other instances, a benefactor might not only negotiate the release of people captured by pirates but also serve as an ambassador to states such as Crete that sponsored piracy. A certain Eumaridas of Cydonia, for example, was awarded a bronze statue in Athens because he ransomed Athenians captured by pirates, then persuaded the Cretan pirates to leave the Athenians alone.

V. The reality of the Hellenistic Age was that individual cities were far weaker than the kings who now ruled territories as large as all of Greece put together. Cities often lacked the means to rebuild after earthquakes or to defend themselves against outside attack.

    A. Because of this vulnerability, the cities relied more and more on their benefactors to protect them. And because the goodwill of the king was so vital to their survival, cities also relied on benefactors to intercede with the powerful kings of the age.

    B. One city in Asia Minor received a governor sent by one of the Attalid kings of Pergamum. Corragus proved to be a valuable intermediary between the local population and their monarch.

1. He negotiated the restoration of the city's ancestral constitution, effectively leaving the city to govern itself.
2. He restored the city's sacred precincts and arranged for royal subsidies to pay for the city's cults.
3. At his own expense, Corragus supplied the city with animals for sacrifice.
4. He convinced the king to extend a tax exemption for the city from 3 to 5 years.
5. He also arranged for the royal treasury to purchase private property for indigent citizens.

VI. Benefaction, therefore, has to be seen as one of the most characteristic and important public institutions of the Hellenistic Age.

Suggested Reading:

P. Veyne, *Bread and Circuses: Historical Sociology and Political Pluralism.*

Questions to Consider:

1. How would the cities of the Hellenistic world have negotiated with the kings of the age had there been no prior institution of liturgical service?
2. In the dealings between cities and kings, who gained more from the kings' desire to act as benefactors?

Lecture Sixteen—Transcript
Benefaction

On a number of occasions in our series of lectures on Alexander the Great and the Hellenistic world, we've had occasion to talk about this concept of benefaction. On a number of occasions we've seen particular Hellenistic kings acting as benefactors of certain states or of certain cities. This concept of benefaction is one of the most crucial concepts and one of the most crucial institutions of Hellenistic life that I'd like to spend one of the lectures in this series discussing the origins of this institution. Where does it come from? What did the Greeks mean by this when they used the term *euergetism*? (Or *benefaction*, as it becomes in Latin.) What was its role in the survival of the cities of the Hellenistic world?

There are a couple of key terms here that we must be familiar with. I've already mentioned the term *euergetism*. This is merely a Greek expression, which in Latin will become *benefaction*. It's an important term to understand, though, because it's often also the title of the Hellenistic king. Many of the kings, many of the Ptolemies and Seleucids were known as Ptolemy Soter (Ptolemy Savior) or Ptolemy Euergetes (Ptolemy the Benefactor). So it is an official title. It has a specific meaning in that range of titles that the Hellenistic kings come to have. Just as they like to be called "saviors" or "gods" this is also one of the most powerful terms in the vocabulary of politics and statecraft during the Hellenistic period.

It was not an original institution, though, founded in the Hellenistic Age. It has roots in the earlier periods of Greek history. In the Classical Age, the city-states of the Greek world had often operated with the help of an institution known as the *liturgy*. When I use the term "liturgy" there is obviously the opportunity for confusion, because we use "liturgy" in English now to mean the words and the ritual practices associated with a religious event. The words of the mass, for example. This is not what the term *liturgy* originally means in Greek. Rather, it refers to an undertaking, a task undertaken by a wealthy individual on behalf of his home state. These *liturgies*, as they were called, these publicly undertaken tasks done for the benefit of the community, were very important in the Classical world (particularly in Classical Athens), as a way of establishing the status of the individuals involved.

In the Classical period, to put the matter at its most simple, cities such as Athens relied on the wealthiest citizens to pay for many of the city's annual expenses. Ancient cities didn't tax at the same rate or in the same way that we do in the modern world. So ancient cities tended to have much lower revenues than contemporary states, and therefore were often in the position of being unable to afford the basic running expenses of the state for a particular year. In this way, by calling upon the wealthy to take on specific tasks for the state, the cities benefited by getting the wealth of the elite. The leading members of society enhanced their position, because instead of simply paying tax at a higher rate, as they may in the modern world, in this ancient system, they were in a position to enhance their own status by very public displays of spending on behalf of the community.

So the ancient concept of the liturgy is an example of something we've seen elsewhere in the Hellenistic world of a set of reciprocal relations. You do something for me and I do something for you. This system of expenditure in the Classical world, of liturgies undertaken on behalf of the public good, was broken into various components. The best known of these liturgies was that of the *choregos*. The *choregos* was responsible for producing the dramatic festivals held in honor of gods such as Dionysos.

When the Athenians went to see their dramas, they didn't do it by simply turning on a TV or even by just buying a ticket for whatever was playing in the theater that night. Instead, they went to a religious event, held at a specific time each year. There they would see a set of plays held on the first day. Another set of plays on the second day. And another set of plays on the third day. Each day's set of performances was paid for by one producer, as we would call him, using the contemporary analogy with Hollywood. This producer commissioned the playwright, he then paid the actors and he purchased all the costumes and all the scenery that were used during the performance. So he really was responsible for every aspect of mounting the production. This is really something undertaken by the wealthy and the ambitious, because you get your name known as a result of doing this.

One of the first public events involving Pericles, the man who, in 5th century Athens will come to stand for the might of the Athenian Empire, is his performance as *choregos*, his taking on of this public liturgy, in 472, when he paid for the production of Aeschylus' play, *The Persae*. So you advertise your arrival in Athenian politics as, say, a thirty-year-old man, having done your military service and now moving into your maturity by producing one of these plays. By spending your money for the benefit of the state.

The other great example of a liturgy in the Classical world, prior to the Hellenistic period, was that of the *trierarchs*. The *trierarchs* were men whose name means exactly "commanders of *triremes*." At one period of Greek history these may have been the actual naval officers who ran the *triremes*, the ship captains, but during much of the Classical period the *trierarchs* were rather the men who paid for the upkeep of a ship.

So, unlike our modern state, where our taxes are spent by the government to support all of our armed forces, in the Greek world (at least in Athens), individual men, each year would take on the duty of paying for the upkeep of a boat. If it was too badly damaged, paying for its complete replacement. Paying for al the tackle that needed to be used every year. The sails and the ropes and the spars that had to be brought from Macedon, or from other parts of the Greek world. They paid also for the crew. So the boat was kept seaworthy and the crew was paid, and it was not done at state expense, but rather it was done by individuals.

I explain this in some detail, even though this all refers to the period before the Hellenistic Age, because I want to establish here the groundwork. This is the institution that the Greeks understand. However, while in the 5th century this system operated on a regular, annual basis, in the 4th century in the Greek world, it began to break down. States began to find it harder and harder to fill the ranks of what can be called the liturgical class. The ranks of the super-rich. The men who can take on these jobs every year. It's that breakdown in the 4th century that really leads us into the Hellenistic period and the informal institution that replaces that of liturgies. Instead of there being definite tasks which must be assigned on a yearly basis, to a certain group of men, in the Hellenistic Age what happens is that *ad hoc* arrangements replace the liturgical system.

In these *ad hoc* arrangements, the super-rich, a very, very narrowly defined elite at the top echelon of society emerges as the group who are wealthy enough and willing to act as the benefactors of the Greek states. They do this, not on a regular yearly basis, but as needed. The term for such behavior is *euergesia*, benefaction. The title of such a person is a *euegetes*, a benefactor. We've seen that it's a term used by (a title used by) many of the Hellenistic kings, but it isn't confined only to the kings. This system, in fact, operates at other levels of Greek society, as well. The title of *euergetes* or "benefactor" can be conferred on an ambitious private individual who performs a function in the service of the state.

It really is, in some respects, the key institution that explains the arrangement of Hellenistic society, because it is fundamentally a hierarchical arrangement. It is based on the vulnerability of the state and the community and their reliance on the good will and the willingness of the leading powers of the day, whether it be the ruling elite or the kings, to save the state. In a way, it allows Hellenistic communities to exist in a state of almost permanent crisis. Always relying upon the good will and generosity of some merchant or some king or some other benefactor.

I think that the prevalence of this institution (because it can be attested throughout the Hellenistic world at all times) points to a widening gap, in the Hellenistic Age, between the community as a whole and the very few powerful men on whom these communities rely for their survival. So I think that in the prevalence of *euergesia* or benefaction, we see a major feature of the Hellenistic Age, which we can compare with the earlier Classical Greek world. The Greek world had been moving in places like Athens towards democracy. We would not see democracy on a grand scale in the Hellenistic world, but we would see local autonomy, where individual communities could continue to act democratically if that's what their local set of laws dictated.

But there is a new level of power that exists above any individual city, and that is the power of the benefactors, these men (whether they be kings or merchants) who can really determine the fate of the city. Because, as is going to become apparent from some of the documents we'll look at, if a benefactor does not step in to save a city, the city will essentially die.

I think that the scale of the Hellenistic world, and the scale of economy, is one that is not merely geographically spread out, but one where we see far greater gaps, or far greater distances between the vast majority of people and the few wealthy, on whom society relied for its continued existence. Benefactions could come in a variety of

©2000 The Teaching Company.

services and gifts. Some states received public buildings. Particularly places like Athens, and particularly the great religious sanctuaries, were given wonderful *stoas*, where people could move away from the hot sun and could get protection from the rain and where they could set up their shops. Or new temples, or new theaters. These are some of the most popular benefactions. But these are the ones that tend to be given by the kings as ways of advertising their power.

What the cities often need is something more practical to survive. For example, shipments of grain. The Hellenistic cities often suffered from grain shortages, as grain was brought in from increasingly greater distances. As cities grew, it became harder and harder for them to feed themselves. At times they would rely on the good will of a benefactor to actually divert a shipment of grain to their city so that people, quite literally, did not starve. New fortifications were regularly given by cities, as they had to build higher and stronger walls as a result of the changes in the techniques of Hellenistic warfare.

A whole series, a whole slew of institutions now in the Hellenistic world (not seen before this) are paid for by benefactions. For example, cities now tend to build more and larger *gymnasia*, where their young men can recreate and where they can take courses of lectures from professors. We also find in the Hellenistic Age many cities establishing a public schooling system, where teachers will be paid for on the public payroll. We even know of acting companies, which, at various times were operating in the red and needed to get assistance. Sounds very much like the modern age. We also know of public doctors, so the Hellenistic world experienced public medicine, rather than just private medicine for the first time. All of these institutions of civic life had to be paid for. It put an increasing burden on the states, and many of the towns were unable to meet their bills and so relied on private benefactors to come in.

We have particularly good evidence about this practice of *euergetism* from two cities located up on the Black Sea: Istria and Olbia. It's particularly ironic that Olbia ended up needing a wealthy man to support them, because Olbia had come into existence hundreds of years earlier as a Greek colony, located in what we would now call the Ukraine, precisely because the region was so rich. In fact, the name of the colony "Olbia" means "wealthy." Yet, by the Hellenistic period, it was often reduced to relying on one man to save it from going under. These two towns, then, have left us a rich legacy of public documents that tell us about the fate of the cities and their survival.

In one inscription, the council and the assembly of the city of Istria record their gratitude to a private individual known as Hephaestion. A very suggestive name, since it's the same name as Alexander's best friend, but it is not the same character, by any means. The city had taken out a loan of 300 gold pieces, but for nearly 20 years, the people of Istria had been unable to repay either the loan or the interest, which, of course, kept accruing. Now, the interest alone, because of the length of time that the debt was outstanding, amounted to 400 gold pieces. So the city was getting into worse and worse financial straits every year, and had no prospect of either balancing its budget or meeting its financial demands. Hephaestion, one single individual, canceled the interest altogether. The loan was owed to him. He basically canceled the interest, worth 400 gold pieces, on condition that the principal be repaid over two years. So here we have an example of a city only being able to balance its entire budget because of the generosity of the one man from whom they had borrowed money in the first place.

In another instance, the people of Istria were suffering from raids by marauding Thracians, people from further north. These Thracians had driven off their flocks. It was a benefactor by the name of Agathocles who served in a number of capacities helping the people of Istria in their dealings with these marauding Thracians. For example, he served as an ambassador to them. He paid the Thracian nomads to leave the city alone. Then when these marauders broke their word, it was Agathocles who went after them in battle.

Let me read you some of the inscription. One of the remarkable features of this is that this inscription as we have it, and it is not complete, is well over 60 lines long. So the inscriptions are getting longer and longer in the Hellenistic world. They also are getting inflated, just like everything else, as you go into more and more detail. It must have been hellish for the stone mason who was cutting this, but it's excellent for us, because we get such detailed information about the events of the day. This inscription talks about when the city was in a state of confusion and a large number of Thracian pirates were attacking the land and the city.

> The harvest was imminent and the citizens were in distress. Our man, Agathocles, was elected commander of the archers. He took in mercenaries. [He paid for more troops.] And protected the land and enabled the citizens to gather in the crops without harm.

So he leads the force that protects the locals. And when the Thracians under King Zoltes came with a larger force to Scythia and the Greek cities under the rule of King Remaxus, Agathocles was elected ambassador. He traveled across enemy territory, passing through many tribes avoiding any danger, and persuading the barbarians not only to not do harm to our city, but even to give back the flocks that they had previously stolen.

The city actually pays over a certain amount of money to this King Zoltes, to prevent the deprivations going any further. So they paid off these marauders to get some security, but what happens? The marauders come back for more. This time, Agathocles, when the Thracians broke their oath of agreement, and made continuous raids, Agathocles was elected by the people to be general over the land, with full powers, and took volunteer troops from among the citizens and barbarians who had taken refuge in the city.

And so it goes on with further instances of his benefactions to the city. The entire city here is relying on the good will of one man. It's very interesting that at one point in the inscription they say he is made commander with full powers. He's almost being made a dictator or a tyrant over the city. The city is so incapable of defending itself that it must almost hand over supreme power to this one man, Agathocles.

The city of Olbia, further north, in the Ukraine, also gives us a very full account of the career of a typical benefactor, a man by the name of Protogenes. His name originally means the "first born." He was clearly a man of substance and importance. The inscription that records his involvement in the affairs of the city is even longer than the one we've just looked at. It goes to over 200 lines. Once again, it gives very precise detail of the way in which he stepped in to save the city in times of crisis. Three times the city was bankrupt. It had simply run out of money. On these occasions, he gives 900 gold pieces to a local chieftan by the name of Citophernes, who was raiding the city. The city is bankrupt because it's been paying off these nomads. Trying to give them money if they will leave their flocks alone. But this doesn't succeed. Each time they come back. They get paid more money. Eventually the city has no more money left and they still have these nomads on their doorstep, ready to sack, plunder, pillage and burn. One man, Protogenes, steps forward and pays money to this local character. The city has gone into hock. It has actually pawned all of its sacred vessels in order to raise cash to give to Citophernes. So it is Protogenes who actually buys back the sacred vessels and redeems them, once they've been pawned.

Twice the city gets interest-free loans from him, when the city is facing starvation, and he pays for the grain out of his own pocket. The city, still in debt because it owes money to various other people as well. He will buy up all the debt and cancel it altogether, forgiving the debt. So he saves the city from starvation. He saves the city from marauding nomads on their doorsteps. In times of war he spends 1500 gold pieces out of his own money to restore the city's walls, its towers and its gates. So this one man is responsible for its physical defense. By the end of his long and illustrious career, Protogenes is owed by the city of Olbia 6,000 gold pieces. A debt which he promptly cancels. Would that the powers that be today would be so generous. Perhaps we should tell the IRS about this policy. I think we must look at these documents with mixed feelings. On the one hand it is wonderful and laudable that there were men willing to step forward and save the day and to step in in these various vulnerable cities. But the fact that the cities were coming to rely on this illustrates, I think, a very dangerous reliance on the super-rich.

The decrees honoring these benefactors of the Hellenistic states provides some of our richest evidence for daily life in the Hellenistic Age, and they also point quite clearly to a period of immense danger, of immense turmoil, when people must have been facing terrifying uncertainty every day. I think it's worthwhile remembering this, given that we've already looked at the Hellenistic romances and the novels, which so often turn on a plot which involves some reversal of fortune, when somebody suddenly is thrown from prosperity into destitution and slavery.

These inscriptions, which are not literary documents, but rather are real productions of these cities, I think illustrate that those novels are reflecting the actual conditions of the time. Many people must have faced dreadful circumstances on a daily basis, and they had to rely on the good will of powerful individuals to step in. I think this also helps to account for the success of the Hellenistic kings in selling themselves as gods. People wanted to have someone powerful in their life.

Some of the most dramatic evidence involving this vulnerability and the reliance on the powerful few, comes from a set of inscriptions that deal with the phenomenon of piracy, which was endemic in the Hellenistic world, and was found in all parts and at all times of the Hellenistic Age. We have a particularly moving inscription that comes from the small island of Amorgos. It's just a dot in the Aegean Sea. But listen to this and try to imagine the situation that it's describing. The council and the people have resolved, as a result of a motion:

> Since, when pirates made an incursion into the countryside at night, and captured a total of more than 30 girls, women, and other people, both free and slave, and scuttled the ships in the harbor and captured the ship of Doriyus, in which they sailed off with their captives and the rest of their booty. When all this had happened, Hegesippus and Antipappus, who were themselves prisoners, persuaded Cycliades, the king of the pirates, to release the free persons and some of the freedmen and slaves, and volunteered to act as hostages on their behalf.

This is really dramatic stuff. These men have been captured, and they've said, "Look. We're very wealthy. We'll go as hostages. Keep us. Let the others go and we'll eventually make sure that you get the money." And they showed great concern that none of the citizen women or men of the city should be carried off as booty and sold, nor suffer torture and hardship, and that no free person should perish. Thanks to these men, the prisoners were saved and returned home without suffering harm.

So the city goes on to vote a crown in honor of these benefactors. I find this a very powerful document to read, because it reminds you that honoring people as benefactors wasn't something that you just did as empty rhetoric. Often, there was a real sentiment of gratitude behind this, because these men had really saved your life and the life of your community.

In another instance, a benefactor might not only negotiate the release of people captured by a pirate, but he might even serve as an ambassador to one of the states that sponsored piracy. Here, once again, the Hellenistic world bears remarkable similarities to our own. We speak customarily of states that sponsor terrorism. The same sort of phenomenon existed in the Hellenistic world. Crete (the island of Crete) and Aetolia in northwestern Greece were notorious regions where pirates lived, and from where they operated, as was the southern coast of Asia Minor in the area known as Cilicia. In fact, there's a very good survey being undertaken right now of that particular region, trying to reconstruct what the daily life of these pirate societies was like.

In one case we know of a certain man called Eumaridas of Cydonia, who was awarded a bronze statue in Athens because he'd ransomed Athenians who had been captured by pirates, and had then persuaded the Cretan pirates to leave the Athenians alone. So the Athenians had actually got an exemption, if you will. If a Cretan boat coming from this particular port saw an Athenian boat, they'd say, "Right. You can go on through." Whereas if it were a Corinthian boat, or a Samian boat, they would then capture it and take the people off. So these pirates weren't just one or two boats flying the Jolly Roger, going around the Eastern Mediterranean. These were often organized fleets of states' ships that preyed on both the ships and even the settlements of other places. You could negotiate with them to actually buy a kind of exemption from them.

Piracy, as I said, was endemic around the Mediterranean. It was, of course, tied to the trade in slavery. This is how the Mediterranean kept up its supply of slaves. Not just by breeding slaves, but by constantly allowing people to be captured like this and to be sold at the great slave markets, as on the island of Delos. So it was an age in which people might truly be terrified that their circumstances in life could change. This is reflected in the novels, and also in the plays of a popular playwright such as Menander.

Once again, as with the novels, the plays often involve someone being a free citizen in one city, going off to a festival and being captured by pirates and then being sold into slavery. As one of the characters in one of Menander's plays says, "Cheer up, my friend. The Sicyonian officer who has bought you is a good man, and a rich man. You'll be well treated." Not much consolation if you really had fallen into the hands of slavers.

The reality of the Hellenistic Age, then, was that individual cities were far weaker than the kings, who now ruled territories as large as all Greece put together. Cities often lacked the means to rebuild after earthquakes. They often lacked the means to restore their walls and to fend off outside attack. Because of this vulnerability, they relied more and more on benefactors to protect them. Because the good will of the king was so vital to their survival, cities also relied on benefactors to intercede with the powerful kings of the age.

We've already commented that many of these kingdoms had between the king and the local communities a network of bureaucrats, of local governors. Of course these local governors then also end up being seen as benefactors, because they can both help a city and intervene between a city and a king. One city of Asia Minor, for example, was sent a governor by one of the Attalid kings of Pergamum. His name was Corragus. He proved to be a very valuable intermediary between the local population and the king back in Pergamum. We know from honors voted to him by the local population that he had negotiated the restoration of the city's ancestral constitution. What that means in practice is that the city was left to govern itself. Provided they paid their taxes when necessary, and didn't cause any disruption, they were left autonomous. Two: he restored the city's sacred precincts and arranged for royal subsidies to pay for the city's cults. So the city was able to restore its temples and its altars, and it even got money from the king in Pergamum to help operate its religious festivities. Three: he himself, out of his own pocket, paid for the beasties that were then sacrificed at these annual festivals. Number four: he convinced the king to extend a tax exemption for the city, from three to five years. So the city was not only getting money coming in from the king in Pergamum, but not having to pay it out. Then, finally, he arranged for the royal treasury to purchase private property to give back to indigent citizens.

So all of the institutions which, in our world, are really incorporated into the state, really here are relying on the good will of individuals. Benefaction, as a result, has to be seen as one of the most important and characteristic public institutions characterizing the Hellenistic Age.

Lecture Seventeen
The Maccabean Revolt, Part I

Scope:

The most well-documented example of a rebellion against Hellenistic overlords by their non-Greek subjects is the Maccabean revolt, beginning in 166 B.C. The revolt came in response to the desecration of the temple in Jerusalem by the soldiers of Antiochus IV. In two lectures we will examine these events, asking how and why this persecution of the Jews arose and what the revolt tells us about the relationship between Greeks and their non-Greek subjects.

Outline

I.   The persecution of the Jews and the triumph of Jewish independence are themes that resonate in our century.

    A. It is difficult to delve more deeply into this subject without bringing some modern analogs to bear on the interpretation, for example, to see Antiochus IV as an ancient precursor to Hitler.

    B. The Maccabean revolt appears as a successful military resistance to what otherwise might have been an ancient Holocaust.

    C. But the ancient and modern persecutions are actually very different.

        1. The Hellenistic world had no clear anti-Semitic context.

        2. No ancient scientific theory existed that posited the biological inferiority of Jews.

        3. The ancient world did not see the gradual imposition of legal restrictions imposed on the Jews analogous to the German laws of 1933.

II. The Seleucids had long dealt tolerantly with Jews who had assimilated Greek practices.

    A. Antiochus repeatedly negotiated with high-ranking Jews who went by such Greek names as Jason, Menelaus, and Lysimachus.

    B. The Jewish community in Judaea was not like a Jewish ghetto in Antioch or Seleucia, or any other Syrian city, but a

        ©2000 The Teaching Company.

separate and completely distinct region within the Seleucid empire.

1. Judaea paid its taxes, sent tribute to the Seleucid king, and had supported the Seleucids in wars against the Ptolemies.
2. Judaea was a peaceful, well-integrated part of the Seleucid realm.
3. The Seleucids ruled a polyethnic empire, and they did so pragmatically; it was not in their interest to antagonize the Jews.

C. The Seleucid persecution of the Jews is a puzzle. We have to ask, why did Antiochus IV turn against the Jews, and what does this conflict reveal about the relations between Greeks and non-Greeks in the Hellenistic world?

III. The oldest interpretation of Antiochus's change of policy is that he saw himself as a champion of Hellenism, which he intended to impose on his entire empire. He tried, it is argued, to create a common culture and worship for all of his kingdom.

A. The justification for this view goes back to the First Book of Maccabees, composed around 100 B.C., in which we read that the king issued a proclamation to his whole kingdom that all were to become a single people, each renouncing his particular customs.

B. This explanation requires a remarkable about-face, because the original Seleucid policy toward the Jews was one of toleration.

1. Earlier, Antiochus III had expressly confirmed the rights of the Jews. Even in 2 Maccabees 3.2, the compiler of the Jewish record of the revolt says, "It came about that the kings themselves honoured the Holy Place."
2. Into the first half of the 2nd century, the Seleucids treated the Jews as a distinct people whose traditions were respected in precisely the same manner as the Seleucids treated their other subjects.

C. Furthermore, it is unlikely that Antiochus had decided to impose Hellenistic uniformity.

1. Local coinage continued to use local symbols and types; Hellenistic motifs were not suddenly adopted.

2. Nothing in the records or documents from Uruk or Babylon or elsewhere in Mesopotamia shows a sudden adoption of Hellenistic practices.

3. Across the Seleucid realm, the record after 167 B.C. reveals a continuation of the same local and indigenous cults, practices, and titles as before 167 B.C.

D. If Antiochus did issue a royal edict demanding the Hellenization of the entire Seleucid kingdom, the only place where we have evidence of this is the very place that chose to resist. This has led many to suspect that the royal edict is a fiction or at least that the Maccabean version is quite different from whatever the king actually decreed.

E. Some scholars have argued that what we really have is an attempt by Antiochus to foster a ruler cult in Jerusalem, that he wished to be worshipped as the incarnation of Zeus Olympius, but this explanation, too, falls short of the mark.

1. Antiochus encouraged the worship of many gods and even presented himself as a god made manifest, *epiphanes*, but the practice of all the Hellenistic kings was to graft this worship onto existing religious systems or to encourage it among subjects who shared the outlook of the Greeks.

2. It is hard to reconcile that flexibility with Antiochus's heavy-handed attack on the Temple.

IV. The Maccabean interpretation sees the persecutions by Antiochus as evidence of a clash of cultures, Greeks versus Jews. In fact, strong evidence suggests that other conflicts lay behind the rebellion, involving not just Greeks on one side and Jews on the other, but Jews against Jews in Jerusalem and Jews in the countryside against those in the city. There were three major contributing factors.

A. The first factor was the plummeting fortunes of Antiochus IV, which made him amenable to a change in policy toward the Jews.

B. The second was a power struggle in the ranks of the leading families in Jerusalem, most of whom had Hellenized.

C. The third factor was a widening gulf between the urban Jews of Jerusalem and those of the countryside, to whom Hellenism was anathema. This volatile mix led to the persecution of the Jews in 168–167 B.C. and the Maccabean revolt immediately thereafter.

V. The Seleucid realm underwent a series of setbacks in the generation before the Maccabean revolt.

    A. In 189 B.C., at the battle of Magnesia in Asia Minor, the Romans defeated Antiochus, and the following year, in 188, the Syrian king signed a peace treaty at Apamea that essentially gave up all the Seleucid territory in Asia Minor. Rome also imposed a crushing indemnity on the Seleucids.

    B. In 168, Antiochus IV embarked on a campaign against Ptolemy in Egypt, where he was met by a Roman magistrate, Gaius Popillius Laenas.

        1. Antiochus was ordered to quit Egypt. He left, humiliated.

        2. As if to show the world that Egypt and Rome were of no consequence to him, Antiochus mounted an extraordinary demonstration of his power—a parade comprised of 50,000 men in armor; 800 cadets wearing gold crowns; 1,000 cattle for sacrifice; statues of gods, nymphs, and heroes; and gold and silver plates and vessels.

        3. This display was to show the world that Antiochus had suffered no setback, but the reality was that he had. He had been bluffed by a solitary Roman magistrate and had failed to conquer Egypt.

        4. The date of the persecution of the Jews overlaps with these events entirely and not coincidentally.

Suggested Reading:

V. Tcherikover, *Hellenistic Civilization and the Jews*.

Questions to Consider:

1. Had Antiochus III not been defeated by the Romans in 189 would the Jews have been pushed toward revolt one generation later?

2. What was to be gained by reversing the earlier Antiochid policy of tolerance toward the Jews?

Lecture Seventeen—Transcript
The Maccabean Revolt, Part I

The picture of the Hellenistic Age that I've been painting in the last few lectures has not been a particularly attractive one. We've been looking at an age which was marked by coercion. Where ordinary people were often afraid because of the uncertainty of the times. We've seen an age where cities were frequently left vulnerable and where they had to rely on the good will of benefactors and kings to save them. And we've seen a world in which the power of the government was quite simply oppressive; where people faced constant daily danger; where there was a threat at any moment of being carried off by a pirate and having your life end up as that of a slave.

We might wonder if the Hellenistic Age was as bleak as the picture I've been painting. Why did more people not revolt? Why did they not try to change the system that they had been given? There are a couple of answers to this. One is that conditions in the ancient world had always been like this. Once you moved beyond the confines of a city, and you were out in the countryside, it was frequently a dangerous place to be. Governments were frequently oppressive and kings were often oppressive. There really wasn't much of an alternative that offered itself to the power structure of the Hellenistic Age.

Another answer is that rebellions did break out. Quite frequently. When probably the greatest of the kings of the Seleucid dynasty, Antiochus III, came to the throne in the early 220s, he faced a period of approximately seven years when he lost much of Asia Minor to Achaeus, a usurper who proclaimed himself king. And then later on, almost as soon as Antiochus had finished with that threat, he then faced the threat of another would-be king, the self-proclaimed King Molon, who ruled in Media, east of Syria, for another three years, from 223 down to 220. So many of the kings did face rebellions within their domains.

Possibly the most interesting of these is that by a man by the name of Aristonicus, who tried to take over the realm of the Attalids, after the death of Attalus III, in 133 B.C. You will recall that I mentioned in an earlier lecture that Attalus III, wanting to save his kingdom from being torn apart, actually bequeathed the entire kingdom to the Romans, but Aristonicus would have none of this. He raised a revolt,

©2000 The Teaching Company.

appealing to the poor, the destitute, and even appealing to slaves, to whom he offered freedom. They called themselves the "Men of the Sun State", the *Heliopolitae*, until the rebellion was finally put down.

But the one revolt about which we have the most information, the revolt which tells us most about the conditions of the Hellenistic Age and how people resisted Hellenism, in some cases, is that of the Maccabees—the revolt that took place in Judaea. It's the best-documented case, so we should look at it in some detail. The revolt came in response to the desecration of the Temple in Jerusalem by the soldiers of Antiochus IV. In the next two lectures I'd like to examine the events of this revolt in greater detail, asking how and why the persecution of the Jews took place in the mid-2nd century B.C., and what their response to this and the revolt of the Maccabees tells us about the relationship between Greeks and non-Greeks. In other words, about conditions in the Hellenistic world.

First of all, it has to be said that the persecution of the Jews by Antiochus IV and the eventual triumph of Jewish independence as a result of the Maccabean revolt are, of course, a story that resonates deeply in our century. It's very difficult for any historian to delve deeply into this story without bringing some modern analogues to bear. To put the matter quite simply, it's very difficult to read the accounts of Antiochus IV without thinking of him as, in some ways, an ancient precursor of Hitler's.

By the same token, the Maccabean revolt has attracted a good deal of attention in the 20th century because it appears as an example of a successful military resistance to what might otherwise have culminated in an ancient version of the Holocaust. So there are many ways, then, in which the Maccabean revolt resonates in our time and in our age and demands our attention.

But—and here's the important point—although there are similarities, I want to suggest that, in fact, conditions in the mid-2nd century were very different, and that the phenomenon that we're examining is not really comparable to the modern persecution of the Jews, at all. In the first place, there was no clear anti-Semitic context to these events in the Hellenistic world. The Greeks had not developed a sense that the Jews were an inferior race, or even a culture to be dismissed. Up until the late 4th century, the Greeks knew very little about the Jews at all. And when they did come in contact with them, we have an account from one of the earliest Greek historians to have any substantial contact with Judaea, a man called Hecataeus, who wrote at the very end of the 4th century, and his account is really quite remarkable. Because, in his account, he tells a story, clearly familiar with the Jewish story of the exile in Egypt, and the return, eventually, to Israel. According to Hecataeus's account this same flight out of Israel led to other foreigners going, some of whom ended up in Greece. So in Hecataeus's account, the origins of the Greeks are really quite analogous to the origins of the Jews in Israel.

Hecataeus writes at great lengths about a law-giver, comparable to a Greek figure like Solon or Lycurgus. Of course, it is Moses. So there was no sense in which there was a prior history, as there was in the case of the anti-Semitism that has been an unfortunate feature of European culture for hundreds of years. There was no ancient scientific theory that ever posited, in the worst way of the Nazis, that the Jews were biologically inferior to any other people. Certainly not the Greeks. And, there was no prior history, before the events of the Maccabean revolt of any legal restrictions placed upon the Jews within the empire of the Seleucids, analogous, for example, to the notorious laws passed against the Jews in 1933 in Germany.

In fact, the exact opposite pertains in the ancient world. The Seleucids, the kings in Syria, whose empire included the area of Judaea, had long dealt tolerably with Jews, particularly Jews who had assimilated Greek practices. Antiochus repeatedly negotiated with high-ranking Jews in Jerusalem who went by such names as Jason and Menelaus and Lysimachus. These were men who, clearly, spoke Greek, who presented themselves to the world as Greek. They were, in our parlance, assimilated. They had adopted the practices of Greek culture. It was very easy, then, for the Seleucid kings to deal with these people, because they didn't see them as entirely foreign at all. The Jewish community in Judaea was not a Jewish ghetto, in the cities of Antioch or Seleuceia or any other Syrian city. The Jewish community in Judaea was a separate and completely distinct region within the Seleucid Empire. The Seleucids were quite familiar with dealing with different ethnic groups. This was a region that paid its taxes on time. That sent tribute to the Seleucid king each year. And that had supported the Seleucid kings in their wars against the Ptolemies.

Judaea, quite simply, in the 2nd century B.C. was a peaceful, well-integrated region within the Seleucid realm. The Seleucids ruled a

©2000 The Teaching Company.

polyethnic empire. They had many different people under their control, in Bactria and in the Upper Satrapies, and in Babylon, and in Asia Minor, for a time. Their attitude, as we've seen on an earlier occasion, was utterly pragmatic. They let people be autonomous as far as possible. And they respected local tradition, as far as possible. So it was not in any shape or form in the interest of the Seleucid kings to antagonize the Jews. Quite the opposite. We have quite concrete evidence of exactly this policy of toleration that I've been trying to chart in the Seleucid realm. It comes in a letter from King Antiochus, written to his governor in Judaea, and it's recorded for us in Josephus, in his work the *Jewish Antiquities*. I'd like to read you part of this, because it's very important to keep in mind that this is the background out of which the persecution will grow.

> King Antiochus to his governor. Greetings. Since the Jews, when we entered their country, at once displayed their enthusiasm for us, and when we arrived at their city, received us magnificently, and came to meet us with their senate, and have provided abundant supplies to our soldiers and elephants, and assisted us in expelling the Egyptian garrison on the citadel—we thought it right to repay them for these services and to restore their city, which had been destroyed by the accidents of war, and to repeople it by bringing back to it those who had been scattered abroad.

And he goes on to detail (in quite astonishing detail) all of the steps to be taken to help the Jews back on their feet, by sending them wine, oil, frankincense, wheat, salt, pieces of silver. And he says, "I wish these grants to be made to them in accordance with my instructions, and the work on the Temple to be completed together with the *stoas* and anything else which needs to be built." We're actually finding here, a Seleucid policy of helping to rebuild the Temple that's been damaged. "The timber for the woodwork shall be brought from Judaea, from the other nations, and from Lebanon. No one shall charge any duty on it." So a tax-free importation of the necessary goods for rebuilding the temple. Here, Antiochus III goes on to say (and this is a very important clause):

> All the people of the nation shall govern themselves in accordance with their ancestral laws, and the senate, the priests and the scribes of the Temple, and the Temple

singers, shall be exempt from poll tax, crown tax and salt tax.

And he goes on to give further examples of his beneficence. And later on, Josephus goes on to add that there was another clause in the letter from Antiochus. Again, this is quite remarkable. He says:

> No foreigner shall be allowed to enter the precinct of the Temple, which is forbidden to the Jews, except for those who are accustomed to doing so after purifying themselves in accordance with the ancestral custom.

Fairly clearly, what this document seems to show is that there is a policy, not just of tolerance, but of actual respect on the part of the Seleucid kings. Antiochus says:

> No one shall bring into the city the flesh of horses, mules, wild or tame asses, leopards, foxes and hares, and generally of any of the animals forbidden to the Jews. Only the sacrificial animal used by their ancestors, necessary for a propitious sacrifice to God, shall they be allowed to use. Whoever transgresses these rules shall pay to the priests a fine of 3,000 drachmas of silver.

So if that's the context—if that's the policy of Antiochus III—it makes the Seleucid persecution of the Jews under Antiochus IV even more of a puzzle. We have to ask, Why did Antiochus IV turn against the Jews? Why did he turn against them? And what does the conflict between the two sides reveal about the relations between Greeks and non-Greeks in the Hellenistic world?

The oldest interpretation of Antiochus' policy is that Antiochus saw himself as a champion of Hellenism, which he intended imposing on his entire empire. In other words, his father's policy had been absolute toleration. One man turns around and says, "We're going to change that, and instead we're going to impose Hellenism on the entire kingdom. The justification for this view goes back to one of the Jewish texts dealing with the revolt, the First Book of Maccabees. In the First Book of Maccabees, we read that the king issued a proclamation to his whole kingdom that all would become a single people and each was to renounce his own particular customs. So here we have in I Maccabees (I'm reading verbatim), "The king then issued a proclamation to the whole of his kingdom, that they should all form one people, and that they should give up their own customs."

And the author of I Maccabees goes on to say:

> All the nations acquiesced in this royal edict. Many Israelites accepted his worship and sacrificed to idols and profaned the Sabbath. The king also sent letters by messenger to Jerusalem and the cities of Judaea that they should follow customs alien to their lands; banish holocausts, sacrifices and libations from the sanctuary, and profane the Sabbaths and Festivals; defile the sanctuary and the holy men; build altars and sacred enclosures and idols' temples; sacrifice pigs and unclean animals; leave their sons uncircumcised; defile themselves with every kind of impurity and abomination so as to forget the law and change all their ordinances.

And he goes on to talk about the further desecrations that took place as a result of this change in policy. So that, on one particular day in one particular month, the First Book of Maccabees records that they built "The Abomination of Desolation" on the altar. And in the cities of Judaea around, they built altars and offered incense at the doors of the houses and in the streets. Any books of the law that they found, were torn up and burned.

So this is a radical change in policy, with each of the various states within the Seleucid realm having to abandon its ways, and particularly the Jews being afflicted by this persecution. This explanation, of course, requires a remarkable about-face in Seleucid policy, because the original Seleucid policy, as we've seen, had been one of toleration. We've already read in great detail Antiochus III expressly confirming the rights of the Jews.

In fact, even in the Second Book of Maccabees, one of the other accounts of the rebellion that we have—the author of this, who, of course, is sympathetic to the Jewish side, has to concede that, up until now, the policy has been one of great friendship and respect. Second Maccabees says:

> While the Holy City lived in perfect peace and the laws were strictly observed because of the piety of the High Priest Onias and his hatred of evil, the kings themselves honored the place and glorified the Temple with the most magnificent gifts.

Into the first half of the 2nd century, the Seleucids were treating the Jewish people as a distinct ethnic group within their empire, whose traditions were to be respected in precisely the same manner as the Seleucids treated their other subjects.

So the abrupt change in policy is very hard to understand. Furthermore, there's actually very little evidence that there ever was such an official change in policy throughout the entire empire. Remember the account we had of Antiochus IV said that he forced all the nations to abandon their customs. But there doesn't seem to be any evidence supporting this. Local coinage throughout the empire continued to use local symbols and local types. It wasn't as if everyone suddenly started minting a Hellenistic Greek-style coinage. Throughout the other parts of the Seleucid realm, in Uruk, and in Babylon and in Mesopotamia, there are no changes in the records or in the documentation to show any kind of sudden adoption of Hellenistic manners and practices.

Across the Seleucid realm, the record after 167 B.C. reveals a continuation of exactly the same local and indigenous practices, local and indigenous cults. The same titles are being used as before 167 B.C. So there's very little evidence to confirm this idea of a sudden proclamation of the enforced Hellenization of the entire Seleucid realm, and it's not a policy that would appear to make terribly much sense anyway. So we're in the rather peculiar position of saying that if Antiochus did issue a royal edict demanding the Hellenization of the entire Seleucid kingdom, the only place where we have evidence for this is the one place that chose to resist—namely in Judaea. This, of course, has led many people to suspect that the royal edict that we have in Maccabees is either a fiction, or at least very different from whatever the king actually decreed.

Some scholars have argued that what we really have here is an attempt by Antiochus not to impose Hellenism uniformly across his kingdom, but to foster a ruler-cult in Jerusalem. Certainly we've seen good evidence before of the Hellenistic kings encouraging that kind of worship. According to this theory, Antiochus wished to be worshipped as the incarnation of Zeus Olympius, the Father of the Gods. But this explanation, too, I think, falls short of the mark. Antiochus encouraged the worship of many gods. He even presented himself as a god made manifest. He took on the title of *Epiphanes*, "god right here." But the practice of all the Hellenistic kings, as

©2000 The Teaching Company.

we've seen, was to graft this onto existing religious systems. Or to encourage it among subjects who shared the outlook of the Greeks.

The idea of suddenly going in, desecrating the temple, and erecting a statue of yourself as Zeus, is one that is difficult to reconcile with this policy. So on the one hand we've got a long tradition of flexibility and of respect, and then we have a rather heavy-handed attack on the Temple. How do we reconcile this?

The Maccabean interpretation sees the persecutions by Antiochus as evidence for a clash of cultures. Greeks versus Jews. Most of the treatments that you will read of this will concentrate on only these two elements. But I'd like to suggest to you that a better way of understanding the Maccabean revolt is to think of other conflicts that lay beneath the surface of the simple Greek versus Jew. These other conflicts involve Jews on one side and Jews on another side. Hellenized Jews, who have assimilated Greek culture, and those who have resisted it. And also another level of conflict underlying the Maccabean revolt is the difference between the Jews living in the city and Jews in the countryside, where a whole different range of practices and attitudes was current. I'm going to argue, therefore, that there were really three major contributing factors that gave rise to the Maccabean revolt.

One. The first was the plummeting fortunes of Antiochus IV, which made him amenable to a change in policy specifically involving the Jews. Two. The second contributing factor was a power struggle within the ranks of the leading families in Jerusalem, nearly all of whom had Hellenized. Had assimilated. The third factor I'll suggest was a widening gulf between the urban Jews of Jerusalem and the Jews of the countryside, to whom Hellenism was anathema. To whom Hellenism represented an assault on Judaism. I'll argue that it was this volatile mixture of city versus country, Hellenized versus orthodox, Greek versus Jew, and particularly the circumstances of Antiochus' rule that led to the persecution of the Jews in 168 and 167, and the Maccabean revolt that broke out immediately thereafter.

Let's start to work our way progressively through these different factors. First of all, Antiochus IV found himself in a difficult situation. The Seleucid realm in the generation before his coming to the throne had suffered a series of serious setbacks. In 189 B.C., you may recall, at the Battle of Magnesia, in Asia Minor, the Romans had defeated Antiochus. Remember, they had been coming east. And in the following year, 188 B.C., the Syrian king Antiochus III had to sign a peace treaty at Apamea, which essentially gave up all of the Seleucid territory in Asia Minor. We have an account of the conditions of this peace treaty, the Peace of Apamea in 188. The terms of this peace treaty would have crippled anyone with power less than Antiochus III, and it is really quite astonishing that the Seleucid realm managed to survive it. As a result of their military defeat at the hand of the Romans, and of the treaty that they signed the following year, Antiochus was forced to pay a crushing indemnity of 10,000 talents, to be paid over ten years in annual installments of 1,000 talents. Enough to cripple any other kingdom in the Hellenistic world. In addition to this, he was forced to hand over hostages. He was forced to cede land to King Eumenes.

Seleucid power in Asia Minor evaporated overnight. Virtually all holdings north of the Taurus Mountains, virtually all of what we call modern day Turkey, ceded at one blow. So this was a devastating defeat to the power of the Seleucids, as they lost virtually all of their western holdings. In 168 B.C., shortly after Antiochus IV had come to the throne, he embarked on a campaign against young Ptolemy in Egypt, where he was met by a Roman magistrate, by the name of Gaius Popillius Laenus. I want to read you the details of the exchange between these two, because it is a most astonishing moment, which will advertise the arrival now of Roman power in the eastern Mediterranean, and will help to explain something of the mind set of Antiochus IV, because of the crushing defeat that he now faced. Not a military defeat like his father's (Antiochus III), but a diplomatic defeat. The details are amazing.

> When Antiochus IV had advanced against Ptolemy VI, in order to take control of Pelusium [which is essentially the Gaza Strip] he was met by the Roman commander Gaius Popillius Laenus. The king greeted him by voice from a distance, and offered him his right hand. But Popillius presented to him the tablet he had in his hand, which contained the Senate's decree.

So it's a lovely theatrical moment. The king puts out his hand, and instead of receiving the hand of the Roman magistrate, the Roman hands him a scroll and says, "Read this." Laenus asked Antiochus to read it first. [Before he would even shake his hand.] In my opinion, [writes this historian] he did not want to display any mark of friendship before finding out the intentions of the recipient. Whether he was a friend or an enemy. So this is really a diplomatic standoff between them. When the king had read it [this is wonderful], he said he wanted to consult with his friends on these new developments. Greek diplomatic language meaning, "I want to consult with my court, with my advisors, my friends."

But Popillius in reply did something which seemed insolent and arrogant to the highest degree. With a vine stick which he had in his hand [sort of a field marshal's stick, if you like], he drew a circle around Antiochus, and he told him to give his reply to the message before he stepped out of the circle. This is bravado on the part of the Roman magistrate. The king was astounded at this arrogance, and, after hesitating for a moment, he said that he would do everything that the Romans asked of him. Thereupon Popillius and his colleagues shook him by the hand and all welcomed him graciously. What was it that he had agreed to by the terms of this astonishing act? The decree of the Senate required him to put an end at once to the war with Ptolemy. And so, within a stated number of days, Antiochus withdrew his army to Syria, deeply distressed at what had happened, but yielding to present circumstances. Popillius and his colleagues settled matters in Alexandria and urged the kings to preserve harmony.

This story is fascinating at many levels. Not only does it clearly show us signs of the Romans insinuating themselves in the affairs of the eastern Mediterranean, and becoming now the power brokers. Two Hellenistic kingdoms: Seleucid Syria and Ptolemaic Egypt, and who settles it with a line drawn in the sand? A Roman magistrate. But even more than this, it gives us a remarkable look at the humiliation suffered by one of these great Hellenistic kings. Antiochus had been ordered to quit Egypt without winning his campaign. Without winning anything to show for the massive effort. Without even having fought at all. He had simply been bluffed by a Roman magistrate. His reaction to this humiliation in the following year was to show, or to try to demonstrate, at least, to the world, that Egypt and Rome were of no consequence to him. So he mounted an extraordinary demonstration of his power back in Antioch, imitating the grand procession of Ptolemy Philadelphus, that I've described to you in an earlier lecture. Here, once again, a parade with all of the wealth of a great Hellenistic kingdom on display. Fifty thousand men in armor. The full Seleucid army. They may not win a battle in

Egypt, but at least they could look good turned out on parade. Eight hundred cadets wearing gold crowns. A thousand cattle for sacrifice. Statues of the gods, of heroes, of nymphs. Gold and silver plated vessels. A great display, just like that of Ptolemy. It was a display that said he hadn't suffered any kind of setback at all.

But of course, the reality was exactly the opposite. Within a generation, the Seleucids had lost all of their wealthy western realms, and they had been bluffed by a solitary Roman commander, and had failed in their attempt to conquer Egypt. This is the setting now, that will lead to and overlap with the persecution of the Jews, and the Maccabean revolt. It's to those events that we will return in the second lecture on the Maccabean revolt.

Lecture Eighteen
The Maccabean Revolt, Part II

Scope:

In December of 167 B.C., agents of the Seleucid king, Antiochus IV, entered the Temple in Jerusalem, piled unclean offerings on the altar, and forced Jews to eat sacrificial animals and to parade wearing ivy wreaths in honor of Dionysus. Copies of the Torah were burned. The Temple was rededicated to Zeus Olympius. Ten days later, after a pagan altar had been erected in front of the Temple, a pig was sacrificed, a deed that has been described as "an act of unspeakable desecration of the people of Judaea." We have seen that this persecution must be set against the collapse of Seleucid fortunes in the eastern Mediterranean between 190 and 167. Now we examine these events from the point of view of Antiochus's Jewish subjects.

Outline

I.   Through much of the 3rd century, Judaea had been under Ptolemaic rule, and the generosity of Seleucid policy toward the Jews had been prompted by an awareness that Judaea was a buffer between Egypt and Syria. The arrival of the Romans in the eastern Mediterranean, the defeat of Antiochus III in 189 B.C., and the prospect of an alliance between Rome and Ptolemaic Egypt all represented severe threats to the power of the Seleucids in this region.

   A. In 168, Antiochus faced the prospect of a Roman-Egyptian alliance.

   B. This alliance could be expected to prosecute territorial claims to Judaea, which would leave Rome or its allies in control of the seacoast from Byzantium to Cyrene with Syria the one exception.

   C. Under those circumstances, the luxury of an autonomous Judaea could no longer be afforded. The shift in policy, then, from Antiochus's point of view, was a pragmatic, cold-hearted political decision.

II. Already following his first campaign in 169 B.C., Antiochus had carried off treasures from the Temple, making it clear that his policy of generosity could be withheld or reversed when more pressing needs, such as an empty war chest, arose.

A. While campaigning in 168, Antiochus received the news that rebellion had broken out in Judaea. In fact, the violence in Judaea was the result of civil unrest between rival Jewish factions and was not an uprising against Antiochus at all. To Antiochus, however, it must have seemed as if the Jews had turned on him when he was most vulnerable.

    1. Furious, he returned to Jerusalem, where his armies slaughtered 40,000 Jews.

    2. The following year, a Seleucid general named Apollonius was dispatched with 22,000 men to Jerusalem, where they occupied the citadel known as the Akra.

    3. From the Jewish point of view, preserved in Maccabees, soldiers were sent to terrorize the population, with orders to kill all the men and enslave the women.

    4. This did not happen, although innocents were killed.

B. Once again, if we strip away the preconceived notion of Greek and Jewish antipathy, we can find a more plausible explanation for the event. Apollonius's army was sent to establish a Seleucid garrison deep in Judaean territory and to secure this region against a combined Egyptian-Roman attack or a rebellion of the local population against Antiochus or both.

C. According to this interpretation, territorial and geopolitical considerations were vastly more important to Antiochus than the questions of Hellenism, Judaism, or any other -ism.

III. What about the Jewish attitude toward the revolt? Resistance to the Greeks must be put in the context of contemporary Jewish anxieties over assimilation.

A. Religious Jews railed against "Apostates from the Law," that is, Jews who had lapsed in their observance. Yet, many Hellenized Jews lived in Jerusalem.

B. These Hellenized Jews in Jerusalem sought to reach an understanding with the pagans around them.

C. They approached Antiochus IV and were authorized to introduce Greek social practices.

D. It was Hellenizing Jews, not Greek colonists, who built a gymnasium in Jerusalem and who disguised their circumcision.

E. These Hellenized Jews were blamed by observant Jews for many of the ills that befell Judaea on the grounds that they had deserted Judaism. Nevertheless, the translation of books of the Torah into Greek suggests that many thought that Judaism and Hellenism were not irreconcilable.

IV. In this society of Hellenized Jews, factional rivalries broke out that would be catastrophic. The key rivalries were among members of a powerful clan, the Tobiads.

    A. Early in his reign, Antiochus IV was approached by a Hellenized Jew named Jason, brother of the high priest, Onias.

        1. He offered to give the king 360 talents of silver if, in return, the king recognized his claim to the high priesthood.

        2. Onias was deposed and Jason took his place.

    B. Jason seems to have renamed Jerusalem as Antioch. Rather than being a Jewish city, it would become a Seleucid city, leaving Jason, the loyal vassal, free to rule Jerusalem and the Jews.

    C. In turn, Jason was deposed by his brother, Menelaus, in exactly the same way.

        1. Menelaus went to Antiochus and outbid his brother for the high priesthood.

        2. Antiochus sold the high priesthood to the highest bidder, Menelaus, who took power, forcing Jason to flee.

    D. In 168, when a false report came back from Egypt that Antiochus had been killed, Jason crossed the Jordan River with 1,000 troops, chased Menelaus into the citadel of Jerusalem, and laid siege unsuccessfully until he was forced to flee back across the Jordan.

    E. Each of these factional disputes involved only the urban, Hellenized Jews, who saw themselves as being both Jewish and part of the Greek world. Their advocacy of Hellenistic culture was part of their strategy for winning power in the framework of the Hellenistic Near East.

V. In the countryside and away from Jerusalem, by contrast, Hellenism must have looked much more foreign. The rebellion against Hellenism began as a guerilla opposition to the persecutions of Antiochus. The rebellion started in the countryside, where antipathy toward the Greeks and Hellenizing Jews was fuelled by the antipathy of the country for the city.

    A. In Jewish tradition, the city was distrusted as the place of power, the place of taxes, the place of royal authority.

        1. The story of the Tower of Babel represents a deep aversion to city life, as does the story of Sodom and Gomorrah.

        2. For a culture whose ideology equates foreign cultures with bondage, it is no surprise that the opposition to Antiochus should take root in the countryside and grow from there.

    B. The first campaigns of the resistance were glorious victories. Supported by his loyal brothers Simon, Joseph, and Jonathon, Judas Maccabaeus defeated the army of Antiochus and captured a number of Seleucid fortresses.

    C. The Maccabean revolt continued until the death of Antiochus IV in 163. During its course, Antiochus attempted to resolve the revolt diplomatically with a letter invoking the age-old goodwill of the Seleucids and Jews toward each other.

    D. But the revolt had set the Jews on the path toward independence, and the purification of the Temple by Judas Maccabaeus in 164 must surely have had an extraordinary political effect on the Jewish conceptions of their own separateness and power.

VI. Nominally, Seleucid governors continued to be appointed to control Judaea, but hostilities were renewed in the reign of Antiochus V and would continue for the next generation.

    A. Eventually, a series of compromises would be worked out. These compromises tell the real story of Hellenism and Judaism.

        1. In 159 B.C., the leaders of the Maccabees, Jonathon and his brothers, were granted amnesty on the condition that they leave Jerusalem alone.

    2. In 153, faced with a pretender in his own realm, the Seleucid monarch, Demetrius I Soter, was forced to make more concessions and withdraw the Seleucid garrisons from Judaea.

    3. The pretender, Alexander Balas, offered an even better incentive to the Maccabees and offered Jonathon the robes of the high priesthood.

B. The family that had led a revolt against those who had bartered the high priesthood for their own profit and power was now complicit in the same world of political maneuvering they had rejected.

    1. Jonathon continued in his position until 142, by which time the last Seleucid garrison in Judaea, occupying the citadel of Jerusalem, had been withdrawn.

    2. Judaea had been released from all tributary obligations.

VII. Jonathon was succeeded by his son Simon, who in 140 B.C. was crowned in the manner of a Hellenistic king. Soon his domain would display a bureaucracy full of Greek names, a professional army, a calendar based on his ruling years, a royal mausoleum in the village of Modin (where the first Maccabean resistance had begun), and the unmistakable sign of Hellenistic kingship: royal coinage with Greek inscriptions issued in the name of the dynasty, the Hasmoneans.

VIII. The history of Judaea in the 2nd century reveals a mosaic of different cultural positions, beliefs, classes, and tensions.

A. One strand of Judaism would continue to oppose any accommodation to non-Jewish practice, whether it was the Hasidim of Judah Maccabaeus's day or the Pharisees of the 1st century. For other groups within Judaism, throughout the diaspora but especially among the elite of Jerusalem, Hellenism was not an alien wisdom.

B. It is in that multiplicity of meaning that the relationship between Greek and Jew foreshadows the complexities of the modern world.

Suggested Reading:

E. S. Gruen, "Hellenism and Persecution: Antiochus IV and the Jews," in *Hellenistic History and Culture*, P. Green, ed.

Questions to Consider:

1. Why was it important for Jewish tradition to maintain that Antiochus IV was mad?

2. What does the evolution of the Maccabean rebellion into the Hasmonean dynasty reveal about Hellenism and power?

Lecture Eighteen—Transcript
The Maccabean Revolt, Part II

Hello and welcome back. This is our second lecture on the topic of the Maccabean revolt. I commented last time that in the case of the Maccabean revolt, which broke out in 167 B.C., we have more detail concerning a rebellion in the Hellenistic world than we have for any other similar episode. So it's necessary to look in great detail to understand what we can learn from this.

I commented that in the past, people have tended to view the Maccabean revolt as resulting from the conflict between Hellenistic culture and Jewish culture. I argued that in fact, the causes of the revolt are somewhat more complex than that, and I've tried to isolate three sets of factors that contribute significantly to the events of 168 and 167 B.C.

The first series of conditions was created by the declining fortunes of the Seleucid dynasty in the first half of the 2nd century B.C. We've already seen that Antiochus III, although he was an enormously powerful monarch (he was famous in the ancient world for having marched all the way across to India and virtually replicating the march of Alexander), nevertheless, had been defeated in the Battle of Magnesia in 189 and in the following year at Apamea had signed a peace treaty with the Romans in which he had essentially given up all territory in Asia Minor, allowing for the creation, really, of the independent Attalid kingdom. This had seriously weakened his kingdom, particularly because his kingdom now had to pay a massive indemnity, at the rate of 1,000 talents per year for a decade.

We also saw that Antiochus IV had also suffered setbacks recently. He had campaigned in Egypt to try to take advantage of the arrival on the throne of a new young ruler, Ptolemy V, but here we had seen that Antiochus IV was essentially challenged or bluffed, if you will, by a Roman magistrate, Gaius Popillius Laenus, who had drawn a line in the sand and said, "Give me your response before you cross that line." The response had been total capitulation.

Antiochus IV had withdrawn from Pelusium, from the Gaza Strip, with nothing to show for two seasons of campaigning. The other conditions that I also pointed out, and which we'll be exploring in more detail today were the tensions within Judaism, within Judaea, between the Hellenized Jews, who really had assimilated Greek practices, and the orthodox, to whom this was absolutely an abomination. The other tension, which usually gets less attention from experts, and that is the conflict between the city and the country, and the different approaches that one finds to Judaism between those two regions. Events came to a head in 167 B.C. In that year, in December of 167 B.C., agents of the Seleucid king, Antiochus IV entered the Temple of Jerusalem. They piled unclean offerings on the altar, they forced Jews to eat sacrificial animals, and to parade wearing ivy wreaths in honor of Dionysos. Copies of the Torah were burnt. The Temple was rededicated to Zeus Olympius.

Ten days later, after a pagan altar had been erected in front of the Temple, a pig was sacrificed. An act which has been described as "an act of unspeakable desecration" for the people of Judaea. This persecution that's triggered by these events, must be set against the collapse of Seleucid fortunes in the eastern Mediterranean, as we've seen. Now it's time to see these events from the point of view of Antiochus' Jewish subjects. How did they perceive these events? It is important to keep in mind that throughout much of the 3rd century B.C., (the 200s), Judaea had been under Ptolemaic rule. In other words, it had been the far northeastern edge of Egyptian territory. The generosity of the Seleucids and Seleucid policy towards the Jews had been prompted by an awareness that Judaea was a buffer state, between Egypt to the south and southwest, and Syria to the north. It was what some people would call a contested borderland.

The arrival of the Romans in the eastern Mediterranean, the defeat of Antiochus III in 189, the prospect of an alliance between the Romans and Ptolemaic Egypt, all represented severe threats to the power of the Seleucids in the eastern Mediterranean. Because in 168 B.C., Antiochus IV faced the prospect of a Roman-Egyptian alliance. Even at the same time, as a new independent kingdom, that of the Attalids in Asia Minor, had also come onto the scene as an ally of Rome. So it was possible, now, in the 160s, that the kingdom in Syria controlled by the Seleucids could face enemies, prosecuting territorial claims, to Judaea. Enemies that would control the entire seacoast from Byzantium, all the way down (today) the western coast of Turkey, the southern coast of Turkey, and then in the south, along the coast of Libya, Cyrenaica, Egypt, and the Gaza Strip. In other words, the Syrian kingdom was facing a coalition of enemies on its western front, north and south, as well.

It is under these circumstances that the luxury of an autonomous Judaea could no longer be afforded. So I would assert then, that the shift in policy that we find between Antiochus III and Antiochus IV comes not from any change in religious or cultural conditions. It is not an attempt to impose Hellenism, at all. It is, in fact, a pragmatic, cold-hearted political decision, designed to bolster Seleucid control of what we've called a contested border zone. It can no longer be independent and allied. It must now be under their direct control. Already, following his campaign in 169, Antiochus had carried off some treasures from the Temple. He had shown that his policy of generosity could be withheld or reversed when more pressing needs, not vague cultural notions, but specific, pressing needs, such as an empty war chest arose. That's what dictated his policy.

While Antiochus was in the south, campaigning on the edges of Egypt in 168, he received the news that a rebellion had broken out in Judaea. Probably this violence was actually the result of civil unrest between rival Jewish factions. It was not really an uprising against Antiochus at all. But to Antiochus, who was out of his kingdom, and was campaigning south of Judaea, it must have seemed as if the Jews had turned on him when he was most vulnerable. Furious, he returned to Jerusalem, where his armies (so it is said) slaughtered 40,000 Jews. The following year, a Seleucid general named Apollonius was dispatched with 22,000 men to occupy Jerusalem, and specifically the citadel known as the *acra* (the high point). From the Jewish point of view preserved in the Book of Maccabees, this campaign and occupation were designed to terrorize the population. According to Jewish sources, these men came with orders to kill all the men and to enslave the women. This, in fact, did not eventuate, although, of course, some innocent people were killed. But if we strip away the preconceived notion of Jewish and Greek antipathy, that always bedevils the discussion of these events, I think we can find a more plausible explanation.

It is this: Apollonius' army was being sent to secure, to establish a Seleucid garrison deep in Judaean territory. That is to say, deep into the region to the southern side of Syria, to secure this region against either a combined Egyptian-Roman attack or a rebellion of the local population against Antiochus on his vulnerable southern flank, or both. One could image easily a triumphant Ptolemaic campaign of an army marching across the Gaza Strip and up into what is now modern-day Israel and heading towards Syria and promising liberation to the Jews if they would join in on the attack on the Syrian kingdom of Antiochus. Such a thing had happened in the 3rd century, certainly, when much of this region had been under Ptolemaic control. So according to this interpretation, I would suggest, that is territorial and geopolitical considerations that were vastly more important to Antiochus than the questions of Hellenism, Judaism, or any other –ism. There are no cultural philosophies at stake here. It is simply a matter of securing territory.

That's fine and good, but what about the Jewish attitude toward the revolt? Again, here, resistance to the Greeks must be put into the context of contemporary Jewish anxieties over assimilation. Religious Jews, those who held close to the Law, railed against the men they called apostates, the people who had given up their traditional Jewish affiliation, and who had lapsed in their observances. And yet, there were many Hellenized Jews in Jerusalem. It was Hellenized Jews in Jerusalem who sought to reach an understanding with the various pagans around them. They had approached Antiochus IV and they had been authorized to introduce Greek social practices.

We have an account of this in one of the books of the Maccabees. Of course, this is told from the point of view of the Jewish sources, so their attitude towards the Hellenization of the Jews is essentially one of condemnation. But we can see that there were actually many Jews in Jerusalem who believed that Greek culture was the culture that they preferred for themselves. We have a description here of Jason, the Hellenized high priest, who, it says, "…quickly established a gymnasium at the very foot of the acropolis, where he induced the noblest young men to wear a Greek hat." So these men are going to a gymnasium, a Greek institution, where they will probably exercise naked, which is something of an affront to traditional Jewish sensibilities. They're wearing Greek clothes, such as this Greek hat.

The craze for Hellenism and foreign customs reached such a pitch through the outrageous wickedness of the ungodly pseudo-high priest Jason that the priests no longer cared about the service of the altar. Disdaining the Temple and neglecting the sacrifices, they hastened at the signal of the discus-throwing, to take part in the unlawful exercises of the athletic field. They despised what their ancestors had regarded as honors, while they highly prized what the Greeks esteemed as glory.

He goes on to talk about these various practices. If this had been anywhere other than Judaea, it would simply have been described in neutral terms as the local population beginning to act more like Greeks, because they had adopted this culture. Because our sources are Jewish and are from a very orthodox point of view, they see this, of course, as a rejection of traditional Judaism. A betrayal of it, in fact. So much of the Hellenism going on in Jerusalem had not been imposed, but rather had been adopted, willingly. It was these Hellenizing Jews, not Greek colonists, who had built the gymnasium in Jerusalem. In some of our sources we're told that they had disguised their circumcision, a clear sign in the eyes of many that they had turned their back on traditional Judaism. These Hellenized Jews were blamed by many of the observant Jews for the ills which befell Judaea, on the grounds that they had deserted Judaism. They had turned their back on the Law.

And yet, the translation of the Torah into Greek, which took place (as we know) in Alexandria, suggests that there were some people who felt that Judaism and Hellenism were not absolutely irreconcilable. We saw in an earlier lecture that Josephus, also seemed to suggest that there were those both on the Greek side (such as Hecataeus) and on the Jewish side who felt that the two cultures really were comparable and could fit together. That assimilation did not mean a betrayal of Judaism. It was merely a different expression of it.

Be that as it may, it was in this society of Hellenized Jews that the factional rivalries broke out, which would eventually be catastrophic. The key rivalries that we know of were among members of a powerful clan known as the Tobiads. Early in his reign, Antiochus IV was approached by one of the Hellenized Jews of Jerusalem, a man named Jason, who happened to be the brother of the high priest. So clearly he was a man of great standing and influence. He came from this leading family. But Jason came to Antiochus with an extraordinary offer. He offered the king 360 talents of silver if, in return, Antiochus recognized his claim to the high priesthood. We know that at this time the Seleucid kingdom was strapped for money, and we know that they were engaged in expensive campaigns. You can probably guess the result of this deal, this bargain. The money was paid to Antiochus and in return, Onias was deposed and Jason took his place as high priest in Jerusalem.

Jason, this Hellenized Jew, seems to have renamed the city of Jerusalem as Antioch. What he was trying to do was to recast the city now as a Seleucid city, just like the other Antiochs and Seleucias locate further north in Syria. Of course, in the contractual arrangement of Hellenistic kingship, if Jason were to be the loyal vassal, ruling in a city that was a Seleucid city like those of Syria, he would be left free to rule Jerusalem. Quasi-autonomous, if you will, in charge of the Jews.

But—the story gets even murkier. Because in a further round of intrigue, Menelaus, the brother of Jason, went to Antiochus and outbid his brother for the high priesthood. Antiochus once again sold this position to the highest bidder, Menelaus, who took power, forcing Jason to flee. So we have no great clash of cultures here. We have, rather, a factional dispute within this one family, of influential and powerful Hellenized Jews in Jerusalem.

When, in 168 B.C., a false report came back from Egypt that Antiochus had been killed, Jason crossed the River Jordan with 1,000 troops, chased Menelaus into the Citadel of Jerusalem, and laid siege to the city unsuccessfully, until he once again was forced to flee back across the Jordan River. Each of the disputes that we've talked about so far, and these are setting the stage for the full revolt that is to come. Each of these disputes involved only the urbanized, Hellenized Jews, who saw themselves as being both Jewish and part of the Greek world. Their advocacy of Hellenistic culture was part of the strategy for establishing their own power within the framework of the Hellenistic Near East.

But in the countryside, away from Jerusalem, things looked very different indeed. Out there, Hellenism seemed much more alien. Much more foreign. The rebellion against Hellenism began, in fact, as a guerrilla opposition to the persecutions of Antiochus. It started in the countryside, where antipathy towards the Greeks and the Hellenizing Jews was fueled by antipathy—the antipathy of the countryside for the city. This is a traditional feature of early Jewish culture. Jewish tradition had distrusted the city, as a place of power. The stories of Sodom and Gomorrah, for example, recall this. The story of the Tower of Babel recalls this. There are, in the Old Testament, stories that show how the culture of the early Jews maintained that there was something suspect and suspicious and corrupting about life in the city.

©2000 The Teaching Company.

For a culture whose ideology equated foreign culture with bondage, it is no surprise that the opposition to Antiochus should take root in the countryside and grow from there. The city people had given in, but not in the countryside. We get a strong suggestion of this in the First Book of Maccabees, because it's here that we get an account of the actual events when the revolt broke out. I want you to notice the location of this. What happens is that as a result of Antiochus' attempt, and Jason's attempts, also, to impose Hellenistic culture now—what happens is that there is a reaction in the countryside. I Maccabees says, "The officers of the king in charge of enforcing the apostasy [the turning away from traditional Judaism] came to the city of Modein, to organize the sacrifices." "City" is a rather glorified term there. It's really a village.

> Many of the people of Israel joined them. But Mattathias the son of John and his sons, gathered in a group, apart. Then the officers of the king addressed Mattathias: "You are a leader and an honorable and great man in this city [this village] supported by sons and kinsmen. Come now, be the first to obey the king's command, as all the Gentiles and the men of Judah and those who are left in Jerusalem have done. Then you and your sons shall be numbered among the King's Friends [once again the vocabulary of the Hellenistic kingship] and shall be enriched with gold and silver and many gifts."

And here's the answer that he receives:

> Mattathias answered, 'Although all the Gentiles in the king's realm obey him, so that each forsakes the religion of his fathers, and consents to the king's orders, yet I and my sons and kinsmen will keep to the covenant of our fathers. God forbid that we should forsake the Law and the commandments. We will not obey the words of the king, nor depart from our religion in the slightest degree.'

Out here in the countryside, these people are not having anything of this nonsense of Hellenizing, the way that the Jews of Jerusalem have done. As he finished saying these words, a certain Jew came forward in the sight of all to offer sacrifice on the altar in Modein, according to the king's orders. When Mattathias saw him, he was filled with zeal. His heart was moved. His just fury was aroused. He sprang forward and killed him upon the altar. That murder, that act of bloodshed is the act that ignites the Maccabean rebellion, since it is the sons of Mattathias who are known as the Maccabees.

So it begins in the countryside. As the country Jews resisting Hellenism, resisting the policies being implemented in the city of Jerusalem, stand up to oppose anything that reeks of Greek culture or Hellenism. I wish to emphasize that, because I want you to keep that in mind for when we get to the very end of this lecture, and where we'll end with the Maccabees at the end of their history. It begins as these orthodox Jews strongly resist any Hellenistic policy coming down from the king or from the Hellenized Jews of Jerusalem.

The first campaigns of the resistance were glorious. Supported by his brothers Simon, Joseph and Jonathan, the leader of the revolt, Judas Maccabeus, the son of Mattathias, defeated the army of Nicanor, a general dispatched by Antiochus, and succeeded in capturing a number of Seleucid fortresses. The Maccabean revolt continued even after the death of Antiochus IV in 163. There was even a time when Antiochus attempted to resolve the revolt before his death diplomatically, with a letter invoking the age-old good will of the Seleucids and the Jews towards each other.

But they had been set on their path of revolt. And the path of revolt led eventually to independence. The purification of the Temple by Judas Maccabeus in 164 B.C. must surely have been one of the most extraordinary moments in Jewish history. It must have had an extraordinarily powerful effect on Jewish conceptions of the independence of their own country, the separateness of their culture, and the potential power that lay within themselves.

From the late 160s onwards, nominally, Seleucid governors continued to be appointed to control Judaea, but in effect the country was already established as a kind of independent state on the outskirts of the Seleucid realm. Hostilities would be renewed in the reign of Antiochus V, and they would continue down for the next generation, through the 150s and the 140s. Eventually, a series of compromises would be worked out. It's actually in the compromises, not in the revolt, that I think we get the true story of the relationship between Hellenism and Judaism. So while most stories of the Maccabees stop with the purification of the Temple, I would like to go a little further, and take us into the generation after the Maccabees.

In 159 B.C., the leaders of the Maccabees, Jonathan and his brothers, were granted amnesty on the condition that they leave Jerusalem alone. (A perfect illustration: the city is one thing, the countryside is another.) In 153 B.C., faced with a pretender in his own realm, the Seleucid monarch (and the later Seleucids were very weak by comparison with the earlier kings)—this Seleucid monarch, Demetrius I Soter (Demetrius the Savior) was forced to make even more concessions and to withdraw the Seleucid garrisons from Judea altogether. So, in effect, because there's no Seleucid military presence, the country is really independent.

The pretender to the Seleucid throne at this time, a man called Alexander Balas, offered an even greater incentive to the Maccabees. He offered Jonathan Maccabeus the robes of the high priesthood. So we've reached a point where the very family which had led a revolt against those who bartered the high priesthood for their own profit and power was now complicit in exactly the same world of political maneuvering that they had rejected. The revolt had begun with the Maccabees standing fast for orthodox law and against Hellenism. But now, they are trading for the high priesthood as badly as Jason, Menelaus and any of the others who had come before them. Jonathan continued in his position of high priest until 142 B.C., by which time the last Seleucid garrison in Judaea had been withdrawn, leaving the citadel of Jerusalem empty. Judaea by this stage had been released from all tributary obligations. Let's take the story a little further, because it continues to get even more interesting, in my opinion.

Jonathan was succeeded by his son Simon. Is this beginning to sound dynastic perhaps? With generations succeeding generations? And Simon in 140 B.C. was crowned in exactly the typical manner of a Hellenistic king. Soon his domain would display a bureaucracy full of Greek names. A professional army. A mercenary army. A calendar which took its date from the regnal years ("in year such-and-such of King X"). A royal mausoleum put up in the village of Modin, where the entire revolt had begun. So the dynasty has the place that it goes back to and from which it begins and where all the kings are to be buried. And the unmistakable sign of Hellenistic kingship: coinage, with Greek inscriptions, issued in the name of the dynasty, the Hasmonean kings of Judaea.

We've really come full circle. What began as a revolt against Hellenism, which began particularly amongst those Jews who opposed not only the Hellenism of the Greeks, but particularly the Hellenism of the Jews who had assimilated, in the space of only a generation or two, even less than thirty years, had finally culminated, yes in the independence of Judaea, to be sure, but independence on what terms? It is now a Hellenistic kingdom that in every way imitates the very thing which it sought to reject in its origins.

That, I think, is the true and the underlying story of the relationship between the two cultures. Not a simple one of apostasy or rejection or cultural resistance, but rather an astonishing mosaic, is what we find in the second century. A mosaic with all sorts of conflicting cultural positions, all sorts of conflicting beliefs, all sorts of different classes and tensions, with none of them properly reconciled. Although one strand of Judaism would continue, of course, to oppose any accommodation with non-Jewish practice, whether this be the Hasidim of Judas Maccabeus' day, or the Pharisees of the 1st century B.C. But there would also be another strand of Judaism that ran throughout the Diaspora, but especially among the elite within Jerusalem, and I think also particularly in Alexandria, for whom Hellenism was not an alien wisdom.

It's in this multiplicity of meaning that I think we get the true relationship between the Greeks and the Jews. In fact, it's almost wrong to be using simplistic terms like "the Greeks" and "the Jews," as if they were two simple groups. In fact, both sides of the equation included a multiplicity of positions and opinions. In that respect, the complexities of the Maccabean revolt, I think, very provocatively foreshadow the complexities of the modern world, where the same debate really exists. To be Jewish, does one have to be orthodox? Or are there other ways of expressing that particular identity? That's never really been reconciled in the modern world, and I don't think that it was ever reconciled in the world of the 3rd, 2nd or 1st centuries B.C., either. But I think in the story—the paradoxical story—of a revolt and a rebellion, that ended up establishing a Hellenistic kingdom, we have a suitable paradox to stand for the way that cultures spoke to each other in the Hellenistic world.

Lecture Nineteen
Rulers and Saviors

Scope:

In the Hellenistic world, traditional Greek religion developed in new ways. An emphasis on personal faith and experience led to the flourishing of mystery cults. At the same time, religion became one of the principal means of recognizing the immense power of Hellenistic kings. The public face of religion changed as more and more rulers were hailed as saviors.

Outline

I. Mystery cults were not a foreign import entering the Greek world from the East, as has often been argued. Such cults existed in Greece long before Alexander expanded the horizons of the Hellenistic world.

   A. Dionysiac cults had long offered an intense religious communion with the god, based on divine madness and possession.

   B. Orphism was another mode of early Greek religious practice that dealt with demonic possession and offered hope for improving one's lot in the afterlife.

   C. Most famous among mystery religions was the cult of Demeter and Kore at Eleusis. This sanctuary was dedicated to the earth goddess and celebrated the fertility of the soil and the gift of grain.

      1. Successive temples were built here from the Geometric period to the Roman Age, attesting to the ever-increasing popularity of the cult.

      2. Initiates of the cult were purified before a midnight ceremony during which wall torches suddenly illuminated the hall of initiation.

      3. At the climax of the ceremony, the initiate witnessed an epiphany, as the goddess manifested herself. This was not a metaphorical appearance but a literal one.

II. During the Hellenistic period, the Greeks enthusiastically adapted existing cults in the newly "Hellenized" territories.

A. A prime example of this adoption is Cybele, an Anatolian mother goddess. Her worship is known in Greece as early as the 5th century B.C., where she was easily associated with Demeter.

B. Cybele was attended by a younger consort, Attis, who was remembered as a mortal lover who died and was mourned. Originally, the cult was concerned with the cycle of the seasons, but increasingly it dealt with issues of salvation and the afterlife.

    1. The worship of Cybele in the Hellenistic world was encouraged by the Attalid dynasty, which offered sumptuous endowments to the sanctuary of Cybele at Pessinus, in northern Asia Minor.

    2. The cult of Cybele reached Rome in 204 B.C. and became immensely popular there.

    3. Much of the popularity of the cult rested on its exotic appearance. The priests of Cybele were eunuchs and were remarkable for their colorful robes, music, and dancing.

III. The most daring example of the synthesis of Greek and non-Greek elements is found in the cult of the Egyptian gods Serapis and Isis.

A. Serapis was a figure from Egyptian religion created from the fusion of Osiris and the Apis bull. His cult was popular and important in Egypt. In the 4th century, immediately before the arrival of the Macedonians, the Serapeum at Memphis was extensively refurbished. The Ptolemies understood the significance of the cult and attempted to Hellenize it.

    1. Greek priests were commissioned to write hymns and prayers to Serapis in Greek.

    2. A Greek sculptor was commissioned to create the cult statue.

    3. Serapis was thus made to look like the Greek god Hades, and his cult was rendered accessible to the Greeks.

    4. Similarly, Imhotep and Aesclepius merged into a syncretized god who combined elements of both cultures.

B. A second deity of Egyptian origin who gained immense popularity throughout the Hellenistic world was Isis. Like Serapis, she was already an established figure in Egyptian religion at the time of the Macedonian conquest. During the Hellenistic period, her worship would outstrip that of Serapis and even the earlier Olympian gods.

1. Prayers composed in her honor and singing her praises became popular throughout the Greek world.
2. Like Demeter, Isis was associated with the fertility of the land.
3. She was seen as a protector of the family and was often shown nursing her child, Harpocrates.
4. In Apuleius's poem, *The Golden Ass*, the narrator tells how the goddess appeared to him and promised him salvation. In her address to Lucius, the goddess explains that she is the same goddess, whether she is called Minerva, Athena, Venus, Aphrodite, Demeter, or Cybele.
5. Her cult demonstrates the syncretistic quality of Hellenistic religion as different gods and goddesses, both Greek and non-Greek, were gradually fused.

IV. Aside from the wide interest in personal religious experience, the other principal feature of Hellenistic religion was the emergence of ruler-cults. In these cults, Hellenistic kings were offered the honors appropriate to gods or semi-divine heroes.

A. Once again, the origins of this practice lie as much in the Greek world as in the East. Characters such as Heracles were believed to have been human but were assumed into heaven because of their glorious deeds. The Spartan general Lysander had been honored as a hero, receiving cult sacrifices at the end of the 5th century B.C.

B. Alexander experimented with this same status after his visit to the oracle of Zeus Ammon at Siwa.

C. Among Alexander's successors, establishing the cult of a dynastic founder was a vivid and practical way of legitimizing Macedonian rule.

1. Ptolemy II established a cult in honor of his father that was gradually extended to include the reigning ruler and his sister-wife as well.
2. Ruler cults allowed the ruling dynasty to deal with the existing priestly caste, as is illustrated by the Rosetta stone. In this trilingual inscription, Ptolemy V is honored by the priests of Memphis, who, in return, were offered

all kinds of concessions and tax breaks by the young king.

3. Ruler cults also served as a medium for international diplomacy. The League of the Ionian Islands, which was dominated by Ptolemy II in the 3rd century, acknowledged the suzerainty of the king by agreeing to make an annual sacrifice, the Ptolemaieia, in honor of the house of Ptolemy.

V. It is too easy to dismiss the ruler cult as a political tool, designed by rulers to enhance their prestige. Although some Greeks resisted the notion of divine honors for living men, many had no qualms about offering divine honors to the powerful men who controlled their lives.

A. When Demetrius Poliorcetes, the first of the successors to claim the title of king, sailed into Athens in 291 B.C., the local population greeted him with religious songs and dances and exclaimed: "How the greatest and the dearest of the gods have come to the city!… For the other gods are either far way, or don't hear us, or don't exist, or ignore us. But you we can see. You are not made of wood or stone. You are real."

B. Ruler cults allowed the Greeks to frame the power of Hellenistic kings in terms of a reciprocal relationship: honor for the king and leniency for the community.

Suggested Reading:

S. R. F. Price, *Rituals and Power*.

Questions to Consider:

1. In what ways are ruler cults and benefaction parallel institutions?

2. In what ways can the religious developments of the Hellenistic period be said to have influenced early Christianity?

Lecture Nineteen—Transcript
Rulers and Saviors

Hello and welcome back to this our 19th lecture now in this series on Alexander the Great and the Hellenistic Age. So far in our series of lectures overviewing the Hellenistic Age, we've had an opportunity to see on a number of occasions the importance of religious ideas and religious practices. We've seen the way that Hellenistic kings were often treated as living gods in their own lifetime. We've seen the way, also, that much of the popular art of the period (the sculpture, the novels and the poetry, also) reflect new interests in the workings of fate, destiny and fortune, for example. So I think it's probably a good occasion now for us to stop and to look more systematically at the nature of religion in the course of the Hellenistic period.

What we're going to find is that during the Hellenistic Age, religion really develops in two ways. First of all, we're going to see a strong emphasis on personal faith and individual experience, which will lead to a flourishing of the so-called mystery cults, which we'll discuss in some detail. We're also going to find that religion also moves into a very public sphere. It had always been a central part of the communal life of the Greeks, but now it's also going to be a prime vehicle for expressing the power of the Hellenistic kings. So let's look today at both the private face of religion and the public face of religion in the Hellenistic world.

We should begin, really, with the so-called mystery cults. You will often find that mystery cults are treated as if they were a foreign import. In other words, that when the Greeks came into contact with the older civilizations of the ancient Near East, they were gradually infected by this contact, and mystery cults moved from the East to the West. This type of interpretation is (or was) particularly prevalent in the studies of the Roman Empire where, again, it was argued that the pristine religion of the Italian peninsula was eventually overtaken in the course of the Roman Empire, by the contact between the Romans and the ancient civilizations of the ancient Near East.

And yet, this is almost certainly incorrect at every level. There had been many such mystery cults in the Greek world long before their contact with the civilizations of the ancient Near East. Just to give a couple of examples of these cults that existed long before Alexander expanded the margins and the horizons of the Hellenistic world. First of all, the cult of Dionysos. Dionysos to the Greeks is a god who actually comes into your spirit. Our word in English "enthusiasm" comes from the Greek *enthusiasmos*, which refers to that state you are in when the god actually possesses you.

The Greeks already had a long tradition of this, and if any of you have read Euripides' play *The Bacchae*, you'll know that even as early as the late 5th and early 4th century, long before the Hellenistic period, the Greeks were fascinated by this phenomenon. By the notion that a person could be taken over by a god. This is what we would call "spirit possession." It is a significant part of Greek religion. When Agave comes onto the stage holding a pole that has on the top of it the head of her son, she is horrified when she realizes what's there, because she actually killed her son and tore his body apart and stuck that head on a pole while she was actually possessed by the god. She had no idea of what she was doing.

There were quite well-organized cults of these followers of Dionysos, or Bacchus, as he's also called. Particularly a cult known as that of the *thuiades*, which regularly roamed over the tops of Mount Parnassus in a state of possession. We have a very graphic description in Plutarch, written in the 2nd century A.D. of an event where, on one occasion these women had been out "wilding," as we might call it, and had woken up after their experience, in the middle of the town of Amphissa, not knowing where they were or how they got there. So this kind of possession, which, in previous generations we've often thought of as being somehow eastern and barbaric, not really fitting in with our notion of the glorious elevated Greeks, this kind of possession really went on in Greek religion. Of course, the oracle of Apollo worked in much the same way, actually going into the *pythia*, the priestess, who then spoke in the voice of the god and her utterances were the god, delivering his oracle to mankind.

In the 4th century we have some evidence (it's not very detailed evidence) of another mode of early Greek religious practice that was centered on the semi-mythical figure of Orpheus. You'll remember the legend of Orpheus, that he was able to charm the animals and the very rocks, and he had almost succeeded in bringing his wife Eurydice back from the underworld, only to fail at the last moment by turning around and looking at her and losing her forever. That myth is associated with a whole religious cult, a series of practices that involved, again, a kind of spirit possession. It seems to be a cult

©2000 The Teaching Company.

that offered some kind of hope for improving one's lot in the afterlife.

The notion that the Greeks had an entirely pessimistic view of the afterlife is not entirely correct. In the course of the 4th century, and particularly in the Hellenistic Age, more and more of these cults developed that seem to offer one an opportunity if not of actual redemption, at least a life after death. A kind of spiritual resurrection. Without doubt the most famous of the cults of this sort in the Greek world was the mystery cult which was based at Eleusis, about six miles west of Athens. Here, the cult of Demeter, the mother of the Earth itself and Kore, her daughter, was an immensely popular cult. We know from the archaeology of the site that there were temples going back certainly to the Geometric period, in early Greek history (900-800 B.C.). The site grew gradually larger, with more and more elaborate temples and gateways and *stoas* being built and added on, particularly in the Roman Age, which, in cultural terms we can really regard as late Hellenism, if you like. So the cult grew in popularity. It, in a way, is the model for all of the mystery cults that became popular in the Greek world.

We know that at Eleusis, initiates of the cult were purified. They went through various ceremonies as they went up the hierarchy of initiation, before, finally the entire process culminated in a midnight ceremony. The initiates had probably not only been purified but had fasted for a couple of days, and may have been under the influence of some kind of hallucinogenic (we're not clear about that, but there are arguments to suggest this), when, in the middle of the night (during this midnight ceremony), in the hall of initiation, suddenly the priests and the devotees of the cult would come in with torches illuminating the hall and in the middle of the night, all of a sudden, the night would turn to day. At that moment, at the climax of that ceremony, the initiate would witness the goddess manifest right there. It was not taken metaphorically. It was not a suggestion that we were supposed to imagine the goddess. These people were psychologically primed and ready to believe that the goddess was actually there.

It's particularly interesting to find that in Easter ceremonies in the Orthodox Church, one will still go to a midnight service and find the priest coming out after a long ceremony, with candles, declaring "Christ is risen!" To which the people in the ceremony will reply,

"He is truly risen!" and will each light their candle off the candle of someone in front of them. So this idea of the god appearing at midnight accompanied by light in the middle of the night is still, in fact, a part of Christianity and certainly has its roots as a ritual practice going back to the ancient world.

During the Hellenistic period, the Greeks enthusiastically adapted existing cults they came into contact with in the territories that were newly Hellenized. A prime example of this is that of the cult of Cybele. There's good evidence that in Anatolia, that is to say, the central part of modern-day Turkey, the highland plateau in the middle of the country, there is a long tradition of the worship of a mother goddess. The Greeks were familiar with her certainly as early as the 5th century B.C. In typical Greek fashion, when the Greeks came into contact with her they tended to think of her as being another version of the goddess they already knew in their own pantheon. So she is often associated with Demeter. Following a very common Near Eastern model, this earth goddess was also associated with a younger consort, sometimes known as "the dying god," a god whose death tends to suggest the passing of the seasons, as summertime moves into fall and then into wintertime.

This younger consort is known as Attis. He was remembered as a mortal lover of the goddess, who had died and was now mourned. Originally, then, the cult was concerned with the cycle of the seasons, the way the earth responds to the changing seasons, analogized her to the mourning of a woman for her dead lover. Clearly it fits into the Greek mindset, thinking of the pattern of the seasons, as well, because a similar story existed in relation to Demeter and her daughter. Remember that Kore, or Persephone as she's sometimes called, had been dragged off to the underworld by Hades. It was while her mother was in mourning that the Earth, then, experienced wintertime. When she was able to negotiate the release of Kore, the Earth came back to life once again.

These are similar myths, similar stories, that are designed etiologically to explain, in other words, the origin of the cycle of the seasons. In the Hellenistic period, this original model to do with vegetation and the seasons, was increasingly adapted in a new way to express a belief in an afterlife and in the notion of salvation. Not just a cosmic principle of the way life operates in the movement of the seasons, but in the individual promise of an afterlife for the initiate into the cult. The worship of this particular goddess, Cybele, in the Hellenistic world, was encouraged (as often these cults were), officially by the ruling dynasty of the region. In this case, the Attalids.

We know that the Attalid kings of Pergamum offered sumptuous endowments to the sanctuary of this mother goddess Cybele at her most important sanctuary in Asia Minor at the place known as Pessinus. The Attalids even seem to have plugged into this idea of an important mother-goddess, because we have inscriptions that attest to cults in honor of their mother, as well. So the mother of the dynasty is really analogized to the mother-goddess.

This cult of Cybele would become extremely popular around the Mediterranean world. It would even reach Rome and would become quite important in the Roman Empire. It was immensely popular in Rome. Much of the popularity of the cult (and this is another feature worth keeping in mind in relation to Hellenistic religion) is that it was extremely exotic in appearance. The Greeks came in contact with other cultures and really responded to them in the way that we find foreign cultures exotic, as well, which, I think, explains some of the popularity of Egyptian culture during this period.

The priests of Cybele were eunuchs, often who had castrated themselves in their possession (as the goddess possessed them). They wore strange and colorful robes. Their ceremonies were attended by weird music, played on instruments that were unusual to the Greeks, and by strange dancing. I sometimes think that this must have looked (to a sober Greek, or particularly to a sober Roman audience) the way the early devotees of Hare Krishna must have appeared in counties like England and America in the 1960s and 1970s when they first became widely popular. Local populations would join these cults. But for the majority of people they looked very strange, and very odd. That was sort of a part of the cachet. It was as if there was some sort of secret wisdom being conveyed by this foreign cult. By far the most daring and the most widespread example of this synthesis of Greek elements and non-Greek elements in the popularity in the Greek world of a non-Greek cult is that of the Egyptian gods Serapis and Isis.

Serapis was a figure from Egyptian religion, who was created from the fusion of the god Osiris and the Apis bull, which received its own cult. This fusion of Osiris and Apis had become quite popular in the later and more recent stages of Egyptian history, in, say, the 5th and the 4th century. This cult was popular and important in Egypt. Immediately before the arrival of the Macedonians, the Serapeum, that is, the shrine of Serapis at Memphis, was extensively refurbished. So it is an Egyptian cult, which is already quite popular. The Ptolemies understood the significance of this cult, and they attempted to Hellenize it. So, for example, they imported priests from the Greek mainland, who were commissioned to write hymns and to write prayers to Serapis in Greek. They were Hellenizing an Egyptian cult that way.

A Greek sculptor was commissioned to create the cult statue. The cult statue was always important in Greek religion because even though it is not the god himself, it is meant to be a representation of the god, to which people can make their devotions. But the statues that were created of Serapis (and these were copied widely in the Hellenistic period and later on in the Roman period) looked nothing like earlier Egyptian models, and certainly do not look like a bull god in any shape or form. Rather, Serapis is made to look like the Greek god Hades, the god of the underworld. His cult is rendered much more accessible, then, to the Greeks.

In Egypt, this god Serapis was often treated as a therapeutic god. He was a god who helped to heal people when they were sick. He often did this by appearing to them in dreams. What happens now is that the Egyptian version of Osiris and Apis together, and the Greek version, come together and we find a syncretism, a blending of the two, as Serapis becomes to the Greeks a healing god, who appears to them in their dreams. There are other examples of this kind of synthesis of the Greek and the Egyptian.

Another one (a very famous one) is that of Imhotep. This is a Hellenized version of an earlier Egyptian god, who is linked to Aesclepius, the great Greek healing god. We actually have examples of people recording the dreams that they get from this combination of Imhotep and Aesclepius. These are interesting. These are particularly revealing because they are dreams recorded by Greeks. So I think this tells us that this cult is not merely an official cult. It is one that actually works for people, because they're actually seeing this god in their very dreams, and expressing this, then, as they write out the account of it in Greek.

I want to read you one example. It comes from a fellow called Ptolemais. His name is the same as that of the kings (Ptolemy), so he's clearly a Greek. He kept a diary in which he recorded many of the petitions he sent off to local officials, letters that he sent off to his friends, and even accounts of his dreams (a very Greek practice). A dream book, in which you record what happens to you. This is what he writes:

> After my mother had been seized by an ungodly sickness that had plagued her for three years, we finally came to our senses. We presented ourselves as suppliants before the god, entreating him to vouchsafe a cure from the disease. The god, ever propitious to all, appeared in dreams and cured her with simple remedies. We rendered the due sacrifices of gratitude to our savior.

A very Greek practice, of having a dream, and the god appears to you and he says, "hey, you ought to be healed." But of course it's actually addressed here to a god who is a synthesis of Greek and Egyptian.

> Not long afterward, I was suddenly seized with a pain in my right side. I rushed to the helper of the human race [which is how he's addressed], and he again readily heeded the call of pity and displayed even more effectively his particular influence, which I will confirm as I recount his awesome powers. It was night, when every living creature was asleep except those in pain, and divine influence could manifest itself more effectively. I was burning with a high fever and convulsed with panting and coughing caused by the pain emanating from my side. Heavy in the head and drowsy with pain, I was dropping off into sleep, but my mother was by my side, and she suffered my tortures without sleeping a wink.

Now listen to this:

> Then, suddenly, she saw him. It was no dream. She was not even sleeping, for her eyes were wide open, though not sharply focused. There came to her a divine apparition, which so startled her that it easily prevented her from observing either the god or his servants closely. Anyway, there was a figure, taller than any human, clad in shining

raiment, carrying a book in his left hand. It only looked at me from head to foot two or three times, and disappeared.

And he goes on to describe then how he is actually healed. But what I find particularly interesting here is that we have an example of the actual appearance, to his mind, of the god, not in a dream, but in an actual waking experience. So this gives us an idea of the true religious sensibilities of these people as they really do feel as though they're in direct contact with their gods.

Dreams were a very important part of that connection. Here, the Egyptian culture of pre-Ptolemaic Egypt and the Greek culture brought from Macedon and Greece actually fit together perfectly, because both cultures had a tradition of dreams as an experience where the gods spoke to you directly. I want to read you one to give you an idea of what they're like. Again, it's from Ptolemy's own writing; that is to say, Ptolemy the ordinary citizen, not Ptolemy the king. He says:

> On the fourteenth, I seemed in a dream to be in a big tower in Alexandria. I had a handsome face, and I didn't want to show my face to anyone because it was so beautiful. An old woman sat down by my side. A crowd gathered to north and east to me. They shouted that a man had been burnt to a crisp. The old woman said to me, 'Wait a minute and I will lead you to the god Cnethis and you can worship him.' [He then has a further experience.] I seemed to be saying to an old man, 'Father, do you not see the vision that I beheld?' And I told him in detail. He gave me two reeds. I looked through them and soon saw Cnethis.

So he comes in direct contact now with the god. And he says:

> Rejoice, o my friends! I shall soon have my release. I have beheld other visions, but these are altogether more beautiful. I worry about nothing else.

He goes on to describe how the god explained to him that the original dream that he'd had was something that he needn't worry about. It's very interesting. He'd actually dreamt that his two daughters were in danger. He dreamt about them in their school room with the teacher present. A parent's anxiety about kids being off at school and not knowing whether they're being taken care of.

The god actually appeared to him and assured him that everything was perfectly all right.

A second deity of Egyptian origin who gained immense popularity during this period was Isis. Like Serapis, she was already an established figure in Egyptian religion at the time of the Macedonian conquest. But during the Hellenistic period, she would become much more Greek and Hellenistic in style. The worship of Isis and Serapis together would far outstrip the worship of virtually any of the earlier Olympian gods. We have, for example, hymns written in honor of Isis by her devotees, in which they sing her praises as being the mother of all mankind. The "Giver of Laws"; the "Giver of Harmony"; the "Founder of Cities". The Solace of women as they're giving birth to their children, and the protector of men as they go off to war. So she becomes a kind of universal mother figure throughout the Hellenistic world.

Like Demeter, she is associated with the fertility of the land. She is often seen as the protector of the family. It's very interesting, because she's often called things like the Star of the Sea, and she's seen with Osiris and with her son Harpocrates, as being a kind of divine family. I think that the model of that you can see is going to be highly influential in the way that the early Christians think about Christ, Mary and Joseph. So some of the stories and traditions about Christ bear a Hellenistic influence, if you will.

She was an extremely powerful goddess in the Hellenistic world. In one extraordinary work, *The Golden Ass*, written by Apuleius, the narrator, who has had the misfortune of being transformed into an ass, and who tries to explain to people his dilemma, but can't because when he opens his mouth, all they hear is his braying— eventually tells us how the goddess appeared to him and promised him salvation. So she appears to him. It's similar to one of these midnight ceremonies, where people are initiated into her cult.

It's very interesting because she says to him in the course of this appearance that she is the same goddess around the world, whether she be called Minerva, Athena, Venus, Aphrodite, Demeter or Cybele. So there is a strong tendency in the Hellenistic world to think of all these various goddesses, which had once been quite separate as really being expressions of the one single, same deity. It's a kind of incipient monotheism going on here.

Aside from this very personal religion, which I wanted to concentrate on, because I think we haven't dealt with it in sufficient detail, before today. The other major face of Hellenistic religion, of course, is not its private face, but its very public face. Here I want to return once again to the topic of the ruler cults so often discussed. In these cults, Hellenistic kings were offered the honors appropriate to gods or to semi-divine heroes. Again, people have often said this is really an Eastern influence on Hellenism. But that's not the truth. In origins, the idea that a man could actually be elevated beyond mortal status and be seen as a god, as a superman, or as a hero—the origins of this lie back in the Greek world, as much as in the East. Characters like Heracles were remembered as originally human beings, who by dint of their extraordinary accomplishments (in his case, his labors) had been assumed into heaven. One of the most popular motifs in the pottery of the late 6th century is the apotheosis, the entry into heaven, of Heracles.

This wasn't simply in the realm of myth for the Greeks. The Greeks prior to the Hellenistic Age had already done this for living human beings. The Spartan general Lysander (the victor over the Athenians at the end of the Peloponnesian War) had been honored as a hero, receiving cult sacrifices at the end of the 5th century. So the Hellenistic Age is really only taking a pre-existing Greek practice and taking it up to another level by certainly making it more widespread. But there had been already embedded in Greek thought this notion of what Plato would call the *theos aner,* "the godly man", or as we would probably think of it, "the super-man."

Alexander, as we've already seen, experimented with this same status after his visit to the oracle of Zeus-Ammon at Siwa. Among Alexander's successors, establishing cults of this sort was a vivid way of legitimizing their power. We've seen Ptolemy II established a cult in honor of his father, who then was known as Ptolemy the Savior (one of the typical titles). Then Ptolemy II extended this practice to include he himself and his sister, who were known as the brother and sister gods.

Ruler cult allowed the ruling dynasty also to deal with an important group within the Hellenistic kingdom, and that was of the priestly caste, particularly in Egypt, where priests for so long had held power and had been the rulers of the land below the level of the Pharaoh. One famous inscription is the Rosetta Stone, which deals with this, and people know about the Rosetta Stone, because, as a trilingual inscription, it allowed us finally to translate hieroglyphs. But people rarely stop to actually read what's in the inscription and to find out what is of historical significance.

The Rosetta Stone records the honors voted to Ptolemy V, a young pharaoh, by the priests of Memphis. In Hellenistic fashion, it is an immensely long document. What it does is to specify his honors and then, in return for the honors offered to him, the tax breaks that are given to the priests of Memphis. It's this contractual nature of Hellenistic kingship that we've spoken about before. The Rosetta Stone says:

> … the priests of all the temples throughout the land have resolved to increase greatly the honors existing in the temples for King Ptolemy. Ptolemy, The Ever-Living, The Beloved of Ptah, god manifest and beneficent, and also those of his parents, the father-loving gods, and those for his grandparents, the benefactor-gods, and those for the brother-sister gods and those for the savior gods.

By now, every Ptolemy and every queen who has been on the throne has been honored in some way. And here is what he did for them:

> He has freed the temples from the tax of one *artaba* for each *arura* of sacred land [So the tax on the sacred land is gone] and also the tax of a jar of wine for each *arura* of vineyards. He has bestowed many gifts on Apis and Mnevis, and the other sacred animals in Egypt, much more than the kings before him, showing consideration for what belonged to them in every respect. For the burials he gave what was needed, lavishly and splendidly. What was paid to their special shrines with sacrifices and religious assemblies, and other customary observances, he has maintained the privileges of the temples of Egypt in accordance with the laws. He has adorned the traditional temples. [And it goes on to specify what else he has done.]

It was a way of negotiating between the ruling dynasty and their priests. It was a medium for international diplomacy, as we've seen on another occasion when we looked at the league of the Ionian islands, where they offered to Ptolemy a sacrifice known as the

Ptolemaieia, in return for which they are given virtually local autonomy.

It is often dismissed as a political tool, but I want to finish off by suggesting to you that this kind of cult is not a political tool at all. Really, though it serves the interests of the kings, it also serves the interests of the people with whom they are dealing. This is a poem, a song written and sung in honor of Demetrius Poliorcetes in 291. Listen to what it says about traditional religion.

> How the greatest and dearest of the gods have come to the city! The hour has brought together Demeter and Demetrius. She comes to celebrate the solemn mysteries of her daughter Persephone, while he is here full of joy, as befits the god. Fair and laughing, his appearance is majestic. Hail son of the most powerful god Poseidon [and] Aphrodite. For the other gods are either far away or they do not have ears, or they do not exist, or they do not take any notice of us. But you we can see here present. You are not made of wood or stone. You are real, and so we pray to you, Demetrius.

The Hellenistic Age was an age in which religion truly flourished, in many different ways. But it was an age where, particularly, people were seeking to find expression for their belief, whether it be at the personal level or at the communal level. It's for those reasons that the religion of the age was such a complex phenomenon.

Lecture Twenty
Economic Growth and Social Unrest

Scope:

The Hellenistic world witnessed a rapid expansion of economic activity but also an increase in social distress and even resistance to the status quo. This lecture explores evidence for these developments and shows how similar the Hellenistic Age is to our own.

Outline

I. The ancient economy was always, in comparison with the modern one, a rural economy. Most people were concerned with farming and raising stock. Nevertheless, changes in organization, technology, and trading practices meant that the economy was critical to the stability of the eastern Mediterranean.

   A. The production of staples increased as the result of the introduction of newer, faster-growing varieties of wheat. Other new varieties of fruits and crops were also encouraged by the Hellenistic kings.

   B. More iron ploughs and new types of olive presses increased production.

   C. Irrigation expanded from traditional areas, such as the Nile valley, to regions further afield in Ukraine and Bactria.

   D. The mass production of pottery increased on a scale previously unknown in the Mediterranean. Luxury trade, lower in volume than staples but potentially more lucrative, also increased dramatically.

   1. Because many amphora types are readily identifiable, it is possible to trace trade patterns across the Mediterranean.

   2. Staple goods, including wine, oil, and grain, were traded from such regions as Egypt and the Black Sea to cities unable to feed themselves, such as Alexandria, Athens, Pergamum, and even Rome.

   3. Luxury goods included spices from India, slaves and ivory from sub-Saharan Africa, Baltic amber, and tin from Cornwall.

4. Many of the most precious goods originated outside the Mediterranean, adding to their exotic and economic value.
5. A notable increase in shipwrecks dating after 250 B.C. attests to the increasing volume of sea-borne trade in the Hellenistic Age.

II. The increase in economic activity did not lead to increased prosperity for all.

A. Reliable evidence in the coins minted during the 3rd and 2nd centuries suggests that money was consistently losing its value.
   1. The Ptolemies gradually lightened the silver tetradrachm from 17 grams of silver to 15, then 13.
   2. Gold and silver coins tended to be used for international trade only; internally, copper was used.
   3. In effect, the profits in international trade were often channeled into the hands of the royal dynasties that monopolized production, their agents, and the cities that acted as free trading ports, especially Delos and Rhodes.

B. Devaluation also went hand in hand with inflation.
   1. A measure of wheat that cost 75 copper coins in the 3rd century cost 350 coppers a century later.
   2. At the same time, the ratio of copper to silver had plummeted from 1:60 to 1:455.
   3. Most hoards of Greek coins date to the Hellenistic period, revealing that people wanted to keep coins for their bullion value.

C. Other factors limited the development of a free and healthy economy.
   1. Salaries were often paid partially in produce and partially in artificially low wages, making it difficult for the soldiers and low-level bureaucrats to improve their economic positions.
   2. Credit was available but expensive, varying from 10%–12% interest to 18%–22% in times of disturbance.
   3. Insurance was hardly known, except in the case of bottomry (maritime loans), where its cost often added between 20% and 30% to the cost of the loan.
   4. Taxation was highly unpopular, not only because taxes are inherently unpopular, but because of the method of

collection. Tax collectors not only gathered taxes but also took an extra 5% to 10% as their commission.

III. As a result of these factors, the Hellenistic period saw widespread social unrest, expressed in a variety of ways.

    A. The most startling evidence of social unrest was the widespread phenomenon of piracy. Originating from Aetolia, Cilicia, and Crete, pirates preyed on the shipping lanes of the entire Mediterranean and often came ashore to raid. They were responsible for much of the trade in slaves that occurred throughout the Mediterranean.

        1. Pirates were not simply single marauding ships, acting on their own. They were often highly organized, their fleets consisting of hundreds of men. They operated wherever central authority was weak and offered an attractive alternative for those who were tired of the taxes and oppression of the Hellenistic kingdoms.

        2. In response to the dangers represented by piracy, many states and sanctuaries agreed to recognize each other's right to grant *asylia* (the right of asylum). Some of the worst areas of piracy negotiated this right.

        3. The *catochi* (recluses) were those whose response to piracy was simply to run away and live in a monastery.

    B. Similar in significance was the widespread phenomenon of mercenaries, a different reaction to social unrest. Such men had always been a part of the Mediterranean world, but they become much more numerous and prominent in the Hellenistic Age.

        1. Hellenistic monarchs often relied on mercenary forces, preferring them to national armies who might agitate against their Greek overlords.

        2. After the battle of Raphia (217 B.C.), the first battle in which the Ptolemies relied on Egyptian forces, widespread rebellions weakened the Greek dynasty and forced Ptolemy V to make concessions to the Egyptian priests.

    C. One of the most interesting forms of resistance to the status quo in the Hellenistic world was through popular literature.

        1. The *Sesostris Romance* promised a rebirth of Egyptian power at the expense of the "belt-wearers," apparently a reference to the sword belts worn by Greek soldiers in their midst.

2. The *Nectanebo Romance* was like a historical novel, in which the Egyptian pharaoh Nectanebo was presented as the father of Alexander the Great.

3. The *Potter's Oracle* was dramatically set back in the XVIIIth dynasty and prophesied a future when the Greeks would kill each other and the Nile would once again flow full and straight.

IV. The institutions of the Hellenistic world had originated either in the cultures of the ancient Near East, such as Egypt and Babylon, or in the city-states of Greece during the Archaic and Classical periods. They were not particularly well adapted to rapid social change.

Suggested Reading:

S. K. Eddy, *The King Is Dead.*

M. I. Rostovtzeff, *The Social and Economic History of the Hellenistic World*, 3 vols.

Questions to Consider:

1. Why did economic theory remain entirely outside the interest of Greek intellectuals?

2. What influence did Egyptian apocalyptic literature have on other literary genres in the Hellenistic period?

Lecture Twenty—Transcript
Economic Growth and Social Unrest

The focus of our lectures so far has been almost relentlessly on the political life of the Hellenistic Age and the social life of the Hellenistic Age. We've been looking at poetry, at sculpture, at religion, at novels, at the political history of the various dynasties established by Alexander's successors. But there is, of course, another very important aspect of the Hellenistic world that we really must address, and that is that of economic activity. How did the Greeks experience a world in which their culture and their economy (their settlers, their production, their relations of production) were now scattered over a much larger area. What effect did this have on economic activity? How did they respond to this?

We're going to see in the course of this lecture that we see an expansion of economic activity, but, as is so often the case in history, it does not mean that the prosperity created by this is evenly distributed to everyone. So we're going to explore in the course of this lecture both the economic activity of the Hellenistic Age and the social tensions created by this great wealth but its unequal distribution. In some respects we really are seeing a Hellenistic Age that seems to resemble our own world.

The first thing that must be said in any lecture about any aspect of the ancient economy at all is that the ancient economy, in comparison with the modern economy, was, by and large, a rural economy. The vast majority of people were engaged in simple subsistence farming. The vast majority of people, certainly at least 90%, of the people of the ancient Mediterranean, lived the same kind of life in the countryside, whether we are talking about Archaic Greece, the Hellenistic world or the Roman Empire. Most people are going to be concerned for most of their lives with farming and with raising stock.

Nevertheless, even if we accept that the vast majority of people are engaged that way, there are significant changes in organization in the economy, the technology of the ancient economy and trading practices, which together will mean that the economy is critical to the stability of the eastern Mediterranean, and will undergo significant changes in the Hellenistic Age, despite the fact that most people carried on life as before.

For example, we know that the production of staples during the Hellenistic Age increased as a result of newer, faster-growing varieties of wheat, producing more crops and more productive crops. Other new varieties of fruits and crops were being encouraged by the Hellenistic kings, as well. So we have a greater control of the economy and experimentation in new crop types. We also know that, at the level of technology, more iron plows were being used, and newer types of presses (for olive production, for example) were introduced, and this increased the productive capacities of the eastern Mediterranean at this time.

Another significant change in the period, which surely had a major impact on the economy, was irrigation, which was expanded. We have evidence from archaeology at various Hellenistic sites, of course, both in the Nile Valley (where irrigation had been a traditional feature of cultivation) and up into other areas such as the Ukraine (with its broad, rolling wheat fields), and even far east into Bactria (the so-called Upper Satrapies), where irrigation was either introduced or (if it was already in existence thanks to the Persians) dramatically expanded under the rule of the Hellenistic kings. So this would have brought more land into production, and it would have made more productive land that was already under cultivation.

There is mass production going on in the Hellenistic world: the mass production of pottery. It increases on a scale previously unknown in the Mediterranean. This you can measure archeologically in shipwrecks. You can measure it in the volume of pottery from different periods that you find, which you can then compare, at sites. Luxury trade, as well, also increases, even though it is lower in volume than the trade in staples. There is much more wheat and grain being sent around the Mediterranean, than, say, cedar wood or perfumes. It's lower in volume, but it's potentially much more lucrative. You can get a much higher return on luxury trade because you can charge very high prices for materials and goods that are scarce and rare and have been brought long distances. This also increases dramatically in the Hellenistic Age.

We know some of this because of different *amphora* types that are readily identifiable. This allows us to chart trade patterns across the Mediterranean. In particular the shape of an *amphora*, the shape of its neck, the shape of the point of its foot or the shape of its handle. These are highly distinctive. It allows you to see goods being transported across the Mediterranean because we have an idea of where they came from, thanks to their *amphora* types. We know staple goods such a wine, oil, and grain that are being traded from productive areas such as Egypt and the Black Sea that are then moving to areas which are less capable of feeding themselves. The great *metropoleis*, the great cosmopolitan cities that are now emerging in the period: say, Alexandria, Athens, Pergamum, and even (and particularly, later on) Rome.

So we've got lots of good evidence, lots of reliable evidence, for an increase in production and an increase in trade. There is simply more stuff being moved around the Mediterranean. As for luxury goods, we have spices coming all the way from India, we have slaves and ivory being brought up from sub-Saharan Africa, we have amber being brought down from the Baltic, and tin coming from as far away as Cornwall. So the lines of production extend way beyond the Mediterranean, out to the Atlantic, down into Africa, and across into Southeast Asia. Because these precious goods—because many of them are originating from outside the Mediterranean, they are therefore exotic, of course, and of high economic value. So they bring a great return on the investment for someone who can bring in a shipment.

The final bit of good, concrete evidence that attests to the increase in trade in the age, both in staples and in luxury goods, is the notable increase in shipwrecks. We simply have many, many more shipwrecks after 250 B.C. If we think that shipwrecks remain a constant proportion of the shipping going on (and that seems fairly logical), then it would tend to suggest that there was an increase in volume of sea-borne trade going on in the Hellenistic Age.

So there's more going on. More being produced. More being brought in. More being shipped. But more, more, more—an increase in economic activity—does not lead to an increase in prosperity for all in the Hellenistic Age. There is reliable evidence, for example, in the coins minted during the 3rd and the 2nd century that money was consistently losing value. The Ptolemies gradually lightened the silver *tetradrachm*, from 17 grams of silver down to 15 grams of silver down to 13 grams of silver. So a devaluation in the actual value of the currency.

Furthermore, gold and silver coins tended to be used only for international trade, whereas for ordinary people in the countryside in many parts of the Hellenistic world, and particularly in Egypt, copper coinage was used. So many people, even by the very currency they were using, were excluded from the kind of prosperity being brought in by international trade.

We have some quite graphic evidence of the way that the Ptolemies tried to keep control of this coinage as they made it necessary for people, as they came into Egypt, to have their coinage reminted. It was a way of constantly dipping into the coinage coming in and using it to add to the value of Ptolemaic coinage. Not that it was always successful. As with any other great bureaucracy, there were glitches, and some of our best evidence for the tight control of the Ptolemaic economy comes from the petitions and letters that we have that attest to the moments when it broke down. For example, here is a letter to Apollonius, a high-ranking official in the Ptolemaic government, coming to him from one of his agents, a man named Demetrius. The letter says:

> If you are well, that is good. As for me, I am devoting myself to what you wrote to me to do. [So this is a lower functionary reporting to his boss.] I've received 50,000 drachmas of gold, which I minted and returned. We would have received many times as much, but as I've written to you before, the foreigners who come here by sea (the merchants and the forwarding agents and the others), bring their own fine local coins, to get them back as new coins in accordance with the ordinance which instructs us to take and mint them. But as Phileretus [we're not quite sure what exactly his rank is, but he's some sort of minting official, by the looks of it] does not allow me to accept them, we have no one to refer to on this matter.

So a low-level functionary has been given one order, but the man he's going to be dealing with, to put this into practice, in other words to take the money of the foreigners and to remint it, won't help him. So this junior official doesn't know quite what to do.

> The men are furious, since we refused the coins at the bank, and … [The document breaks off for a moment and then it resumes] They cannot send their agents into the country to purchase merchandise, but they say that the gold lies idle and they are suffering a great loss, since they brought it from

©2000 The Teaching Company.

abroad and cannot easily dispose of it to others, even at a lower price.

Nobody in Egypt will take their money because it hasn't been reminted as Ptolemaic coinage. So the Ptolemies, by controlling the exchange are really controlling the economy. And as for people in the city of Alexandria, they're all reluctant to use the worn gold coins, the older ones. None of them knows who he can refer to. And so the letter goes on. Unfortunately, we don't know what the response was, although I would think that, given the nature of the Ptolemaic economy, they found a solution to make it more efficient to gouge out their little bit of profit.

Effectively, then, profits in international trade (and that's really where the profits lay), were often channeled straight into the hands of the royal dynasts, who monopolized production and of course, the other people, the jackals around the lion and its carcass, who also fared at this table (to mix some metaphors) were the agents of the dynasts. Their agents, such as Demetrius and Apollonius, who would get their cut. And then, of course, the cities, which would be the ports at which this trade would be funneled. Place such as Delos and Rhodes and, of course, Alexandria.

So once again, the cities, which are the sites of Hellenistic and Greek culture would profit from this. The dynasts and their functionaries would. But the people in the countryside probably saw very little increase in their prosperity as a result of this. We've seen devaluation going on in the coinage. Of course it goes hand in hand with inflation. There were no economic theorists in the ancient world who were able to understand adequately the mechanisms of the economy and to be able to deal with this. But we've got dramatic evidence for periods of rampant inflation during the Hellenistic Age. A measure of wheat which cost 75 copper coins in the 3rd century, 100 years later cost 350 copper coins.

At the same time, the ratio of copper to silver had actually plummeted from one to sixty to one to 455. So the combination of inflation and devaluation certainly meant that the ordinary people who couldn't get their hands on silver coinage were kept right out of the loop as far as prosperity was concerned. When people did manage, fortunately, to transfer some of their copper coinage or some of their produce into real silver or gold, which had genuine value, they hung on to it. As a result, we have most of our hoards of

Greek coins from Greek history, coming from the Hellenistic period. That's when people finally got their hands on gold and silver and put it underneath their mattress, or put it in the jar and buried it under the floor. People wanted to keep coins because these gold and silver coins had real value as bullion.

There were other factors that were important in limiting the development of a free and healthy economy as we would know it today. First of all, salaries. Salaries were often paid partly in produce and partly in artificially low wages, making it difficult for soldiers and low-level bureaucrats to improve their economic position. They weren't actually getting much in valuable coinage that they could then trade. Rather, they were basically paid in kind (given food and sustenance) and then a small allowance, as it were.

Secondly, and we know this is an important part of the modern economy, credit. Credit was available, but it was very expensive in the ancient world, varying from ten to twelve percent interest rates to 18-22% in times of unrest and disturbance. So it was difficult to be able to borrow money to be able to invest and take part in the economic activity of the age.

Related to this, insurance is virtually unknown in the Hellenistic world. There is really only one category of insurance that exists, and that's a *bottomry*, that is to say, maritime loans. But because moving stuff by sea was a hazardous business (you never knew when a fleet would go down), correspondingly the cost of a maritime insurance policy was extraordinarily high. Twenty to thirty percent. So it was an expensive proposition to be able to invest in a fleet and then to guarantee by insurance the material that you were shipping by sea.

We cannot talk about economic activity in any period of human history without, of course, mentioning taxation. Taxation, you may be surprised to hear, was unpopular in the ancient world. It was unpopular not only because taxes are inherently unpopular, but also because of the method of collection. In the ancient world, taxes tended to be collected, not directly by a government official, but rather by a private person who had signed a contract with the government to collect taxes. That way, the government was guaranteed their money, because the tax collector actually forked it over. But then, of course, the tax collector was in a position of adding a commission to the original taxation amount, so that he could make a profit out of it. So people who were being taxed were even paying for the privilege of being taxed by fellow citizens. The name for this, of course, in Latin, for these tax collectors, is *publicani,* and that is why often in translations of the New Testament we hear of "publicans and sinners." It does not mean that hotel keepers had a bad reputation in the ancient world. It's because "publicans" is a funny translation for "tax collectors."

We have a very startling piece of evidence regarding the degrees of taxation. We know that in Egypt, taxation was more rigorous and at a higher rate than anywhere else in the Hellenistic world. But also because of the sand of Egypt and the papyri that we have, we have very detailed evidence of how taxation worked there. For example, here is a document that records goods that were brought in across the Gaza Strip, a boat that sailed down the coast of Lebanon and Israel and across round toward Egypt. And it entered Egyptian territory at the site of Pelusium, near what today is Gaza City. As the ship came into Egyptian territory it came into port. A Ptolemaic customs agent would go aboard and he would read the bill of lading and he would check all the contents of the boat, record everything, and then present the captain with a taxation bill on the spot. Fortunately, this would be in duplicate, and then the captain would be able to show later on to the owners of the goods what he had paid in taxes.

This is just to give you an idea of what was being taxed on this boat. The boat is captained by a man called Patron. The bill of lading includes grape syrup, filtered wine, ordinary wine, white oil, kein jars of wine, half jars, Phasian jars, jars of wine from other areas, and some jars of dried figs. Now, what do you suppose would be the taxation of those goods as they came in? The import tax on them was 33-1/3rd percent. Fairly drastic. Then a boat captained by a friend of his (they came through together, at the same time) a fellow by the name of Heraclides, has on board such things as wild boar meat in a jar, a pot of the same, two large jars of venison, a couple of small pots of goat meat, a basket of hard sponges, and cheeses and various other goods of this sort, and they're taxed at 25 percent.

So taxation, which was ubiquitous, was not popular. In Egypt it must certainly have had an effect on limiting the amount of goods that could be brought in, except by those agents of the king. The total effect of this, the total effect of the coercive nature of government, of the disproportionate allocation of the prosperity of the age, led (along with a number of other factors, of course) to widespread social unrest. This is a feature of the age that we really need to spend some time looking at. The most startling evidence for this, of course, is the widespread phenomenon of piracy. We've already had an opportunity to look at this and to see how some people responded to it. We saw that in one case from the island of Amorgos when a group of women and some citizens of the state were carried off, the men offered themselves as hostages to the pirates to negotiate the release of the women slaves and their fellow citizens. You'll remember that I remarked in dealing with that particular instance that piracy was very well organized.

It tended to originate from well-identified areas: Aetolia in northwestern Greece, Crete, Cilicia. These pirates preyed on the shipping lanes of the entire Mediterranean. If you regard a map of the Mediterranean and look at these locations, you'll see that any trade which goes by coast from the eastern Mediterranean to the Aegean (in other words, from the coast of Syria and Lebanon and Israel and Egypt around into the Aegean—the western coast of Turkey and to Greece), must go past the southern coast of Turkey, or Cilicia. So the pirates there were absolutely perfectly situated to be able to just sail out and grab anything that went past.

Similarly, if you go from the eastern Mediterranean and across towards the west, the other places that you will go past will be Crete (boats sailing from there can nab anything that goes past). And if you sail up the west coast of Greece, and start heading across towards the heel of Italy and around the toe of Italy, you will have to go past Aetolia, where again, the pirates will simply be able to sail out and grab anything. So they weren't simply single marauding ships. Rather, they were highly organized fleets, often with hundreds, even thousands of men.

They are a particularly interesting phenomenon because I think they explain to us that power in the Hellenistic world tended to be effective only as far as it could be enforced. Only as far as the troops of a Hellenistic king could go. Central authority, then, was based on towns. And beyond that, all bets were off. It has sometimes been pointed out that in the story of the Good Samaritan in the New Testament, we have the suggestion of robbers operating on a major road in Judaea, not terribly far away from major cities. But as soon as you're outside the walls of the city, it's possible that you're going to move into bandit territory. These pirates are like an alternative society, for those who are tired of the taxes and the oppression of the Hellenistic kingdoms. They just go off and act as marauders.

In response to the dangers presented by piracy, I pointed out in an earlier lecture, that many states and sanctuaries actually agreed to recognize each other's rights. They refer to this in the Hellenistic world as *asylia*, or the right of asylum. They actually will negotiate with pirate states, saying, "Allow us to be free of piracy," and presumably they would pay something over for that right. So places had to deal directly with the pirates.

But what about if you're not a city or a kingdom? What about if you're an individual? What do you do in this world where at any time you could be robbed and beaten? Where policing is essentially ineffective and where if you're outside of the city you might find yourself grabbed by slavers, ending up on the auction block on Delos or Rhodes? For many people, who simply got tired of this, the answer was, to flee. To run away from society. In Egypt in particular we have a widespread phenomenon in the Hellenistic world, of people not becoming priests of cults and joining the temple estates, but becoming almost a lay brotherhood associated with the Temple estates. These are known in Greek as *catochi*, which means "recluses."

We have an example of this from the great Serapeum, the temple of Serapis at Memphis, where one Greek individual named Ptolemy (again, not the king, of course, but just the same name)—where he went and lived for a number of years, claiming that he was "in detention." This phrase, which turns up in many of the documents seems to mean that he'd had some kind of epiphany, some kind of dream or visitation from the god, where the god had said, "I want you to come to my sanctuary." And he's kept there for a number of years. While he was there, he didn't manage to avoid the sort of random attacks that people are afraid of. He says, in his petition to the local governor,

> I've been living in detention for a number of years. While I was in detention at the Serapeum, I was attacked. Some men with stones in their hands and others with sticks, broke in. They tried to force their way in in order to seize the opportunity to plunder the temple and to put me to death because I was a Greek. [This is very interesting because it's

an example of the tension between the various ethnic groups.]

Like men laying a plot against my life. But when I anticipated them and shut the door of the temple and shouted to them to withdraw in peace, they didn't go away, even so.

One of the other Greeks, who's also in detention, eventually expresses indignation at this, and comes to his assistance. So we're reading about a brawl that's actually going on in what is meant to be the safest haven that you can imagine: the temple of Serapis. Even there, you weren't safe.

Similarly, another response to the upheavals of the time, apart from piracy and becoming a recluse and simply running away, was the phenomenon of mercenaries. Some men simply said, "Why stay in Greece, and die a slow death of starvation, when I can grab my shield and my spear and I can sign up?" Of course, there was always ready work for them, because, as we've seen, the various Hellenistic kings tended to rely on mercenary armies. Such men have always been a part of the Mediterranean world. But they become much more numerous and much more prominent in the Hellenistic period.

Hellenistic monarchs relied on these mercenary forces. We have lists from Egypt, for example, and from Syria where we find men drawn from all of the old towns in old Greece coming to serve their new Greek and Macedonian overlords. There is a dramatic change towards the end of the 3rd century in relation to this when, after the Battle of Raphaea in 217 B.C., the Ptolemies start including more and more forces in their army. They actually have Egyptian battalions at the Battle of Raphia. But the effect of this is to weaken their dynasty. There are more and more rebellions going on after this period as the Greek dynasty becomes weaker. So we can imagine some people running off to become mercenaries, some people running off to become pirates, some people running off to temples to become recluses, and some people just raising arms in rebellion against their king. Here's a description of one such rebellion from 160 B.C. It occurs in the area known as the Thebiads, the region around Egyptian Thebes.

Yet another disturbance took place in the Thebiad [writes Diodorus, the historian], as a revolutionary fervor fell on the masses. [Note the language in this, the reference to Greeks and Egyptians.] King Ptolemy advanced against him with a large army and easily restored control over the other parts of the Thebiad. But the town called Panopolis is situated on an ancient mound. Because it is difficult to access, it is thought to be a strong position. So the most active of the rebels gathered there. Ptolemy, seeing the desperation of the Egyptians, and the strength of the place, laid siege to it, and after enduring every kind of hardship, he captured the city, punished the culprits and returned to Alexandria.

It's very much the work of an occupying force, coming down from Alexandria (a Greek and Macedonian army under Ptolemy), coming to reassert its authority in the Egyptian zone. So it's another example of a strong sense of divide between the two cultures. One of the most interesting ways in which the unrest of the time finds expression is through popular literature. I'm not talking now just about the Greek novels, although we have seen motifs there of shipwreck and capture by pirates. But we actually have in the Hellenistic Age what is sometimes referred to as resistance literature. Texts that demonstrate that people were writing about their oppression and were opposed to it. The *Sesostris Romance*, as it's called, from Egypt, constantly refers to the belt-wearers. The belt-wearers seem to be the Greeks. It is a reference to the fact that the Greeks in their midst were wearing their side-arms, their swords, hanging from their belts.

Another interesting example is called the *Nectanebo Romance*. It's an historical novel in which the Egyptian pharaoh, Nectanebo, is presented as the father of Alexander the Great. So in this way the oppressed Egyptians are claiming that really, the great man of the age, Alexander, was one of them. He's not really one of the Macedonians at all. The *Potter's Oracle* is set even further back. It's set back in the time of the 18th Dynasty, so it's a historical novel going back a long way. Back in the 18th Dynasty, according to this oracle, there is a prophecy of a future time—a future time when the Greeks will kill each other, and once again the Nile will flow full and straight. Like many such documents, of course, it is about contemporary events, but is set in the past and then projects forward into the future an alternative to current conditions.

So what we find, then, in the Hellenistic Age is that there were many different responses to the economic developments. The rich got richer, but the poor didn't. Their response to that was either to run away and live in a monastery, and in fact, the monastic impulse, which will become important in Christianity really originates at this time. Or they join an army and go after Ptolemy and become one of his mercenaries. Or, in some even more imaginative instances, they write an historical novel, but a novel which predicts the end of the Hellenistic world.

Lecture Twenty-One
The Mood of the Hellenistic Age

Scope:

The Hellenistic Age saw cultural contact on an unprecedented scale, as the Greeks established control of areas once ruled by Egyptian pharaohs and Persian kings. The result was something radically different from the Classical Age of mainland Greece. This lecture identifies some of the most characteristic features of the Hellenistic world: internationalism, individualism, and a fascination with fate.

Outline

I.   The Greeks of the Hellenistic world were well aware of the fact that the Greek world was much larger than Greece itself.

   A. Their word for this larger world was the *oecumene,* meaning "the commonwealth." It refers to a cultural zone that existed wherever there were Greek communities and corresponds very closely to what in more modern times we would call the Levant, the world of the eastern Mediterranean.

   B. *Koine* is the term used to describe the Greek language of the age. As Greeks from different parts of the Greek world migrated to new places, their language began to lose some if the distinctive features of its separate dialects, and a new standardized Greek began to emerge.

      1. *Koine* Greek is the language in which the New Testament was composed, although Aramaic elements are also present.

      2. Jewish scriptures were also translated from Hebrew into *koine* Greek at the order of Ptolemy II. Tradition holds that the translation was performed by 70 scholars, from which derives the name of the Greek translation of the Old Testament, the Septuagint.

      3. *Koine* did not emerge overnight, however, and differences in pronunciation could still be heard. Theocritus's poems include one, Idyll 15, that captures the broad vowels of Doric Greek spoken by two ladies from Syracuse now living in Alexandria.

C. To the Hellenistic world, however, internationalism did not mean fusing with other Greek cultures so much as exporting a uniform Greek culture to a larger area. This exportation was accomplished by a number of new institutions that were characteristic of the age.

   1. Many Greek states employed doctors, architects, and gymnastic trainers on the public payroll. These professionals repeated the same pattern of Greek culture wherever they went, encouraging cultural homogeneity.

   2. Greek drama was now performed by professional troops of actors—also a religious brotherhood—who traveled from city to city, the so-called *technitai* of Dionysus.

   3. Professional teachers brought Greek education wherever Greeks settled. The usual setting for education was the gymnasium, and the presence of a gymnasium and theatre became one of the hallmarks of a Greek city, whether in Greece or Afghanistan. The *gymnasiarch* became an extremely important public official.

II. The Greeks and Hellenized non-Greeks had international meeting places: sanctuaries. Panhellenic sanctuaries, such as Delphi and Olympia, had long been important meeting places for the Greeks, but now other shrines became just as important.

   A. Delos emerged as one of the largest and wealthiest sanctuaries of the Mediterranean.

      1. Between 300 and 166 B.C., the island was independent and enjoyed prosperity, thanks to its central location and the prestige of the sanctuary of Apollo.

      2. In 166, Rome took control and gave the island to Athens, but the loss of independence was compensated by its tax-free status, making it the busiest port in the Aegean for the next century.

   B. Various sanctuaries of Asclepius, a healing god, also gained in popularity from the 4th century B.C. onward.

      1. At Epidaurus, a magnificent complex (an *asclepieum*) included a temple and a dormitory/hospital. People came from all around Greece to be cured by the healer god and left inscriptions giving their thanks.

      2. On Kos, another *asclepieum* was located, not far from a famous medical school where doctors were trained in the

Hippocratic tradition. The sick could choose their cures, either from the god or from scientific medicine.

C. Sanctuaries benefited from the generosity of Hellenistic kings and repaid their largesse by conferring prestige on their patrons. The cult of the Cabiri on Samothrace was popular with many Macedonian dynasts, as well as the Ptolemies, and was endowed by them with gates, fountains, and buildings.

III. The international character of the age was balanced by an increasing interest in individualism.

A. We have already seen this is in our study of Greek sculpture, in which we saw a type of realism not witnessed in the Classical Age.

B. The interest in individualism emerged in our look at Greek philosophy, which increasingly concerned itself with freeing the individual from emotional disturbance.

C. The work of major writers also shows an interest in individuality.
    1. Theophrastus wrote a comic treatise that examined different types of characters: the Suspicious Man, the Conservative, and so forth.
    2. Menander's comic plays, unlike the earlier broad farce of Aristophanes, were about familiar and recognizable family problems, the ancient forerunners of modern sitcoms.

IV. Many of the writers of the age explored a theme than runs through all Hellenistic art and culture, namely the unpredictability of fortune.

A. In Greek novels, heroes and heroines constantly suffer reversals of fortune. They are reunited, only to be separated once again by a storm or a pirate attack.

B. Many historians of the age also emphasized the role of fortune in determining the course of events.
    1. Both Duris and Phylarchus were notorious for writing highly dramatic and emotional histories that emphasized the feelings of the protagonists.
    2. Polybius, possibly the best Greek historian after Thucydides, deplored this emphasis on sensationalism

and the role of fortune in what was sometimes called "tragic history." Occasionally, even he refers to the role of fate.

C. The Greek term for fortune was *tyche*; from the 4th century onward, the goddess Tyche received cult honors in Athens and abroad.

    1. In the east, Tyche was associated with a Semitic goddess, Gad, and sometimes with Isis.

    2. Although she could be capricious and malevolent, her power was also harnessed for the protection of cities.

    3. Statues that show her wearing a crown representing the walls of the city became common in the Hellenistic east, and Tyche was often treated synonymously with the spirit of the city.

D. This was a culture in the eastern Mediterranean that could genuinely be called "international."

Suggested Reading:

J. J. Pollitt, "Introduction: Hellenistic Art and the Temperament of the Hellenistic Age," in *Art in the Hellenistic Age*.

F. Walbank, *Polybius*.

Questions to Consider:

1. What does the emphasis on fortune tell us about the mood of the Hellenistic Age?

2. In what ways did the Hellenistic Age explore individual experience differently from the Classical period?

Lecture Twenty-One—Transcript
The Mood of the Hellenistic Age

Welcome back to our series of lectures on Alexander the Great and the Hellenistic Age. We have tried to break the Hellenistic Age down into a series of discrete compartments or units that would allow us to conduct our survey a little bit more thoroughly. We've looked at the politics of the age, beginning with Alexander's career and the establishment of the various Hellenistic kingdoms. We've also looked at the culture of the age. We've examined its sculpture, its poetry, its philosophy, and we've looked at its art. More recently, we've been looking at the economy of the age. I've tried to suggest that though the economy grew during the Hellenistic period, it was also a period of great social unrest. A period of great upheaval.

There are some aspects of cultural activity, cultural production that almost defy general categorization. I've actually put some of these together into one lecture. They are aspects of the Hellenistic Age which in some ways relate to each other, but which can only be generally lumped together by calling it "The Mood of the Hellenistic Age."

What I would like to do in this lecture is to examine the way in which the atmosphere of the Hellenistic period, the general appearance of the age, the *zeitgeist*, if you will, is somewhat different than we find in the earlier periods of Greek history, whether it be the Archaic or, more recently, the Classical. If we approach it from this point of view, trying to broadly encompass the entire age and to make generalizations about it, I think that there are at least three major features of the age that are distinctive and deserve closer attention.

One is what we might call internationalism. It is an age in which, because Greek culture is extrapolated over such a larger area, there are now institutions which are repeated in new areas. Institutions that make people Greek, whether they be in Greece or whether they be in Afghanistan or in Upper Egypt. So we're going to talk about what constitutes "internationalism," in a moment. It's also an age in which a fascination with the individual is very important. I want to look at some of the areas in which that is expressed, in, say, the writing of history and in some of the philosophical works. Then, finally, we'll look at the fascination with Fate. And although these three areas look disparate, they are all, I think, very characteristic qualities that mark the Hellenistic Age as something distinct and separate from earlier periods. The Greeks of the Hellenistic world were well aware of the fact that theirs was a Greek world. A Greek culture much larger than the actual territory of Greece. They had a word for this. They referred to it as the *oecumene*, the commonwealth, as we would call it. Sometimes also referred to just more simply as the *koine*, the "common" world, the world that was culturally Greek. *Koine* coming from the Greek adjective meaning "common." This term, then, refers to a cultural zone, which existed wherever there were Greek communities. It corresponds very closely to what, in more modern times we would call the Levant. That is to say, the eastern Mediterranean.

Koine referred not only to the o*ecumene*, the commonwealth, the Greek area. It also referred to the language spoken in that cultural zone. That language was, of course, Greek. But the Greek that had been spoken back in the Greek mainland in earlier periods had been marked by many different dialects. We know this from the early inscriptions from Greece. Greek is a phonetic language, so if there are changes in pronunciation in northern or southern or eastern or western Greece, these will be marked by different spellings on our inscriptions. It was a language that originally had very distinctive dialectical differences, but now what happens in the Hellenistic Age is that a more standardized, a more common form (*koine*) of Greek begins to emerge.

It really is a phenomenon somewhat similar to the spread of the English language in modern times, where it is now possible to find a kind of standard English spoken, at least in the southeast of England. It's very different from all the various dialects of English spoken there, and which is sometimes assimilated to Californian English or other varieties of English, producing a fairly neutral accent. *Koine* Greek worked the same way. It was a standardized form of Greek. It's the language in which the New Testament is composed, even though there are some Aramaic elements in the language of the New Testament, as well. But it's a good example of the spread of this common Greek so that even the people of Judaea are acquiring this, and it's being used for writing down the Gospels. The Jewish scriptures, also, we've seen already, were translated from Hebrew into Greek, and the Greek that they're translated into is, once again, *koine* Greek, the common Greek of the Hellenistic Age. Supposedly this was done on the order of Ptolemy II, and tradition maintains that it was performed by seventy scholars who came to Alexandria for the task. It's from the term for "seventy" that the Greek translation of the Old Testament takes its name, the Septuagint. It means, "the seventy."

Koine, of course, did not emerge overnight. Differences in pronunciation could still be heard in the Hellenistic period. In fact, a poet with a good ear for language, like Theocritus, seems to have been particularly interested in dialectical differences, so that, in one of his Idylls (in fact, it's the one I read to you, involving the two women, Gorgo and Praxinoa, who are rushing off to the palace to hear a recital), one of the pleasures of reading that in the original is that the actual language spoken by those two women is Doric Greek, the broad Greek associated both with Sparta and also with Syracuse, the city from which they originally come, before they had moved to Alexandria. So the differences didn't die out altogether, and the poet here seemed to be interested in getting that down on paper and showing how these people spoke. I imagine it would be a little like Alexander Pope writing a poem and trying to capture the brogue of either a couple of Irish ladies or perhaps some women who had come down from Glasgow.

To the Hellenistic world, internationalism was not simply a matter of a standard form of Greek. As I've argued on a number of occasions during this course of lectures, it also did not really mean fusing with other Greek cultures. Internationalism in the Hellenistic period really means a kind of exportation of Greek culture, and a uniform Greek culture which can be replicated, whether you are in Macedon, whether you are in southern Greece, whether you're on the Nile, whether you're on the Orontes, whether you're in Mesopotamia or out in Bactria.

This was accomplished thanks to a number of institutions which are characteristic of the Hellenistic period. For example, many Greek states now employed doctors, architects, teachers and gymnastic trainers. These professionals tended to repeat the practice of Greek culture, wherever they went. The introduction of public education is one of the interesting developments of the period. We have good evidence for it from a number of Greek sites. The city of Teos, for example, in Asia Minor, leaves us an inscription from the 2nd century that includes the following stipulations:

Every year at the elections, after the selection of the scribes, three schoolmasters are to be appointed. They are to teach the boys and the girls. The first person, to teach the first class, will get 600 drachmas per year, the second class 550, and the third class will get 500 drachmas.

There are also to be two physical trainers, so the boys and girls are to get their exercise at the school, as well as their learning. There is to be a lute player, so music is an important part of their education. They are to be taught music. There is also to be a good drill sergeant. So military training is meant to be part of their education, as well, and they will be taught archery and javelin throwing. And so it goes on with various regulations about how the school is meant to be organized.

So we have an idea here that what's emerging is a kind of standardized curriculum. A Greek boy in Macedon and a Greek boy in Sparta, a Greek boy in Alexandria and a Greek boy in Mesopotamia is likely to be going to school, reading the same poets, being exercised in exactly the same way, learning the same kind of musical scales. Doctors also helped to export Greek culture, because they ended up being employed far and wide around the Mediterranean. We have, for example, an inscription that comes from the island of Samos, which talks about the good work done by their public doctor. It says:

> Since Diodorus, son of Dioscorides, who took over among us the task of public doctor, has for many years in the previous period through his own skill and care looked after and cured many of the citizens, and the others of the city who had fallen seriously ill, and since he took care of people when the earthquakes took place, many of us had suffered painful wounds of every sort, because of the unexpected disaster, but he assisted all of them. ...

It goes on in typical Hellenistic fashion to vote him a series of honors. What this inscription reveals to us is that we've got doctors (often coming from the island of Cos) operating all around the Greek world.

Another institution which contributed to this sense of similarity, of homogeneity, if you like, in Greek culture and Greek practices, was that of Greek drama. Not only do we have now the great plays of

Aeschylus and Sophocles and Euripides being performed all over the eastern Mediterranean, but we have bands of travelling performers known as the *technitai*, the technicians, if you like, of Dionysos. Yes they are actors, but they are also a religious brotherhood. A religious brotherhood that travels from city to city, and on the occasion of the festival of Dionysos will put on a performance of plays in honor of the gods. Since Greek drama was always enacted in honor of the god. They are an interesting phenomenon. One of the inscriptions we have—I won't read it. It's far too long. It's one of the longest inscriptions to come to us from the Hellenistic period. It is hundreds of lines long.

What it shows us is that these technicians of Dionysos, this guild of actors, which is really the best way of expressing it in English, felt vulnerable, because they traveled a lot. As we've already seen, there was always the risk of being captured by pirates. So what do they do? They get a royal patron, who gave them money to help them, and also wrote them a document which they could show in case they came under attack by pirates, saying that they were being offered *asuleia* (that is to say, asylum) and *asphaleia*, that is to say, safe passage), guaranteed by the king of Egypt. It's a good example of how many of the features we've seen are coming together: the unsettled nature of the times, the importance of the power of the king in being able to guarantee, in this instance, at least, the safety of these itinerant actors.

Professional teachers brought Greek education wherever the Greeks settled. It wasn't merely a matter of Greek teachers or professors being employed, but an entire institution that was associated with Greek education. That institution, of course, was the gymnasium. This is where young men go for their education. The presence of a gymnasium in a city, which is usually fairly easy to find archeologically—the presence of a gymnasium and the presence of a theater, tells you that you've got a Greek city. A city that regards itself as being Greek.

You'll recall that when we looked at the revolt of the Maccabees, when the Hellenizing Jews in Alexandria came to power, what they attempted to do was to put up a gymnasium in the city. In other words, to advertise that this was no longer merely a Jewish city, but it was now also a Hellenistic city. A city with Greek culture. One finds these both in Judaea, and in Alexandria, and all the way across to Ai Khanum, where a gymnasium also has been found.

As a result, the man in charge of the gymnasium became one of the most important public officials in the Hellenistic state. He's usually known as the *gymnasiarch*. Again, we have inscriptions from many parts of the Greek world, hundreds of lines long. We don't have them back into the Classical or Archaic period, but in the Hellenistic period, many of these, dealing with the establishment of a gymnasium. One that we have comes to us from Macedonia. It has extraordinarily detailed stipulations about how the *gymnasiarch* is to be selected, how he is to run the gymnasium, who the supporting officials are who are to work with him. How he is to take care of things.

> Concerning the boys: None of the youngsters may enter among the boys nor talk to the boys. Otherwise, the *gymnasiarch* shall find and prevent anyone who does any of these things.

It goes on to talk about the physical trainers. It goes on to talk about how the *gymnasiarch* has to make sure that certain people are not allowed into the gymnasium. He's acting *in loco parentis*.

> No one may enter the gymnasium or take off his clothes if he is a slave, if he is a freed man, if he is the son of either of these, if he has not been to the wrestling school, if he's a pederast, if he's practiced a vulgar trade, if he's a drunk, or if he is mad.

So this is an institution that is being set up for the first time to train all the boys of the city on a regular basis. People are making sure that they've got someone of good, sound, moral character running the whole show. For the Greeks and those who adopted Greek culture (those who were Hellenized) there were other institutions which helped in this process. Not institutions that were replicated in the cities, but rather institutions to which people came. Most important here is that of the Greek sanctuaries.

Sanctuaries had always played an important role in Greek culture. Remember that in the earlier period of Greek history there was no united Greece. The Greeks were never politically united, but they were culturally united. One way in which this was expressed was by the meetings that took place on a regular basis at places such as

Nemea, Isthmia, Delphi and of course, Olympia. These places are known as pan-Hellenic shrines. In other words, they are places where all the Greeks meet together. Now, in the Hellenistic Age, other shrines attempted to attain a status that was equal to this. In fact, there is now, for the first time in Hellenistic Greek, an expression *Iso-Olympiakos*, which means "equal in status to the Olympics." So if your sanctuary attained that status, then you now became essentially a pan-Hellenic shrine as well.

One of the places that emerged as a large and wealthy sanctuary that really flourished in the Hellenistic period as never before, was Delos. Hellenistic Delos gives us a good idea of the connection between trade, economy and culture going on in the Hellenistic period. Between 300 B.C. and 166 B.C., the early Hellenistic period, in other words, the island was independent. It enjoyed a great deal of prosperity thanks to its central location, and the prestige of the sanctuary of Apollo. In 166 B.C., smack bang in the middle of the Hellenistic Age, Rome took control of the island and gave it into the safekeeping of Athens. The small island of Delos lost its independence, but this was compensated for by being given a tax-free status. This made Delos the busiest port in the Aegean for the next century. This we might regard as merely a matter of economics. It is something like the Singapore, if you will, of the ancient Aegean, sucking trade into it as people come here.

We know, for example, of many slave ships that came in. There are estimates of 10,000 slaves per day being sold on the island of Delos. But it isn't merely a matter of crude economics of that sort. We know that as the island gained in economic status, and because it already was a sanctuary dedicated to Apollo, it also increased in religious status at the same time. One of the most remarkable documents in this respect, takes us back to a cult that we've already looked at, the cult of Serapis.

You'll remember that I mentioned in an earlier lecture that the cult of Serapis, this fusion of Greek and Egyptian elements, was actually a successful export from Egypt, and became popular around the Hellenistic world. We in fact have a document that gives us the ground zero for when that cult left Egypt and landed on the island of Delos. It comes in a letter recorded by a man called Apollonius. This Apollonius (it's a good Greek name) comes from a long family of men who were priests. Interestingly enough, in this letter he talks about his grandfather, whose name was also Apollonius, but he says his grandfather was an Egyptian. So somewhere along the line, earlier in the family's history, they've dropped their Egyptian names, and adopted Greek names. We do have other letters, inscriptions and petitions that show this, with people sometimes having a Greek name and saying "Also known as 'X'," followed by an Egyptian name. Greek and Egyptian. This man says that his grandfather lived to the age of ninety-seven, and then his father succeeded his grandfather, and worshiped the gods in the same way, and he lived for sixty-one years. They are priests of Serapis in this family, and the priesthood is passed on.

> When [says Apollonius] I inherited the sacred objects and devoted myself carefully to the cult, the god told me in my sleep that a *Serapeum* [a shrine of Serapis] of his own must be dedicated to him, and that he must not be as before in a rented building. He said he would find a spot himself where he should be set, and that he would point it out.

So they've rented a little shrine on Delos, but this isn't enough for the god, so he finally said to Apollonius, "This won't cut it. I need to have my own shrine." So he appears to Apollonius, and he points out to him exactly where the spot is to be.

> This spot was full of dirt, and was advertised for sale in a little notice on a passage to the *agora*. As the god wanted this, the purchase was completed and the sanctuary was rapidly built in six months. When some men joined against us and the god and introduced a public suit against the sanctuary [they're sued for trying to put up their local church] and me, involving a penalty or a fine, the god promised to me in my sleep that we would be victorious. Now that the trial has been completed, and we have won a victory worthy of the god, we praise the gods and repay them adequate thanks.

So here the story has a happy ending and the shrine was successfully built and continued to flourish for some time afterwards. So shrines represent, as they pop up like mushrooms, the exporting of these fused Hellenistic religions. They're exported all around the Mediterranean. There are a number of gods of the period (not only gods, like Serapis, who are new to the Greeks), but there are a number of other gods who gain even greater significance in the period. Their popularity once again, I think, attests to this international culture.

The one who is probably most important at this time is Asclepius. Asclepius had been known to the Greek prior to the Hellenistic period, and certainly in the 4th century he was treated as a god, although it appears that in earlier periods he may have been regarded as a hero and as a very powerful man, rather than a god. But by this time, in the Hellenistic Age, he is certainly being treated as a healer-god, a god who can step in to help people. The best known instance that we have of his worship comes from Epidaurus, the site, of course, of one of the great theaters in modern Greece still to be seen.

What people often don't know is that at Epidaurus there was an Asclepium, a shrine in honor of the god Asclepius. It wasn't merely a temple. It included a dormitory where people would come and where they would sleep overnight. They would experience the kind of dreams that we've already seen in some of our documents. In these dreams the god would either appear and heal them, or he would give them indications of the course of therapy they would undergo later on. People came from all around Greece to be healed by the god.

There were a number of shrines in his honor. This is only the most famous. One of the reasons it is famous is that after people were healed, they left testimonials, saying "this is what the god did to me." These testimonials were then engraved, they were inscribed on stone, so as you walked into the sanctuary, you got to read the stories of all the people who had been cured. Here's a couple of them:

> Cleo was pregnant for five years. After already five years of pregnancy, she came as a suppliant to the god, and went to sleep in the innermost sanctuary. As soon as she came out of it and was outside the sanctuary, she gave birth to a boy, who, as soon as he was born, washed himself in the fountain and walked about with his mother.

I mean, he was five years old. Of course he was able to walk. After being granted this favor, she wrote the following inscription on her dedication: "It is not the greatness of the tablet that deserves adoration, but the divinity. As Cleo was pregnant with child in her womb for five years, until she went to sleep and the divinity restored her to health."

So this both attests to the strong sense of the real involvement of the gods in your day-to-day life, something that we've talked about already, but the fact that this was replicated through so much of the Greek world also talks to our idea of internationalism. These stories would circulate around the Greek world.

On the island of Kos, there was another Asclepium, another sanctuary of Asclepius. What is most fascinating about that particular sanctuary is that it was located on the same island and not very far away from, a medical school. A medical school which had been founded by the followers of Hippocrates. Hippocrates, of course, of the Hippocratic Oath. What I think this strongly suggests is that on the island of Kos, when you arrived, you could take your choice, either of going to the sanctuary and trying to get a religious cure, a divine cure, or else go in to the doctors for a scientific and secular cure. I am absolutely convinced that there were many people who tried one, and if it didn't work they went over and tried the other. It makes absolutely good sense.

Sanctuaries benefited from the generosity of the Hellenistic kings, and the sanctuaries repaid the largesse of their patrons by conferring great prestige on these kings. So the sanctuaries act as a way of replicating this Hellenistic power relationship that we've seen so often. The cult of the Cabiri, for example, is a rather obscure mystery cult. We don't know the details of what was involved here, or what the myth or the story was. We do know that it was located on the island of Samothrace. It was the largest international sanctuary, if you will, located near Macedon. So it had become quite popular with the Macedonian dynasts. There's even a story that Philip and Olympias (the parents of Alexander the Great) met here. It also became quite popular later on with the Ptolemies. It eventually was endowed with all sorts of magnificent buildings, with fountains, with monumental structures and temples, all in honor of various members of the Ptolemaic and other dynasties.

We've talked a lot about the international character of the age, but I also wanted to talk about the individualism of the age. We find here (and we've seen this already in the sculpture of the age, and we've seen it to some extent in the philosophy, as well, with an interest in the individual), but there are other works that are particularly interesting here.

Theophrastus, for example, who was a student of Aristotle, came to write a comic treatise that dealt with different types of characters: the suspicious man, the oligarchic man, the conservative man, and so forth. He was exploring here different types of character. Menander's comic plays also are interested in individuals. They're not interested just now in the affairs of the city-state, as had been the plays of Aristophanes, which were largely plays about democratic life in Athens. Menander's plays, instead, are somewhat more like modern-day sitcoms. They're about recognizable families. They're about the dilemmas that families face. What happens if a parent dies and a child is left without a guardian, for example. And, imitating many of the themes of the Hellenistic novels, what happens if a boy and a girl meet, fall in love, but then get separated. So there's an individualism there, in the plays of the time and in Theophrastus' work as well.

But then that other theme that we can't ignore, that runs throughout the whole Hellenistic period is this notion of the unpredictability of fortune. In the Greek novels, as we've seen, heroes and heroines are constantly suffering a reversal of fortune. They are constantly being reunited, only to be separated again by a storm or a pirate attack. But this idea of fortune wasn't something merely used by novelists or poets. It was an idea very seriously explored also by historians. They were pursuing the idea that capricious fortune might play a role in destiny and history.

Two historians, Duris and Phylarchus, both were notorious for writing histories that highlighted the role of fortune. A dramatic change in circumstances, leading to the collapse of fortunes of one of the great leaders. These highly emotional histories that they produced were then often referred to as "tragic history," because they really blurred the line between a kind of dramatic story that you would expect on the stage and a sober history.

Polybius, who's probably the best Greek historian after Thucydides, deplored this emphasis on sensationalism and the dramatic impact of fortune, decrying this tragic history. And yet, even Polybius, ironically enough, often refers to the role of Tyche or, as the Romans would later call her, Fortuna, in history. The Greek term for this, as I've just said, is Tyche. From the 4th century onwards, it's not merely a concept. It's not merely an abstract noun, as the word "fortune" is in English. She's a goddess. She's a personified goddess. She actually receives cult honors. People can go and worship at a shrine, to make a dedication to Tyche, in Athens, from the 4th century, and further abroad, as well.

In the East she becomes, as is so often the case, incorporated with other goddesses. There is a Semitic goddess Gad, who is often regarded as being similar to Tyche. Once again, all of these will be assimilated into Isis on various occasions. She could be capricious. She could be malevolent. But by the same token she could also be the protector of cities. So one increasingly finds during the Hellenistic period, then, statues, engraved gems, in some cases terra cotta plaques or glass bowls, on which one will see a woman representing the city. She may be crowned. With the crown, though, showing the walls of the city, representing the city. She becomes the kind of genius or the guardian spirit synonymous with the spirit of the city itself.

So this is a very complex age when it comes to new developments that make it different from the period that came before. The Greeks, yes, had always believed in a healing god and, yes, they had always believed in Fortune, and, yes, they had always been fascinated by the individual, and by what makes up Greek culture. All of these elements, yes. But one finds many of these elements being given fresh interest and fresh impetus in the work of the Hellenistic Age. An age that produced a culture, which, for the first time, probably, in the eastern Mediterranean, which can genuinely be called international.

Lecture Twenty-Two
Hellenism and the Western Mediterranean

Scope:

Following Alexander, the Macedonians marched all the way to the Hindi Kush, yet the western Mediterranean, much nearer to Greece and Macedon, was never politically under the control of Alexander's successors. What prevented Hellenism from moving west? What was the relationship between the Greeks and their western Mediterranean neighbors?

Outline

I. Hellenism was tied to Alexander's dream of conquering Persia, because the Persians had been the ancestral enemies of the Greeks for 200 years. The territorial limits of Hellenism were first determined by Alexander's agenda: the conquest of an empire to the east.

   A. Even so, at the time of Alexander's death, he is reported to have had plans for a campaign to the western Mediterranean.

   B. The authenticity of these plans has been doubted, but Alexander was always happier campaigning than administering.

   C. It is quite possible that he intended to take an army west once he returned to the Mediterranean from Babylon.

II. A second reason for the indifference of the Hellenistic world to the western Mediterranean was that it would not have been an easy region to conquer, because Carthage already existed as a superpower there.

   A. Established as a Phoenician colony as early as 800 B.C., Carthage sat at a nodal point where the Mediterranean narrows between Italy, Sicily, and North Africa.

   1. From here, the Carthaginians exercised control over most of the western Mediterranean, sailing and trading from the North African coast west and north up the coast of Portugal and Spain.

   2. The presence of Carthage acted as a buffer, discouraging further Greek expansion beyond Sicily.

B. If, during the Classical period, the eastern Mediterranean was littered with Greek cities and colonies, at the same time, Carthage exercised the same position in the west.

    1. For that reason, Greek colonization of the western Mediterranean never went much beyond what it had reached between 700–600 B.C.

    2. Sicily was the frontier between these zones of power: the eastern side was largely Greek; the interior, largely indigenous; and the west, largely Punic.

III. One part of the western Mediterranean did attract the attention of one of Alexander's successors. This was Italy, and the man who tried to conquer it was Pyrrhus, the king of Epirus.

    A. Pyrrhus was from the same northern Greek world as Philip, Alexander, and the Macedonians. The world of northern Greece was one in which kings ruled, not democracies, and kings were constantly facing the threat of a challenge from the barons and lords who formed their courts.

        1. Pyrrhus's early life reflects this instability. As a child, he had to flee Epirus with his mother as the result of intrigues at court.

        2. As a young man, he was a sort of prince in exile, never giving up his claim to the throne of Epirus but serving first in the army of Antigonus and Demetrius and later living in Egypt as a well-treated, royal hostage of the Ptolemies.

        3. He was trained as a warrior; some said he was the best general after Alexander.

    B. In the 290s, while still in his twenties, Pyrrhus set about reclaiming Epiros. He fought with his former patron, Demetrius Poliorcetes, and the 290s and 280s saw the two men invade each other's territories with varying degrees of success. In 280, the people of Tarentum called on Pyrrhus to cross into Italy and fight as their ally against Rome.

        1. Over the next 6 years, Pyrrhus fought campaigns in southern Italy and Sicily, once reaching as close as 40 miles south of Rome.

        2. He probably won more times than he lost, but an invading army is always limited by its own size and the success with which it can win support from the local population. The defending army, on the other hand, has easier access to supplies and reinforcements from its own territory and population.

3. After one particularly bloody victory, when he was congratulated by one of his generals, Pyrrhus remarked, "Another victory as costly as that and we'll have lost the war."

4. Eventually, he did in fact lose the war, quitting Italy entirely in 274 B.C. and dying in 272 in mainland Greece in an attack on the city of Argos.

5. His campaigns represent probably the only chance of Rome and Italy to fall under the political control of a Hellenistic dynast.

IV. Pyrrhus's failure marks a turning point in the history of Hellenism, because it is the first confrontation between a Hellenistic power and Rome.

A. In military terms, these were the first full-scale campaigns in which Roman legions fought against Greek armies trained in the Macedonian style and led by a general thoroughly imbued with the tactical lessons of Philip and Alexander.

1. The short-term result had been even, with some battles won by the Romans and some by Pyrrhus, but the long-term result was a clear Roman victory.

2. As Plutarch notes, shortly after this, Rome was to conquer the rest of Italy and Sicily.

3. The campaigns of Pyrrhus may have contributed to Roman ideas of territorial expansion.

B. In cultural terms, the victories of the Romans over Pyrrhus also played a significant role in determining the complex response of the Romans to Greek culture. In the aftermath of Rome's defeat of Pyrrhus, Greek culture acquired a foothold in Rome.

1. Some of this was the direct result of Rome's military victory. For example, in 275 B.C., following his victory over Pyrrhus, the Roman general Manlius Curius Dentatus put on a triumph, a victory parade in which hundreds of Greek art works captured during the campaign were displayed.

2. This display encouraged an attitude toward the Greeks that the Romans never entirely lost, namely, that Greek

culture was a commodity and that it was part of the spoils of victory.

3. When Rome sacked the Greek-speaking city of Tarentum in 272, all the statues and other art works, bronze vessels, paintings, silver plate, and so forth were carted off to Rome.

4. This attitude remained remarkably consistent throughout the Republic, so that by the 1st century, the Roman general Sulla was exporting not just statues but also the entire temples in which they were housed.

V. The Roman response to Greek culture was not limited to sacking of Greek treasures. Because Greeks began to enter the population of Rome as merchants, prisoners of war, slaves, and ex-slaves, they also brought with them Greek ideas, Greek beliefs, and Greek letters.

A. Roman religion easily adapted the gods and goddesses of the Greeks, fusing them with their own deities in an act of syncretism.

1. In 293 B.C., after a plague broke out in Rome, the Romans dedicated a temple to the god of healing, whose Greek name, Asklepios, was changed somewhat into the Latin form of Aesculapius.

2. In 249, the Greek divine couple Hades and Persephone were honored in a celebration in Rome commemorating the victory over Tarentum. Again, the Greek name Persephone was slightly altered to the Latin Proserpina.

B. A cultural transformation was also set in play, thanks to the contact between Rome and its Hellenistic neighbors.

1. Livius Andronicus, a Greek from Tarentum brought to Rome as a slave, translated Homer's epic poems into Latin.

2. He also wrote and produced 10 tragedies for the Roman stage, plays based on Greek stories.

C. Regarding this cultural contact with the Greeks, the Romans were quite ambivalent. They brought home spoils of war, all the while cringing from feelings of cultural inferiority.

1. In 155, Carneades, a Greek philosopher, came to Rome and delivered two lectures over the course of two days, both for and against the possibility of justice, a display of the power of sophist oratory.

2. Cato, the Roman censor, was so alarmed by this that he had the ambassadors expelled from Rome, worried about their corrupting influence. Yet the speeches were delivered in Greek and could only have corrupted those who understood Greek.

   3. Furthermore, although Cato called the Greeks a vile and unteachable race, he himself knew Greek and was able to read and speak it fluently.

   4. Whether they liked it or not, the Romans were being Hellenized.

D. Set in motion were two opposite trends: the Hellenization of Rome and the Romanization of the East.

Suggested Reading:

E. Gruen, *Studies in Greek Culture and Roman Policy* and *Culture and National Identity in Republican Rome*.

Questions to Consider:

1. How would Rome's position in Italy have been affected had Pyrrhus been victorious?

2. Why did the Romans experience such anxiety in dealing with Greek culture?

Lecture Twenty-Two—Transcript
Hellenism and the Western Mediterranean

The Hellenistic world that we've been examining is a cultural zone that extended over the eastern Mediterranean. As we know, at times it went even further, across into Central Asia. But the heartland, we've seen, was essentially that of the eastern Mediterranean, corresponding to the region referred to in more recent times as the Levant.

But there is no natural barrier between the eastern and the western Mediterranean. There is no mountain chain that makes it impossible to get from one side to the other. If one can sail in a boat from Alexandria to Greece, surely one can sail on to Sicily, and even on to Marseilles and or to Gibraltar. So an interesting question, that deserves some examination (and we're going to see why it's so important in a moment) is the question of why Hellenism did not move into the western Mediterranean. The reason this is going to be an important question to address is because it is from the western Mediterranean that there will eventually come a political and military force that will overwhelm the Hellenistic world—namely, that of Rome.

So I'd like to look in today's lecture at the question of the relationship between the Greeks (the Hellenistic Greeks in particular) and their western Mediterranean neighbors. This is to set the stage for our final lectures, which will examine in more detail the specific relationship between Rome and the Hellenistic world.

Hellenism, as we know, was tied to Alexander's dream of conquering Persia. He had inherited from the rest of the Greeks the notion that the Persians were the ancestral enemies. As we've seen, it was already before Alexander's time, in the generation before him, a notion being played with by Greek intellectuals such as Isocrates, that to take a Greek army east against the Persians might be the one way of unifying a people who, up until then, had never been politically unified. So it is historical circumstances, then, that dictate that Hellenism will originally move towards the east. The territorial limits of Hellenism are first determined by Alexander's agenda. As in so many other ways, it's the great man here who establishes the future course of development.

But even though it may seem fairly obvious that Hellenism should go east because of those conditions, it is the case that at Alexander's death, he apparently had plans to move into the western Mediterranean, or at least so we're told by the ancient sources. We have a quite extraordinary account in Diodorus that gives us the details of Alexander's intentions. Alexander's so-called "last plans."

The following were the largest and most remarkable of these plans. It was intended to build 1,000 warships larger than *triremes* in Phoenicia, Syria, Cilicia and Cyprus, for an expedition against the Carthaginians and the other inhabitants of the coastal area of Libya, Africa, Spain, and the neighboring coasts as far as Sicily. To build a coastal road in Libya as far as the Straits of Gibraltar [across all of North Africa, in other words], and, as required by such a large expedition, to build harbors and shipyards at suitable places, to build six expensive temples at a cost of 1,500 talents. In addition, to settle cities and transplant populations from Asia to Europe, and vice-versa from Europe to Asia. The temples just mentioned were to be built at Delos, Delphi, Didona and in Macedon. And there was to be a temple of Zeus at Dion, and likewise a temple at Troy in honor of Athena. A tomb for his father Philip was to be constructed which would be as large as the greatest of the pyramids in Egypt, which some reckon the Seven Wonders of the World.

According to our sources, the Macedonian generals after Alexander's death came across these plans written down. They looked at them. They weren't too sure about whether any of this would be acceptable. But they also knew that they couldn't suppress them. So they read them aloud to the Macedonian army. This is the response:

> When the plans had been read out, the Macedonians, although they approved highly of Alexander, nevertheless saw that the plans were extravagant and difficult to achieve, and they decided not to carry out any of those that had been mentioned.

So we have a tantalizing prospect here. It is possible that Alexander was seriously contemplating a western campaign. So this is one of these moments when we can ask, "What if?" What if Alexander hadn't died at Babylon? It's quite possible that Alexander would have marched all across North Africa, and that the whole nature of the Hellenistic world, and the Mediterranean, the relationship between west and east, and between Rome and the Greeks, between

Latin and Greek—the entire nature of European culture and world history would have been different. But he died. The plans were shelved. The plans may not actually have been authentic. It's very hard to tell. But I think it is quite likely that he was planning some kind of western campaign and that after his death all plans for that were dropped.

There is another reason why Hellenism maintained an eastern orientation and not a western. Not just the fact that Alexander died before he could go there. It's because there already was a superpower in the western Mediterranean: Carthage. Carthage had been established as a Phoenician colony as early as 800 B.C. Its name, *Kirjath-Hadeschath*, in Semitic is basically identical with Naples. That is to say, *Neopolis*—New City. A nice, easy, colonial name. It sat at a nodal point in the Mediterranean, where the Mediterranean narrows because there are only a few hundred miles between North Africa here, Sicily and then the toe of Italy. It was from this important and nodal point that the Carthaginians exercised control over much of the western Mediterranean, sailing and trading from the North African coast west and then north up the coasts of Portugal and Spain.

So the presence of Carthage to the west must have acted as a kind of buffer. It certainly did for earlier Greeks, because it discouraged much Greek expansion beyond Sicily. There were one or two Greek colonies in the western Mediterranean, Marseilles, of course, being the most notable. But it is certainly the case that during the Classical period, while the eastern Mediterranean was littered with Greek cities and Greek colonies all the way around the coastline of southern Italy and all the way up the Aegean and up into the Black Sea, and around the east, at the same time, Carthage exercised that sort of control in the western Mediterranean. So on the western side of the Mediterranean, the coastline is dotted with Carthaginian colonies, not Greek colonies. It's for that reason, then, that Greek colonization had never really advanced much beyond the stage that it had already achieved between 700 and 600 B.C. So Carthage acted as a buffer.

The important frontier between these two zones of power (and I really think we can think in terms of spheres of influence here, the western Mediterranean and the eastern Mediterranean), the frontier between these two is Sicily. The colonization of Sicily even reflects this, because the eastern side of Sicily (which is basically shaped like a triangle, you may recall), the eastern side of Sicily is essentially dotted with Greek colonies. The interior of the island is largely made up of local, indigenous populations, and the western side (both on the northwestern side and on the southwestern side) is largely made up of Punic colonies. So in Sicily we find the westernmost expansion of Greek culture. We find the easternmost expansion of Carthaginian culture, and the poor Sicles (the native population) squeezed into the center.

There was, however, one part of the western Mediterranean that did attract the attention of Alexander's successors, and there was one successor in particular who was interested in trying to conquer this region. The region that I'm speaking of is, of course, Italy. The man involved was Pyrrhus, King of Epirus. Epirus is the Greek kingdom located immediately to the west of Macedon. Pyrrhus, therefore, though not a Macedonian himself, came from exactly the same northern Greek world as Philip and Alexander and Alexander's other successors.

This world of northern Greece, as you'll recall, was one in which kings ruled, not democracies. Kings were constantly facing the challenge of other barons and other lords who formed their court. Pyrrhus's early life reflects this kind of commotion and upheaval. As a child, he had to flee Epirus with his mother, as the result of these intrigues at court, and, as a young man, he'd grown up largely in exile. He never gave up his claim to the throne of Epirus, but in fact as a young man he served for a long time in the army of Antiogonus and of Antigonus's son Demetrius Polyorchetes. Later he even lived in Egypt with Ptolemy, as a well-treated royal hostage.

So we have a man cut from the same mold as the other Hellenistic rulers, although someone who had to fight to claim his ancestral right as king of Epirus. He was trained as a warrior by the very best generals of the day (Antigonus, Demetrius, Ptolemy), certainly the very best. There were many men of the age who believed that he was the nearest thing to Alexander. That he resembled Alexander in his flair, in his tactical skill, in his bravery. On one occasion, Antigonus was asked who he thought was the finest general, and he replied, "Pyrrhus, if he lives to be an old man." So there was also this sense that he, like Alexander, might burn out. A blazing star.

During the decade of the 290s, while he was still in his twenties, and while he was still trying to reclaim his kingdom of Epirus, Pyrrhus fought with his former patron, Demetrius Polyorchetes. The 290s and the 280s saw the two men, Pyrrhus on the west and Demetrius on the east, invading each other's territory of Epirus and Macedon, with varying degrees of success. This was an example of the typical stalemate of wars that we've seen in the early Hellenistic period.

Pyrrhus might have perished in one of these wars and become a footnote of history, but for the significant fact that in 280 B.C., the people of Tarentum, modern-day Taranto in southern Italy, called upon him, asking him to cross over the Adriatic into Italy and to help them fight their enemy, the Romans. This was going to be the first confrontation between a Hellenistic successor, a Hellenistic prince, and the Romans. So it is a monumental event. Over the course of the next six years in the 270s, Pyrrhus fought a series of campaigns in southern Italy and in Sicily, once reaching as close as forty miles south of Rome. It's a little like Hannibal, in that he got very close to the gates of Rome. This, of course, is before Hannibal, by a good 60 years.

He probably won more battles than he lost, but an invading army is always limited by its own size and by the success with which it can win the support of the local population. While the defending army (in this case the Romans) is always fighting on its own soil. It has easier access to supplies, and of course can be reinforced from its own territory and by its own population. So the six-year campaign becomes a kind of war of attrition, to see who can win. The brilliant general or the dogged Romans, who can survive defeat after defeat. After one particularly bloody victory, when he was congratulated by his generals, Pyrrhus is supposed to have remarked, "Another victory as costly as that and I'll have lost the war." The origin, of course, of our expression in English of a "Pyrrhic victory." One that is too costly in the long run.

Eventually, in fact, he did lose the war. He quit Italy entirely in 274. He died not long afterward, in 272, during yet another one of these marauding raids and attacking southern Greece and the city of Argos. His campaigns (those six years in the 270s) represent probably the only chance (and this is one of the reasons why I think it's significant) of Rome and Italy falling under the direct political control of a Hellenistic dynast. If Pyrrhus had been successful, Italy would have become a Hellenistic kingdom, like Syria and like

Macedon and like Egypt. But it didn't. So history took a very different course, indeed.

Pyrrhus' failure marks a dramatic turning point in the history of Hellenism, since, as I've said, it's the first confrontation between a Hellenistic power and Rome. In military terms, these were the first full-scale campaigns in which Roman legions fought against Greek armies trained in the Macedonian style, with the Macedonian *phalanx*. The army of Pyrrhus was led by a general who was thoroughly imbued with all of the tactical lessons of Philip and Alexander. So from a military point of view, it's a confrontation between two very different styles of warfare.

The short-term result had been even, with some battles won by the Romans and some battles won by Pyrrhus. But the long-term result had been a Roman victory, as Pyrrhus was gradually worn down. As Plutarch notes, shortly after this, Rome was to go on and conquer the rest of Italy and the rest of Sicily. So I think that one of the important features of Pyrrhus' campaigns (apart from the fact that they signify the first confrontation between Hellenistic east and Roman west), is that they may have contributed to the idea in Rome of territorial expansion. Shortly after this they took over the rest of the Italian peninsula and moved into Sicily, as well, which became their first overseas province.

In cultural terms, the victories of the Romans over Pyrrhus also played a significant role in determining the very complex response of the Romans to Greek culture. Now we turn our attention a little away from political machinations to talking about how the Romans treat Hellenism as a culture. In the aftermath of Rome's defeat of Pyrrhus, Greek culture acquired a foothold in Rome. How so? Some of this was a direct result of Rome's military victory. For example, in 275 B.C., following the victory over Pyrrhus, the Roman general Manlius Curius Dentatus put on a triumph. A triumph, of course, is a great procession held in downtown Rome in which the glorious general is brought in victory through the streets of the city with his soldiers coming along behind him, followed by a great display of the booty won in battle.

In this triumph, this victory parade, there were hundreds of Greek artworks on display. Greek artworks that had been captured by the victorious Romans. What I think this probably encouraged, and it certainly found fertile soil in Rome, was the attitude toward the

Greeks that the Romans never really lost ever after: that was, that Greek culture was a commodity. It was statues and bronze and gold bowls and marble statues. And that this Greek culture was something which was really theirs as the spoils of victory. The Romans deserved this because they had defeated the Greeks.

When Rome sacked Tarentum in 272, and please recall, the city we're talking about, Tarentum, is not an Italian city. It's located, yes, on the Italian peninsula, but from the point of view of the Romans, it's Greek. Its inhabitants speak Greek. When Rome sacked Tarentum in 272 B.C., after Pyrrhus had been kicked out, all the statues and all the other artworks, the bronze vessels, the paintings, the silverplate and so forth, were all carted off to Rome. So the Romans from the early 3rd century got used to the idea of seeing these victory parades in which Greek culture was on display as something that had been won by a victorious Roman general, conquering these effete Greeks.

This attitude remained remarkably consistent throughout the Roman Republic. This idea that Greek stuff was stuff to be plundered, to be brought back, to be shipped back. So by the 1st century, the Roman general Sulla was exporting not just statues or paintings. That was small fry. His men actually dismantled entire temples, put them on board boats and shipped them back to Rome. (One of them actually sank along the way, so somewhere south of Italy there's a Greek temple in the water, waiting to be excavated and put back together again.)

The Roman response to Greek culture was not limited to the sacking of Greek treasures, because the other booty that came back was, of course, prisoners of war. Slaves and ex-slaves began to enter the population of Rome. People who had come to Rome as captives of war. People who stayed on, then, with Roman families, even after they were given their manumission and liberated. Of course there were Greek merchants as well. Greek free men, as well as freed men and slaves.

As the population of Rome began to receive this infusion, quite literally, of Greek blood, and Hellenistic blood from all parts of the eastern Mediterranean, what this brought to Rome was an increasing exposure to Greek ideas, Greek beliefs, Greek culture, Greek letters, in other words.

This exposure, in some instances, was relatively easy for the Romans to manage. Roman religion, for example, could easily adapt to the gods and the goddesses of the Greeks. Like other ancient religions Roman religion was essentially one that worked by syncretism. If your god and my god appear to be similar, then we fuse the two and see it essentially as two names for the same thing. There was not this exclusivity, this dogmatic approach to deity that we find in monotheistic and modern religions.

For example, in 293, a plague broke out in Rome and the Romans dedicated a temple, of course, to the god who helped them to get over the plague, a god of healing. We've already spoken about this god in his Greek context as Asklepios. We've already talked about the cures at the Asklepieum. The Romans worshiped him as well. They just simply Latinized his name, changing Asklepios in the Greek into Aesculapius, in Latin. But it's essentially the same god with his name merely transformed a little. In some cases they didn't even bother to change the name much at all. Apollo was worshiped under the same name in Rome as he was in Greece. Jupiter is nothing more than a Latin pronunciation for Zeus-Pater, Zeus the father of the gods, which of course is exactly what Jupiter is, as well.

In 249 B.C., the Greek divine couple of Hades, god of the underworld, and Persephone, the daughter of Demeter, who he had carried off, this divine couple was honored at a celebration at Rome, commemorating the victory over Tarentum. Again here, all that happens is that the Greek name Persephone is slightly changed into its Latin form of Proserpina. So at a religious level, the exchange between the two cultures was very easy to manage, because they already spoke a similar religious language, if you will.

What about at the level of cultural transformation, because we are really talking now about hundreds and thousands of Hellenistic Greeks gradually coming in to the city of Rome itself, bringing with them their Greek culture. We actually know of quite specific instances of cultural transformation taking place in Italy and specifically in Rome as a result of this process. A man named Livius Andronicus (his name is interesting because Andronicus is, in fact, a Greek name, whereas Livius is a Roman name). This character originally is from the Greek south, from Tarentum, but comes to Rome and comes into the household of a Roman family and eventually gets a Roman name. This transplanted Greek from

Tarentum, who was brought to Rome as a slave, translates Homer's epic poems into Latin. So here we have, now, from the early part of the third century, the Romans reading their own version of the *Iliad* and the *Odyssey*, but not in Greek. In Latin.

Livius Andronicus also wrote and produced at least ten tragedies for the Roman stage. Each one of them, interestingly enough, was based on a Greek story. So the Romans, from this early stage in the 3rd century can go to the theater and what they're seeing on stage, not the stories of their heroes fighting against the Etruscans, but rather heroes such as Ajax and Achilles. Good Greek heroes, but now being packaged for Roman consumption on the stage.

This contact between the two cultures left the Romans quite ambivalent. On the one hand, they're importing all this stuff as the spoils of war. It's the stuff that they've won because they're superior to the Greeks. On the other hand, culturally the Greeks come from a long and glorious tradition with wonderful poetry and great art work. So in some ways the Romans looking at the Greeks feel a kind of cultural cringe, almost a sort of inferiority, at the same time as they feel a kind of moral superiority. It's a very tortured and ambiguous attitude. I think the nearest one can find in more recent times is perhaps in the strange relationship culturally between America and England. The sort of thing captured by Henry James, where there is sometimes a sense that the English culture may be older, but the American culture is more vigorous and new. It's an analogy you may wish to play with.

Let me give you some instances, though, of exactly how the Romans in their early stage of contact with the Greeks dealt with this. In 155 B.C., an embassy came from the Greek world to deal with the Romans. The Romans by now were one of the major powers in the Mediterranean. It was led by a Greek philosopher named Carneades. Over the course of two days, Carneades wished to demonstrate the power of Greek philosophy and the power of what the Greeks called heuristics. Essentially, the science of debating. As we all know, the essence of good debating is that you can take any proposition and in one speech argue in favor of it, and on another occasion, in a second speech, argue against it. This is exactly what Carneades did. It was a good example of what the Greeks, in their traditional curriculum would call epideictic oratory. Display oratory. It's an attempt to show people what the power of oratory is, by speaking on the subject of justice one day (that justice is possible) and then the next day demonstrating that justice is an illusion and is impossible.

From a Greek point of view, this is a good example of how to display the powers of oratory. It's meant to show people that you should really learn oratory because it will equip you with these skills. From the Roman point of view, it was infuriating, because it meant that these Greeks or these *Graeculi* (these "little Greeks" as the Romans often termed them) were essentially duplicitous. That they were dishonest and you really couldn't trust them. That when a Greek spoke, you never knew whether he was telling the truth or whether he was just putting one over you.

Cato, the stern Roman censor, was so alarmed by this that he had the ambassadors instantly expelled from Rome. This was really regarded as, somehow, a deep moral threat to the integrity of Roman culture, because he was worried about the corrupting influence of this (essentially) university professor. And yet, think a little further about this, and we find it's a very interesting episode, because the speeches delivered by Carneades were delivered in Greek. The only people that they could corrupt were people who spoke and understood Greek. In other words, there already was a contact between the two cultures. There was an audience for this kind of material.

Cato called the Greeks a "vile and unteachable race." And yet, he himself knew Greek and he was able to speak Greek and to read Greek fluently. So, whether we like it or not, the Romans already were being exposed to Hellenistic culture, and, in a sense, were being Hellenized even against their will.

In the lectures to follow, I'm going to pursue this even further, and also map the specific political circumstances that led to the Roman involvement in the Greek world. But I want to finish with something slightly different, because I want to give the last word today to Pyrrhus, this wonderful, Alexander-like king who has dominated our story so far. The reason I want to finish here is because we have an anecdote involving Pyrrhus which I think absolutely sums up how the Hellenistic kings saw their mission. It's a story that involves the West, so it gives us an idea of what they thought about going west towards the Romans.

This is a story that involves Pyrrhus and a Greek philosopher named Cineas. We've already talked on previous occasions about the way in which philosophers are often seen to be the moral equivalent of kings. They are often their advisors. See what Cineas does with Pyrrhus in this little exchange.

> When Cineas at this time saw that Pyrrhus was eager to sail to Italy, finding him at leisure, he started the following conversation. "Pyrrhus, the Romans are said to be good soldiers and to rule many warlike peoples. Should a god grant us success over them, how shall we use our victory?"

> Pyrrhus replied, "Cineas, the answer to your question is obvious. Once the Romans are defeated, no barbarian or Greek city there can resist us. We shall immediately secure control over the whole of Italy. And how large, strong and powerful she is, I imagine you know better than anyone else."

> Cineas paused a little and said, "Sire, once we've taken Italy, what shall we do?"

> Pyrrhus, not seeing yet what Cineas was leading to, replied, "Sicily, nearby, stretches out her hands to us. A wealthy, populous land, easy to capture. There's nothing there Cineas, but revolution, anarchy in the cities, and excitable demagogues, now that Agathocles is dead."

> So Cineas replies, "Well yes, that seems quite plausible. But is the capture of Sicily the end of our expedition?"

> Pyrrhus replied, "May god grant us victory and success. That will be a preliminary to a great achievement. Libya, Africa and Carthage would then be within easy reach. Who could keep us away from them when Agathocles, who secretly escaped from Syracuse and crossed over with a few ships, very nearly captured them. Can anyone dispute that once we have conquered these, none of our enemies will be able to resist us?"

> "Certainly not," said Cineas. "Clearly with such power behind us we will be able to recover Macedon and to rule Greece. When we've established our domination everywhere, what shall we do?" [This is the essence of the wonderful exchange between the king and the philosopher.]

Pyrrhus laughed and said, "We shall have ample leisure. Life, my friend, will be a daily drinking party, and we shall entertain each other with conversation."

At which point, Cineas interrupted Pyrrhus and said, "Well then, what prevents us from having a drinking party now? And enjoying leisure among ourselves if we so wish? The possibility is already there and costs no effort, so why achieve the same result through blood, toil, and danger?"

Of course, Pyrrhus had no response to that.

It's a wonderful story, at so many levels. It exemplifies the relationship of king and philosopher. It also gives us an idea of why Pyrrhus was looking to the west. Simply, he was trying to do another Alexander. That's all. To conquer the West. The great irony of his entire career is that while, of course, he was militarily unsuccessful, he actually set in train a series of events that would eventually lead to the Hellenization of Rome and the Romanization of the East.

Lecture Twenty-Three
The Freedom of the Greeks

Scope:

The political end of the Hellenistic world came about once the Greek kingdoms of the eastern Mediterranean were incorporated into the expanding Roman Empire. How was Rome able to exert the kind of control that no single Hellenistic king had wielded since Alexander? By what stages did Rome come to dominate the Greeks? Was it a planned campaign of imperialism, or do other factors explain Rome's inexorable rise to power?

Outline

I. After Rome's first serious contact with a Hellenistic ruler, Pyrrhus of Epirus, in the 270s, Rome had little time to deal with the major Hellenistic kingdoms of the eastern Mediterranean. The great power in the western Mediterranean during the 3rd century B.C. was Carthage.

   A. During this century, the Romans fought two serious wars against Carthage. Both wars witnessed developments in Rome's approach to warfare and territorial expansion that would set the stage for the Roman expansion eastward in the 2nd century. The First Punic War (264–241 B.C.) came after Rome had united most of the Italian peninsula under Roman control.

      1. The First Punic War saw the emergence of Rome as a maritime power, winning sea battles at Mylae and Cape Ecnomus.

      2. The Romans demonstrated their ability to win a war of attrition that lasted over 20 years against a tough and wealthy adversary.

      3. The Romans amassed a huge amount of booty and acquired their first overseas province, Sicily, as a result of the victory.

   B. The Second Punic War was also a protracted conflict, lasting from 218–202 B.C. Provoked by differences between the Romans and Carthaginians over the Roman alliance with the Spanish town of Saguntum, the war prefigured much of Rome's involvement with the Hellenistic East.

1. Although historians often look for economic causes for the war, there is little evidence that the Romans responded to such pressures as competition over natural resources.
2. The Romans, however, did take seriously the alliances that bound them to smaller and weaker states.
3. Hannibal, the charismatic Carthaginian commander, resembled Alexander the Great and saw the Romans in much the same way as Alexander saw the Persians.

II. Rome's victory over Hannibal at the Battle of Zama (202 B.C.) coincided with Rome's emergence as a state that resembled other Hellenistic states but was also in some ways quite different.

A. Unlike the Hellenistic states, which relied heavily on mercenary armies, the Romans had extended the franchise to much of the Italian peninsula, thereby dramatically increasing the manpower available to the Roman army.
1. Polybius reports that the Romans were able to muster over 700,000 men when Hannibal crossed the Alps into Italy with 90,000.
2. The Romans survived defeats inflicted by Hannibal at Trebia, Lake Trasimene, and Cannae, where perhaps 25,000 men perished. Any one of these defeats would have demolished most Hellenistic states.
3. The Romans were able to hold out against Hannibal in Italy for 14 years, while opening new fronts in Sicily and Spain.

B. Rome was also different from Carthage and other Hellenistic states from the point of view of its constitution. Polybius, a Greek historian living in Rome in the 2nd century B.C., emphasized this as the key to Rome's success—an effective government that included elements of kingship, aristocracy, and democracy.
1. The Hellenistic east was ruled by kings descended from Alexander's generals; mainland Greece was dominated by regional federations, such as the Achaeans and Aetolians. But the Romans had a mixed constitution.
2. The principle of kingship in Rome was represented by the two consuls, who shared power and were elected for a single year.

3. The oligarchic principle was represented by the power of the Senate, which came to dominate foreign policy in particular and was made up of ex-magistrates.

4. The democratic principle was represented by the voting assemblies and the public meetings of the Roman populace, where matters of policy were debated openly.

5. By creating a mixed constitution, Polybius believed, Rome resolved the tension of competing models of government.

C. The Roman aristocracy emerging in the late 3rd century B.C. would also exert a powerful influence on Roman policy toward the Greek east.

1. Power circulated in a small coterie of families. The scions of these families felt an enormous pressure to wage war and win glory for their families and for Rome.

2. As a result, such families as the Fabii and the Scipios came to see overseas campaigns as their duty and an expression of Rome's good faith toward its allies.

III. With the defeat of Hannibal and the Carthaginians in 202 B.C., the Romans were drawn into affairs in the eastern Mediterranean.

A. Rome's first eastern involvement had been prompted by piratical raids in the Adriatic, originating in the kingdom of Illyria in the vicinity of modern Albania, Montenegro, and Croatia. Rome fought two Illyrian Wars, in 229 and 219 B.C., ending both through treaties rather than by military campaigns.

B. Rome also became directly involved at this time in the affairs of the Greeks. The Romans wished to prevent Hannibal from receiving aid from his ally, Philip V of Macedon.

1. To keep Philip in check, the Romans formed an alliance with the Aetolians, in northwestern Greece.

2. The Roman-Aetolian alliance was also joined by King Attalus I of Pergamum.

3. The First Macedonian War lasted from 214 to 205 B.C. but saw no major battles involving the Romans.

4. The war was concluded by the Treaty of Phoenice, which freed Rome to concentrate on Hannibal without fear of an attack from the east.

5. The war also resulted in Rome's first major alliances in the Greek world.

IV. Once Hannibal was defeated, the Romans were again free to turn their attention to Philip V and affairs in the Greek world of the eastern Mediterranean. Rome's involvement in the Second Macedonian War (199–196 B.C.) illustrates the complexities of Rome's emerging role as a Hellenistic superpower.

    A. A number of factors caused the war. One was Roman resentment at Philip V for his alliance with Hannibal during the invasion of Italy. A second factor was the threat to Rome's new allies, Pergamum and Rhodes, from an alliance between Philip V of Macedon and Antiochus III of Syria.

        1. According to one interpretation, Rome had taken on the role of power-broker in the eastern Mediterranean and was intervening to break up the powerful alliance of Macedon and the Seleucid dynasty.

        2. In this view, Rome was using its *amicitia* (friendship) with its allies as no more than a pretext to stir up another war.

        3. Such an interpretation lays the blame for the war at the feet of ambitious Roman commanders, such as Titus Quinctius Flamininus, who sought lucrative and impressive military commands in the east now that the Hannibalic war was over.

    B. There may be some truth to these charges; however, there is also a danger in assuming a Roman plan for world conquest when more simple explanations apply. The Romans were successful in the war, defeating Philip's Macedonian phalanx at the Battle of Cynoscephalae in 197 B.C., the first victory of a Roman legion over a Macedonian phalanx in pitched battle. But the aftermath of the war tells us a great deal about Rome's plans.

        1. In a widely celebrated festival held at the Isthmus of Corinth, the Roman general Flamininus issued a decree declaring the "Freedom of the Greeks" and guaranteeing the various Greek states the right to live independently under their own constitutions.

        2. The Roman Senate also issued instructions to Flamininus to quit the three key garrisons known as "the Fetters of Greece."

3. By 194 B.C., all Roman troops had been withdrawn from Greece.

C. Taken together, these details strongly suggest that Rome had no long-term plan for the domination of Greece. Rome had been sucked in by its eastern alliances. The same conditions would result in the final incorporation of the entire Hellenistic east into Rome's empire.

Suggested Reading:

E. Gruen, *The Hellenistic World and the Coming of Rome*, 2 vols.

W. Harris, *War and Imperialism in Republican Rome, 320–70 B.C.*

Questions to Consider:

1. How well did the Romans understand the diplomatic language of Hellenistic international politics?
2. To what extent was Roman expansion driven by a desire to extend Roman territory?

Lecture Twenty-Three—Transcript
The Freedom of the Greeks

Welcome back. In our last lecture, I posed the question, "Why was it that Hellenism did not make more inroads into the western Mediterranean?" We supplied a couple of answers to this, saying that, of course, the early thrust of Hellenism had followed Alexander's conquests, and it had necessarily, then, been directed toward the East, towards the old Persian Empire. We then also looked at the career of Pyrrus, the king of Epirus, who, I argued, was the one Hellenistic ruler, the one successor of Alexander, who had a real shot at introducing Hellenism to the West politically. That is to say, he campaigned in southern Italy for about six years in the 270s. Had he been victorious, (here we'll play for a moment "What if?")—had he been victorious, I think that we would have seen a very different history of Rome, because Rome would have been integrated into a Hellenistic kingdom. A Hellenistic kingdom that would have embraced southern Italy, the Adriatic and Epirus. But that was not to be. The Romans were victorious. And though we saw that in the career of Pyrrhus we were able to understand how he was interested in further expansion for its own sake (we went over the story of Kinneas the philosopher interviewing Pyrrhus) and we saw that Pyrrhus was very much like the other Hellenistic rulers and like Philip, we found that his failure meant that politically the tide had turned.

And yet, we tried to temper this picture somewhat by saying that, politically, no Hellenistic state was able to dominate Rome and the Italian peninsula, nevertheless, culturally Rome had begun to come under the influence of Hellenism. We saw this being precipitated by the influx, not only of Greek goods, of properties, of statues, of temples, of artwork and so forth, into Rome, but also even of human beings. People being brought to Rome as captives and as slaves. We saw that these people coming from the wider Hellenistic world, the eastern Mediterranean, brought with them Greek culture. The best example of this was Livius Andronicus, who actually translated Homer and Greek tragedies, essentially, into Latin.

This really sets the stage for what is going to be a complicated story involving the relationship between Rome and the Greeks. Because the political end of Hellenism, the incorporation of these Hellenistic kingdoms into the emerging world empire of the Romans, will mean the end of an independent Hellenistic world or Hellenistic kingdoms. It raises some serious questions. How was Rome, a small town originally, just on the Tiber River, able to exert the kind of control that no king since Alexander had wielded? By what stages did Rome come to conquer the Greeks?

These are vexed questions, because, in the past, some have wanted to argue that there was a fixed plan of world conquest that lay behind the relationship between Rome and the Greeks. As if the Romans, after conquering the Italian peninsula simply went further afield, endlessly looking for more regions to conquer. But we may find that there will be other factors involved here. So what we need to turn to is the fuller story of Rome's interaction with the Hellenistic East and Rome's growth to world power.

After Rome's first serious contact with a Hellenistic ruler, Pyrrhus of Epirus, in the 270s, Rome had little time to deal with the major Hellenistic kingdoms of the eastern Mediterranean. This is because Rome, on the western side of the Italian peninsula, faced an even greater superpower in the western Mediterranean, and that was, of course, Carthage. So the 3rd century B.C., though it does see the contact between Rome and Pyrrhus, is really a century that is much more taken up in the western Mediterranean with the wars between Carthage and Rome. During this century the Romans fought two serious wars against Carthage. Both of these wars witnessed developments in Rome's approach to warfare and territorial expansion that would set the stage for the Roman expansion east, which would then take place in the 2nd century B.C.

The first of these great contests between Rome and the Carthaginians was the First Punic War. It takes its name from the fact that the Romans referred to the Carthaginians as *Punii*, because they were Phoenicians, remember. They'd been colonized by the Phoenicians. This First Punic War lasted from 264 B.C. to 241 B.C. A long, drawn-out campaign which came after Rome had united virtually all of the Italian peninsula under its control. I'm not going to go into the details of the First Punic War, but there are certain features of it that I need to highlight, because they will have a real impact on the future development of Rome.

The first is that the First Punic war saw the emergence of Rome as a maritime power. Up until now, virtually all of Rome's campaigns and conquests, and territorial expansion, had taken place on the

Italian peninsula. But in the First Punic War, the Romans built fleets that successfully engaged the Carthaginians. The Carthaginians, of course, were a great naval power, long used to sailing the sea lanes of the western Mediterranean. At the sea battles of Mylae and Cape Ecnomus, the Romans proved to be their equal in battle on water, as on land. That, of course, would be an ominous development for Rome's future expansion.

Probably even more importantly than the fact that the war had moved from land to sea, was that in the First Punic War, the Romans demonstrated their ability to win a war of attrition. This war lasted for well over twenty years. In it, they fought a tough and wealthy adversary, a major economic force in the western Mediterranean that could afford to pay for mercenary armies. And yet, every year, the Roman levies once again collected, bringing men from the Italian peninsula, ready to fight on behalf of Rome, and every year fresh Roman armies went into the field. There is something inexorable about this, which is distinctively Roman.

The third feature of the First Punic War that I wish to highlight, is that the war saw the Romans amassing a huge amount of booty, including their first overseas province: Sicily, which was acquired as a result of the victory. By the middle of the 3rd century B.C., we have a Rome which is undergoing a rapid expansion, which is moving out onto the water and becoming a naval power the equal of Carthage. An empire that has already acquired a province beyond the Italian peninsula itself.

The Second Punic War, towards the end of the century, would last from 218 B.C. to 202 B.C. Once again it pitted the Romans against their Carthaginian enemies, provoked by differences between the Romans and the Carthaginians over a question of a Roman alliance. This, in a way is going to be typical of Rome's overseas engagements. The Romans enter into alliances and they take these seriously. In this case, the Roman alliance is with a Spanish town, the town of Saguntum. There was a difference of opinion finally leading to war between the Carthaginians and the Romans as to whether or not Saguntum lay within the Carthaginian sphere of influence or the Roman sphere of influence. We won't go into the details of how the war broke out. But the war is important because it will prefigure much of Rome's involvement in the Hellenistic East to come.

In what senses? First of all, historians are used to looking, of course, for the economic causes for a war. But there is, in fact, little evidence to suggest that the Romans responded to pressures such as competition over natural resources. It is not very likely that the Romans went to war with Carthage because they were competing to get the resources of Spain. The reason that they went to war was that they took their alliance with Saguntum seriously. Alliances which bound the Romans to smaller and weaker states. The basis of this was what the Romans called "friendship," *amicitia*. If the Romans did not protect a state to whom they were allied, in their eyes it meant that they had not demonstrated and proved their good faith. These are binding concepts in Roman law.

The other feature of the war that I think is very interesting is that the Second Punic War involved, of course, that most charismatic of generals from the ancient world, Hannibal. Hannibal, a Carthaginian commander who, in many ways resembles Alexander the Great. Rather than sail across the short stretch of water leading to Sicily and the Italian peninsula, instead, in the good style of Alexander, he marched his army up through Spain and across southern France and over the Alps and into Italy, performing a great journey, a heroic journey, worthy of Alexander. He, in fact, saw the Romans in much the same way that Alexander saw the Persians.

The war would end with a Roman victory at Zama (just outside of Carthage), in 202 B.C. It would coincide with Rome's emergence as a state that in some ways resembled other Hellenistic states, but in other ways was quite different from it. I want to highlight both the similarities and the differences that we see in the Second Punic War.

First of all, unlike most of the Hellenistic kingdoms that we've seen, which relied heavily on mercenary armies, the Romans had extended the franchise, they had given citizenship to many of the people of the Italian peninsula. They, in fact, had a very elaborate system of citizenship. Some people were made Roman citizens, some people were made Latin citizens, which was a kind of second status. But the point was that by enfranchising so many people outside of the city of Rome itself, they had dramatically increased the manpower available for the Roman army. So while Hannibal was fighting with mercenary forces and forces culled from different parts of the Carthaginian empire in the western Mediterranean, the Romans were able to bring into battle the men of the Italian peninsula. The numbers are really quite disparate. Polybius reports that the Romans were able to muster over 700,000 men at the time when Hannibal crossed the Alps into Italy with an army of 90,000 men. So while Hannibal's crossing of the Alps lives on in memory as a great event, in fact, the army that he was coming up against was potentially vastly larger than any of the forces he had brought with him.

This was to have a concrete effect, because in the early stages of the Second Punic War, Hannibal was extraordinarily successful year after year but could never defeat Rome. At the Battle of Trebia, at the Battle of Lake Trasimene, and at the Battle of Cannae, three years in succession, the Romans suffered the kinds of military defeats that would have destroyed any Hellenistic kingdom. At the Battle of Cannae alone, up to 25,000 Roman soldiers may have perished in one day. It may have been the single most bloody day of fighting in European history ever. Twenty-five thousand men.

We've seen that great kings, like Antiochus III of Syria, if defeated once by the Romans, as at Magnesia in 189, were forced to make astonishing reparations, paying indemnities of thousands of talents and signing humiliating peace treaties giving up vast tracts of their territory. The Romans' response to these terrible defeats was simply to put more men into the field. Ever larger armies.

Not only that. After they were defeated in these three great battles, the Romans went on to hold out against Hannibal in Italy for fourteen years, and at the same time, to open up new fronts campaigning against the Carthaginian forces, in Sicily and in Spain, before finally, in 204 B.C. being able to send a Roman army by fleet to North Africa and forcing Hannibal to return and eventually defeating him on his own front doorstep. So the resources available to the Romans in sheer manpower dwarfed anything that the Hellenistic kingdoms were able to put into the field. That is to say, not neccessarily in one single battle, but certainly in the long term, year after year. That's where the Romans were well-prepared for their dealings with the eastern Mediterranean.

The Greeks in antiquity well understood that there was something different about the Romans. They were also stunned by the eventual success of the Romans in overtaking their own world. They had an explanation for it, but it was a little different from the one that I've just been offering, of manpower. Polybius, the Greek historian, writing in the 2nd century B.C. (he actually lived in Rome, because he ended up going there as a hostage, so he knew the Greek system and he knew the Roman system very well). As an astute politician and as an historian, as someone trained in all the traditional practices of Greek philosophy, he argued that the success of the Romans was due to their constitution.

Constitutional theory was something that was well-developed and advanced by the time of the 2nd century. The view in the Greek world, in the Greek intelligentsia, the view that had been worked out was that there were essentially six types of constitution. Three good, and three bad. The types of constitutions involved the rule of a single man, secondly the rule of a small elite, and thirdly the rule of a large number of people. The good version of the first, of course, was kingship, which was then debased into tyranny. The good version of the second was aristocracy, which when debased turned into oligarchy. The good version of the third was democracy, which when debased turned into mob rule.

So there is a well-packaged intellectual program, if you will, already in place in the Greek world for understanding constitutions, and then interpreting Rome's success in those terms. What did the Greeks make of this? It's simply this: For Polybius and for other Greeks, the Romans represented a kind of perfect balance of these different types of constitutions. So, unlike the Hellenistic East, which was dominated by great kings such as Ptolemy or Antiochus; unlike the regional federations of Greece, like the Achaeans and the Aetolians, or the old Athenian democracy, the Romans (in their view) had a mixed constitution, blending each of the three elements that we've talked about. The principle of kingship was represented by the two consuls, who shared power and were elected for a single year. This is brilliant, because, being elected every year, they are not kings for life, and because there are two of them, the power of the one is always balanced by the power of the second. So this seems to represent what we would call a check and a balance, if you will.

Secondly, the oligarchic principle was represented by the power of the Senate. This was the body made up of ex-magistrates, so it wasn't open to just anybody. You had to be someone who had served the state. They came to dominate foreign policy. The decrees that were sent out from Rome usually began, "A decree of the Senate and people of Rome." We're familiar with that catch phrase, *senatus populusque romanus*.

Then the democratic principle, which for the Greeks meant the assemblies of the whole population of voting citizens, was represented at Rome by voting assemblies. Laws were ratified by the popular vote of the people. And by the public meetings of the Roman populace. Raucous public meetings where speakers would stand up to debate about current issues of the day. In the eyes of Polybius, Romans have found a way of managing to blend all of these together. So he says in his essay (this is in his essay on the Roman constitution in book six of his work). Polybius says:

> As for the Roman constitution, it had three elements, each of them possessing sovereign power. Their respective share of power of the whole state had been regulated with such a scrupulous regard to equality and equilibrium [checks and balances] that no one could say for certain, not even a native, whether the constitution as a whole was an aristocracy or a democracy or a despotism. And no wonder. For if we confine our observation to the power of the counsuls, we should be inclined to say it was rather despotic. If, on the other hand, the Senate, as aristocratic. And if, finally, one looks at the power possessed by the people, it would seem to be a clear case of democracy.

So the Romans seemed to blend these various elements. The effect of this—it was not merely the theory that there were different types of constitutions that fascinated the Greeks. They also believed that in these various constitutions lay the seeds of revolution and war. That good rule was always going into its debased form. So kingship was always turning into despotism. This was then precipitating war that led to aristocracy and then breaking down into oligarchy. So this was not merely six different constitutions, it was a cycle of conflict and civil breakdown. By creating a mixed constitution, in the eyes of the Greeks, what the Romans had done was to break the cycle, to create a kind of perfect constitution where all elements were in perfect harmony. So Polybius says:

> The result of this power of the several estates [the three different groups], for mutual help or harm is a union sufficiently firm for all emergencies. For whenever any danger from without compels them to unite and work together, the strength which is developed by the state is so extraordinary that everything required is unfailingly carried

out by the eager rivalry shown by all classes to devote their whole minds to the needs of the hour. And to secure that any determination come to should not fail for want of promptitude.

We might be inclined to dismiss this purely as theorizing by a professor of Greek philosophy or a theoretician, but we must remember that the man who wrote this lived in Rome. He saw this system working in Rome. So even though he's using the Greek apparatus for explaining the Romans, I think we have to credit him with having some insight into the way that the Romans were successful. They managed to have power devolved into different institutions and areas, balancing each other.

Nevertheless, it would be naïve to buy this entire interpretation. The fact is (and Polybius doesn't give us all the details of this), but the fact is that in the 3rd century an aristocracy was emerging in Rome that would come to dominate Roman policy towards the East. Power in Rome was held by a small coterie of families. For example, in about 100 years of what historians call the Middle Republic (say, the 3rd and 2nd century), 50% of the consulships, 50% of the magistrates of Rome came from eight families.

So there is a very narrow aristocracy here. The scions of these families, the young men coming to the fore and making their reputations, felt an enormous pressure to wage war and win glory for their families and for Rome. So it was that men like the Fabii, and the Scipios came to see overseas campaigns as their duty and as an expression of Rome's good faith towards its allies. Personal ambition and state policy married perfectly.

With the defeat of Hannibal and the Carthaginians, the Romans were now drawn more comprehensively into the eastern Mediterranean. Rome's first eastern involvement had been involving once again, the pirates—those ubiquitous pirates we've spoken of so often. There was a pirate stronghold in the kingdom of Illyria, in the vicinity of what is modern-day Albania, Montenegro and Croatia, the eastern side of the Adriatic. The Romans intervened to put an end to piracy here in 229 and 219, although both of these campaigns ended with treaties, rather than with military campaigns. So we see the Romans still a little wary about moving east.

Rome became more directly involved in eastern affairs (in the affairs of the Greeks to the east) as a result of the war with Hannibal, because Hannibal was allied with the king of Macedon, Philip V. So to keep Philip out of the war, so that they could concentrate purely on Hannibal, the Romans formed an alliance of their own with the people of Aetolia, of northwestern Greece. This Roman-Aetolian alliance, meant to keep Philip out of the war, was joined by King Attalus of Pergamum. So it was as a result of a war in Italy that the Romans form alliances with various Greek and Hellenistic states.

This first war, taking the Romans into the eastern Mediterranean, is the First Macedonian War, which lasted from 214 to 205 B.C. If you remember the dates of Hannibal's invasions, you'll see that that war corresponds entirely with the time when Hannibal was in Italy. So while the Romans were nominally at war with Philip, they really were involved in no major battles at the time. They eventually concluded a peace with Philip of Macedon (Philip V) in 205, the so-called peace of Phoenice. This freed the Romans to concentrate on Hannibal and affairs in the Italian peninsula. But the war, even though it had no military impact at all on Rome's involvement in the east, did result in Rome's first major alliances in the Greek world. The kingdom of Pergamum and the Aetolians.

So in the short term, Rome had a very miniscule involvement in Greek affairs at this time, and then withdrew. But it had set the stage for much more comprehensive involvement now in the 2nd century. Once Hannibal had been defeated, the Romans were free to turn their attention to Philip V and affairs in the Greek world and the eastern Mediterranean. This came to a head in the Second Macedonian War, fought between 199 and 196 B.C. The details of this illustrate the complexity of Rome's emerging role as a Hellenistic superpower.

The war was caused by a series of factors. One was Roman resentment at the fact that Philip V had made an alliance with Hannibal during the invasion of Italy. Since Hannibal was their enemy, Philip V was their enemy, and they wanted to—it was payback time (let's put it that simply). A second factor was a threat to Rome's new allies Pergamum and Rhodes, from an alliance between Philip V of Macedon and Antiochus III of Syria. What we're finding here, quite simply, is that there is a shifting series of alliances involving the states of the eastern Mediterranean. The Hellenistic kingdoms and the powerful trading ports, and so forth.

Rome is being sucked into this, thanks to its alliances. Not seeking to acquire an empire, but being drawn in to the complex diplomatic world of the eastern Mediterranean.

According to one interpretation of these events, Rome had now taken on the role as power broker in the eastern Mediterranean, and Rome was intervening to break up a powerful alliance of Macedon and the Seleucid dynasty. In this view, Rome was using its *amicitia*, its friendship with its allies, such as Rhodes and Pergamum, as just a pretext. That really what it was after was breaking the power of the Seleucids and of Macedon. In this interpretation, the people who are usually most blamed are the successive Roman commanders; particularly Titus Quinctius Flamininus, a flamboyant commander who is supposed to have sought lucrative military commands, impressive military commands in the east. The Hannibalic war is over. There's no glory to be had there, so (the argument goes) these Roman generals are pushing for war out in the east so that they can get a chance to go out on campaign and to make a name for themselves and to win their booty. There may be some truth to these charges that the Romans were forcing the war, both for public and for private reasons.

But there is a danger in this interpretation that we may see a Roman plan for world conquest, when they are actually much more simple explanations which apply. The Romans were successful in the Second Macedonian War from 199 to 196. They defeated Philip's Macedonian phalanx at the Battle of the Cynoscephalae, (the Battle of the Dog's Head is what it means in English) in 197. This was the first victory of a Roman legion over a Macedonian phalanx. Not the forces of Pyrrhus of Epirus, but a Macedonian phalanx in a pitched battle.

But the aftermath of the war is what I think is most instructive. Let's examine what happens after the Roman victory to see if we can understand Rome's aims before the war. In a widely celebrated festival held at the Isthmus of Corinth, the Roman general Flamininus, this supposed war-monger, declared the freedom of the Greeks in an event which absolutely stunned the Greek world. I want to read you a description of this, because it's quite amazing.

> The expectation of what would happen at the Isthmus drew the men of highest rank from nearly every quarter of the world. [Meaning every quarter of the Greek world.] There

was a great deal of talk on the subject from one end of the assembled multitude to the other.

What are the Romans going to do? They've defeated Philip. The whole of the Greek world, at least mainland Greece and Macedon is in their hands. What are they going to do? Some said that from certain of the places and towns, it was impossible that the Romans could withdraw. The Romans are going to leave their garrisons here. Of course they are. Others asserted that they would withdraw from those considered most important, but would retain others that were less prominent, though capable of being quite as serviceable. So people are going on, saying, "The Romans are going to stay." "The Romans are going to go." "The Romans are conquering." Whatever.

This is what happens. In the middle of this hubbub, the herald comes out, blows his trumpet, and when there is silence, he delivers the following proclamation:

> The Senate of Rome and Titus Quinctius, proconsul and imperator, have conquered King Philip and the Macedonians in war. They declare the following peoples free, without garrison or tribute, in full enjoyment of the laws of their respective countries. Namely: Corinthians, Phocians, Locrians, Euboeans, Achaeans …

And so forth. They start to list all the people of Greece. And there is an absolute outcry, as people cannot believe that the Romans are seriously saying, "We've conquered Philip. Now you're free." Of course there were many who claimed that the Romans really didn't mean this at all. But consider these factors. The Macedonians had maintained control of Greece thanks to the use of three key garrisons, known as "the Fetters of Greece." The Romans now took over these as a result of their victory over Philip V of Macedon. And what did they do? The Senate sent orders to Flamininus to quit the garrisons and to leave them alone.

And then, this (and I think that this really is the most important point): The Freedom of the Greeks was declared in 196 B.C. By 194 B.C. there was not a single Roman soldier on the Greek mainland. The Romans did not have a long-term plan for the Roman domination of Greece. Rome would be sucked in by its eastern alliances. It would be these conditions that would lead to the final incorporation of the Hellenistic East into Rome's emerging empire.

Lecture Twenty-Four
Pax Romana

Scope:

Between 196 and 146 B.C., Roman attitudes toward the Hellenistic east changed dramatically, setting the stage for the final century of Roman expansion. After the defeat of Macedon and the Seleucid dynasty in Syria, Rome would become preoccupied in its own civil conflicts, with the Hellenistic east serving as the backdrop for the final conflict between Antony and Caesar's heir, Octavian. Antony's alliance with Cleopatra, his Hellenistic queen, raised the prospect of a joint Roman-Hellenistic hegemony of the eastern Mediterranean, but this passed with their defeat at the Battle of Actium in 31 B.C.

Outline

I. In the aftermath of the Roman declaration of the "Freedom of the Greeks," the Romans found that their former allies, the Aetolians, resented the failure of the Romans to reward them. As a result the Romans looked on as the Aetolians appealed to Antiochus III of Syria to liberate the Greeks. Antiochus's invasion of Greece in 191 B.C. precipitated the First Syrian War (191–188 B.C.).

   A. Antiochus and the Romans had no natural enmity. Nor did the two powers experience any clash of economic or even strategic interests.

      1. Antiochus had hosted Hannibal after his defeat, but this was hardly a cause of war in the eyes of the Romans.

      2. The Romans had already demonstrated they were not interested in annexing Greek territory.

   B. Instead, the war resulted from the increasing entanglement of the Romans in the shifting and unsteady system of alliances that existed throughout the Hellenistic world.

      1. Rome remained loyal to her ally, Eumenes II of Pergamum.

      2. Roman generals may have looked on this as another opportunity to win glory and booty, but the Senate still demonstrated no desire to acquire more territory.

C. Antiochus was defeated at the battle of Thermopylae by L. Cornelius Scipio, brother of the man who defeated Hannibal. Antiochus's army withdrew to Asia Minor, where the Romans were once again successful at the Battle of Magnesia (189 B.C.). The peace treaty that followed, the Peace of Apamea (188 B.C.), dramatically altered the geopolitical map of the eastern Mediterranean.

    1. The Romans collected a massive amount of booty, including a large indemnity from Antiochus.

    2. Antiochus was forced to cede virtually the entire western portion of his empire, the region known as Asia Minor, corresponding to much of modern western Turkey.

    3. The Romans granted this new territory to their allies, Eumenes of Pergamum and the people of Rhodes.

II. The change of heart in the ruling class of Rome in relation to the annexation and administration of foreign territory began in the generation following their victory over Antiochus III. The Senate came to be persuaded that military solutions were not long lasting. The events that started this change of thinking occurred during the Third Macedonian War (171–168 B.C.).

    A. In 179, Philip V of Macedon was succeeded by his son Perseus, who was concerned with restoring the prestige of Macedon and its influence in Greece. During the next eight years, Perseus fought a series of campaigns in Greece and was denounced by Eumenes II, who feared the threat to his own kingdom of Pergamum if Macedon once again grew powerful.

        1. The Romans accepted the charges laid against Perseus by Eumenes and dispatched an army to Greece.

        2. In the fourth season of the war, Perseus and the Macedonian army were crushed by the Roman legions at the Battle of Pydna (168 B.C.).

        3. Perseus was captured, sent to Rome, and paraded in the triumph of the victor, Lucius Aemilius Paulus.

        4. Macedon was partitioned into four republics.

    B. Gradually, after the partitioning of Macedon, it is possible to detect a hardening in the Roman attitude toward the endless internecine fighting of the Greeks.

        1. Following a fresh revolt in 148 B.C., the Romans lost all patience.

2. Once the revolt of Andriscus had been put down, the Roman victor, Quintus Caecilius Metellus, disbanded all forms of autonomous rule, and Macedon became a Roman province, ruled directly by a Roman governor.

C. As Roman attitudes toward Greece changed, so, too, did the Greek attitude toward Rome sour. In 196 B.C., the Romans had been hailed as liberators and saviors. Now they were denounced as hypocrites. As a result, one final war of resistance flared up, organized by the Achaean League, in 146 B.C.

    1. The war ended with the Roman sack of Corinth. The city was leveled and later rebuilt as a Roman colony.

    2. In the same year, the Romans also faced a final conflict with their old enemies, the Carthaginians. This war also ended with the sack of the enemy's city.

    3. The sack of Corinth and Carthage in 146 B.C. dramatically marks the Roman conquest of the Mediterranean, leaving only Syria and Egypt of the old Hellenistic kingdoms still independent.

III. The emergence of Rome as the greatest single power in the eastern Mediterranean coincided with the annexation of Greece, which was transformed into the province of Achaea in 146 B.C., and with the weakening of the older Hellenistic dynasties during a century of instability.

A. New kingdoms, such as Pontus, Bithynia, and Cyrenaica, were emerging on the edges of the old kingdoms.

    1. The kings of these domains often styled themselves *philoromaios*, or lovers of the Romans, as if in recognition of Rome's superpower status.

    2. When Prusias of Bithynia appeared before the Roman Senate in 165, he wore chains, acting the part of a suppliant and even a slave to Rome.

B. Rome's position in the east gradually solidified as a result of a series of extraordinary episodes.

    1. In 133 B.C., Attalus III of Pergamum died, bequeathing his entire kingdom to Rome, creating the Roman province of Asia Minor.

    2. In 96 B.C., Cyrenaica also passed to Rome as a bequest.

    3. In 75 B.C., the kingdom of Bithynia on the Black Sea passed to Rome on the death of its king, Nicomedes IV.

C. Roman expansion was also helped by the weakness of the Seleucids in Syria. This kingdom had lost its western holdings to Rome and Pergamum and was further buffeted by change.

    1. In the east, the rise of Parthia in Mesopotamia and Persia cost the Seleucids their eastern provinces.

    2. Even closer to home, the Maccabean rebellion in Judaea eventually resulted in the founding of the Hasmonean dynasty.

    3. Within the dynasty, as well, was much dissent, as rival claimants weakened the power of the kingdom.

D. The Ptolemies came under increasing Roman influence during the 1st century B.C.

    1. Ptolemy XII Auletes required the intervention of a Roman army to secure his throne, and Roman officers became advisers and officials in the upper echelons of the Ptolemaic bureaucracy.

    2. The last of the Ptolemies was Cleopatra VII, the famous lover of Caesar and Marc Antony. Her career, however, has to be seen against the backdrop of Rome's final annexation of the east.

IV. Between 100 and 31 B.C., a succession of commanders emerged in Rome who were willing to use overseas campaigns as the basis for establishing their power in Rome.

A. During the 60s B.C., Pompey asserted Roman military might throughout the eastern Mediterranean.

    1. He swept the pirates out of the Aegean in 67 B.C.

    2. Between 66 and 62, he established a network of provinces and client kingdoms across the east.

B. Pompey's one-time ally and later enemy was Julius Caesar.

    1. The civil war between their armies was fought in Greece, and after his defeat, Pompey fled to Alexandria, where he was killed.

    2. Caesar followed Pompey to Egypt and intervened to help Cleopatra keep her throne.

    3. As a result of their affair, Cleopatra bore a son whom she named Ptolemy Caesar.

    4. Her visit to Rome, however, did little to win over popular opinion.

C. After Caesar's assassination, in the final round of Rome's civil war, Marc Antony made Egypt his base of operations. With Cleopatra, he had three children. Their royal family was the last expression of independent Hellenistic kingship.

    1. After pacifying the western provinces, Caesar's heir, Octavian, marched east to confront Antony and Cleopatra.

    2. At the Battle of Actium, Antony and Cleopatra were defeated.

    3. They fled to Alexandria and, with their suicide, Egypt was annexed as a Roman province.

D. Though Rome had triumphed, it had been thoroughly Hellenized in the process, as seen in such writers as Ovid and Virgil. This was the real irony of the Hellenistic world: a people that had lost their political independence would live on as a powerful culture.

Suggested Reading:

E. Badian, *Foreign Clientelae (260–70 B.C.)*.

M. Grant, *Cleopatra*.

Questions to Consider:

1. At what point did the rulers of the Hellenistic world recognize that Rome was more powerful than any other Hellenistic state?

2. From the point of view of the Egyptians and the Ptolemaic dynasty, was Cleopatra a successful ruler?

Lecture Twenty-Four—Transcript
Pax Romana

Hello and welcome to the last in our series of our lectures on Alexander the Great and the Hellenistic Age. In the final lectures in this series, we've been looking at the gradual encroachment of Roman power into the eastern Mediterranean. We've seen that originally the Romans were little interested in the affairs of the Greek world, being rather more preoccupied with, first, the domination of the Italian peninsula and then their conflict with the great superpower of the western Mediterranean, namely Carthage.

But we've also seen that gradually, as a result of the alliance between Hannibal and Philip V of Macedon, during the Second Punic War, that the Romans were gradually brought in to the eastern orbit of affairs. I argued that if we examined closely Rome's involvement here, both during the First Macedonian War at the end of the 3rd century, and in the Second Macedonian War, when they were finally and completely victorious over Philip's army at Cynoscephalae, that if we examined these events and this period, we'd be able to see that the Romans really demonstrated no long-term plan for a conquest of the Hellenistic world or the eastern Mediterranean. I remarked that in 196, at the Isthmus of Corinth, the Romans issued a proclamation. It came from the Senate, and it was in the name of the Senate and of Titus Quinctius Flamininus, declaring the Greeks to be free.

The "Freedom of the Greeks". To live without Roman garrisons or anyone else's. To live without tribute (taxes paid to any overlord). And to live according to whatever laws they chose to for each of their own separate states. I strongly suggested that this was not merely the political rhetoric of the age, although it is true that a phrase like "the freedom of the Greeks" had been bandied about by earlier so-called liberators. But I argued that in this case, the Romans remained true to their word. The final proof of this was that two years after these events, the Roman troops were gone from Greece. They had given up the three great garrisons known as "the Fetters of Greece." They had not attempted to annex any territory. No Roman provincial governors had been sent out. In fact, the Romans had remained true to their word.

In the next fifty years, there would be a dramatic shift in the attitude of the Romans towards their allies and their enemies in the eastern Mediterranean. That fifty-year period would set the stage for the final century of the B.C. era, the final century of Roman expansion into the eastern Mediterranean, which would see the defeat of Macedon. The defeat of the Seleucid dynasty in Syria. With Rome, however, becoming more and more preoccupied with its own civil conflicts, and the Hellenistic East serving then finally as the backdrop, both for the culmination of Rome's civil wars and Rome's conquest of the Hellenistic East. The two stories are utterly intertwined and cannot be separated.

Antony's alliance with Cleopatra, so well known to us from Shakespeare (Cleopatra the Hellenistic queen) raised the prospect at the very end of Hellenistic independence, of a Roman-Hellenistic hegemony over the eastern Mediterranean. But that would pass into history with their defeat at the Battle of Actium in 31 B.C. A victory for Octavian, soon to be known as Augustus, whose power would extend over the entire Mediterranean, both west and east, witnessing the final collapse of the Hellenistic kingdoms, and the beginning of a more profound Hellenization of the Roman Empire. So it's a complex and convoluted story that we want to try and chart in our last lecture.

In the aftermath of the Roman declaration of the freedom of the Greeks, the Romans found that their former allies, the Aetolians, resented the failure of the Romans to reward them. So it was that in the late 190s, Roman legions were once again in northern Greece. But now they were dealing with Aetolians who were unsure whether they were friends or enemies of the Romans. There is one episode that we have recorded in this period that I think tells us a great deal about the way in which two cultures, in this case the Greeks and the Romans, could look at each other, could speak to each other, and could totally misunderstand what the other side was saying.

These events occur in 191 B.C. At this moment, an Aetolian embassy is talking to a Roman general named Valerius. In the typical fashion of the Hellenistic period, these Aetolian ambassadors start by waxing long and lyrical about the long contact between their two countries and the great previous services that the Aetolians had done to Rome.

Valerius cut this line of argument short by saying that such justification did not apply to the present circumstances. For as these old friendly relations have been broken off by the Aetolians, and the existing hostility was owing entirely to the Aetolians themselves, the services of the past could be of no assistance to them in the present. Typically Roman, brusque, uninterested in any of the folderol of Greek diplomatic language. They must therefore abandon all idea of justification, adopt a tone of supplication and beseech the consul's pardon for their transgressions. After a long discussion on various details, the Aetolians eventually decided to leave the whole matter to Achilleus, and to commit themselves without reserve to the good faith of the Romans.

What follows is Polybius' comment on this episode and the decision of the Aetolians, written by someone who understood the Greeks and understood the Romans. This is what he has to say. Remember, they've committed themselves without reserve to the good faith of the Romans. They had no comprehension of what was really involved. But they were misled by the word "faith" into supposing that the Romans would thereby be more inclined to grant them terms. But with the Romans, for a man to "commit himself to their good faith," is held to be equivalent to surrendering unconditionally. So just as, at the beginning of this course of lectures we saw the Greeks and the Persians misunderstanding each other, so too now we find at the end of the Hellenistic period the Romans and the Greeks utterly misunderstanding each other.

As a result of this misunderstanding, the Romans looked on as the Aetolians appealed now to a new liberator of the Greeks. In this case, Antiochus III, king of Syria. Antiochus duly therefore proclaims that he was coming to "liberate the Greeks" once again. The Greeks must have gotten very tired of all these liberations. Antiochus' invasion of Greece in 191 B.C. precipitated the First Syrian War, a war between the Romans and Antiochus of Syria, from 191 to 188 B.C. This war is an interesting one for us to pause and consider for a moment. Unlike earlier conflicts with, say, the Carthaginians, with Hannibal, or even with Philip V, there was no natural enmity here. No history of conflict between Antiochus and the Romans. No clash of economic interests, as there may possibly have been in Spain between the Romans and the Carthaginians. There were not even strategic interests involving the two of them, because Antiochus' whole sphere of influence, the eastern Mediterranean, was outside of Rome's sphere of influence. So why do they go to war?

Antiochus had hosted Hannibal after his defeat. (Hannibal eventually died at the court of Antiochus.) But this was hardly a cause for war in the eyes of the Romans. The Romans had already demonstrated that they were uninterested in annexing Greek territory. Instead, the war resulted from the increasing entanglement of the Romans in the shifting and unsteady alliances that existed throughout the Hellenistic world. By now, the Romans were allies of Eumenes, the king of Pergamum. It is that alliance, I think, that accounts for their decision to come east again.

And of course, Roman generals may have looked upon this as another opportunity to win glory and booty. But still the Senate demonstrated no desire to acquire more territory. Antiochus was defeated at the Battle of Thermopylae, by Lucius Cornelius Scipio, brother of the man who had defeated Hannibal. The great military commanders even come from the same families. Antiochus' army withdrew to Asia Minor, where the Romans pursued him, and, as we know, defeated him at the Battle of Magnesia in 189 B.C. A battle that we've mentioned on a number of occasions in this series.

You'll recall, also, that the Peace of Apamea, which was signed the following year, in 188, dramatically altered the geopolitical map of the eastern Mediterranean. We've looked at this from the point of view of the Seleucid monarchy on a number of occasions. Now we have to consider it from the Roman angle. The Romans collected a massive amount of booty, including an indemnity of 10,000 talents from Antiochus, crippling the Seleucid kingdom as it was forced to pay this off over the next decade.

We've seen also that Antiochus was forced to cede virtually the entire western portion of his empire, the region known as Asia Minor, corresponding to much of western modern-day Turkey. But did the Romans establish now a province? Still the answer is "no." The Romans granted all of this territory cut off from their enemy to their allies: Eumenes of Pergamum and the people of Rhodes. So even now, down into the 180s, even though the Romans have been brought east once again, thanks to their alliances with various Greek states and Hellenistic kings, they still demonstrate a willingness to fight wars but no desire to actually annex territory. They are not seeking an empire at all.

But there was to be a change of heart. A change of heart in the ruling class of Rome in relation to this business of eastern campaigns, territorial annexation and the administration of foreign territory. It began in the generation following the defeat of Antiochus III in 189

B.C. The Senate now would come to be persuaded that military solutions were not long-lasting. Defeat one of these kings once, and you would still be called back a year or a decade later in yet another war involving them. The events that I think precipitated this change of thinking and a change of policy on the part of the Roman Senate, occurred between 171 and 168 B.C., during the Third Macedonian War.

In 179 B.C., Philip V of Macedon had been succeeded by his son Perseus. Perseus was concerned with restoring the prestige of Macedon and its influence in Greece. During the course of that decade of the 170s, Perseus had fought a series of campaigns in Greece and was denounced constantly, year after year, by Eumenes II, king of Pergamum, who feared the threat to his own kingdom of Pergamum if Macedon once again grew powerful. So you have to imagine a situation in which the Romans year after year are hearing these denunciations. "You must do something about Perseus." The Romans accepted the charges laid against Perseus by Eumenes and finally dispatched an army to Greece.

In the fourth season of the war between Perseus and his Macedonian army and the Roman legions, the Romans were successful in bringing him to battle at Pydna, and in 168 B.C. at the Battle of Pydna, the Macedonian phalanx was wiped out. Perseus was captured. He was sent to Rome. He was paraded in chains in the triumph of the victor Lucius Aemilius Paulus.

But—and this is the most important point—not the humiliation of a Macedonian king; Macedon was partitioned into four separate republics, and the kingship was abolished. This is one of the first instances of the Romans stepping in and changing the actual constitutional arrangement of a territory that they've now conquered in war. Gradually, after the partitioning of Macedon, it's possible, I believe, to detect a hardening in the Roman attitude towards this endless cycle of internecine fighting between the Greeks and the Hellenistic kingdoms.

So we find that in the coming years, the Romans simply lose patience and now begin to act much more decisively. In 148, a fresh revolt breaks out in Macedon, and this time, when the revolt of a certain Andriscus has been put down, the Roman victor Quintus Caecilius Metellus disbands all forms of autonomous government in Macedon and Macedon becomes a Roman province, ruled directly by a Roman governor. This, I think, comes about as a result of the exasperation of the Romans with the people of Macedon and the Greek world.

And of course, as Roman attitudes towards the Greeks are changing, as they're becoming more exasperated, so too, the Greek attitude towards the Romans is beginning to change, as they turn sour on their Roman liberators. In 196, the Romans had been hailed as liberators. People had cheered so much at the Isthmus of Corinth that they'd forced Flamininus to read the decree a second time. But now, fifty years later, they're denounced as hypocrites.

As a result, one final war of resistance flares up, organized in the Peloponnese by the Achaean League, in 146 B.C. The Roman response to this is very instructive. The war finishes, not merely with a Roman victory in the field, against a Macedonian phalanx or a Greek army. The war ends with the sack of Corinth. One of the oldest and most prestigious cities in the Greek world, leveled to the ground. Later to be rebuilt, in fact, as a Roman colony.

Perhaps even more dramatically, and this year, 146, is really one of the great turning points in European history—in this very same year, the Romans also face a final conflict with their old enemies in the western Mediterranean, the Carthaginians, who have raised the battle standard once again. That war also finishes with the sack of the city.

So I think we've got here, a Rome which is dramatically marking its position in the world of the Mediterranean very differently from the way it has behaved in the century beforehand. Because with the sack of Corinth in the east and the sack of Carthage in the west, the Romans really mark their conquest of the Mediterranean, leaving only Syria and Egypt of the old great Hellenistic kingdoms still independent (and some smaller states around the edges of this). The emergence of Rome as the single power of the whole of the Mediterranean now coincides with the annexation of Greece. With the defeat of the Greeks in 146 and the sack of Corinth in that year, Greece, like Macedon, is annexed, and it is turned into a Roman province. Thereafter, from 146 onwards, it is not even known as Greece any longer. It is called the Roman province of Achaea.

This phenomenal growth of Roman power and its assertion and its domination over both east and west, also corresponds at the same time with a century of instability in the older Hellenistic kingdoms.

So if we want to think in terms of Tyche or Fortune as the people of the Hellenistic Age would think, Rome's Tyche is in the ascendant, while that of the Hellenistic states is declining.

New kingdoms were sprouting up on the edges of the disintegrating older Hellenistic empires. Kingdoms such as Pontus, up on the Black Sea; Bithynia, a little west of that; and Cyrenaica, west of the Ptolemaic domain in Egypt. The kings of these domains are very interesting. They are local potentates asserting their independence. But what do they call themselves? In their titulature, they are now *Philoromaios*, that is to say, they are "lovers of the Romans." They are declaring themselves to be allied to Rome, because they recognize now, in the later half of the 2nd century B.C. that Rome is the one superpower left in the Mediterranean world. This is dramatically illustrated by an event in 165, when the king of Bithynia, a man called Prusias, comes before the Roman Senate. But rather than wearing the robes of a Hellenistic monarch, he comes in dressed as a suppliant, with chains on, as if he is a slave of the Romans.

Rome's position in the East gradually solidified as a result of a series of extraordinary episodes, and I doubt that the Romans could have had much control over this. This is where the hand of Fortune is working on their behalf. In 133 B.C., when Attalus III of Pergamum died (and Pergamum by now, you'll recall, is a kingdom that embraces all of Asia Minor), he dies and bequeaths the entire thing to Rome, creating in one blow the Roman province of Asia Minor. So between about 150 and about 130, Rome has acquired Macedon, Greece and Turkey (to use modern terminology), and these are all now Roman provinces. Macedon, Achaea and Asia Minor.

Similarly, in 96 B.C., Cyrenaica, the area around Cyrene on the north coast of Africa, on the Libyan coast, is also passed to Rome as a bequest by its last king. Then finally (and the habit seems to have taken off), in 75 B.C., the kingdom of Bithynia up on the Black Sea also passed to Rome on the death of its king, Nicomedes IV.

So the older kingdoms are being replaced or broken up like mice nibbling away at the edges, and these smaller independent kingdoms are allying themselves to Rome, actually become part of the Roman domain, as their powerful kings die and bequeath them to Rome.

Then, what about the older Hellenistic kingdoms? The main ones of Syria and Egypt? Roman expansion into the East is being aided here by the weakness of the Seleucids in Syria. The kingdom had lost its western holdings to Rome in 188, and to Pergamum, as well. Now, it was further buffeted by change. In the East, the eastern satrapies of the old kingdom, the rise of Parthia in Mesopotamia and Persia cost the Seleucids their eastern provinces. So we're ending up with a rump state, involving just really the region of Syria.

Bounded by Pergamum and Asia Minor to the north, bounded by the Parthians to the east, bounded by desert and Judaea to the south, and of course, as we know in Judaea, the Maccabean rebellion eventually results in the founding of an independent dynasty, the Hasmonean kingdom in Judaea. Then within the very heartland of Syria (Coele-Syria, as the Greeks call it, or hollow Syria), in that very area, too, the dynasty is rent by dissension between rival claimants, weakening, therefore, the power of the kingdom.

In Egypt, a similar story. The Ptolemies come under increasing Roman influence during the 1st century B.C. One of the weakest of the Ptolemies, Ptolemy XII (Ptolemy Auletes or Ptolemy the Flute-player, as he's called) required the intervention of a Roman army in order to secure his throne. Roman officers become advisors at the court of Ptolemy, and they become officials serving in the upper echelons of the Ptolemaic bureaucracy. So there is a way in which Ptolemaic Egypt is almost being sucked into Rome's orbit, and Roman officials are almost taking over the running of the state.

The last of the Ptolemies, of course, was Cleopatra VII, the famous lover of Caesar and Marc Antony. We'll talk a little more in a moment about her career. But I suggest that it has to be seen against the backdrop of Rome's final annexation of the East. Cleopatra was fighting a rear-guard action. She's the last Hellenistic ruler, trying to find some way to salvage the power of the Hellenistic East in the face of an inexorable advance of Roman power.

We've looked at affairs in the Hellenistic East during this period, but we need to backtrack for a moment, because the story is also driven by the internal affairs of Rome. The two will eventually come together. The strand we need to follow for a moment is the history of Rome between about 100 B.C. and 31 B.C.

Even as the Hellenistic kingdoms are getting weaker and weaker, Rome is experiencing a succession of supreme commanders who are willing to use overseas campaigns as the basis for establishing their own power at Rome. Men like Marius, and men like Sulla, who fight overseas campaigns in order to win greater glory and to then assert that control of Rome. During the 60s B.C., Pompey asserted Roman military might throughout the eastern Mediterranean. So it is he who finally represents the power of Rome sweeping away the last vestiges of independence in the eastern Mediterranean. He sweeps out pirates from the Aegean in 67. The fact that a Roman supreme commander had to be given that job, I think, gives us some idea of how endemic piracy had been in the eastern Mediterranean.

Between 66 B.C. and 62 B.C., he established a network of provinces and client kingdoms across the East, that acted either as allies of Rome or buffer states between Rome and the people further beyond, such as the Parthians to the east. So the entire East has been incorporated into the Roman provincial structure. But it is not done smoothly, because Pompey is for a time allied to and then an enemy of Julius Caesar.

The civil war that is going to be fought between them, and the last rounds of civil war that afflict the Roman Republic, will not be fought only in Italy, but will be fought across the Mediterranean, and particularly in the eastern Mediterranean. So the Hellenistic world is finally going to become the backdrop for Roman civil wars. The civil war between the armies of Pompey and Caesar was fought primarily in Greece. After his defeat there, in the battle of Pharsala, Pompey fled to Alexandria, where he was killed. Caesar followed Pompey to Egypt, only to arrive and find that his opponent had been slain.

Then Caesar stayed on, involving himself in the internal affairs of Egypt. First, helping Cleopatra to keep her throne, and then fighting a war against the Alexandrian mob through much of 47. One of the toughest campaigns of his career. Ever. During the course of this time as he was there, helping the young Egyptian queen to establish her authority, he also, as we know, had an affair with her. Cleopatra bore a son whom she named Ptolemy Caesar. The very last phase of the connection between the Hellenistic East and Rome would come about once again as a result of the civil wars of the Romans and Cleopatra's position in Egypt.

After Caesar's assassination in 44 B.C., a final round of civil war broke out, involving Marc Antony, who had been Caesar's right hand man, and Caesar's heir, Octavian. For some time they had managed to partition the Mediterranean between them, with Octavian campaigning largely in the West, and with Marc Antony campaigning largely in the East, with Egypt as his base of operations. There he, like his old friend Caesar, fell in love with Cleopatra, and the two of them together had three children. A royal family, if you will. With each of their children being given a nominal Hellenistic kingdom in the East.

But after pacifying the Western provinces of the Empire, Caesar's heir Octavian finally marched east, to confront his one remaining enemy, Antony, a man who, by now, had almost completely given up the manners of a Roman general and was behaving as a Hellenistic king. He and Cleopatra together held sumptuous banquets. He is sometimes referred to as the last prince of the East.

At the Battle of Actium, off the western coast of Greece, in 31 B.C., Antony and Cleopatra were defeated. They fled to Alexandria. With their suicide, the last remaining Hellenistic monarch and the blood of Ptolemy, namely Cleopatra, died. Egypt was annexed and became thereafter a Roman province. By 31 B.C., the Hellenistic world is now entirely a subset of the Roman Empire.

It would be wrong, I think to finish our series of lectures on the Hellenistic Age by concentrating only on the political demise of the Hellenistic East. Because it is important to remember that Rome, really, by now had become thoroughly a Hellenistic Empire. The great poets of Hellenistic culture, men such as Catullus and Tibullus and Ovid were writing poetry in Latin, but using the meters of Greek poetry, regarding the Greeks as their masters. So Virgil, who produced the finest epic ever produced in Latin poetry can really be seen as a Latin inflection, if you will, of Greek epic.

The epic that he writes, the *Aeneid*, is a poem that's produced during the reign of Augustus, the man who finally incorporated all of the Hellenistic East into the Roman Empire. It is a poem which is, in a sense, a national celebration of Rome's genius. There is a moment in the *Aeneid* when Virgil will have one of his characters turn to Aeneas and say, "This, Roman, will be your genius." "To throw down the proud and to spare the conquered." In that one line, we get

©2000 The Teaching Company.

a more perfect expression of Rome's imperial mission than anywhere else in Latin literature.

And yet, the *Aeneid*, the national epic in honor of Aeneas, the founding hero of Rome, is essentially a work that could not have been made possible had it not been for Greek epic before it. Because the whole first half of the *Aeneid*, which tells the story of Aeneas' arrival in Italy after his journey from Troy, is essentially modeled on the *Odyssey*. The entire second half of the work, accounting for the foundation of his dynasty, which eventually will give Rome its kings and the glory of Rome, is essentially modeled on the story of the *Iliad*.

So it is with Virgil, I think, that we get a perfect expression of the great irony of the Hellenistic world. That a world which passed into history in the realm of politics and lost its independence by 31 B.C., would, nevertheless live on as a culture influencing first the Romans and later the rest of western European civilization.

The more we look at the Hellenistic world, in conclusion (it seems to me), the more we find an age that continues to exert subtle but strong influences on our own age.

Timeline

359 ....Philip II comes to the Macedonian throne.

356 ....Birth of Alexander.

338 ....Philip and Alexander defeat the Greeks at Chaeroneia.

336 ....Assassination of Philip and accession of Alexander the Great.

334 ....Battle of the Granicus River.

333 ....Battle of Issus.

331 ....Alexander's visit to the oracle of Siwah; Battle of Gaugemala.

330 ....Death of Darius, King of Persia.

329 ....Alexander's Bactrian campaign.

326 ....Mutiny of Alexander's army at the Hyphasis River.

325 ....Alexander's return through the Gedrosian desert.

324 ....Mutiny and banquet of reconciliation at Opis.

323 ....Alexander dies in Babylon; beginning of the Wars of the Diadochi.

321 ....Death of Perdiccas during campaign against Ptolemy; division of Alexander's empire at Triparadeisus.

317 ....Murder of Philip Arrhidaeus by Olympias.

315 ....Coalition against Antigonus.

311 ....Peace treaty signed by Antigonus and the other Diadochi.

310	Cassander murders Alexander IV.
306	Ptolemy defeated off Cyprus; Diadochi assume the title of kings; Seleucus cedes eastern borders to Chandragupta in exchange for war elephants.
301	Death of Antigonus at Ipsus.
283	Death of Ptolemy I; death of Demetrius, son of Antigonus.
281	Death of Seleucus I; defeat and death of Lysimachus (Battle of Corupedium).
280	Pyrrhus of Epirus crosses to southern Italy.
274	Withdrawal of Pyrrhus from Italy.
272	Sack of Tarentum by Rome.
264–241	First Punic War.
263	Eumenes I succeeds Philetaerus (Pergamum).
246–241	Third Syrian War (Ptolemy III versus Seleucus II).
241–197	Reign of Attalus I (Pergamum).
240	Diodotus of Bactria assumes title of king.
238–227	Attalid victories against Celts (Galatians).
229	First Illyrian War.
219	Second Illyrian War.
218–202	Second Punic War.
217	Battle of Raphia.
215	Alliance of Philip V (Macedon) and Hannibal.

31 ....Battle of Actium; defeat of Marc
                                Antony and Cleopatra.

Glossary

akatalepsia: Sceptic doctrine that holds that absolutely certain knowledge is impossible.

amicitia: Roman term for friendship; often applied to Rome's alliances with foreign kings and states.

Asclepieum: Any sanctuary of the healing god Asclepius, often including buildings for the diagnosis and treatment of disease.

asylia: Inviolability, especially the right of sanctuaries to be left unmolested, formally recognized by other states.

ataraxia: Imperturbability, a state of calm sought by many Hellenistic philosophical schools.

aulos: The court of a Hellenistic king, including his advisors, military officers, and officials.

basilikoi laoi: Royal peasants, i.e., peasants living on and tied to estates owned by the king.

catochi: Recluses. Individuals who withdrew from life in the world at large to live wholly within a temple precinct.

choregos: Citizen responsible for paying for a dramatic production at a religious festival.

dioiketes: A high-ranking government official responsible usually for taxation and financial affairs.

epiphanes: An epithet applied to Antiochus IV meaning "god made manifest."

epoche: A term from Sceptic philosophy asserting the need to suspend judgment because of the impossibility of absolute knowledge.

euergesia: Benefaction. The institution of public assistance offered by the wealthy to Greek states, especially in times of crisis.

euergetes: Benefactor. A term applied to wealthy citizens who assisted a city with gifts of food or money; often adopted as a royal title.

gymnasia: Cultural institutions, common in Greek cities, combining athletic training, poetic performances, and philosophy lectures.

gymnasiarch: Official in charge of the gymnasium, appointed by the city to oversee the training of young men.

heroon: A shrine dedicated to a man of heroic, i.e., semi-divine, status.

hoplite: Heavily armed Greek infantry soldier.

koine: "Common" Greek, the dialect of Greek based on the Attic (Athenian) dialect, common throughout the eastern Mediterranean.

laoi: The people, but usually used in Hellenistic times to refer to non-Greek peasants.

logistes: An official of the Hellenistic kings primarily concerned with record-keeping and accounts.

megalopsychus: An Aristotelian doctrine that identified the great man as the possessor of a "great soul."

oecumene: A general term referring to the sphere of Greek culture and language extending throughout the eastern Mediterranean.

palaestra: The wrestling ground of a gymnasium where young men took their exercise and underwent military training.

pezetairoi: Literally "foot companions." Elite infantry battalions of the Macedonian army.

phalanx: The massed formation of heavily armed infantrymen, equipped with pikes, forming the core of the Hellenistic armies.

philoi: Literally "friends." The noble companions of a Hellenistic king; the core of his military and administrative staff.

philoromaios: A term increasingly adopted from the 2nd century on, meaning "Rome lover," used by Rome's allies to advertise their friendship with Rome.

pothos: A popular expression in the ancient literature about Alexander meaning "yearning" or "desire," often linked to Alexander's divine status.

stoas: Open colonnaded buildings popular in the Greek world as public buildings for commerce, judicial hearings, and civic administration.

technitai: A general term for craftsmen but often used specifically for the guild of actors known as the technitai of Dionysos.

trierarchs: Citizens who undertook the task of manning and equipping a trireme or warship.

tyche: Fortune. A popular deity of the Hellenistic Age; often associated with either personal destiny or the fate of an entire community.

Bibliography

Badian, Ernst, *Foreign Clientelae (260–70 B.C.)* (Oxford, 1958).

Bernard, Paul, "Aï Khanum on the Oxus," *PBA* 53 (1967): 71–95.

Borza, Eugene N., *In the Shadow of Olympus: The Emergence of Macedon* (Princeton, 1990).

Bowman, Alan K., *Egypt after the Pharaohs, 323 B.C.–A.D. 642* (Berkeley, 1986).

Canfora, Luciano, *The Library of Alexandria: A Wonder of the Ancient World* (Berkeley, 1990).

Eddy, Samuel K., *The King Is Dead* (Lincoln, 1961).

Errington, R. Malcolm, *A History of Macedonia* (Berkeley, 1990).

Fowler, Barbara Hughes, *Hellenistic Poetry: An Anthology* (Madison, Wisconsin, 1990).

Fox, Robin Lane, *Alexander the Great* (London, 1973).

Grant, Michael, *Cleopatra* (London, 1972).

Green, Peter, *From Alexander to Actium* (Berkeley, 1991).

Gruen, Erich S., *Culture and National Identity in Republican Rome* (Cornell, 1992).

———, "Hellenism and Persecution: Antiochus IV and the Jews," in *Hellenistic History and Culture*, ed. P. Green. (Berkeley, 1993).

———, *The Hellenistic World and the Coming of Rome*, 2 vols. (Berkeley, 1984).

———, *Studies in Greek Culture and Roman Policy* (Berkeley, 1990).

Hägg, Thomas, *The Novel in Antiquity* (Berkeley, 1983).

Hammond, N. G. L., *Philip of Macedon* (Baltimore, 1994).

Hansen, E. V., *The Attalids of Pergamon* (Ithaca, 1971).

Harris, William V., *War and Imperialism in Republican Rome, 320–70 B.C.* (Oxford, 1979).

Herman, Gabriel, "The Court Society of the Hellenistic Age," in P. Cartledge et al. (eds.), *Hellenistic Constructs: Essays in Culture, History, and Historiography* (Berkeley, 1997).

Inwood, Brad, and L. P. Gerson, *Hellenistic Philosophy: Introductory Readings* (Indianapolis, 1988).

Lloyd, Geoffrey, *Greek Science after Aristotle* (New York, 1973).

Long, A. A., *Hellenistic Philosophy: Stoics, Epicurans, Sceptics* (Berkeley, 1986).

Narain, A. K., *The Indo-Greeks* (Oxford, 1957).

Pearson, Lionel, *The Lost Histories of Alexander the Great*, American Philological Association Philological Monographs 20, New York, 1960.

Piper, L. J., *Spartan Twilight* (New Rochelle, 1985).

Pollitt, J. J., *Art in the Hellenistic Age* (Cambridge, 1986).

Price, S. R. F., *Rituals and Power* (Cambridge, 1984).

Reardon, Brain P., ed., *Collected Ancient Greek Novels* (Berkeley, 1989).

Roisman, Joseph, *Alexander the Great: Ancient and Modern Perspectives* (Lexington, Mass., 1995).

Rostovtzeff, M. I., *The Social and Economic History of the Hellenistic World*, 3 vols. (Oxford, 1941).

Sherwin-White, Susan, and Amelie Kuhrt, *From Sardis to Samarkhand* (Berkeley, 1993).

Stoneman, Richard, ed., *The Greek Alexander Romance* (Harmondsworth, 1991).

Tcherikover, Viktor, *Hellenistic Civilization and the Jews* (New York, 1959).

Thompson, Dorothy, *Memphis under the Ptolemies* (Princeton, 1988).

Veyne, Paul, *Bread and Circuses: Historical Sociology and Political Pluralism* (London, 1976).

Walbank, F. W., *Polybius* (Berkeley, 1972).

Notes

Notes